TeleVisionaries

This is book number ____
of a limited edition of 1000.

Jim Robertson

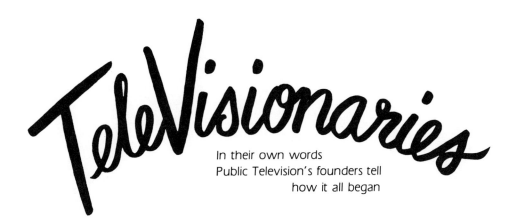

In their own words
Public Television's founders tell
how it all began

TABBY HOUSE BOOKS

Manufactured in the United States of America

Library of Congress Number: 92-062246

ISBN: O-9627974-8-0

TABBY HOUSE BOOKS
4429 Shady Lane, Charlotte Harbor, FL 33980
813-629-7646 • 813-627-6938

This book is dedicated to

Anabel Graves Robertson

As my life partner for more than fifty years and also my most discerning critic, she traveled 19,000 miles with me to interview the fifty-five individuals quoted in these pages—and then typed the transcripts of the audio tapes resulting in nearly 3,000 pages of personal reminiscences about the very beginnings of public television. Without her at my side, this work never would have been accomplished.

Contents

21—THE LATE BLOOMERS   **201**

New York steals a channel from New Jersey, the Nation's Capital struggles to overcome the disadvantages of a UHF channel, and Los Angeles is born again.

22—THE NATIVES ARE GETTING RESTLESS AGAIN   **215**

The traditional insistence on local independence interferes with the development of a stronger national network—evidence of the nature of public television station managers, especially their diversity.

23—NAEB IN CRISIS AND THE RETURN OF SCOTTY FLETCHER   **225**

Division within the NAEB and ETV's need for leadership other than NET result in Fletcher's return to stage the first national conference involving both station managers and board representatives—all of which results in recommendations leading to the first Carnegie Commission on Educational Television.

27—HAS YOUR DREAM BEEN FULFILLED OR BECOME LOST?   **257**

Public Television's Parents express their thoughts as they look back over several decades of Public Television.

Epilogue   **271**

Granting all of these past efforts, still no adequate funding solution, and the onrush of multi-channel technology, where does Public Television go from here?

The author's own views—based in part on the opinions of the heads of CPB, PBS, and America's Public Television Stations—with a few serious words of advice for the reader.

Introducing:
Public TeleVisionaries

Since the individuals who were interviewed in 1981-82 provide most of what you will be reading, I would like to introduce them individually in the order that they come in the text. These are the people to be thanked for initiating a totally new kind of television in America. For easy reference, all fifty-six Public TeleVisionaries are listed alphabetically in the Index, which also shows page numbers of their respective comments.

RALPH STEETLE, as director of the Joint Council on Educational Television (JCET), was present at the dedication of the first ETV station and helped scores of other stations to get on the air. He then headed public television in Oregon before retiring to the Oregon coast— a move typical of his good judgement.

GEORGE ARMS was a staff member of the first ETV station (KUHT Houston), and served later in St. Louis, St. Paul, Minneapolis, and South Carolina. He always was mindful of the dream he shared with his colleagues of what television could mean in American education.

ROY BARTHOLD, also on the staff as KUHT went on the air in Houston, eventually became its manager. In that position he did the best he could to build the station into something significant, despite fiscal problems at the university.

JACK McBRIDE visited KUHT as he prepared to begin his life-long career as head of public television in Nebraska. Subsequently he built Nebraska's state network, acted as a consultant to other states as they built theirs, and demonstrated dozens of innovations possible in education through the use of emerging electronic technology.

HYMAN GOLDIN held many key positions through the years at the Federal Communications Commission, providing him with many opportunities to evaluate public television's progress. He served subsequently on the staff of the 1966 Carnegie Commission on Educational Television.

EVERETT CASE became interested in broadcasting in the 1920s and continued this interest throughout his distinguished career as the head of Colgate University and the Sloan Foundation, serving as a board member and frequently chairman of PBS' predecessor, National Educational Television.

PARKER WHEATLEY entered radio before radio had any commercials. All his life he campaigned for fine cultural and educational programming, specifically as founding manager of Boston's WGBH-FM and the first manager of WGBH-TV. He was one of the true idealists in the early days.

ROSEL HYDE served as a member of the Federal Communications Commission under four different presidents and twice was appointed chairman. He was highly respected for his professionalism, evident in his reputation for fairness, objectivity, and a willingness to consider all points of view.

GERTRUDE BRODERICK, as a staff member of the U.S. Office of Education, was instrumental in promoting the use of radio in education, once serving as national president of the Association for Education by Radio. Even after retirement, she helped to promote Washington's WETA.

HAROLD McCARTY was the heart and soul of educational radio and television in Wisconsin for forty years, during which he frequently emerged as an idealistic spokesman who could stir the spirits of everyone at national conventions of the NAEB, of which he was president in the 1930s.

LEONARD MARKS, hardy perennial among communications attorneys, befriended the educators early on. In more ways than may ever be known, he brought about federal support for educational broadcasting—including passage of the first Public Broadcasting Act.

MARCUS COHN was a partner with Leonard Marks in one of the most influential and useful law firms that educational broadcasters could ever have wished for. Like Marks, he was an early proponent of educational radio and subsequently of educational television.

I. KEITH TYLER, from his academic position at Ohio State University, played many key roles in the growth of educational broadcasting, including direction of annual gatherings in Columbus, securing of Congressional witnesses, and conducting studies and workshops in instructional TV.

JOHN C. CRABBE progressed from early participation in educational radio to become the father of KVIE-TV in Sacramento, after having served as one of the first Program Associates for the Educational Television and Radio Center, the earliest effort toward national programming.

ARTHUR HUNGERFORD entered television at NBC in New York, developed instructional television for the U.S. Navy, assisted many early stations while he was a field man for the JCET. Then he courageously maintained a holding operation in New York City until others were able to acquire Channel 13 for noncommercial use, after which he served at Pennsylvania State University until his retirement.

JAMES MACANDREW headed New York City school broadcasting as manager of WNYE radio for many years, then was called upon to develop the comprehensive school television service known as The Regents' Project even before Channel 13 become public, providing great leadership in ITV nationally as well.

MARTHA GABLE pioneered school television in Philadelphia on commercial stations prior to her long term at WHYY-TV, and showed many others how to do it as well, through demonstrations at national meetings and countless workshops for teachers as well as for TV professionals.

ARMAND HUNTER secured his early TV experience at commercial stations in Philadelphia, went on to fight the lengthy battle for an ETV station at Michigan State. He furnished many a fellow pioneer with both solace and inspiration—a great motivator.

DAVID M. DAVIS, one of public television's most competent producers, learned his trade in Philadelphia commercial stations, then provided strong leadership in North Carolina, Michigan State, and particularly at WGBH-TV in Boston during its critical formative years.

JIM ROBERTSON, author of this book, started in radio in Wisconsin and began his television career at the Milwaukee Journal stations in 1947. In 1955, he moved to Chicago to help establish WTTW, then to NET as Station Relations head, then to Los Angeles to get

KCET under way, returned to Wisconsin to help strengthen WHA-TV and to get its state-wide ETV network started, headed NAEB's radio division until National Public Radio became organized, finally was consultant to many Public Broadcasting clients before taking on this oral history project.

JONATHAN RICE edited early TV newscasts for KTLA in Los Angeles, then joined San Francisco's KQED and presided over perhaps the most adventurous group of producers ever known in public television. His partnership with James Day made KQED unique in more ways than can be counted.

RICHARD B. HULL was one of the great statesmen in early battles with the FCC to gain reserved channels for both FM and TV while he also was managing WOI radio and then WOI-TV, forming the JCET, and serving as president of NAEB. In later years he was responsible for educational radio and TV at Ohio State.

ROBERT B. HUDSON came into noncommercial broadcasting from CBS, guided the programming efforts of the fledgling Educational Television and Radio Center, then became program head for National Educational Television (NET)... a quiet, thoughtful man, devoted to the cause.

G.H."BILL" GRIFFITHS was chosen vice president of the Ford Foundation's Fund for Adult Education, and in close association with C. Scott Fletcher supervised scores of grants to help new stations get started. He also had a hand in early funding of the Educational Television and Radio Center.

STANLEY NEUSTADT was chief of staff for the FCC's first woman commissioner, Frieda Hennock, and thus recalled more about this phenomenal female than anyone else—even though she obviously impressed everyone she met in her fight to reserve TV channels for educational use.

WILLIAM G. HARLEY, announcer and program manager for WHA Radio, was appointed the first general manager of WHA-TV, then became president of the National Association of Educational Broadcasters and moved its headquarters and activities to Washington, D.C., where for years he was a seminal force in the growth of educational/public television and radio.

M.S. "MORRIE" NOVIK, while head of New York's municipal radio station WNYC, persuaded Mayor LaGuardia to read the funnies on radio. His powers of persuasion and his connections in organized labor also resulted in many political victories for educational broadcasting in Washington, D.C. and elsewhere.

JOHN F. WHITE was best known as president of NET, the national agency which preceded PBS. From his years in the academic field and his term as manager of Pittsburgh's WQED, "Jack" knew the territory and saw what was needed to bring ETV into the national arena— the right man at the right time.

JAMES DAY created San Francisco's KQED out of almost nothing except enthusiasm, partly by his own capabilities and partly by derring-do. Along with Jonathan Rice, he brought forth the most unusual public television station in the country during his years in the Bay Area.

RAYMOND WITTOFF caught The Dream very early and enlisted influential folks in St. Louis to establish KETC. His philosophy of what television could achieve influenced his fellow board members at the Educational TV and Radio Center and later at NET.

FRANK SCHOOLEY epitomized educational radio at the University of Illinois, served as an early president of the National Association of Educational Broadcasters. He accepted TV when it arrived, was always a fixture at national meetings, and ultimately became a member of the first board of directors of the Corporation for Public Broadcasting.

C. SCOTT FLETCHER, as president of the Ford Foundation's Fund for Adult Education, gave ETV a tremendous impetus through grants to get stations started. "Scotty" also established and briefly headed the first national program center. Years later he was called out of retirement to help establish the first Carnegie Commission study, which led to the first Public Broadcasting Act.

ROBERT J. BLAKELEY helped activate early stations as a staff member of the Fund for Adult Education. Subsequently he devoted years to researching and writing about this kind of television and its potential.

JAMES R. KILLIAN, while chancellor of MIT, served as a trustee of WGBH in early days, headed the 1966 Carnegie Commission on Educational Television, and subsequently chaired the board of directors of the Corporation for Public Broadcasting.

HARTFORD N. GUNN may have been the most farsighted professional in public broadcasting—from his days as manager of WGBH and founder of the Eastern Educational Network to his major contributions as the first president of the Public Broadcasting Service (PBS).

KENNETH OBERHOLTZER, more than any other American school superintendent, grasped the instructional possibilities inherent in public TV. He saw to it that Denver got a station, encouraged the formation of ITV program libraries, and served several terms on the board of directors of NET.

NORMAN COUSINS found time in his busy life as writer/editor/lecturer/publisher to serve several terms on the board of NET when it was the national program service. He also played a vital role in securing Channel 13 to serve the New York City area as a key public television station.

JAMES W. ARMSEY was the Ford Foundation's man in charge of educational/public television during the late 1950s and the early 1960s. He probably fought for and won more dollars for public television than anyone else ...a conscientious strategist.

NEWTON N. MINOW headed the Federal Communications Commission at a critical time in public television's development. He played a leading role in supporting federal legislation to strengthen ETV and in finding ways to assure reserved channels for stations in New York, Washington, and Los Angeles, and subsequently served on the boards of PBS and Chicago's WTTW.

CHALMERS "CHUCK" MARQUIS left commercial TV in Chicago to become senior producer at WTTW, then its program manager, then moved to Washington where for more than twenty years he was public broadcasting's "Man on The Hill"...a dedicated representative if ever there was one.

JOHN W. TAYLOR, lifelong educational administrator, was executive director of Chicago's public television station from its inception in 1955 until the early 1970s. A dignified and unusually capable Kentucky-born gentleman, he imparted his prestige to a new way of educating people.

RHEA G. SIKES built the school service of Pittsburgh's WQED into perhaps the finest in the land, helped encourage exchange of instructional materials among stations, and counseled many professionals in the best ways to use ETV.

DONALD TAVERNER got into public television to improve education in the state of Maine, became president of WQED in Pittsburgh for a time, then held a similar position at WETA in Washington, D.C. His Down East humor lightened many a heavy moment.

KENNETH CHRISTIANSEN, as a field representative for the Southern Regional Education Board, helped start many southern states on the road to public TV. In the late 1950s, he played an important role in the creation of the first national program service. Subsequently he settled in Gainesville, Florida, as manager of WUFT and a highly-regarded professor at the University of Florida.

GERARD "JERRY" APPY introduced Dick Van Dyke to commercial TV in Atlanta, then was called to help build the University of Georgia ETV station, WGTV, Athens. Subsequently a key officer in two national educational television agencies, (ETS-NAEB and then NET), he completed his career as head of Oregon Public Broadcasting.

RAYMOND HURLBERT was plucked from schoolwork by Alabama's governor to head that state's ETV Commission and build the country's first state-wide educational television network, not a simple task in a state with limited funds. But Ray caught a glimpse of The Dream and never lost it.

HENRY J. CAUTHEN saw the possibilities for educational improvement through television in South Carolina, and over the years built one of the most comprehensive state-wide systems of TV instruction anywhere in the United States.

WILLIAM J. McCARTER participated in the very beginnings of TV in Philadelphia for he was a television professional prior to his stint as program director of WHYY-TV, then learned about underwriting at NET before heading Washington's WETA and subsequently Chicago's WTTW.

LOREN STONE got out of commercial radio with no intention of doing what he did do later. He built and ran the University of Washington's public station, KCTS-TV, Seattle, and served with distinction on many national committees and boards for the next two decades.

KEITH ENGAR was asked by the president of his University in Salt Lake City to put together an ETV station, and he did—so effectively that he was called to head the Educational Broadcasting Branch of the FCC for a brief time, an assignment which afforded him some unusual insights.

LEE A. FRISCHKNECHT was one of the stalwart group at Michigan State's WKAR-TV, then joined National Educational Television in New York as head of Station Relations—a tough assignment during the "growing pain" years of public television. Subsequently president of National Public Radio, he then served many years at Arizona State University's KAET in Phoenix.

ELIZABETH CAMPBELL saw what a public television station could mean to education in the nation's capital. Despite problems which would have daunted others, she succeeded in founding WETA in Washington—and actively worked with it for several decades.

JAMES L. LOPER marshalled the diverse elements of the educational community in Southern California to help establish KCET, continued there as the one most responsible for instructional television, then became president and general manager of this important station in the public television system.

LEE A. DuBRIDGE, as president of Caltech, was one of the catalysts around whom major citizens gathered to make Los Angeles' KCET possible. He subsequently served on the board of NET and was a member of the Carnegie Commission on Educational Television in 1966.

FREDERICK BREITENFELD was drafted to help run a conference of ETV managers and board members in Washington and was available when Maryland was looking for a lively and capable young fellow to build their state-wide system. This he did so well that Philadelphia later called him to be general manager of WHYY.

HARRY J. SKORNIA was the one-man staff of the National Association of Educational Broadcasters during much of the time it headquartered at the University of Illinois in Urbana —but his major contributions to the field lay in the many books and articles he wrote, based on his shrewd analysis of the implications of the broadcast media in society.

Acknowledgments

Special thanks to four individuals, without whose encouragement, inspiration, and support, I would not have been afforded the experiences which not only made this book possible, but have given me a most interesting and satisfying professional life.

Harold B. "Mac" McCarty, who invited me to participate at WHA in Madison while I was in high school; who first encouraged me to utilize radio and television for high purposes; who trained me in the techniques of broadcasting and the proper use of the public's airwaves; who cheered me on wherever I went, and who saw to it that I became his successor in Wisconsin when he retired in 1967.

John W. Taylor, educator extraordinaire, who knew he would need experienced broadcasters around him to plan and operate Chicago's WTTW so that there could be a successful "marriage" of education and television, and from whom I learned what skillful adminstration means. Here Dr. Taylor is paying close attention to advice from Director of Engineering Duane Weise (right), Dr. Colby Lewis, production manager, and from me.

John F. White, my colleague on the early NET Affiliates Committee, who called me to become his station relations head when he became president of NET. Jack taught me how important enthusiasm and a large measure of dreaming can be in any enterprise. Despite our reliance upon each other, he released me from NET when Los Angeles called, and came out to KCET for its dedication as we went on the air in 1965.

Lee A. DuBridge, who maintained his confidence in me during KCET's stormy beginnings and upheld the decisions of his general manager, even when none of us was certain where we were headed. Dr. DuBridge's reputation for integrity and his escalating interest in and support for public television encouraged all who worked with him, at KCET and later when he served on the board of NET and on the Carnegie Commission on Educational Television.

Also, my heartfelt thanks to every individual with whom I was privileged to share the excitement and the challenge of establishing these two great stations.

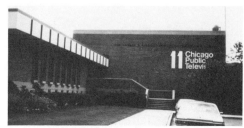

WTTW Channel 11 Chicago

KCET Channel 28 Los Angeles

Further Acknowledgements

For initial encouragement: the late Norman Cousins.

For early endorsement and continuing reassurance: Dr. Everett Case, Newton Minow, Sylvester L. "Pat" Weaver, Dr. Donald R. McNeil of the National Public Broadcasting Archives, and Dean Edward J. Pfister of the School of Communications at the University of Miami. Also, station manager-statesmen Henry J. Cauthen and Lloyd Kaiser, and long-time professional colleagues David Brugger of America's Public Television Stations and James A. Fellows of the Central Educational Network and the National Association of Educational Broadcasters.

For providing the grant which made our initial trip possible, supplementary funds for preparing transcripts and duplicating audio tapes, and a subsequent grant to cover much of the preparation of this book: the Corporation for Public Broadcasting; for other supplemental funding, the Benton Foundation, Marcus Cohn and Leonard Marks. For reading early drafts of several chapters: James W. Armsey, George Bair, Steve Behrens, Ronald C. Bornstein, Edwin Cohen, John C. Crabbe, David M. Davis, Dionne and Roger Jones, Jack G. McBride, William J. McCarter, Ruth Morton Miller, Judith Prier, Rhea G. Sikes, Arthur L. Singer, Jr., and Parker Wheatley.

For assistance in searching for, locating, and providing photographs: Association of America's Public Television Stations; John L. Boor of KCTS-TV Seattle; Broadcast Pioneers Library and its director, Catharine Heinz; Broadcasting Magazine; Kenneth Christiansen; Marcus Cohn; David M. Davis; Lee Frischknecht; Marlow Froke; Arthur Hungerford; Raymond D. Hurlbert; Rosel H. Hyde; KUHT's Jeff Clark and Jill Pickett; Leonard H. Marks; the MIT Museum's Sally Beddow; Stanley S. Neustadt; Photo/Graphics of Pennsylvania State University; Jonathan Rice and KQED; the *San Francisco Chronicle-Examiner* and freelance cartoonist Dan Perkins; Arthur L. Singer, Jr.; South Carolina ETV's John Scruggs; The State Historical Society of Wisconsin's Mass Communications History Center; Donald V. Taverner; WETA's founder, Elizabeth P. Campbell; WGBH Educational Foundation, WGBH-TV's picture researcher, Debby Paddock; WHA's Ralph Johnson; WOI-TV's Bob Helmers and Bob Phillips; WQED's Russ Martz; and WTTW's William J. McCarter.

For meticulous word processing, April L. Card; for editorial review, perceptive and enthusiastic suggestions and careful editing, Chester Baum; for cover design, art work and photographic services, Joy and Art Duperault; for laborious proofreading, Anabel G. Robertson; for painstaking typesetting, Bob and Earlene Lefebvre; for empathetic yet objective professional guidance in all aspects of the publishing art, Linda and Jim Salisbury, publishers of Tabby House Books.

Jim Robertson
Port Charlotte, Florida
November, 1992

Prologue

Is television a blessing or a curse? Or are you among those who ignore it?

How is television affecting all of us—our families, our children, our society?

In the very earliest days of television in America, even before it had entered many homes, there were a few people who dreamed that television could become something of tremendous value in our democratic way of life. They did something about it.

They formed the basis for what we now call public television.

Although something similar to public television was foreseen by a very few as early as the 1920s, it actually came into being when the first few noncommercial educational television stations went on the air in the early fifties.

Since then our world has changed in many ways. Now, we live in an electronic communications universe far different from what we experienced in the 1950s. Public television today and in the future faces an entirely different set of circumstances than did those pioneers who created it four decades ago.

Those of us who purchased the first television receivers, in the 1950s, were lucky if we were able to watch one or two of the twelve available VHF channels. Today, we choose from among dozens of channels from UHF as well as VHF broadcasting stations and typically fifteen to fifty or more additional channels of cable programming. Moreover, in a rapidly increasing number of back yards and rooftops there are home satellite receiving dishes. With a VCR (videocassette recorder) we can capture incoming programs and later play them back at will. And there are hundreds of other video materials to rent or purchase at the neighborhood video store.

These options have fractionalized what once was referred to as "the television audience," an audience comprised of people who regularly watched programs on local TV broadcasting stations—stations which were either affiliated with one of the commercial or independent networks, or their local public television station. Now the audience pie is being cut into more and more pieces.

What does this fractionalization portend for public television? It means that the more than three hundred public television stations now face a fight for survival and significance even more daunting than the odds they struggled to overcome earlier.

Recognizing such a state of affairs, I find it useful to look at the 1920s—when broadcasting's first proponents were horrified by the thought that the airwaves might be used for advertising—to try to understand what public television's founders saw in this amazing medium which they thought might bring great benefits to every American.

This story of the history of public television, as told by its founders, is not without humor, political maneuvering, personal foibles, failures, and triumphs. It is a story of a social enterprise which was not mandated by government or imposed from the top, growing instead as a "people's movement" in many regions of our nation at the same time. It is the story of individual American initiative on the local level, from its beginnings in 1953, until the Congress of the United States finally recognized its value in the Public Broadcasting Act of 1967.

It is the story of real people who tell their own story in their own words. Sometimes it is funny. Often there is rivalry and confrontation. Occasionally it is pathetic, and most of the time it reflects a kind of idealistic naivete which can only be applauded. Now and then it appears incredibly primitive when compared with the sophisticated and expensive TV world of today. In the end it is somewhat sobering, as these "parents" reflect upon what has happened to their hopes and dreams — their "child" — in the years since the first ETV stations went on the air.

After seventeen years in commercial radio and television, I became involved in what was then known as "Educational TV." It was my privilege to have worked at one time or another with most of the others in this book. As time went by, it became evident that if someone didn't capture the essence of their efforts in their own words, the opportunity would be lost. Many of my colleagues urged me to do the interviews because I had been through the period, was no longer managing a station and had the time as a free-lance consultant.

Thanks to the Corporation for Public Broadcasting, acting in accordance with its archival responsibility, we were able to develop a project to interview as many ETV pioneers as we could find, record their recollections on audio tape and furnish verbatim transcripts of these interviews for deposit in telecommunications archives. At the outset, no one envisioned that a book might evolve.

Anabel

My wife, Anabel, and I purchased a motor home and pre-arranged our interview appointments with fifty-five of the founders. We left Florida in March 1981 and returned in November, traveling more than 19,000 miles to chat with these people on their home grounds. Perhaps because I was a former colleague who understood their hopes, dreams and frustrations, the pioneers responded in an unguarded, almost confidential manner, providing their memories and incidental sidelights to main events. I believe this gives their accounts a certain charm as well as validity.

As I drove, and for the next eight months, my wife transcribed the interviews into three thousand pages of typewritten, verbatim material to complete the project for CPB.

The idea for the book came from many of those I interviewed. "Are you going to do a book about this?" was a common question. The seed began to grow. Then, when I interviewed the late Norman Cousins at his home in Beverly Hills, I asked him, "Is there a book in this."

"There most certainly is," he said, "and you are the one to do it!"

I had both the material and the encouragement I needed. However, I did not start writing the book for several years, partly because I was employed full-time in public relations for a full-service retirement center. And perhaps more importantly, I felt I was too close to the topic to judge what should be included or omitted from the transcripts. I felt a time gap from gathering the material to writing the book would give me a greater perspective not only on the origins of public television, but on its direction. This book does *not* pretend to be a comprehensive and carefully balanced history which gives properly proportioned weight to every step in the development of public television. Rather, this book is intended to be a sharing of personal recollections by many of those who first caught a glimpse of a dream. This is a period in American television now long past. There are glimpses also of an ideal which may still be attainable if enough concerned Americans today can be brought to see that television is capable of accomplishing far more now than it was in its first fifty years.

The fifty-five individuals whose recollections are included represent a cross-section of those who contributed in a significant way to the beginnings of this unique "alternative service" in American broadcasting.

What a Huge and Varied Country for Public Television to Serve

Since public television pioneers we interviewed lived in many different places across America, our motor-home trip gave us an unusual opportunity to sense both the greatness and the diversity of our nation, and to ponder how widespread was the initial urge to utilize television for the benefit of people of all ages wherever they lived—then, now, and into the future.

On the Road

School L.B.J. Attended

Snow in Arizona

California Redwoods

Gloucester Fisherman

Pacific Shore

On the Mall in the Nation's Capital

New England Church

Oregon Coast

Midwestern Farm

New York Skyline

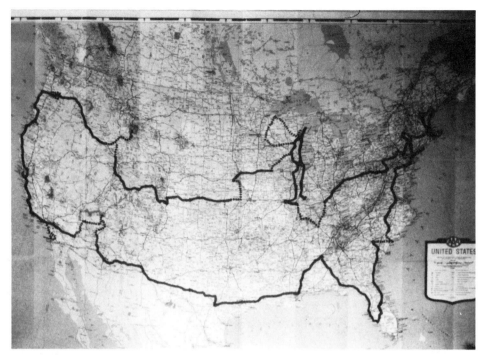

Jim and Anabel Robertsons' well-worn travel map

As indicated in the introductions which precede this prologue, many of those interviewed were outstanding citizens in their own right, in addition to playing key roles in the development of educational television. Dozens more were directly involved in early station management and operations.

From their comments it has been possible to provide accurate profiles of a few founders I was unable to interview personally, such as the late Frieda Hennock, the first woman member of the Federal Communications Commission; Ralph Lowell of the New England Lowell family, founder of Boston's WGBH-FM and WGHB-TV, who was involved with other significant activities in the early days of educational television; and John C. Schwarzwalder, manager of the very first educational television station. My apologies to any others who might feel that they were overlooked.

It is more than whimsy to call these people "TeleVisionaries," or "the parents of public television" for they dreamed of a new creation with great promise. They tell of the circumstances they had to face in the early years and offer their assessments of how their dream was doing in the early 1980s.

The birth of a dream has its parallels in human life. I find it amusing that just as a newborn baby is smacked into life by the attending physician, educational television was literally kicked into being when the first station went on the air—as the "parents" relate.

1

Kick the Transmitter!

Those who watch public television today—and perhaps most of those who work in it and those who support it—may be astonished when they compare present circumstances with those surrounding the very first moment when noncommercial educational television flickered onto a very few TV screens. That moment occurred in Houston, Texas, late in the afternoon on May 25, 1953, when KUHT, Channel 8, was about to go on the air.

Among those crowded into a small radio studio in the Cullen Building on the campus of the University of Houston for the dedication ceremonies were three of the visionaries of public television.

Two of them, George Arms and Roy Barthold, were part of the station staff. The third was one of several dignitaries who had flown from Washington, D.C. to participate in the dedication. He was Ralph Steetle, executive director of the Joint Council on Educational Television. He came from Louisiana State University, where he had been director of broadcasting and would later play a major role in the development of ETV.

STEETLE: I remember its inauguration. All the brass from Washington goes down. There is Frieda Hennock with her shoes off. The set director has covered the studio with an acre of flowers. It looks like a funeral!

Ralph Steetle

ARMS: Bill Davis, the first chief engineer—a rangy, rawboned fellow who always wore high-heeled boots, cowboy boots they called them—was having trouble with the transmitter about two hours before the five o'clock air time. It had suddenly developed a broad black band across the face of the screen, starting about

George Arms

four inches from the top and extending to about four inches from the bottom.

Frieda Hennock, who was one of the great heroines of educational television in those days, was to make the opening address, and we all had these horrible visions of Frieda's hair-do at the top of the screen and her bosom at the bottom of the screen...and a big black bar in between!

None of the engineers had any experience with television. They were all radio people. Of course, we'd surreptitiously had the transmitter on the air two or three times, but maintenance and trouble-shooting they didn't know anything about.

It got closer and closer to five o'clock. Finally, about twenty minutes to five, Bill lost his temper and kicked the transmitter. The black band disappeared and we never saw it again!

~

In my interview with Steetle, he confirmed the episode with this description of the event:

STEETLE: He [Davis] put his foot back and he whopped with all of his might the back of the transmitter. All of the needles sprang into action...so educational television, Jim, was literally kicked into existence!

Other sources say that John C. Schwarz-walder, manager of KUHT at the time, later claimed that he was the one who administered the kick.

Why Houston Was First

Why was the University of Houston the first to activate such a station when several other universities with greater prestige and far greater financial resources had been more active than Houston in educational radio? The only reason, apparently, was that opportunism was more alive in Texas than elsewhere.

STEETLE: There was a combination of a kind of mustang president in W.W. Kemmerer, and a mustang former opera singer in the form of our friend, John Schwarzwalder, and I guess a mustang millionaire [Hugh Roy Cullen] with oil money, and a private institution in the process of becoming public, and an interested school system which couldn't carry the load by itself.

I think Kemmerer was miscast as a university president.

He got so interested in television that when he wasn't looking, he was fired. He was a superior man. I was very fond of W.W. Kemmerer.

We were on our way over to the ceremony, riding in his [Kemmerer's] big black Cadillac. As we pulled in beside another black Cadillac, he says, "Ralph, I want to tell you the difference between a rich man and a poor man in Texas. See how shiny and clean his Cadillac is? That belongs to so-and-so," and he named a local millionaire. "See how dirty my black Cadillac is? I'm a poor man."

KUHT Mobile Unit: One of KUHT's most-watched programs in early years was live coverage of the Houston School Board meetings using this 1950-style truck containing two or three tons of portable but cumbersome television equipment.

KUHT Building: The present-day KUHT building completed in 1965 on Cullen Boulevard in Houston was a great improvement over the cramped quarters where KUHT operated for the previous twelve years.

Although Steetle and Arms had long since left Houston, Roy Barthold was found to be retired and living not far from the present-day KUHT studio building on Cullen Boulevard. Roy had lost his larynx to cancer but was able to talk to us using a battery-powered speech aid which, when held to his neck, produced a "synthetic voice."

In the KUHT conference room over coffee, Roy answered our questions about the eagerness of President Kemmerer to use television at the University of Houston.

Roy Barthold

BARTHOLD: Kemmerer had two prongs. First, he had strong feelings about the idea of cultural transmission on a universal scale as opposed to highly commercialized television as it was then. Then, here he had a private university with burgeoning enrollments. The university was very shy on space as well as personnel for teaching these big loads, especially at the freshman and sophomore levels.

So his concept was to teach a major part of the required freshman and sophomore courses — the mass enrollment courses: English, math, biology, government, and history — so that gradually it became a concept of two television lectures and one lecture on campus per week. This would theoretically allow us to handle three times as many students with the same space and the same personnel.

ARMS: The lecturers were to be on television, and he didn't care where the kids watched them...at home, in classrooms, in a bar. He didn't care.

Now, there were regularly scheduled conferences and tutorials. It was kind of an anticipation of the British Open University system.

But what he had going for him was administrative sanction. If there is no other way to take biology than by television, you're not going to have the argument about whether television courses are better than classroom courses.

Dr. Kemmerer saw with very clear vision the real possibilities for educational television in the service of an institution. Besides that, he didn't argue with the faculty very much. Maybe that's why he didn't last very long.

~

Two other factors apparently were vital to Dr. Kemmerer's audacious plan. One was personified by oil millionaire Hugh Roy Cullen, the other by a daring and skillful practitioner in the arts, John C. Schwarzwalder.

ARMS: Cullen looked and acted like a farm-hand. And he hadn't much money. He'd been a wildcatter all his life, and he'd struck it rich relatively late in life.

He was not a wealthy man by present-day or even Texas standards. Of course he had two or three million dollars in the bank, but that was small change.

Kemmerer had come when the University of Houston was a two-year junior college of the Houston Independent School District. Kemmerer had this dream of making it into a real four-year college, and he hit Cullen on a day when they resonated.

At the time that the station went on the air and Kemmerer was president, Cullen was the financial root—the root, singular.

He had a very sincere populist feeling about the virtue and value of education for the common man. That's the way he thought about KUHT.

John Schwarzwalder As Head

BARTHOLD: The pragmatic side of the thing was developed through John Schwarzwalder. He was already here as chairman of the Radio-Television Department, at the time that the television thing came up. And then Kemmerer grabbed the ball and ran with it.

He [Schwarzwalder] realized that he had a large resource, which was the large and rapidly growing student enrollment in the Radio-Television Department, and that became the operational focus. "Here's volunteer help to run the thing under faculty supervision!" So what he had there was his Radio-Television faculty, each of them assigned to certain areas, with a crew of volunteers.

ARMS: There had been a group of students—the likes of which will probably never be seen again—who had hung around the University of Houston for a couple of years, waiting for the television station to get started. They were relatively mature, as were all students after World War II almost, but even the ones who hadn't been to war were mature because they had hung around. They were goal-oriented.

They were the entire operating force at the station for two or three years. As soon as they finished a directing course, they would become directors.

Early Staff At KUHT: Some of the KUHT staff in its early days. General Manager and principal sparkplug John Schwarzwalder is on the left next to the TV camera. Roy Barthold is standing to the left of the microphone boom.

John reasoned wrongly that you could operate a television station at a very low cost, relying on student help. It won't work, as we know now, for a variety of reasons. It worked there as long as the original group of fifty or seventy-five kids were there. When that motivation, that calibre, that goal-orientation vanished and they got replaced, then you had to start paying them or they wouldn't show up.

But it was a marvelous experience those first couple of years....

I got something like $4200 to go as associate professor. And we taught a full schedule. We taught fifteen [credit] hours a week and ran the television station in addition. We were young then.

McBride Senses the Spirit

Jack McBride, who at the time was attempting to develop a plan for educational television at the University of Nebraska, recalls visiting KUHT in Houston during those years.

McBRIDE: There was a buoyant spirit about it. They knew they were pioneering something. There was a marvelous camaraderie among the people John [Schwarzwalder] had assembled. They were just caught up in the spirit of it, and it was easy for yourself to get equally caught up in it.

Jack McBride

They were operating in makeshift quarters, a studio that was way too small. It undoubtedly had been built as a radio studio, and they were on an upper floor, and they had far too little space—but it didn't matter. They were producing programs and they were sending pictures out and they were on to something and they knew it!

ARMS: The studio was about—I forget the exact size—twenty-five by thirty feet, or something like that, very small by today's standards, and with a very shallow roof. It had not been built as a television studio.

Of course, there was no videotape in those days, [so] we tried to do a live program and then [run] a film. But occasionally we would do three programs, back-to-back, live. And that meant that because there were four corners in the studio, whatever program you were doing had to be based in one of the corners and expand out from there. And they would change pieces of sets after you got started with the program, if necessary.

But it was hot and it was all live and it was exciting. And in a way, I wish that could come back to television because it enhanced the feeling of communication that isn't there now, when you punch a button and a videotape plays or a film plays.

I think unless public television—and probably commercial television—recaptures the feeling of "communication now," they're going to lose their birthright. Because as cable and other means of distribution get going, the only thing [broadcast] television will have going for it is the capacity for instantaneous distribution over a wide area, and the capacity to produce fairly complicated programming live.

If we lose that sense, we will have sold our birthright—but we had it then.

~

George Arms was describing the beginning of noncommercial educational television in the early 1950s. To gain a reasonable perspective on this event, it helps to go back more than thirty years to the beginnings of radio broadcasting in America—when a few of the visionaries sensed the educational possibilities of electronically-transmitted communication capable of reaching virtually everyone in the world.

2

Advertising on the Air? Never!

More than a generation before Schwarz-walder, Kemmerer, and Cullen tried to use television for specific educational purposes in Houston, some of the people in American broadcasting were trying to envision what this industry would eventually become. Unfortunately, most of them failed to see that it would develop into a gigantic money-making enterprise profoundly affecting American life.

At first, radio consisted of experiments in university physics laboratories and in shacks or garages owned by electrical engineers fascinated with sending messages through the air without using wires—first by dot-dash code and then by voice transmission.

A few university extension people in the Midwest began to see radio's value for disseminating weather information and market reports to farmers. In the East, the big electric companies, busy making small household appliances, had not yet dreamed of the market they soon would discover for the sale of radios in homes.

After World War I, unregulated transmissions filled the American air. The amateurs and hobbyists who built radio receivers and donned headphones were less interested in actual program than they were in vying with each other to tune in stations from the farthest distance.

Broadcast transmission is such that if two or more stations are using the same frequency, that is, the same spot on the dial, they will interfere with each other if they are geographically too close together. In other words, to assure listeners a clear signal, some sort of regulation was going to be required.

Hoover's First Radio Conference - 1922

Herbert C. Hoover, later President of the United States but then Secretary of Commerce under President Warren G. Harding, became aware of this impending chaos and convened the first Washington Radio Conference in 1922 to see what could be done. As Eric Barnouw comments in the first volume of his *History of Broadcasting in the United States:*

"Pandemonium was on its way. An industry scarcely out of its swaddling clothes had its first national meeting."[1] Because the primary matter to be dealt with was regulation to avoid interference, the matter of programming was scarcely mentioned. Even more interesting in retrospect is the fact that apparently there was only minor concern about commercialization. As Barnouw reports, "the idea of ether advertising" was mentioned but with disfavor. One of those who did so was Secretary Hoover, who said, "It is inconceivable that we should allow so great a possibility for service to be drowned in advertising chatter." His remark caused little comment at the time. [2]

Three of public television's "parents" confirm the early expectation that broadcasting would not be an advertising medium—that it would be mainly a service of informational and cultural value.

Hyman Goldin, who served on the staff of the Federal Communications Commission in various roles over a period of twenty-two years, undertook a study of the early days.

---

[1] Barnouw, Eric, "A Tower in Babel," page 94.
[2] Barnouw, ibid., page 96

GOLDIN: As a historian, the first thing that I did when I came to the FCC [1943] was to find out about the background, and I looked into that period in the 1920s and 1930s.

Hyman Goldin

One of the interesting things is that the notion of a noncommercial service was something that [David] Sarnoff thought was the way broadcasting was going to go....

He had that notion that if radio was to go anywhere it had to be culturally uplifting. It was going to be positive, and it was going to serve all of these great purposes.

He even tried to organize a support system by the manufacturers [of radio sets] for a fund for cultural programs, because he didn't see how it was really going to be sponsored.

~

Another individual who occupied an advantageous position from which to view the development of broadcasting in the 1920s was Everett Case. In more recent times, Dr. Case was president (later, president emeritus) of Colgate University and subsequently a president of The Sloan Foundation.

Everett Case's Home, Van Hornesville, New York.

Dr. Case received us warmly in his beautifully-furnished living room of Van Horne house in the little community of Van Hornesville, New York, where he and his wife, Jo, had been reading the proofs of a book they had written about her father, the late Owen D. Young.

Owen D. Young Creates RCA, Hires Sarnoff

In the 1920s Case was assistant to Owen D. Young when Young was head of both General Electric and RCA. He recalled Young's selection of David Sarnoff to be head of RCA and the forming of the National Broadcasting Company [NBC] and explained the business reasons behind these moves after World War I.

CASE: We had the edge on Britain in natural resources of oil. Britain controlled ocean transportation, and Britain controlled the cables. Hence, if there was to be a standoff, we needed the wireless preeminence...and Young's response was to create the Radio Corporation of America [RCA].

To do that, he had to acquire control of American Marconi, which was a virtual subsidiary of the British Marconi company. He did that and then brought in the telephone company [AT&T], which also had patents that were needed to create the best devices for both receiving and sending.

So that was the origin of RCA—except for a fellow named Sarnoff, who had been general manager at American Marconi.

~

Dr. Case also recalled how Westinghouse had begun radio broadcasting over its experimental station in Pittsburgh, which became KDKA, with a broadcast of the election returns in November 1920. He confirmed that Westinghouse—then only a manufacturer of electric toasters and other household appliances—was among the first to see, along with Sarnoff and Young, the commercial possibilities in "the little black box."

CASE: This attracted attention, and it had the General Electric engineers climbing the wall because they let Westinghouse get ahead of them.

And then it just caught like wildfire, the radio set and the beginning of broadcasting. Sales of "the little black box" suddenly boomed, and the revenue from this began to shoot far ahead of the increasing revenue from wireless communication.

I did not master all of the intricacies of the General Electric Company, but by that time RCA had set up the National Broadcasting Company. Young had drawn the specifications for it and made the announcement as chairman. He was then chairman of both GE and RCA. He had also set up—well, let's go back a minute.

The question when you set up a national broadcasting company was whether you were going to follow the European model, with government control and government financing, or whether you were to do this on the basis of private initiative. Young chose the latter but recognized that there were pitfalls. So he set up an advisory council to the National Broadcasting Company, which was comprised of such members as Elihu Root; Charles Evans Hughes; John W. Davis; Edwin Alderman, then president of the University of Virginia; Julius Rosenwald; Mrs. John Sherman, who was president of the Women's Clubs; representatives of the Protestant, Catholic, and Jewish faiths, and William Green for labor.

~

I commented to Case, "The nature of that board seems to suggest that Mr. Young had a somewhat different notion of what broadcasting would become than what it has become in latter years."

CASE: You can say that again...very different. And so, as a matter of fact, did Sarnoff.

They both agreed, separately and together, that this new instrument was of such importance, going into the home, that the greatest care had to be exercised not to commercialize and exploit it so it turned the home into a bazaar—which

Everett Case

it has since become, a bazaar with a midway! And therefore, advertising was not the ideal form of support.

Sarnoff Proposes A Tax On Radio Sets

CASE: What Sarnoff himself proposed was that RCA set aside—I don't remember whether this was just RCA or whether it was to be a tax on all producers, perhaps it was—a 2 percent tax on the sale of sets.

And that would be sufficient, because they were selling like hot cakes, sufficient probably to finance the broadcasting company, at least initially. And, sooner or later, he thought that foundations would come in, and the broadcasting company could build up capital and reserve sufficient to do its job.

If advertisers came into the picture—and they were clamoring to—the rule would be that they could announce that they were sponsoring such-and-such a program, but no sales talk—and never any mention of the price at which things were to go....

In any event, as one looked over—as I did at the time—the programs developed and listed in the report to the Advisory Council of NBC, one had the feeling that this was very much like what public radio [and television] is now supposed to be and sometimes is.

The "Walter Damrosch Music Appreciation Hour" reached I don't know how many hundred thousand schools all over the country and encouraged students of the violin, for example, to get the violin score and play with the orchestra. Ditto for the flute, the clarinet, and so forth. This was a terrific thing, opening the ears of students to music as a performing art, not just listening.

I might say that some of us younger critics were by no means satisfied with the quality of the programs, even at the peak that I'm talking about. We were very critical. We thought some of it was just geared to mass tastes, and not picking out the best and feeding the best to the public at all.

The other thing that Young saw in this was a new medium for poets, artists, musicians, which would encourage creative work by younger artists and writers and musicians—that would make this another Elizabethan Age.

There are those who would disagree and say that they [Young and Sarnoff] talked the importance of culture but raked in the shekels on the other hand from the advertisers, that they talked a good game. I think there may be truth in that as far as some of the individuals concerned go....

But by this time [1932] the only profit-making adjunct of RCA was NBC, and they had to go for all the advertising they could get. The cards, in a sense, were stacked in favor of the advertiser. The pressures became irresistible. It became more and more difficult to assure cultural programs in prime time.

Commercials On Radio Will Not Be Allowed!

These two recollections are confirmed by the reminiscences of Parker Wheatley, a lifelong broadcaster whose idealism always seemed to show. In later years he led the establishment of Boston's WGBH-FM and participated in the beginnings of WGBH-TV but in 1928 was an announcer for WFBM in Indianapolis.

In 1981, Parker was on the air for CBS radio in St. Louis, alerting his listeners to important issues in the area. We met in the KMOX conference room, and as he and I reflected on those long-past days, he seemed almost surprised by his own recollection.

WHEATLEY: I actually lived in broadcasting when you could not put a commercial on the air!

I lived at a time when Herbert Hoover and David Sarnoff both thought it quite unthinkable that this great system of communication, education, enlightenment, entertainment—there was a great deal of good music on the air then, and so on—should ever be turned to commercial purposes.

Parker Wheatley

Herbert Hoover said that, and so did David Sarnoff. And David Sarnoff hoped that some day broadcasting could be supported by gifts, such as public libraries had been supported by Andrew Carnegie's largesse. But that didn't happen.

~

Recalling his principal activities when he subsequently became program director for Westinghouse's KYW, which was then in Chicago, Wheatley demonstrated the hopefulness which apparently was still alive among broadcasters at that time.

WHEATLEY: As program director of that station, I was out digging around for ideas, for something which had inspired me in the first place about broadcasting—to bring to people who otherwise would never have the means, great music, the great ideas of the world, and the great thinkers and artists and scholars. I had a kind of uplift mission.

~

The idealistic hopes and dreams related by Public TeleVisionaries were kept alive by others as well. Had this not been so, we might not have anything like public broadcasting today.

3

Gimme a Channel and I'll Show You

If you set out to operate a radio or television station, you can't just choose a channel and go on the air. You can start a newspaper (if you can find the financing) and print and distribute it without being licensed to do so. The same applies to starting a magazine or almost any other kind of commercial enterprise. If you have the money, the talent and the courage, you just go ahead.

Not so with a broadcasting station—for technical reasons. These reasons became clear in the early 1920s and led to Herbert Hoover's Washington Radio Conferences. By that time it also had become clear that if you held a broadcast channel, you had a license to make money. Even though it wasn't nearly as clear then as it is today, the shrewd ones saw the possibilities and plunged into the fray to assure themselves a choice piece of the eventual profits.

But those who conceived of broadcasting as a medium for public benefit forced the regulatory authorities to face two major problems: how to minimize technical interference between stations, and also how to allocate the limited number of available frequencies among all of those interests—commercial and otherwise, including educational—who began to clamor for licenses.

The Federal Radio Commission, established by Congress in 1927 to deal with this situation, didn't manage to please anybody. In what broadcast historian Eric Barnouw has called "the gold rush atmosphere," [1]

those who could see even dimly the potentials in broadcasting for educational and cultural purposes were aghast at the manner in which commercial interests gobbled up available frequencies.

By 1929 the National Committee on Educational Radio was formed, with Joy Elmer Morgan, editor of the National Education Association's *NEA Journal*, as its chairman. The committee's first task, in Morgan's words, was "to save or recover for the uses of education a fair share of the radio broadcasting frequencies."

The following year saw the organization of another action group with a name so similar as to cause considerable confusion: The National Advisory Council on Radio in Education. Its position was that educational needs could be served adequately by commercial broadcasters; thus educators did not need to have their own channels.

Rosel Hyde Describes Early Regulations

One of public television's "parents" who began his career in 1928 as a staff member of the old Federal Radio Commission recalls the furor of the time. Rosel Hyde spent virtually his entire professional life in broadcast regulation, from 1928 until he retired from the Federal Communications Commission in 1969. First appointed an FCC commissioner by President Harry Truman in 1946, he successively served in that capacity under four U.S. presidents and was FCC chairman during several terms. Because of Hyde's extensive experience, his comments take on special significance.

---

[1] Barnouw, Eric, op. cit, page 282.

HYDE: There was a considerable broadcast industry—enough to cause chaos on the air—before the Radio Commission of 1927 was created.

Rosel Hyde

Then, in connection with the new administration of Franklin D. Roosevelt, often referred to as the New Deal, there was a considerable examination of government functions generally, and a proposal to regulate communications in one place was undertaken. And so legislation was introduced which resulted in the Communications Act of 1934. [2]

The Communications Act of 1934 provided that the commission should study the proposition that a fixed percentage of channels should be reserved for educational purposes. The commission was ordered to report on this suggestion by February 1935. One of the items on the first agenda of the new commission was to conduct an investigation. In fact, they held oral hearings, and many came in to represent various viewpoints. [This was] my first opportunity to view some of the pioneers in educational broadcasting.

The recommendation to the commission out of those hearings was that no reservations should be made, the view being that all licensees had a responsibility to serve all elements, all factors of society.

This seems like a very narrow position in the light of present-day conditions, but at the time of this recommendation there were—oh, perhaps seven hundred stations. And one of the problems that the new commission had to deal with was reducing the number of stations in order to reduce interference.

Their finding was not without its supporting arguments. But they did not comprehend the possibilities for expansion both in the spectrum and in the number of stations that later developed.

The Federal Radio Education Committee

Apparently there were those on the commission who were sympathetic to the pleas of educators. Gertrude Broderick, a long-time civil servant in the U.S. Office of Education, speaks of a subsequent development which seems to have kept the educators' vision alive.

BRODERICK: Out of those hearings and the testimony of many educators and broadcasters, the FCC decided to appoint a committee—a committee of forty men and women from broadcasting and education.

Gertrude Broderick

That was known as the Federal Radio Education Committee, or FREC. Dr. John W. Studebaker was the commissioner of education at that time, and he was named chairman of this big committee of forty people.

In due time, he called the committee together for what turned out to be its first, last, and only meeting.

It was made up of pretty high calibre people both in broadcasting and education. Mr. [William S.] Paley, the head of CBS, was a member, as was his counterpart at NBC, whose name escapes me at the moment, and Harold McCarty represented the NAEB.

~

Harold B. "Mac" McCarty had begun his lifetime love affair with radio six years earlier at the University of Wisconsin's pioneering educational radio station, WHA.

McCARTY: That was a genuine effort on Studebaker's part to enlist the participation of leaders—from the land-grant institutions, from state universities, from a whole cross section of the educational enterprise—for consideration of some of these things. One of the leaders was from [Studebaker's] own office:

Harold McCarty

Franklin Dunham. You had leaders such as Arthur Adams from adult education, and Belmont Farley, and Joy Elmer Morgan....I could never figure out why a man would be named Joy. But oh, what respect I had for him, and what affection.

[2] This act did away with the old Federal Radio Commission and created the Federal Communications Commission, which has been the regulatory agency for broadcasting ever since.

When I was feeling low at one point, I recall, he took me aside with arm on shoulder and said, "McCarty, don't be discouraged. You really have a more important assignment than President [Glenn] Frank of your university."

And I said, "Oh, come on!" And he said, "I'm serious about that. President Frank doesn't have the access to the people that you do. With your station and with the possibility of a state-wide network, you have the opportunity...."

And suddenly I began to see in greater perspective the possibilities of the medium reaching into every home of the state, making the university come alive, helping people to solve

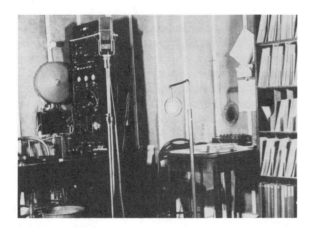

WHA Studio 1929: The "corner room in Sterling Hall," served as the radio studio, office, and transmitter room. The grand piano is outside the photo, but the apparatus behind the standing microphone is the transmitter, the shelves on the right are the music library, and the desk in between was McCarty's office. Author Robertson visited this studio while a high school student in the 1930s.

their problems. Joy Elmer Morgan was one of those people who helped me to see that.

Pioneering Educational Radio at WHA

McCARTY: [The physical conditions at the early station were] primitive! Extremely so! It was operating in a corner room in Sterling Hall. It was hung with some old faded velvet drapes. It housed the grand piano, a panel of equipment—the amplifier and control equipment—in the same room which also served as my office. I was the whole staff except for a part-time student operator who operated the transmitter in the basement. And everything took place there. When we were on the air, I'd take the telephone off the hook so we wouldn't be interrupted!

That was 1929. The station had been on the air for ten years, not with an impressive schedule but with a constant, continuing effort to offer mainly three types of programs: specialized information for farm listeners which we called "The Farm Program"; information for homemakers called "The Homemakers' Hour," which was really only a half hour, from 10 to 10:30 in the morning; and programs of general interest—music, and a talk arranged by Professor [William H.] Lighty of University Extension.

I think that credit should be given in the beginning to a real pioneer, a programming pioneer, Andrew Hopkins, who was chairman of Agricultural Journalism. He had developed the farm program, the homemakers' program, and he encouraged the people of University Extension to contribute. He would line up these

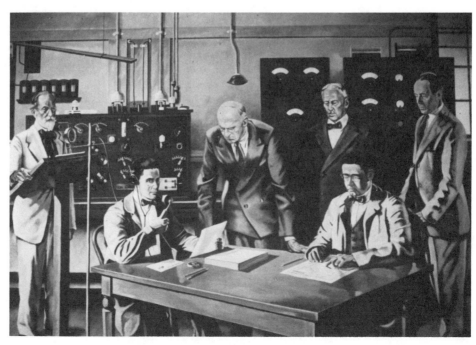

WHA Mural: Shown in this portion of a larger mural at WHA are key individuals in its history, mentioned by McCarty. Left to right, Prof. William H. Lighty, student engineer Malcolm Hansen, and Professors Andrew W. Hopkins, Edward Bennett, Earle M. Terry, and Henry L. Ewbank. The technical apparatus in the background appears similar to the actual experimental gear of 9XM when it began broadcasting in 1919.

features, send the people over to the studio. I would greet them, announce them, and put them on the air.

The programs of general interest were arranged by Professor Lighty, who was director of University Extension. He was imbued with the idea enunciated by a former president of the university: "I shall never rest content until the beneficent influences of the university are available to every home in the state."

I got caught up with that philosophy and thought this was just absolutely inspiring—to share with the people of the state the advantages of learning on the campus.

That was what we had in mind when we formed the "College of the Air" in 1933. In 1931 we had established the "Wisconsin School of the Air" to provide enrichment and specialized learning for schools of the state.

We started out with only an hour and a half a day, but before long had come to occupy the entire daytime schedule.

It's good to see the enthusiasm with which they do it now. In the beginning there was indifference, there was a certain—well, everybody was a little in awe of this magic instrument of radio. They needed to be encouraged and instructed in some elementary principles.

Educational Radio's First "Conventions"

McCarty recalls the first-ever attempt of educational radio practitioners to get together in the early 1930s—all part of a long preamble to the subsequent development of public broadcasting.

McCARTY: The Association of College and University Broadcasting Stations—which was a mouthful for any radio man, no matter how nimble he might be—was formed in the early thirties.

We had several so-called national meetings, which really consisted of small conferences of the Midwest representatives—from Iowa to Ohio State, then Michigan, Indiana, Illinois, Wisconsin, and Minnesota.

These were the chief proponents because of the commitment of these institutions to public service to their state under the land-grant college idea of taking the university to the people.

We gathered annually to console each other, and to compare our budgets, and to gain what comfort we could from the realization that the other fellow wasn't much better off than we were.

We had a convention called a "national convention" in the early thirties in Kansas City at the Hotel Muehlebach, and as I tell the story there were fourteen of us. This is disputed by some, who claim there may have been as many as two dozen at this "national convention."

It was there that I suggested that a name change would be highly desirable, because we had this awkward name. I remember vividly, standing at a blackboard accepting suggestions and putting them on the board until we had about eight or nine suggestions for a name for the organization.

And I believe I was the one who said, "Look, the commercial guys are organized as the National Association of Broadcasters; why don't we just put an "E" in there—NAEB—the National Association of *Educational* Broadcasters?"

So it was agreed and adopted, and from then on bore that name.

~

For nearly half a century thereafter, the NAEB was unquestionably the seminal force in the gradual growth and development of what is now known as public broadcasting.

NAEB's central position in many subsequent situations will be reflected in the words of many of the Public TeleVisionaries —particularly during the efforts in Washington, D.C. to secure a reasonable share of broadcast channels, both in radio and in television. And the emergence of FM gave NAEB its first real chance.

4

How About FM For You Educators?

One way to get your piece of the future is to grab what you want before anyone else realizes they might want it. This seems to have been the nature of the next step in the long march toward public television. Broadcast frequencies for noncommercial educational use needed to be set aside.

Educators and others who saw in broadcasting a remarkable way to enrich the lives of the American people lost the battle for AM radio frequencies to the commercial broadcasters in the 1930s. But in the 1940s a new method of radio transmission—frequency modulation, or FM—became available as a result of the engineering research of one Major Edwin H. Armstrong.

RCA, the Radio Corporation of America, elected not to push FM because of David Sarnoff's greater interest in television. World War II also commandeered nearly all FM engineering know-how for military purposes. Frequencies allocated for FM broadcasting, therefore, were not quickly taken up by commercial interests. This gave the educators a second chance.

HYDE: Dr. Armstrong's development of FM offered a new opportunity, and you will notice that the commission did allocate certain frequencies in the FM band for the development of educational stations. I think that's an example of planning ahead. I think the commission should be given credit for statesmanship in this.

~

Leonard Marks, in the 1940s, was assistant to Rosel Hyde when he was FCC general counsel. Marks was to become the hardy perennial among communications attorneys. His early befriending of the educators

developed into a lifelong support of educational broadcasting that has been of incalculable value.

Leonard Marks

MARKS: As the war was winding down, it became apparent that we ought to develop rules and regulations to encourage two new industries, one the FM field and the other television. It became my responsibility to head a small task force to prepare rules and regulations, hold public hearings, and carry this out. We were of the opinion that education should play an important role in the development of these new technologies.

When the standard broadcast band was being perfected, universities, colleges, and public institutions that desired to use [AM frequencies] found that because they took longer to get organized, because many of them did not have adequate capital, the wonderful opportunities disappeared and the choice frequencies were assigned to department stores and seed companies and venture capitalists. And the broadcast industry started without the full participation of the educational community.

We wanted to avoid a recurrence of that, and so we included in the original thinking a reservation of channels for FM broadcasting.

In fact, the FCC in 1945 reserved twenty channels, from eighty-eight to ninety-two megacycles, for noncommercial educational FM broadcast service, the portion of the FM dial where one now finds National Public Radio.

Marks left the FCC in 1946 to become the partner of Marcus Cohn, also formerly with the FCC, in a law firm which played a key role in assisting fledgling educational broadcasters for decades thereafter.

Educational Radio Folks "Babes In the Woods"

Cohn's recollections shed light on the nature of both the educators and the FCC during those days.

Marcus Cohn Brooks photo
Marcus Cohn

COHN: At the time, the noncommercial broadcasters were really babes in the woods. They really didn't know what was going on in Washington. They didn't know the procedures of the FCC. They didn't know rule-making proceedings. They didn't know about decisions in the FCC.

One of the things they needed most was a bridge between their local concerns and Washington. And that bridge had to be people, hopefully such as ourselves, who were experts in the field who could help them along the way.

While obviously I wanted to succeed as a person practicing in the communications field, and success would normally be denominated in terms of economic security and income, nevertheless, because of my background and the number of different things that I did and my family did in terms of helping those who needed help and couldn't pay, I felt a commitment—a devotion to this.

These were struggling, young, energetic, dynamic, intelligent people who were trying to do something, and yet they didn't know the realities of this Frankenstein here in Washington. They were innocent...they were innocent babes.

Fortunately, certainly during the days of the New Deal, the complexion of the commission was one where at least you weren't automatically rebuffed. There was an empathy toward this phenomenon of public broadcasting.

There was a far greater brotherhood—it's a good word—because of that feeling, that empathy, toward these poor struggling educational institutions, which needed a helping hand. And

that was really, I suppose, the gratification we got from helping these poor babes in the woods with whatever expertise we had in the field.

~

Franklin Dunham and Gertrude Broderick in the U.S. Office of Education also did what they could to alert the educational community to the potentials of FM radio in education.

BRODERICK: There was a growing interest on the part of the educational broadcasters in the possibility of reserved radio frequencies for noncommercial use. So the Office [of Education], through its newsletter and through its participation in workshops and other activities, helped to stimulate interest in the reservation of FM channels. We didn't appear as witnesses who needed assistance.

Commercial FM was something way off, you know. But there were some folks who recognized a genuine possibility in the further uses of radio if there was a special reservation of channels.

~

One of those folks was I. Keith Tyler of the Ohio State University. He qualifies as one of the visionaries of public television for a number of reasons. Although he was never a station manager, he played many supporting roles—researcher, encourager, evaluator, and strategist—in several of noncommercial broadcasting's battles. He described his part in the effort to persuade the FCC to reserve FM frequencies.

I. Keith Tyler Begins to Help

I. Keith Tyler

TYLER: Cleveland had been experimenting, in cooperation with local commercial radio stations, in school broadcasting ...direct instruction by radio: arithmetic, music, various things.

But they began to run into the usual problems. Their time would be changed on them, or as radio became more popular and [the stations] could sell more time, the schools would lose their air time. So they began to explore the idea of developing their own station.

At about this time the FCC was exploring the possibilities of FM. And so we helped [Cleveland] get a grant for their initial station.

As far as I know, the first FM educational station was WBOE in Cleveland.[1]

About this time, the NAEB was beginning to look at this new band of frequencies and suggesting they ought to reserve channels there for education. Here was our chance.

I had the fortunate circumstance that my chief, the president of Ohio State University at that time was Dr. Howard Bevis. He was also chairman of the radio committee of both the Land-Grant College Association and the American Association of State Universities. And I wrote his reports on various things.

I would write in there what I thought were reasonable things that the associations of higher education ought to be doing. Bevis usually bought this and he'd deliver these papers. So Ohio State got committed, and so did the associations, you see. I will take credit for a lot of that.

When they were having hearings with regard to setting aside these channels in FM for education, Bevis and I went down to Washington, and he was called on the witness stand, and he was telling why they should do this. At one point he stopped and said, raising his voice, " That's right, isn't it, Keith?" And the commissioner said, "You can't do that unless he's sworn in!"

Anyway, they didn't have long hearings, but the educators were united on this. There were no problems. There wasn't much commercial interest in FM.

But we wanted to get there first, and we did.

~

Californian John C. Crabbe, one of the first program associates for the Educational Television and Radio Center and later the founder of KVIE-TV in Sacramento, remembers how one local educational radio professional felt about those circumstances.

John C. Crabbe

CRABBE: That was going on during World War II, a lot of that activity. I was in the navy and was based in Baltimore for a period of time so I was able to get right close to that. A whole lot of us were mixed up in that whole reservation fight.

Up to that point, nobody knew an awful lot about FM. NAEB was kind of a focal point of it.

The Situation in the 1940s

Wisconsin's H. B. McCarty furnished a summarizing comment on radio's circumstances in the mid-forties.

McCARTY: The idea of reserving a portion of the spectrum exclusively for educational noncommercial purposes was an anathema to the commercial broadcasters, who felt that they had a proprietary interest.

Many of them sincerely believed that if there was something worth doing educationally, they could do it—and could even do it better because of their so-called expertise. This argument was accepted by many people because there was no great clamor on the part of educators themselves.

I think we must be absolutely honest about it. Educational institutions and educational leaders were slow to grasp the opportunities provided by broadcasting. It took some stirring up, and the NAEB was the chief stirring-up agency, and had a great role to play when the FCC faced the problems of how to utilize frequency modulation.

It was realized, because of the clamor for licenses immediately after the war, that the AM band could never accommodate all those who wished to broadcast. So there were several abortive attempts to get started on FM and divide up the frequencies. Finally, because it offered the possibility for establishing so many stations, far beyond the dreams of the commercial broadcasters then, they didn't protest too much at a reservation of a portion for education.

But that became very important when television came along. Indeed it did!

~

McCarty was right. Precedent is significant in any kind of legal or regulatory matter. The foot in the door which educators achieved in securing the reservation of FM channels could be considered the first stage in what became a larger campaign to reserve television channels—without which, of course, there would not be public television today.

---

[1] As early as 1939, the FCC had granted noncommercial educational licenses to WBOE in Cleveland and WNYE in New York. The FM reservations hearings, however, were in 1945.

And who knows? Hopefully FM reservations in the 1940s and the TV reservations in the 1950s will form precedents which can be applied to allocations of other scarce portions of the electronic spectrum as our communications technologies continue to expand in the future.

As the NAEB leadership marshalled the forces of education to secure FM radio channels for noncommercial use, a new technology was being born.

5

Hot Lights, Gooey Makeup, and No Big Audience—Yet

Many of those who produced the earliest programs on noncommercial educational television stations had been among the first to learn television production at the country's first commercial stations.

Eighteen years before the first educational television station went on the air, one of the visionaries of public television graduated from the Massachusetts Institute of Technology and promptly got a job with NBC. Little did he realize at the time what the professional path before him would be like. He could not have imagined the experiences which he was shortly to enjoy. He made this clear nearly fifty years later, prior to his retirement as a faculty member at Pennsylvania State University.

Seven other founders also were participants during the 1940s as the first few commercial TV stations came on the air, but Arthur Hungerford's experiences even prior to television's debut at the New York World's Fair of 1939 pre-dates them all.

Arthur Hungerford

HUNGERFORD: I graduated in 1933, which wasn't a very good year to get a job, but I wasn't out of a job at all. I went right from MIT to NBC. In only a little time, we started a little thing called the Television Research Institute. Three of us took the magazines from England—which was the leader then in television experiments— and we collected all that information, and we got out each month an offset sheet—a summary sheet—of the television going on in the world. We sent this to all the heads of advertising agencies, the heads of the biggest banks in New York, and all over the city, because we really wanted to get into television.

After this had been going on for about eight months, the vice president in charge of sales at NBC, Ed Kobak, called us into his office. We were shaking in our boots. We knew something was up.

He said, "David Sarnoff sent this down and said 'What are you guys doing down there? My friends are showing me this thing and I never heard of it before. What's this?'"

So we told him what it was, and that all we wanted to do was to get into television.

He said, "Look, I'll make a deal with you." By this time we really were shaking. He said, "If you will give up this magazine and I put you in television, would that be a fair deal? I'm going to put you in with Jimmy James [who was head of promotion at NBC,] and you two guys will go down and join the staff in the television studio." And that's the way we got in...in 1935.

We had a very secret studio, 3H, on the third floor of the RCA building. It was being converted with large lights, and we had a basic camera there, only one, an old iconoscope camera. And every once in a while the engineers would bring up new tubes from [the RCA plant in] Camden, and we'd try them all out and take the best one we could get to work. That's the way it was.

The big day was July 7th in 1936. This was the first high-definition television program in the United States, and we had quite a group there. We had Ed Wynn, we had Henry Hull from "Tobacco Road," David Sarnoff from RCA, we had three Rockettes [we could only use three of them because there wasn't much room in the studio,] and Russell Markert had to come up with a little dance that the three of them could do so we wouldn't have to move the camera very much!

I was working on the microphone boom in that show. Later on I became stage manager and what-not. But that was the very first show, and I have a script of it.

[Lighting] was horrendous. It was a thousand foot-candles. We had air conditioning, but instead of having the anemostats to distribute the air we had it [flowing] down through the chutes right onto the set so that it would cool the people the best it could.

Dinah Shore's Baptism

HUNGERFORD: One time we had a girl performer. I was the stage manager on the show and she was singing. All of a sudden she was in serious trouble, and I could tell because I was, you know, ducking under the camera and taking signals, and I waved to her. I said, "Do you want to get off?" You can't talk, but you can do this all with your hand. She said, "No, I'll stick with it." And we got through...but it turned out the mascara on her eyes had melted and it was dripping into her eyes, and this gal finished her song with that going on. Her name is Dinah Shore. Dinah went on to be the wonderful person that she is.

The other horrible thing was, makeup was black and white. Everybody had white faces and black lips. We wanted to get the maximum contrast, and that was the way we did it.

~

I asked Hungerford about the New York World's Fair demonstrations.

HUNGERFORD: That's where we began television officially. We came on the air then.

President Franklin D. Roosevelt as he appeared on television screens in 1939, opening the New York World's Fair.

We were putting on films all day long. I was in charge of getting all those films at that time. We put them on repetitiously so that the dealers—

well, first of all, so we could demonstrate television at the World's Fair. It started with [Franklin D.] Roosevelt. I have a picture of that. President Roosevelt came up and launched the fair, and we were televising it at that time...the World's Fair of 1939.

And after that we went on with a regular schedule. It was quite an active schedule; we were on five days a week. One night would be a play, one night would be a variety show, one night would be wrestling, one night there would be a feature film, and I've forgotten what the other night was—some sort of educational thing usually.

We did that for about a year or so. Then the FCC stopped the sale of sets and we had to retrench. Then we got started all over again, and then the war came.

~

Hungerford's recollections of TV programming prior to the shut-down for World War II reflect an effort to utilize educational materials.

HUNGERFORD: The two shows that I was the most interested in...one was the "Esso News," and the other one was "The Explorer's Club." That was a beautiful show. I had it arranged so that there was one explorer; he'd come in and go over his films with me and we'd decide what they were going to be and he'd narrate these films live when the show time came.

So we telecast this thing, and there were three explorers and the host. Then the next week we had the next guy and three more fellows. So we didn't have to rehearse the show at all. It rehearsed itself each week.

Sir Hubert Wilkins going under the arctic ice—he was one of them. And Julian Bryan—all those folks.

So that was the first way I got interested in education. And then the navy, of course, was the second. Toward the end of the war they gave me a half-million dollars to build a television studio and to try out this idea of teaching by television. That's why I didn't go back to NBC.

Armed Forces Begin Teaching By TV

Hungerford presided over extensive experiments in the use of television as a teaching tool for the U.S. Navy during the late 1940s and maintained careful research data to show conclusions.

HUNGERFORD: It came out with the famous phrase, "There's no significant difference" in the television [instruction], whether you do it live or, you know, you have the students there.

One other thing we found that was fascinating...and we never promoted this.

We found out that we could take an actor and put him in a sailor suit and have him memorize the script, and we found out that he taught just as well as a competent man in the classroom. We never published that, but that actually happened.

~

Having undertaken this project in televised instruction for the navy, Hungerford and his associates made a proposal to the U.S. Army to teach reserve units. Their contact at CBS was Davidson Taylor.

HUNGERFORD: He said, "Would you like to have Tuesday night, eight o'clock to nine o'clock, for about ten weeks?"

I said, "Sure, that's great. How can we do that?"

He said, "I think I could arrange that." Why do you think we got that time, free? What was on NBC at eight o'clock during those days on Tuesday nights? Milton Berle! Davidson Taylor said, "You guys can have that. We can't program against that guy." Isn't that fascinating? We had that time for ten weeks, and we taught hundreds of those guys.

~

Another perspective on early television in New York is furnished by James Macandrew, for years the key individual in instructional broadcasting in the New York area, who, after many years as manager of WNYE radio, developed the comprehensive New York school television service known as The Regents' Project.

MACANDREW: In the early days, the [television] stations had time that was empty. They couldn't fill the hours they had. I'm speaking of commercial television in the 1940s after World War II, the coming of television and the appearance of television receivers in more and more homes....

James Macandrew

They went to the colleges; they went to Columbia, they went to NYU, and eventually they asked me if the Board of Education might not also be interested in some

television time to do what would be mutually desirable.

Dumont had a channel and a studio in the John Wanamaker store, and suddenly the Board of Education was putting on programs at night for a general audience.

One of my early colleagues, who was tremendously active in the birth of television, was Ed Stasheff. Ed had been in the field of dramatics at Columbia. His heart belonged to the theater and to broadcasting, and I had the great good fortune of having him join the staff at WNYE where he really became the key man in television. When we started putting programs on commercial stations, he was the producer and sometimes the host.

I recall an evening program out of the Dumont studio in the Wanamaker store called "You Be the Judge." This attracted quite an audience. When I think of all the programs which are game programs or mystery programs, I sometimes think of "You Be the Judge," which must have been in 1949 or 1950.

It was the re-creation of a problem in law which came out of history or literature, and the two sides were presented and the viewer was asked, "What would you have done had you been the judge?" At the very end, of course, the secret of what had happened was revealed to the audience. It was a cliffhanger; it was a very attractive program idea.

~

Even before World War II, the Philadelphia area saw some early television, as related by Martha Gable. Initially a physical education instructor for the Philadelphia schools, she became over the years one of this country's foremost proponents and practitioners of educational television, participating in countless workshops and demonstrations at educators' conventions to encourage the use of television for instructional purposes. Retired from the Philadelphia school system in 1974, her 1981 recall of events forty years earlier was remarkable.

GABLE: The Philco Company was manufacturing television receivers, and they had a factory up in the Kensington area of Philadelphia.

In 1941, President Roosevelt appointed John B. Kelly, Sr., Princess Grace's father, to head up the national physical fitness program. And Mr. Kelly asked me to leave the schools for a year, and the Board of Education granted that leave so I could work with him for the women's activities.

Philadelphia Schools and Colleges Use TV

GABLE: Philco decided that they would like to have some sports programs [on their new TV station] to help the physical fitness program along. They were only on the air from seven o'clock to nine o'clock at night and the only receivers in the area belonged to about fifty of their employees. They were interested to see whether the television sets worked!

Martha Gable

So they asked me to do a program on a Tuesday evening for an hour on women's sports and then on Thursday evenings for men's sports.[1]

They had a little studio that wasn't very big. I don't think it was more than thirty by thirty, and they had just cycloramas around, and all the scenery was struck behind the cycloramas.

These days people don't realize how it was to go into a television studio and perform.

The lights were so hot that I used to take a complete change of clothing, because the perspiration would run down into my shoes!

And, you see, the cameras in those days washed out reds and orange, so they made us wear makeup that looked like powdered cocoa, sort of, and then lipstick was in what looked like a shoe shine box and it looked like melted chocolate. And they would put this on our lips so we didn't look like mummies, you see, completely washed out in color. Sometimes I'd forget to take it off, and I went out in the street and people would look at me as though I had Chinese rot or something.

One time I had a couple...a man and a woman on roller skates. Of course, they had a very small area. And he swung her around and hit this cyclorama, and all the piled-up scenery behind the cyclorama started falling down. We could see the cyclorama coming toward us so we ran off the stage, and there was another standing mike over at the other side, and I ran over to that mike and just said, "Well, we brought the house

down with that act. We'll have the next act ready in a minute." And they got the whole thing straightened up.

The men in the studio were terrific in dealing with emergencies and crises; they were used to it.

Shortly thereafter the United States got into the war and they took all the television [facilities] that were inoperative to develop radar.

~

Activity resumed following World War II, at a time when two more of the visionaries for public television were experiencing TV for the first time in Philadelphia.

Armand Hunter, a Nebraskan, who had become interested in radio while securing his doctorate at Northwestern University in Evanston, Illinois, was called to Temple University in Philadelphia in 1947 when Roger Clipp and the Annenberg Foundation encouraged the development there of a new Department of Radio, Speech, and Theater, headed by Dr. Hunter. Many of his students gained experience at WFIL on radio by assisting in the school broadcasts which Martha Gable supervised. And then came WFIL-TV.

HUNTER: WFIL was one of the first of the stations in Philadelphia and in the east to activate a TV station. They also affiliated with ABC-TV at that time, and quite a few of the early ABC-TV programs originated out of Philadelphia and the WFIL studios.

They acquired a former athletic facility in Philadelphia for their

Armand Hunter

new [TV] studios, because at that time sports were a major part of the early days of television. They were operating on the basis that if you had your studios at the arena, you were close at hand for any of the athletic events that normally took place in metropolitan arena facilities and settings.

As educational director for the station as well as chairman of the Department of Radio, Speech, and Theater out at the university, we developed a "University of the Air" series. This brought higher education programs and resources into the picture along with the public school elementary programs, a continuation of the "School of the Air" which went into TV from radio.

---

[1] Preceding and during her professional career in education, Miss Gable showed great interest and unusual proficiency in athletics. She competed nationally in gymnastics, judged Olympic gymnastics, and attended all Olympic Games, except Munich and Moscow, from 1932 to 1981.

David M. Davis, one of Armand Hunter's students at Northwestern University in Evanston [he wrote and conducted the music for Hunter's Ph.D. dissertation with the help of people like Bob Banner, Al Crews and Homer Heck from NBC Chicago], followed Dr. Hunter to Philadelphia and later to Michigan State before spending many years at WGBH-TV in Boston.

His memories of early TV in Philadelphia are sparse, but offer yet another glimpse of those early efforts.

DAVIS: We put together a Christmas Eve television show in 1947 which was called "Christmas In Many Lands" [CHUCKLES]... seen only in local bars. We went on from there.

~

David M. Davis

William J. "Bill" McCarter, who years later managed Washington's WETA and Chicago's WTTW, also got his start in television in Philadelphia at about the same time. His memories reflect the "try anything" attitude of commercial TV in its earliest years.

McCARTER: WCAU, believe it or not, was running live westerns on television in the afternoon! It was called "Action in the Afternoon," and they had a stable, they had horses, they had Indians! Isn't that an incredible story? And I could drive you today to exactly the site where all that programming was made. Action, live westerns in the afternoon.

William J. McCarter

Goes to show you how timid we've become.

It was really a marvelous time because nobody did really quite know what they were doing. That's what made it the golden period because you had a mixture of people from vaudeville—you had Phil Silvers and all those fellows that played the boards—then you had the radio transfers, the guys that were enamored and were coming in from radio. So you had vaudeville and radio, and then you had motion picture people who were pulled over.

Then there were some very broadminded executives who really didn't have to worry so much about losses in those days because it wasn't that expensive and they let us try things and do things.

My Own Recollections of Early TV

In mid-America just after World War II, despite no network service as yet, a few long-time commercial radio broadcasting companies were eager to establish themselves as the first TV stations in their respective areas.

My own recollections of my earliest television experiences prior to establishing the *Milwaukee Journal's* TV station in December of 1947 may help provide an account of what was going on in the Midwest.

My boss, Russ Winnie, and I flew over to Detroit where the *Detroit News* station, WWJ, was planning to get into television, and we went down to St. Louis to KSD, which was the *Post-Dispatch* station.

Both of these were NBC affiliates and were newspaper-owned radio stations going into television like we were at *The Journal*, so the logic of it was, "Let's see what these fellows are doing."

We spent a day in Detroit and they were not on the air yet and wouldn't be for five or six months, and they had twenty full-time television people on their staff, doing demonstrations and experiments and that sort of thing.

Then we went to St. Louis, which again was a comparable situation. But they had been on the air for about three months and they had four full-time people on their television staff. Of course, they raided their radio staff, too.

We learned a great deal from both of these visits, and the upshot, the management decision was, "Heck, we'll do this our own way. Let's use our own people."

I was given full responsibility for finding out what to do and how to do it and for training the program and production people, as well as for generating events which would create interest in the community.

WTMJ-TV Demonstration: During this demonstration at the 1947 Home Show in Milwaukee, the camera on the platform picked up images of the folks seen below the platform, the monitor at the right showed their pictures. Author Jim Robertson is interviewing "Carla," hostess of an early women's show on WTMJ-TV, which was the eleventh TV station in the U.S. to go on the air.

First we did demonstrations. We had the corner store window at Fourth and Wisconsin Avenue, the Boston Store, for a week, and we had fashion models and kitchens and one thing and another, and everybody came and looked. We took the cameras and put them on a high platform at the Home Show in the middle of the Milwaukee Auditorium so people could see themselves on television. And we didn't know what we were doing—we were lucky if we knew which button to push!

But we learned gradually through that year (1947) how to combine the pictures from one camera with the pictures from another, all live, of course.

In the studio we had a big boom microphone similar to motion-picture booms, the kind of thing you see in pictures of early television. There was an operator who stood up on the platform and cranked various cranks to turn the microphone and telescope the boom—let it out and back. Then you had a so-called dolly-pusher, who just wheeled that fellow around to wherever he should be.

The two cameras each had a turret of lenses, no zoomar lenses as yet. Lighting was not so critical with these new cameras as it had been before the war, but you still had to have an awful lot of light.

Our engineers rigged up what I think Bill Eddy at WBKB in Chicago had come up with. You know the kind of sealed lamp that you have now for outdoor yard lights, either floods or spots? They would rig up what was called a light tree—with either nine or sixteen of these—either three each way or four each way, into a kind of quadrangle of lights—a grid of lights. And they would have several of those, which could be moved around the studio. They generated quite a lot of heat.

When we got around to developing commercials for our brewery accounts in Milwaukee, one of the problems we had was that there was so much heat that the beer wouldn't pour properly! This was all live in those days, you know; you had to pour the beer right at the moment when the announcer was talking about it, and it took some doing to get that beer to get just the right head on it under that heat!

Unexpected Episodes On Kitchen Shows

I remember that we had a kitchen program—as almost every early television station did, I guess, and the kitchen was not a fully-equipped kitchen. We had an arrangement of rolling platforms on which to put the essentials of a set for a given show such as a kitchen. When we didn't need it, we rolled it into the corner of the studio and brought in something else.

As a result, the sink was not equipped with running water. There were pans of water underneath. And Breta Griem, who was a fabulous character—a predecessor to Julia Child in that she was superb in knowing what she was doing, also very entertaining and very natural—was doing her kitchen show one day, and she got a frog in her throat.

She just reached underneath for a glass of water, took a drink of it and realized that it was the soapy dishwater that she had washed the dishes in. But nobody knew that until

passenger elevators, a wire cage business, where on the ground floor you push a button and a bell rings in the whole building so somebody will come and get the elevator.

Julia was twenty minutes into her first show—and the elevator bell rang.

I was in the [remote] truck, and I thought, "What are you going to do?"

Julia was whipping away at something. She said, "Oh, somebody's at the door but I'm much too busy."

We knew we had something.

~

There is nothing to match the appeal of animals on TV, and early practitioners learned this quickly. I remember we had a little thing with the Humane Society where

Julia Child kitchen show: From her first program on WGBH-TV, Julia Child became public television's first popular "star." Initially known as "The French Chef," she subsequently demonstrated many kinds of cooking, not only on public TV stations from coast-to-coast, but in more recent years as a feature on ABC-TV's "Good Morning America."

after the program. She didn't miss a syllable. She didn't grimace or make any face. But it was that kind of circumstance under which this early television got going.

Several years later, in the early days of WGBH-TV in Boston, a very similar episode involving Julia Child, "The French Chef" as she was called in those days, is described by David M. Davis, who witnessed Julia's very first television program.

DAVIS: This [took place] in a demonstration kitchen on the second floor of the Cambridge Power and Light Building, part factory and part office. It had one of those combination freight/

they would bring in three or four dogs or cats for adoption. The simple thing to do was put the animal up on a table, and Gus Utke from the Humane Society would talk about it.

One such time in particular we had a darling little puppy—I can't remember what breed, but it was terribly appealing. We got a nice closeup shot of the dog—just as close as you could get, because Gus's hand was keeping him from falling off the table.

Gus explained the breed and how old he was and how they happened to have him, and he said, "And of course, he's already housebroken." At just that point, the dog piddled all over the table! So you never knew ahead of time, and you couldn't go back and do it over again, there it was!

First TV News In Los Angeles

Also in 1947, another of public television's visionaries (who had been a war correspondent and photographer in the Pacific for Acme-NEA, then a combat correspondent in the Marine Corps, and then a picture editor for *LOOK Magazine*,) was a friend of a vice president of Paramount Pictures. Paramount had put KTLA on the air in Hollywood and was looking for a TV news editor. They found Jonathan Rice.

RICE: At that point I had seen half of one inning of one baseball game—in a store-window television set! That is all the television I had seen in that part of 1947. So when I was hired to become news editor, I came out to Los Angeles. There were three thousand sets. If we'd had enough nickels, we could have called everybody and said, "How did you like that show?" But we didn't have that many nickels.

Jonathan Rice

My first job the first day was to edit a bunch of quarter-inch ticker tape, which was the United Press feed, so that it could be run across the screen for an hour, on sixteen millimeter reels. I had to take out the typos and terrible words like "divorce" and "venereal disease" and "prostitute"—of which there weren't many.

It took me almost eight hours to do the chores with that copy. And I went home and told my wife, "You know, I think as news editor I'm expected to do something else, but this took me eight hours!" The happy ending to that is that five years later when I was leaving, my assistant was away and I had to do the same job, and I timed myself, and it took me sixteen minutes.

But I was there as news editor for five years, and my programs won all sorts of awards, and I learned an enormous amount about television.

The man I worked for—it's probably very unkind to say anything nasty about a man on tape—but Klaus Landsberg, who was "Mr. Television," taught me more than anybody could have taught me and he was a total bastard. I had been told that he would be jealous of everything I did, and he was.

I became the world's best man at putting new news over old still pictures, because there were no films. Until there was cross-country cable service, my news program was the highest rated in Los Angeles. We had a superb guy named Gil Martin from Paramount News as the voice, and it was a fine program.

I also did something called "Magazine of the Air," which was a bunch of features of the kind that were eventually going to become public television—educational television *series*, not features. Klaus bugged me, because he really took credit for everything. One year my shows won five Emmys, but I wasn't allowed to go to the Emmy Awards banquet, much less accept, and I wasn't mentioned in any of his acceptances!

My budget for that "Magazine" was twenty-five bucks!

~

Jon Rice enters the story later as the program wizard of San Francisco's KQED in partnership with James Day. Like all of the seven other founders whose recollections have contributed to this chapter, Rice was to put these early experiences to good use as one of the prime builders of public television today.

Meanwhile, some of the leaders in the field of educational radio began to flirt with television during the late 1940s and were about to embrace this new communications medium for their own noncommercial purposes.

6

Let's Get Our Act Together

Those involved in broadcasting for educational purposes did not understand too clearly at first exactly what they were capable of doing, but they were trying. Representatives of both commercial and noncommercial broadcasting participated in the effort.

One fondly remembered approach to better understanding was an annual event held at the Ohio State University in Columbus, known as the Institute for Education by Radio—later the Institute for Educational Radio and Television. The individual most closely identified with the IERT (because from 1935 to 1962 he organized and ran it), was Ohio State University's I. Keith Tyler. He tells of the institute's origin.

TYLER: In 1930, Dr. W.W. Charters, who was then head of the Bureau of Educational Research at Ohio State, and Judith Waller, who was educational director for the National Broadcasting Company in Chicago, conceived of the possibility of getting educators and broadcasters together to look at the educational uses of the [radio] medium as it was developing on both commercial and noncommercial stations.

They decided to hold a conference in the summer of 1930. I think this conference lasted about a week or more. They brought over people from the BBC in Britain and various foreign broadcasters and American broadcasters in both commercial and educational and called this the Institute for Education by Radio.

Subsequently they decided these meetings would be held each year. They cut it down to about a three-or-four-day meeting.

There were two kinds of people in the networks and in the commercial stations who came to the institute. One were the people who held educational jobs. In those days there was a heavy responsibility on radio to perform public service. They had farm directors, they had women's directors, they had directors of children's programs, they had all kinds of these educational people.

The other kind of people who came to the institute were the creative people. The first recognition they would get would come out here when they'd get an Ohio State Award—the oldest award in broadcasting. Norman Corwin was first singled out here. These people came because here was a place where they could talk with creative people and not be confronted all the time with commercial necessity which they had in their own home bailiwick.

In addition, we would get executives, some of them quite broadminded. The president of ABC for a long time used to bring his people out; he felt they needed this.

Memories of the IERT in Columbus

Three more of the Public TeleVisionaries remember the Ohio State Institute.

CRABBE: It was for years the principal showcase and the principal meeting in the nation. An award from the Columbus Institute was—we were pretty darn proud of that thing when we took it home, believe me.

Then, of course, there was the annual meeting. This was the rather typical kind of convention program—although the sessions themselves were very substantive—more content oriented than politically oriented, if I can put it that way. It was a big thing, I can tell you...I used to go to that institute from California every year.

GABLE: That Ohio State thing was great. We were very proud that our "Operation Blackboard" got several prizes in those days. I don't know that we were that good, but there was nobody else doing it. So we got some good prizes and had them framed and put up on our office walls, and everybody was proud as punch.

~

Another regular participant in IERT who also was emerging as a leader of the educational broadcasters was Richard B. Hull, then director of WOI radio and eventually WOI-TV at the Iowa State University in Ames, and from 1947 to 1949 the president of the National Association of Educational Broadcasters. Hull's own recollections, recorded in 1979 prior to his death in 1980, are found throughout this book because of his many contributions to the birth of public broadcasting.

HULL: [The institute] was another great background for educating, and for dispersing ideas. In fact, it was — in my own view — for many years, the Academy.

NAEB'S Earliest Years

Hull's recollections of early meetings of the National Association of Educational Broadcasters were equally descriptive.

HULL: The NAEB was founded in 1926, was mostly Big-Ten and a few Big-Eight radio stations in the Middle West. I remember at an annual meeting at Michigan State, in the cafeteria, we had our banquet. John Dunn, who was then at Oklahoma, at one time an NBC executive, railed at us as a bunch of snobbish Big-Ten Club members...which had certain elements of truth.

Richard B. Hull

At that point we conceived the idea of breaking the nation up into districts, which gave a little autonomy and recognition.

Then the Chicago meeting I'm trying to think of. There was the inevitable old guard and the new guard, and several of us wanted to really get things going, and we thought we could.

It was in 1948, after the districting, that we retained Cohn and Marks as legal representatives, and then we had [as members] educational institutions as well as stations and production centers...so that gave us ninety-five

educational institutions, fifty stations, and thirty-one states, and began the preliminary aspiration of television in education.

~

Leonard Marks, communications attorney, was later advisor to Lyndon B. Johnson in broadcasting matters, and during another period the head of the U.S. Information Agency.

MARKS: The board used to meet in a single bedroom in the hotel where the convention was being held. And the attendance was, of course, very limited. But people there had determination and ambition, and the NAEB became the central organization for the development of educational broadcasting.

~

After the 1948 convention, Hull appointed Harold McCarty of Wisconsin to head a television study committee.

McCARTY: The aim was to study the feasibility of reserving certain television frequencies for education. This was a radical idea in those days, and you had to determine the reasonableness of such an idea...the feasibility of launching such a proposal.

~

Lawyer Marcus Cohn confirmed this NAEB effort of September, 1949.

COHN: There's no question at all that I did file something with the commission asking for reservations.

~

That occurred shortly after the FCC had clamped a "freeze" on granting of any further television channels because it had become obvious in 1948 that the FCC's plan of allocations was wholly inadequate to handle the flood of applications. The NAEB's filing, asking for ten channels in UHF, was the first step taken by the educational community to request reservation of television channels for noncommercial use.

Dissatisfaction With "UHF Only" Proposal

There were some in the NAEB who violently disagreed with the strategy of asking only for UHF. Among those one who stood out was Parker Wheatley, by that time the manager of Boston's WGBH-FM.

WHEATLEY: I was on my feet first, and I said, "If education has to go second class in the reservation of television channels, count us out in Boston! Either we go for V's or we're out, Harvard, MIT, all of us...and there's no more point in my sticking around this meeting if we're going to settle for U's.

Edgar Fuller, representing the Association of Chief State School Officers, was on his feet next. He cheered, in his fashion, and said, "I agree with Parker 100 percent!"

~

Dick Hull was one of the great statesmen in early battles with the FCC for reserved channels for FM and TV while he was managing WOI and later WOI-TV, forming the JCET, and serving as president of NAEB. His words reflect his remarkable grasp of the critical situation at that time.

HULL: The good [Federal Communications] Commission established a late summer deadline for the filing of protest petitions. Now, that date unhappily coincided with the period when most educational institutions are closed— August. And I don't think this was entirely accidental, I don't know. Of course, the commission used to vacation in August, too. In any event, this was a fast little piece of business. Cohn and Marks were the attorneys, and Marcus was the active one then, not Leonard. I requested they petition for UHF channels because I didn't think anybody else would want them.

Keith Tyler, who was very friendly with Bevis, the Ohio State University president, got Bevis in. He was that year chairman of the Land-Grant College Association Radio Committee, and that's a very powerful lobby, and the National Association of State Universities. Tyler was asked to write two supporting petitions to the NAEB petition. So we had three petitioners accomplished without a lot of cumbersome democratic procedures [LAUGHTER] to support this.

So then everybody began to be interested. See, that had been the problem before; the rank and file of the universities thought "too expensive...too impossible...too far off." But it whipped up from then on, and a lot of groups became involved.

If an observer were to find a single time and place where the educational broadcasting movement finally found itself, it would be '49.

The Summer of '49 at Allerton House

In part, Hull was referring to the seminar held at Allerton House, the University of Illinois' conference center, during the summer of 1949, which provided an unusual meeting ground for some of that day's principal planners of educational broadcasting. One of them destined to play a leading role in public television in subsequent years was Robert B. Hudson from CBS. A quiet, thoughtful man, he later joined the fledgling Educational Television and Radio Center and subsequently became program head for National Educational Television (NET).

HUDSON: I came out as representative of CBS because Wilbur Schramm, Dean of Communications at Illinois, and John Marshall, from the Rockefeller Foundation, had agreed that this was a good thing to do...to bring the managers of educational radio stations together to confer and to do a little plotting of what their future was.

Robert B. Hudson

This was a very dynamic meeting. It lasted seventeen days. The managers from nearly all of the educational radio stations were there, plus some key consultants like Paul Lazarsfeld and Charlie Siepmann and several people from the University [of Illinois] like George Stoddard and Wilbur Schramm and Dallas Smythe and some others.

It was a good active series of meetings in which the group formed itself pretty much into working parties, and came up with some strong recommendations, thought a lot about what their role was, and how they could go together further and advance it.

~

Two other participants, also Public TeleVisionaries, shed further light on this seminal summertime gathering in 1949.

Ralph Steetle, who later would play a major role in the establishment of ETV, came up from Louisiana State University in New Orleans where he was then director of broadcasting.

STEETLE: [It] began with a modest aim of "Let's see where we are. Are we all over-drawn in terms of personal knowledge?" And it grew into an intensive self-study. We tended to look for the first time non-defensively at Robert M. Hutchins' statement that "The trouble with educational radio is that the programs are no good."

We said, "My Lord, he's right!" When normally we would have said, "Oh, what a persnickety so-and-so he is." We had some interesting cross-fertilization with network people. It was a ferment time that I think is one of the base lines for the entire movement.

McCARTY: We had, up to that time, been a group of individuals struggling in our way in our own campuses or institutions...getting together, as I said, to comfort each other...but never seeking to establish an "identity."

This is a term much over-used, I think, in present-day sociological and psychological terms. A person is "seeking an identity" or "he hasn't found himself." Well, we certainly hadn't found ourselves.

But I think at the Allerton conference we did. We knuckled down to the very tough problem of defining who we are, what our operations are, how we might reach some of our goals.

the situation we had when we met at this beautiful mansion in the country, totally isolated from all present-day activity...and were required, for about ten or twelve days, to think! This was the first of the think tanks in educational broadcasting. And our aim was to come out with some sense of direction.

We struggled through the heat of an Illinois summer, when I declared you could lie awake at night and hear the corn growing. You really could! But I had the feeling that the rest of us, whether it was the temperature or what, we caught fire. We caught a vision of what we *could be.*

It was from that moment on, it seemed to me, that educational broadcasting came alive. I think I personally stood taller than I had before, and I had the feeling that the others felt the same way.

That was a turning point that ought to be recognized as such in the history and development of this whole movement...the summer of 1949 at Allerton House. Things kind of turned around when a couple dozen lonely broadcast-

Allerton House seminar group: On the terrace of Allerton House, the University of Illinois conference center, in the summer of 1949, four pioneers try to define the mission of educational broadcasting. (Left to right) Seymour Siegel of New York's WNYC, Robert Coleman of Michigan State, H.B. McCarty of Wisconsin, and Armand Hunter of Michigan State.

And we had to begin with a definition. "What is education, first of all?" And you find in the minutes of the Allerton meeting, summarized by Bob Hudson, a very concise statement of education—which aims to enhance, enrich life, to help every individual to realize his own capabilities....

That was a strange experience. I had been brought up in the cornfields of Illinois and I should have been accustomed to or adjusted to

ers from their own individual areas and shops came together and decided: "We really can count. We really can do something worth while." As I look back at it, I had a kind of "born-again" feeling.

Had it not been for the Allerton experience, and for the mutual identification of our goals and this kind of spontaneous resolution to push on relentlessly towards them, I think I could not have been so positive as a witness before the

Federal Communications Commission. After all, this was a fairly awesome experience.

But I know I gained confidence from that, and was able to utter my convictions with more strength and resolve than previously.

I think we started to grow up in 1949, really asserted this in the 1950-51 hearings, and took another step forward in the determination with which we sought the frequencies which then had been allocated—and from modest beginnings, pushed on to the big, expansive, influential, powerful movement which we have today.

~

McCarty spoke those words in the summer of 1981, thirty-two years after the first Allerton House gathering. Ten years later, during the preparation of this book, there might have been some whose assessment of public television today would not be as optimistic as McCarty's—a reminder that educational communications technology is not static.

There is value in looking back. We may sense the changes which have occurred and are occurring and envision the potentials of public television in the future.

TV was just entering the consciousness of educators at the mid-point of the century. Many of the early experiments in ETV were taking place, not in major cities, but in the heartland of America. Iowa.

7

An Island in Iowa: WOI-TV

Back home at Iowa State University, Dick Hull was about to do what others were barely talking about—much to the dismay of commercial broadcasters. In the middle of the FCC's "freeze" on further TV stations and before the effort to reserve channels for education, Hull put on the air in October 1950, the world's first non-experimental, educationally-owned, commercially-licensed television station and the 100th TV station in the U.S., WOI-TV. This was possible because Iowa State had gained its construction permit before the FCC had enacted the "freeze."

HULL: The idea of TV didn't spring suddenly. In a twenty-year report, old man Griffith had suggested to the previous president that they should look into it at the proper time and build a facility. [1]

It began to get hot, I think, in the 1940s. Captain Bill Eddy was playing with his station in Chicago, and Kansas State had an experimental thing.

W. I. Griffith

There was one fussing around in Los Angeles. General Electric had one in Schenectady. I don't remember them now, but no more than about six stations and no more than seven thousand receivers in the whole country. But it was moving fast.

So we applied. I was the enthusiast for it, and the president was a supporter.

We applied for FM and TV at the same moment. WOI radio was viewed as an integral off-campus tool of the college extension program. Only the land-grant colleges had this idea. You go out to the people as part of the job, and the audience does matter.

One night—I think there was some kind of a deadline on filing or something—I spent half the night typing up why we should have a go-ahead for a TV station, and took it to the president, and he said, "Okay." So we started.

This was in the context of serving everybody. That's how he saw television.

Anecdotes on Erecting A Tall Tower

HULL: So we built this tower. You can't imagine the curiosity and interest then. There was one station in Davenport, Iowa, which is really Illinois over there. Here we are, in the center of the state, thirty miles from the capital, and the "freeze" is on, they can't do anything in Des Moines...all are sore as hell at us. And we start to build this tower.

Well, they used guys from the oil fields, you know, derrick workers, for the climbing, and they brought their women and camp followers and kids with them in trailers.

I think one of the funniest things I ever saw in my life—everything is ready now, and they're hoisting up the antenna that was about 150 feet long, a pipe like that [GESTURING], and RCA had welded a great big thing for a pulley hook, but they welded it in the wrong place so it was off balance.

So the foreman gets this hooked in, and it starts up. And all of these women come running out of the trailers saying, "Don't do it. It's going

---

[1] The reference is to the late W.I. Griffith, a school teacher who became interested in visual aids, and as Hull put it, "Visual aids brought him into radio when radio developed enough at Iowa State to require administrative interference!" Griffith was the father of extension radio service in Iowa.

to hit the tower!" This makes the foreman mad, and he curses a blue streak, asks them what the hell they know about it, and sure enough, it goes bang and breaks the batwings off. [LAUGHTER] I thought that was an early triumph of an insightful feminine group! [MORE LAUGHTER]

So, we get the thing built. However, money was limited. We had no cameras to begin with except projection—slides, films—which bore with it a little item or two of interest.

Our nearest thing to a live show was a slide show, like at the Rotary Club. We did quite a few of those, a little bit of an ordeal because the transmitter was four miles out in the country and we had to haul people out there.

There was one man who didn't like television, manager of the college farms. We tried to get him on because he had an interesting story, and he said, "Oh, something will go wrong, it always does." Finally they persuaded him that this would be letter-perfect. He got on, and the first thing they did was to put his picture on upside down!

Dedication Night - Minus One Guest

HULL: The night we went on the air—you see, we were really something—on the front page of the *Des Moines Register*, you know, all over everywhere. We were station number one hundred, you see, the only one in Iowa. So we were dearly loved by the television set dealers, I'll tell you that.

We had only four programs to show that night. We had a color program from the Canadian Film Board, and somebody had broken our color filter so it came through in black and white on an ancient machine. Then we had Stokowsky and the NBC Symphony in an extremely bad kinescope. Then a promo piece that CBS got out, which showed endless rooftops with antennas and TV sets. And I guess there may have been an ag film in there.

We had the customary party after the official evening. While it was going on, everything that had come in were plaudits, but in the middle of all these admiration calls, we get this one from Des Moines from a beer joint somewhere. He identifies it. He said, "I'm the manager. I've got your god-damned station on the air. Take that symphony off. All my customers is leavin'." [LAUGHTER] I just loved that.

The crowning triumph of the evening, though, was that we forgot to ask the [university] president. We forgot to ask him to the party! Isn't that awful?

We operated on a commercial license, because there wasn't any other kind until the reservations in 1953. And because by our policy,

AM was noncommercial and by law FM was noncommercial, we made this, by policy, no local commercials—in order not to offend the merchants in Iowa—Des Moines.

William Kahn photo

Iowa State University President Dr. Charles E. Friley (center) and WOI-TV Manager Richard B. Hull (right) welcomed Dr. Allen Dumont during a visit to WOI-TV in 1952. Dr. Dumont headed Dumont Laboratories and the Dumont Television Network and produced many types of TV equipment in the 1940s and 1950s.

[But] we took commercial network programs, all four networks, Dumont was there. And gradually that began to build into a money operation and we could get our equipment, so we had in short order the mobile unit and everything, and those clumsy old cameras.

It was such a novelty, I suppose because of the educational ownership, that we were nearly visited to death. I finally had to hire one man full time just to handle visitors and prepare hand-out material. Even foreign visitors.

Learning How TV Works —and Showing Others

Hull's remarks do not reflect the unique value of this early television station as a laboratory for the training of personnel from other educational institutions and as an outlet for innovative educational uses of the medium, once the station was properly equipped.

Much of this activity was undertaken on grants from the Ford Foundation's Fund for Adult Education, which also was largely responsible for many aspects of educational television's subsequent development. FAE's vice president was G.W. "Bill" Griffiths, not related to Iowa's W.I. Griffith, but an active overseer of the fund's projects at Iowa State under Dick Hull.

Chatting with me nearly thirty years later in his pleasant home in Santa Barbara, California, Bill gave us another perspective of early WOI-TV.

GRIFFITHS: The great thing about WOI-TV was that it existed. That is to say, it was the place where you could really get your feet wet. Not only on the training side, but we ourselves were to use some of "The Whole Town's Talking" program as evidence of what could be done.

G.W. "Bill" Griffiths

The format, as I recall it, was this: You went into a community which was identified with an actual or a forthcoming community problem. You worked with those who were diagnosing it and who saw possible solutions to it. You document their efforts, how they went at it, what they came up with, their successes, their failures, and in effect provided a prototype pattern for community action which was at one and the same time engrossing as documentary drama.

It was a richly rewarding experience for those involved in the producing side, the writing, the technical side, editing, and so forth. It was an experiment in community education.

WOI-TV was a shakedown situation in terms again of determining a critical mass of equipment and so forth that you needed to have a viable operation. It was getting exposure to linkages with the state legislatures and with the universities. It was a kind of trial balloon type of thing in a way, teasing out some of the problems others would face.

~

Indeed they would. But first would come the marshalling of forces, the briefings, the persuasive arguments, the gathering of data, and the development of the strategy necessary to persuade the FCC to reserve television channels for noncommercial educational use, the achievement without which the public television service available across the nation today could never have been established.

8

The Blond Bombshell on the FCC

It must have been a shock to the somewhat staid gentlemen of the Federal Communications Commission when President Harry S. Truman, in 1948, appointed a blond female Democrat from New York to be one of their number. Had this not occurred, the growth of noncommercial television certainly would have been stunted. Instead, Frieda Hennock forced it to bloom. Some say that without her, the FCC would not have reserved channels for education.

Stanley Neustadt, who later became a prominent communications attorney in the law firm of Cohn and Marks, served as Frieda Hennock's staff assistant at the FCC in earlier times and knew her better than anybody else in broadcasting. Stan took time from his professional duties to brief me on her days at the FCC and recalled the circumstances of her appointment.

NEUSTADT: One of the problems the administration had apparently confronted was the fairly widely bruited-about notion that the FCC was full of "pinkos," if not "reds" at least, too liberal.

On the very last day of the congressional session, in May or June of 1948, the Senate considered some eight hundred or so of Truman appointments —and my understanding is that of the total number, the Senate only confirmed two, and one was Miss Hennock.

Stanley Neustadt

~

Freida Hennock had been politically active as a Democrat in New York, and had hoped to be appointed to a federal judgeship. Her appointment to the FCC was to compensate for her disappointment, but she accepted it with gusto.

NEUSTADT: She told me once that the reason she was confirmed was that she had charmed Senator Robert A. Taft, who at that time was chairman of the Interstate and Foreign Commerce Committee, "Mister Republican," and his word carried an awful lot of weight in the Senate.

When she was testifying before Taft's committee, he had exacted from her a promise that if her nomination was confirmed she would be independent—she would not come under the sway of the people who were then at the commission, particularly the commission staff, because—as I say—there was this fear that the commission staff was much too far to the left. And she promised Senator Taft that if she was confirmed she would indeed be independent.

~

She certainly did carry out her promise of independence—and in the process became a kind of Joan of Arc, leading the campaign to reserve television channels for noncommercial educational use.

NEUSTADT: She was quite a remarkable woman in many ways. She was not exactly a self-taught lawyer, but almost.

She came to this country as an infant with her parents. She was born in Poland. I don't know where she went to college, but I know that she went to one of the less well-known and less highly-regarded law schools in New York, and after having left there went into practice for herself and worked her way up.

At the time she was appointed to the commission, she was a partner in a firm called Choate, Mitchell and Ely, which was the oldest law firm in the United States. She was the only woman partner, she was the only Jewish partner, and she was the only Democratic partner in this—all of which were considerable accomplishments!

I had the feeling from the very first that as the first woman appointed to the agency, and indeed in line with the rest of her background, she was anxious to find a cause of some sort with which she could identify and which would be identified with her.

One of the things she really was desperately worried about was being labeled "pinko" or "red" or anything like that. She wanted something that did not smack of that kind of political labeling, but yet would be appropriate to a woman and which involved some challenge.

Exactly how she came upon educational broadcasting, as it was then called, I'm not certain. But I know that she went out to an IERT meeting in Columbus [Ohio] over a weekend, and I can remember quite vividly that when she got back I said, "Miss Hennock, how was the meeting?"

And she said, "Boy, Stanley, do those educators drink!"

Frieda At the IERT in Columbus

According to I. Keith Tyler, who directed that Institute, Miss Hennock learned much more than that fact during her visit in Columbus.

TYLER: Frieda had been advised by a couple of commissioners who were close to us that if she really wanted to know what was going on in broadcasting, she ought to come to the institute. So, that spring of 1950, she had come out. And she found what she was looking for. She was fascinated. Here were these Catholic nuns, here were these teachers, here were people from the networks, here were a whole conglomerate interested in something besides commercial aspects. No matter where they came from, they were interested in education. So she decided that was going to be her cause.

~

Dick Hull, speaking years later of her first visit to the IERT, remarked on what he saw as her reasons for selecting educational television as her cause.

Frieda Hennock, first woman to be appointed to the Federal Communications Commission.

HULL: Like many people fifty years ago, education per se was valued, even more so if you were a first-generation immigrant—so she believed in the stuff.

So she took this on as her cause. Sometimes there were those of us who felt she took it on too often and too loud. She was, as I say, a remarkable woman, a smart woman, and an interesting one—but difficult! A conversation with her consisted of being cross-examined by her. She was always beating you down.

She could create absolutely terrific attitudes of support or antagonism. There was a man, one-time manager of a station in Cleveland, now dead. I had never seen him behave except as a gentleman in public. This was at the Institute at Ohio State. He so hated her guts that with the aid of one drink more than he needed, he made an effigy of Frieda with a noose around her neck and ran it up and down the halls, till several people thought better of that—and him—and dragged it away.

But she was a delight in other ways. Keith Tyler used to have a group of Columbus Grand Dames—you know, whatever passed for the local Four Hundred—to pour tea. This was supposed to be an honor for those who poured and likewise those who received. Well, Frieda was invited to this.

She was a good-looking woman. Oh, she didn't know how to dress, but she came in this faintly slinky-looking thing, down to this important ceremony, with a hat about like that [GESTURES WIDE]. Some little girl reporter from *The Lantern*, the student newspaper at Ohio State, stopped her and wanted to interview her.

"Sure, honey. Let's go to the bar."

So they go to the bar—and she forgot all about the tea [at which] she was to have been featured! Whisper, whisper: "See Frieda there?" Boy, did they hate her!

BRODERICK: She was by far the most enthusiastic FCC member that ever existed, so far as I was concerned.

She always spoke of the people in education in her typical Brooklynese… [IMITATING]… "You ed-you-kay-tahs," she used to call us.

She came to Columbus one year and was really the hit of the institute. She made quite a name for herself because she spoke out in favor of the reserved television channels and what "you ed-you-kay-tahs" can do if you have these reserved channels.

We were grateful to Frieda because she was the one enthusiastic person on the FCC that had a genuine interest in what we were attempting to do.

~

The Fund for Adult Education's vice president, G.H. "Bill" Griffiths, who also attended the Institute that year, remembered his first impression of Miss Hennock. He chuckled over how he discovered her as he was looking for someone else.

GRIFFITHS: I thought maybe he was in a big meeting they were having in the auditorium, and I started going up the stairs, sort of preoccupied by other things but just generally moving in that direction, when these *sounds* assailed my ears. Without really thinking it, I said to myself, "Why in the world are they running that tape backwards? That's a stupid thing to be doing in a proceeding like this. My God, you'd think they could at least turn off the sound while they're doing this."

Anyhow, I opened the doors to see if Bob might be there and I discovered that what I thought was a tape being run backwards was Frieda Hennock giving a speech!

This is true, literally true. She had that strident manner, loud, fast-talking, high-pitched voice….

If she hadn't been there with that uncompromising, dogged persistence in the FCC, who knows? She didn't have much company, heaven knows, least of all at the beginning.

~

Another of the visionaries of public television whose major role in its development comes a bit later was among the younger attendees at the 1950 Institute, where he experienced Frieda Hennock for the first time. William G. "Bill" Harley was subsequently president of the National Association of Educational Broadcasters but at that time was program director at the University of Wisconsin's educational radio station, WHA. He remembered the 1950 institute this way.

HARLEY: Frieda came down there—well, I should also say that there were commercial broadcasters involved—and Frieda was brutal. I mean, she just ripped up those commercial broadcasters one end to the other. Couldn't understand why they weren't supporting educational television, and so forth.

William G. Harley

So she became a champion of our cause and picked it as a kind of white horse she rode, ultimately a bit too hard, so that she began to annoy her fellow commissioners by her constant insistence upon the importance of educational television and that it should be given more consideration and more support and on and on. Actually it got to be a little embarrassing because she was beginning to alienate people in our cause as well.

But her heart was in the right place, and she did a great deal for us, especially in the earlier aspects of support. And she had a good relationship with [President] Harry Truman, which was helpful as well.

Democrats Help Democrats: Truman, Novik, Hennock

Ralph Steetle shed further light on Miss Hennock's effectiveness with President Truman.

STEETLE: At one stage she had President Truman invite an entire group over to the White House for a conversation. And President Truman in no uncertain terms told them what he felt about educational television. He was for it. It must happen.

~

During her participation in New York Democratic politics, she had become acquainted with Morris S. Novik, another of public television's "parents."

Morrie had come to the notice of Fiorello H. LaGuardia, mayor of New York, because of extensive efforts in labor politics and in journalism and broadcasting. He is said to be the person who persuaded LaGuardia to undertake reading the newspaper "funnies" on the radio. When Novik became director of New York City's municipal radio station, WNYC, he began to fraternize with educational broadcasters, a mutual love affair which continued for many decades. Novik's powers of persuasion and connections within organized labor helped win political victories for educational broadcasting.

Novik recalled with fondness the informal cocktail parties he hosted at one Columbus Institute after another.

Morris S. Novik

NOVIK: Whenever we would meet [in Columbus], I would try to get a larger room. I would buy a couple of bottles of liquor. We would meet in my room and we would talk about NAEB expansion or any ideas that we would have. And we would always try to invite the guest—generally a commissioner. This is how we came to know the Durrs, and the Walkers.[1] They would sit on the bed in the room and just talk, expanding the concept. One of those that came one year was Frieda Hennock.

I knew Frieda from New York, so it was easier for me to act as [her] host. I was the one who educated her as to what educational broadcasting was. She was getting all of the [commercial] propaganda in Washington from the industry, but she knew me.

~

More of Novik's political savvy became evident as he told of his efforts to educate Truman, an effort in which he was joined by Frieda Hennock—all three of them loyal and hard-working Democrats.

NOVIK: I went to see Truman with a very simple idea. I knew he was a historian. I knew that he knew a helluva lot about the original concept of setting up land-grant colleges to educate and to give their areas better help so they could be better farmers.

I said, "Mr. President, what you-all were doing years ago on land-grant colleges, I think this is the role of noncommercial educational stations."

---

[1] Clifford Durr and Paul Walker were successive chairmen of the Federal Communications Commission during those years.

He said, "You mean you use the stations in order to educate the people, just as we do with land-grant colleges?" You know, all you had to do was give him the clue and he started to spell it out.

We were sitting there, and he pressed a button. I don't know who the [FCC] chairman was. Whoever it was, Truman said, "Mr. Chairman, I want to discuss a problem that might be a public policy position later on, but now it's just really in the formative stage. Will you tell Commissioner Hennock to come over here?" In fifteen minutes, Hennock arrived.

The president turned around and he said, "We are just discussing this." And he spells out what I would have liked to have said, had I known as much about land-grant colleges. He spelled it all out, and he drew the picture that we will have these stations, and these would be "noncommercial educational stations." That's the term that we used.

~

Morrie Novik and WNYC, aided by the Ohio State Institute for Education by Radio and Television, clearly gave Frieda Hennock her initial understanding of the future potentials of educational television. But she was tireless in seeking additional ideas from other sources as well as in promoting her own.

NEUSTADT: She spent a lot of time lobbying other people in government, and people outside of government. I remember she talked to Oscar Ewing, who was at that time in charge of what is now the Department of Human Resources. She talked to lots of people throughout the government to get support for the idea of reservations. She made speeches in a lot of places.

~

The FCC's Hyman Goldin recognized another aspect of her approach.

GOLDIN: She was the first one to appreciate the importance of going public. Prior to that time the FCC was primarily within the halls of Congress and Washington rather than in terms of the national [scene]—with the exception of James Lawrence Fly, who first turned the FCC around to a modern stance. He took on the networks and tried to restructure broadcasting. He was not into educational broadcasting, but Frieda made that her cause.

Frieda had this habit of calling in various people in the agency to talk to her. She'd go out to lunch with them, and so forth. And her question always was, "How can we push this?

How can we make it go?"

Frieda became the Joan of Arc in terms of sparking the commission. [Chairman] Paul Walker was very friendly to educational broadcasting, but Paul was by this time not as effective as he had been in the 1930s, and it was really Frieda who led the fight, both at the FCC and the Congress.

And she did it in terms of great emotional appeal. She used all of her emotional charm—and she was very charming in some ways. She drove people absolutely crazy—including staff people and congress people—but, nevertheless, she got the message through.

Her Impact In Local Communities

Frieda Hennock's presence was felt not only in Washington but in many places she visited around the country.

John F. White, later president of National Educational Television, knew of her influences in the formation of WQED in Pittsburgh, the station where he first became prominent in ETV.

WHITE: The combination of Frieda Hennock and Dave Lawrence, who was then mayor of Pittsburgh—the two of them leaned on Leland Hazard to become interested and active in the new thing called public television.

~

John F. White

Jonathan Rice, telling of the days prior to the birth of KQED in San Francisco, quotes one of that station's instigators.

RICE: The AAUW had been very helpful in bringing out Frieda Hennock and arranging for her to meet Vaughn Seidel. There are some women here who really regard themselves as the founders, and one of them had a reception at her home. And Vaughn Seidel subsequently is said to have indicated that "the Frieda Hennock visit was the turning point," and the momentum began from there.

~

Rice's partner and boss at KQED, James Day, told me about a later visit by Hennock to the San Francisco Bay Area.

James Day

DAY: My only recollection is having a drink with Frieda in the Mark Hopkins Merry-Go-Round Bar one night before I went on the air, and I left the meeting quite dizzy—neither from the drink nor from the bar which constantly revolved, but from Frieda, who got me all charged up as well.

The thing I find most interesting about Frieda's role in this is that she had a broader vision, it seems to me, than most of the other people who were involved, if you look at what she said. She saw educational television as a constructive competitor to commercial television, one that would lead commercial television to do things it ought to do, which is the vision I've always had.

~

St. Louis businessman Raymond Wittcoff, who spearheaded that city's long effort to establish KETC and served on the board of directors of the Educational Television and Radio Center, told us:

WITTCOFF: The commissioner with whom I met that made a most lasting impression on me was Frieda Hennock. She was delighted with what we were talking about doing here, and we became instant friends.

Raymond Wittcoff

Tactless, Perhaps—But Triumphant

She also managed to alienate some who were striving toward the same outcome which she herself was encouraging. Martha Gable remembered one bad day in Philadelphia.

GABLE: One Schoolmen's Week I set up a program in the Otterbein Auditorium at Penn. We had Bob Trout [from CBS] and I had Frieda

Hennock, and I had three gentlemen from our local commercial stations.

Bob Trout made a great speech. Then Frieda got up and started lambasting commercial stations—and here the commercial stations were giving us time on the air for our [school] programs!

Our superintendent of schools, Louis Hoyer, couldn't take this. People started booing her. Dr. Hoyer said, "These stations are very generous with us." But she kept right on lambasting. The people got mad and left the auditorium.

Afterwards I said, "Look Frieda, these stations here in Philadelphia are very generous. They are giving us time."

She said, "I can't change my story. If I say anything nice about the commercial people, I'll lose my pitch for FCC. I gotta keep lambasting them."

I said, "Well, you lost your audience, you know that."

She said, "Yeah, I know, but I had to do it this way."

~

Hennock's staff assistant, Stan Neustadt, commented on this characteristic of hers.

NEUSTADT: When she decided that a certain objective was desirable and she decided how to go about accomplishing it, people who wanted to accomplish the same objective but in a different way sometimes antagonized her very much. She was always dubious about whether they really were trying to get to the same objective.

Even during her struggle on the reservation of channels, there came times at which she would split from the people who ought to be supporting her.

I always thought this aspect of her character was unfortunate, because she could always get along better with her opponents than she could with her friends. She was always against the networks; they were the enemy. But when Frank Stanton or General Sarnoff or someone from the big networks would come down, they would get along marvelously. When she was dealing with someone from JCET, chances are they had a terrible big fight. This watered down what should have been a good alliance.

On the other hand, Frieda Hennock could have a big fight with you one day, and you could be the best of friends the next.

~

Her colleagues at the Federal Communications Commission apparently understood her despite some of her unusual personality characteristics.

HYDE: She deserves great credit for her imagination and her enthusiasm for public television. It did give her a cause—a good cause. But the allocation of channels, according to my recollection, was unanimous. No one forced the commissioners to do what they did, but one would have to recognize that the enthusiasm and zest that Frieda brought into this would be a factor.

Paul Walker had previously been an enthusiast for educational television but he was no match for the excitement that Frieda brought into the business.

~

In the months just prior to the FCC hearings concerning possible channel reservations for education, Miss Hennock employed her various talents to alert slow-moving educators to the coming opportunity.

She attended the convention of the National Association of Educational Broadcasters in Lexington, Kentucky, in October of 1950. Robert B. Hudson remembered.

HUDSON: That was the meeting where she came and really talked about it. It opened the eyes of most of us that this thing was looming.

~

The University of Illinois' venerable Frank Schooley, a pioneer educational radio manager and NAEB leader, who ultimately became a member of the first board of directors of the Corporation for Public Broadcasting, also recalled the Lexington NAEB meeting, though with a somewhat different twist.

SCHOOLEY: She [Frieda] was in Lexington, Kentucky, to a meeting...and if you ever saw a female sit on a table with sixteen wolves around it, she was the female—and a lot of my friends were the wolves!

~

Frank Schooley

Another Midwestern educational broadcaster, Wisconsin's H.B. McCarty, contributed this evaluation.

McCARTY: Frieda played a role which should be prominent in the historical records. She had courage, she was aggressive, and she also softened the aggressiveness with a femininity [CHUCKLE] and, uh, charm and appearance, and became very effective, and won over the majority of the commissioners to her view that reservations absolutely had to be made so that the educators would never be subject to the kind of pressures they had been in AM broadcasting, where popularity and numbers were the criteria for allocation.

I think of her as a really powerful, aggressive, incisive person. I would never want to be on the opposite side from her in any kind of legal situation. At the same time, she was a very attractive feminine creature, who—when I shook hands with her once—left the fragrance of her perfume on my hand for the next day or two and I didn't want to wash!

Colorful, Yes—and Convincing

Since Stanley Neustadt, in his capacity as Frieda Hennock's staff assistant, spent more time with her than any of our other public television pioneers, we can accept his summary of the role and personality of the FCC's first female commissioner.

NEUSTADT: You've got to picture this woman. She was kind of short, and while she was still at the commission a little bit on the plump or chubby side. She was young. I think when she was appointed she was forty-three. Very, vivacious, blunt, big flowing hair, flamboyant.

She had certain public relations gimmicks. When we used to have a big banquet—the Federal Communications Bar Association, for example, would have a big banquet, and there were other big banquets—she usually would be seated on the dais when she was a commissioner. She never arrived on time. She never arrived during the cocktail hour. She arrived when everybody was seated. And except during the heat of summer, she would show up wearing a full-length ermine wrap. And she would just s-w-i-r-l up to the dais, and I assure you that however many eyes there were in that room, they were all riveted to this kind of a vision.

And she was, as I say, extremely vivacious, very charming, but very emotional. Some people thought her emotionalism was put on, but I doubt it. When things went badly for her in the commission meetings, for example, she would cry. She would get up and stalk out. She would shout when the occasion warranted it. She would wheedle.

Neustadt also confided that the son of Wayne Coy [chairman of the FCC during part of Miss Hennock's term] told how his father would come home after a day of presiding over a commission meeting, take off his shoes, throw himself into a chair, pick up a martini, and say, "Oh, *that woman!*"

Nevertheless, as Neustadt concludes, hindsight indicates she was a first-class commissioner.

NEUSTADT: On almost every issue on which she took any noticeable position, she was ultimately shown to be right.

She was, as much as anyone I've ever known, aware of her own limitations. She told me often she wouldn't dream of trying to write a brief, for example. She would argue a case but she would never write a brief.

She was an absolutely superb negotiator, not only because she was a woman, not only that she was an attractive woman incidentally...but when she negotiated, she knew what she wanted and she always knew how to get it. She had all of the intellectual tools. She was a good talker when it came to that.

She could wheedle almost anything that she wanted out of people, including sometimes her colleagues on the commission.

But she was a doer. She cared much more about results than she did about how she got them. I don't mean that she was indifferent about how she got them, but what she wanted was to get there.

I have always believed that had it not been for Frieda Hennock and the things she did, we probably would not have the educational reservations, at least in the way we have them. I think she did manage to focus a lot of sentiment in the country and put force in the country behind this in a way which was impressive for the people in government.

I'm not taking anything away from the pioneers who were in the JCET and all of the others who really did all of the nitty-gritty detailed work, but their work would not have been enough. It needed somebody to kind of dramatize, highlight, scream, be inconsiderate, be irrational if need be, to make this point. I think that she did have an awful lot to do with the reservations as we know them. And we're in her debt for that.

9

The Triumph of Virtue

Thanks in part to the deliberations at the Allerton House seminars and to Frieda Hennock's strident pleas for action, broadcasters interested in education and educators interested in broadcasting began at mid-century to prepare for the history-making battle over television reserved channels. This was to take place during the FCC hearings scheduled in the final months of 1950.

From the educational broadcasters' ranks came WOI-TV's Dick Hull, unquestioned leader of the NAEB. He and Franklin Dunham, a former NBC executive with educational credentials (who by then was heading the radio section of the U.S. Office of Education where Gertrude Broderick also was working), took the first joint steps to prepare for the oncoming hearings. Much would be at stake.

HULL: Dunham and I called a meeting of everybody we could think of that might be interested. We sent them quick telegrams because we didn't have any budget!

BRODERICK: One of my functions was to call a conference as president of AER [Association for Education by Radio]. With Dick's help and Franklin's help we brought in people from all over the country, and out of that came the establishment of the Ad Hoc Joint Committee on Educational Television.[1]

~

The coming together of those with related interests for the sake of gaining greater influence had been urged by Marcus Cohn

and Leonard Marks, the communications attorneys who had taken on NAEB as a penurious client a year or so before.

MARKS: We urged that we broaden the base by taking in leading educational institutions and not confining it just to broadcasters, and that was done. Then, representations were made to Congress, testimony was presented, and hearings before the Federal Communications Commission were attended by the consortium, with witnesses being offered from not only the broadcast stations but the educational community itself.

~

Marks attended that first strategy meeting of the Ad Hoc Joint Committee on Educational Television in the fall of 1950.

MARKS: I had the advantage of having been counsel to Congressman, then Senator, Lyndon Johnson, who was very sympathetic to the idea. He was one of the people that we turned to for advice and help on how to accomplish this result.

Dick Hull became the principal actor. Everybody respected him because WOI-TV had been an established institution in AM, FM, and TV. They did not wait for reservation of channels; they applied and received a permit among the early ones in the United States. Dick had a station on the air, and therefore he could be relied upon as an experienced broadcaster. Frieda Hennock became the public champion. But she by no means was the only person on the commission interested in this development. In fact, she was among the latecomers. She was among the junior members.

First Meeting of the Ad Hoc JCET

Ralph Steetle, who also attended that very first joint meeting, recalled who else was there.

---

[1] This ad hoc group, as well as the subsequent permanent JCET, included representatives of the seven key national education organizations in the country.

STEETLE: I'm visualizing that sheet of paper with the results and the names on it. There were people like Franklin Dunham, Keith Tyler, and Dick Hull. Our friend from the Association for Education by Radio was there [Gertrude Broderick]. Probably also at this stage, the beginnings of the NEA people: Belmont Farley was there. Edgar Fuller certainly was there. The American Council [on Education] was also there [Arthur Adams]. This was a broader group than just the NAEB people.

~

Steetle also emphasized the utter importance of combining the influences of both educators and broadcasters in order to build the best possible case.

STEETLE: It's like "war is too important to be left to the generals." Communications are too important to be left to the communicators. Education, even, is too important to be left to the educationists!

So you see here the beginnings of a major growth in the stature of the NAEB. Mostly, organizations tend to think of their first objective: survival. But if you begin to move to program, what it is you are about to do, and you seek other resources to help that to happen, that becomes an organization that is far beyond what the early NAEB was. So the NAEB won its spurs, I think, for all time, in the development and establishment of the JCET.

~

One might wonder exactly what happened at that first gathering of these hitherto uncoordinated agencies.

STEETLE: It was "What are the problems? What do we want? Who can we get to help us get it? What can your organization do? What other organizations should we tap?"

It was a broad scale approach to all of the problems that would come up later—and would be solved in order to get public television.

~

A first-hand report of the outcome and follow-up activities is provided by Ohio State University's I. Keith Tyler.

TYLER: They finally decided we ought to form a group and see if we could get together some testimony. Then the question was, who has the time?

This was a slack time for me. The Institute had ended in May. And I said, "I think my president, because of his commitment to educational broadcasting in these two national associations, will release me on salary to come

down and coordinate this effort, if you people will all cooperate." And that's what finally happened.

I spent five days a week in Washington and weekends in Columbus.

There have been many jokes about my office being the powder room in the old NEA building. In a sense that was partly true. There was this old mansion that the NEA was using, the National Education Association, and they gave me an office in what had been a very large bathroom, but the fixtures were out. It was quite a decent little private office.

The first job was to get some staff. George Probst, who represented the University of Chicago, persuaded the University to endorse us wholeheartedly. They sent down their director of public relations, a little short man who wore a black homburg and was a very colorful character. He was invaluable.

One of the things we needed was money, so they undertook a direct mail appeal, the same thing now being used by various one-issue groups. They got the mailing list through University of Chicago members of the Association of Atomic Scientists. Their contributors were very social-minded people throughout the United States. They wrote this letter over the signature of the president of the University of Chicago, Bob Hutchins. And this one mailing got $42,000. So that was one support we had.

~

Tyler also knew that the two strongest agencies were the American Council on Education, headed at that time by Dr. Arthur Adams, and the National Education Association, whose representative, Belmont Farley, had for some time been encouraging educational broadcasting. Although neither of these agencies had much money, each cooperated to the extent of finding $3,500 to provide the fledgling Ad Hoc JCET with its first "nest egg."

Enlisting the Skills of Telford Taylor

TYLER: The next thing we had to do was get an attorney. Here we consulted Commissioner Frieda Hennock. She said, "There's a guy named Telford Taylor, who was chief prosecutor for the Nuremburg trials, a very prominent person. He's back in Wall Street at his firm. It's just the kind of cause he might want to do. Needs something that would be a cause for his law firm. Why don't you go up to see him?"

He had been chief counsel for the FCC before the war. He knew the ins and outs of the FCC and all about it, so we had a great guy, you see.

Belmont Farley and I went up to New York and bearded the lion in his den and told him what we were going to do.

We said, "We haven't any money. We've raised $7,000 dollars, that's all we have, but we'll share what we have and will pay you whatever we can."

He said, "Fine. Money's not the important thing. I'll have to ask my firm, but I think I want to do it, and I'll let you know." Three or four days later he said, "The firm thinks it's fine... will do." And he devoted himself unstintingly to this.

Later, he took on a co-counsel, Seymour Krieger, and they both worked very hard on this. They were great!

~

One might wonder why the principal attorneys assisting Telford Taylor were Seymour Krieger and his partner, Norman Jorgenson, rather than Cohn and Marks.

MARKS: Marcus Cohn had worked for Taylor and knew him well, but we did not wish to involve ourselves in the entire operation because we felt that diversity would be desirable and bring greater strength.

Norman Jorgenson had been at the FCC; Sy Krieger had also. And they had just left the government and were not yet involved with heavy commercial responsibilities, so they could devote greater time to putting the case together.

We participated. We prepared statements; we suggested testimony. We also went with witnesses to visit individual congressmen and senators to make certain that they were aware of our positions.

We all worked together, but Tel Taylor was chief counsel.

TYLER: My job as director, besides being a front and doing interviews for *The Nation* and various magazines, was to line up witnesses.

I was in a very fortunate position. Through these higher education things, I knew most of the college presidents around the United States...I had no hesitancy, I knew them by their first names and I could get them.

In fact, we said to the commission at one point—or, at least, Telford did—"Look, there's no problem getting witnesses. We just don't want to tire you. We'll bring in outstanding superintendents, we'll bring in countless college presidents, as many as you like."

Then, of course, we got American labor, AFL-CIO, we got the PTA, we got everybody in. We had a staggering list of witnesses. They all came at their own expense. On the whole, these were people who had [educational] radio going on in

their bailiwick: Philadelphia's Martha Gable, Chicago's George Jennings, New York's James Macandrew.

And there were plenty of people who would simply come in to say, "We believe in this kind of a station as an alternative kind of programming because we're disgusted with what commercial television is doing to kids."

That was the PTA point of view. Those were the days when kids were committing suicide after watching a broadcast—jumping off, flapping their wings, you know, after whatever—Robin, or somebody.

We couldn't have had a better time in which to have hearings.

Before and During the Hearings

As the month of December came closer, preparatory activities increased.

STEETLE: We had headquarters in the Willard Hotel, and I was there during those hearings. There was the briefing of witnesses and getting them in before the commission. I did not testify at the time. The level of people we needed was not the broadcasters. But I was involved in the process.

Here, I think, you begin to see the importance of the NAEB's growth to new stature. If you're going to have university presidents, school superintendents, and the like, speaking about a strange subject, they are going to have to have some confidence in this operation—and this will tend to come through their own organizations.

When we had 240 communities to inform about sworn statements and engineering developments and the like—in three weeks, we needed the American Council or the NEA or the Association of School Administrators-people whom they trusted—to say, "Yes, this is important. Do it!"

The fact that we were a part of those other newsletters, not just our own, made a lot of things possible that might not have been possible without them—even getting witnesses for that first testimony. Keith and Dick really did most of sweating that through. Keith was called chairman but Dick was just as much involved.

McCARTY: I know it was one of them—or both of them—who got in touch with me and said, "Mac, we want to present the Wisconsin story as a part of the testimony."

More than that, they got the president of our own university and universities across the country and superintendents of schools to make statements, saying in effect, "Yes, we've been laggard in not utilizing radio opportunities, but we see television as a positive and powerful medium and we intend to do something about it."

~

McCarty recalled clearly his own participation in the hearings as a young, idealistic proponent of broadcasting in education as he was developing it in Wisconsin.

McCARTY: I was in Washington on the 6th of December, actually arrived on the 5th of December...and had a briefing that night for my appearance the next day.

Somebody—I don't know who—gets credit for arranging for Telford Taylor to be there...and, gee, I was so impressed that we had a man of his stature on our side.

I remember the session we had there at the Willard Hotel as we thought about the hearings, which had already begun and were going to be continued the next day. Telford Taylor and Sy Krieger—I think there were a couple of others, too—were helping to outline the testimony that would be important.

Then followed, on the 6th of December, the hearing in which I took part. And I suspect in all modesty that the story of the Wisconsin experience in attempting to improve its position in the AM radio band and failing completely, and then the effort to take advantage of FM frequencies with a well-established state FM network, interconnected—that these two features of the testimony offered some guidance for the commission.

I was helpful because so much of the testimony was theoretical. We were all talking about the promise of television, the great things that could happen, that were going to happen, but we couldn't point to anything specific. There was not a single educational station on the air except WOI-TV in Ames, Iowa, which was operating commercially.

All during those formative years when we were trying to set goals and influence people to support this endeavor, we had to talk in terms of expectations and aspirations instead of actual accomplishment.

~

Nevertheless, the level of public consciousness of the possibilities began to rise as events in Washington were reported through kindred souls all over the country. California's John Crabbe describes how it was in his home area.

CRABBE: Our lines of communication to Washington were, I think, pretty good. We really knew what Frieda Hennock was up to, what FCC chairman Paul Walker was up to, and all of those people. NAEB coordinated a lot of the activity, of course, as did a variety of agencies out of Washington. They kept us all informed.

The thing that we did, mostly, was to generate public awareness of what was going on in terms of carving out this franchise that we really wanted.

We watched our own back yard very carefully, because you got all kinds of different signals as to what channels were going to be reserved where. The table of allocations would come at you, and you didn't like it for this reason or that reason—so you kept the powers that be in Washington informed of how you felt about your particular area. That was one thing.

Another thing. We spent a lot of time generating interest in two ways, in the educational community, on the one hand—the schools, the colleges, the universities—to let them know what was at stake here and what the possibilities were. We did a lot of dreaming, of course. And, in the community agencies as well. You'd go out and make talks to the local Rotary Clubs and that sort of thing, just to generate awareness as much as anything. "Write to the commission or write to somebody and tell 'em how you think!" Getting all kinds of testimonials put together. Somewhere there's quite a substantial document that has quoted in it one after another of those testimonials from all across the country.

MARKS: It was a very well organized lobbying effort, and the case that was presented was based upon fact. It was not confined to any one city or region. It represented a grassroots feeling throughout the United State.

HUDSON: A great many of the radio people and the university and school people came in and testified...although I must say that nearly all of the testimony was kind of "blue sky," and nobody knew quite how we would operate these things or what we would do with them. It was so much "blue sky" that the commission said, "We need some hard data." So it was at this point that the monitoring studies were set up.

The Christmas Week
Monitoring Studies

HUDSON: Dallas Smythe and a chap from the University of Chicago set up the first monitoring study in New York for a solid week, and brought in testimony which showed the great lack of variety of programming material on New York stations. They were able to bring data not only from New York; they also made one in L.A. and one in Chicago.

TYLER: They had people sitting there with seven monitors and simply put down what was on the air. Of course, what you got was all the same. It didn't matter what station you were looking at, you were seeing the same kind of thing—western movies, blood and gore, and all the rest of it. And this was a powerful influence on the commission.

What it intended to show was that in spite of having as many as seven stations, the actual choice for the consumer was very limited because these stations tended to be very much alike.

Simply to say, "Look, they've got seven stations in New York with all these opportunities for variety," wasn't an accurate picture of what the consumer found when he looked for variety or for alternatives. And we were offering a public station as an alternative.

We said we had no quarrel with the commercial stations, they were doing a fine job, but they were not meeting the total need. And what we needed in every community was the opportunity for an alternative service.

~

Tyler and others became convinced that those monitoring studies—conducted during the Christmas holidays and showing that not all programs were about peace on earth—had a considerable impact, not only upon the FCC members but also on the commercial broadcasters, because this was testimony which they had known nothing about.

Commercial Broadcasters' Attitudes

Commercial broadcasters at that time were not in agreement in their attitude toward noncommercial reservations.

TYLER: The commercial industry was divided because those who had channels didn't want any more commercial stations in their town. They didn't want competition, so they were all for us. The people who did not have channels obviously fought us. So the National Association of Broadcasters—the NAB, the commercial trade association—took a very weak stance because their members were divided.

The educators, on the other hand, were a solid group. This had not been true in 1935. In 1935 a lot of those educators came in and testified that it would be foolish to reserve channels. This time they all said it was necessary. They had learned their lesson.

~

Often chance circumstances affect the outcome of proceedings such as hearings.

Both Tyler and McCarty remembered one such incident which demonstrated again the inadequacy of the commercial broadcasters' showing.

TYLER: A fellow named Baker, a professor at Ohio State in marketing or some such thing, was engaged by NAB to be their director of research, so he was to give this testimony.

It was late afternoon, and he made the mistake of bringing his manuscript with him with the necessary twenty copies and distributing it, and then got on the stand. Frieda Hennock started asking him questions and before he could give his testimony, it was time to adjourn for the afternoon.

I got hold of his testimony and discovered it was full of errors. I mean, he was just sloppy! He was using as a source, Frost's *Education's Own Stations*, and his statistics were bad.

Belmont Farley and I analyzed this paper and pointed out these things, and then went to Telford Taylor, and he said, "Boy, this is something!"

The next day, when this fellow gets on the stand, he was cross-examined by Telford Taylor. And they just stripped this guy to quivering bits of flesh. He lost his job and everything else as a result.

At noon that day, Frieda Hennock gave a luncheon for all the participants in the hearings, pro and con, and he was there, but everybody sort of avoided this guy like a pariah because they were embarrassed. What do you do when here's a man professionally destroyed by his own handiwork?

~

Education's Own Stations was written by S.E. Frost, Jr., of the University of Chicago, and provided McCarty with some welcome ammunition.

McCARTY: Oh, how I loved to launch into an attack upon that book...because if one were to read it unquestioningly, it would seem a terrible indictment of the educational establishment that here, at one time, there were over 200 licenses held by so-called institutions of education or staff members of educational institutions, and that now there were thirty-four, or twenty-nine, or what-not. So education doesn't know how to utilize broadcasting; that was the "lesson" of this.

Well, I took the pains to go through the book and to read the names of the licensees. I found that in some cases the institution—the college or technical school or whatever it was—held the license but that in many cases individuals—a professor of physics or a teacher of electrical engineering—people with a mechanical or electrical turn of mind—were seeking the licenses to experiment with the physics of wireless communication. They couldn't care about the listeners. They were experimenting with wireless as a physical phenomenon.

And I used to delight in pointing out that these were not genuine educational stations. By no stretch of the imagination could they be described as similar to the member stations of the National Association of Educational Broadcasters, for example. Our purpose was to extend the educational advantages of the campus, and theirs was to experiment with the physics of wireless transmission.

I think Frieda Hennock made good use of that testimony. It was mentioned later by a network representative as "a piece of damaging evidence" and the comment was, "Certainly you weren't here when Mr. McCarty dealt with that previously!"

~

FCC staff member Hyman Goldin remembered another moment in the hearings when the commercial side appeared to some observers to be reaching pretty far for evidence to support their arguments.

GOLDIN: I don't know who was talking for NBC at the time, but they gave as an example of the educational programming that the networks were doing, "Your Show of Shows," where they had an opera singer!

They would have one or two numbers during this whole two-hour program, and they argued that that was the sort of thing they could do, and therefore there was no special need for an educational channel!

~

While it seemed clear that the major battle to secure educational reservations might be won in those hearings, the outcome of the entire war would depend upon whether the educational community could maintain its united front and continue the work necessary to follow through on whatever might be the FCC's recommendations.

This would require two things: a permanent organization, and money. Both were achieved.

To secure agreement on a permanent organization with even a minimum staff, substantial funding was necessary, especially since the initial monies were almost expended. It was Dick Hull who saw this as a **necessary precondition for further progress.**

His target for funds was the man who soon would become the president of the Fund for Adult Education of the Ford Foundation, C. Scott Fletcher. [2]

C. Scott Fletcher Enters the Field

C. Scott Fletcher

FLETCHER: In February of 1951, I think it was, I received a call from Dick Hull, whom I had never met. He asked if he could see me about a grant to an organization which I had never heard of.

I had known that prior to Dick's calling me, George Probst — who was then director of the "University of Chicago Round Table" —had talked with Bob Hutchins.

And Bob Hutchins had said to him that anything dealing with educational radio and educational television had to be taken up with Scott Fletcher. [3]

So when this was known to Dick Hull, he asked to see me. We took an immediate liking to one another.

~

Hull provided Fletcher with all the pertinent information, including the need for a permanent organization comprised of the educational agencies and interests with seats on the Ad Hoc Joint Committee on Educational Television, that had served as the steering committee for the channel reservation fight so far.

These "sponsors" included the seven most powerful and prestigious national education organizations, an imposing group holding considerable clout: the American Council on Education; the National Education Association; the U.S. Office of Education, which also represented the Association for Education by Radio, the Association of Land

[2] From this point until after the passage of the Public Broadcasting Act of 1967, Fletcher played a significant role in the gradual development of public television. Subsequent chapters are devoted to high points in his efforts.

[3] About this time, Hutchins moved from the presidency of the University of Chicago to become an executive of the Ford Foundation.

Grant Colleges and State Universities, the National Association of State Universities; and the National Association of Educational Broadcasters.

Fletcher was properly impressed.

FLETCHER: We had a long talk, not only about JCET but about him and his unique organization at Ames, Iowa, about educational radio in general, and about the future of educational television if it ever came into existence as a major factor in the lives of American citizens.

Hull completely convinced me that this was a worthwhile project, a genuine foundation risk.

~

This conversation occurred in February of 1951 and the Fund for Adult Education would not be holding its first board meeting until April. But Fletcher already was an employee of the Ford Foundation, headed at that time by Paul G. Hoffman, formerly the president of the Studebaker Corporation—where Fletcher had served as one of Hoffman's lieutenants.

FLETCHER: I went to Paul Hoffman direct and asked him if he would approve a $15,000 presidential grant to JCET. In most large foundations, the president is given the right to use what are known as discretionary funds. He can make discretionary grants between board meetings if items of an urgent nature arise.

Hoffman said, "From what you tell me, this is a good start for ETV and a sound idea. Go ahead."

I called Dick and told him his request had been approved and sent him a check. This took place before the Fund for Adult Education came into being.

The directors of the fund, at their first meeting in April, decided to make a $90,000 grant to the JCET. Later they made two other substantial grants, much larger.

These grants proved to be one of the best so-called foundation investments that we made, for the JCET was a major factor in the early days of educational television.

The JCET Becomes Permanent

This fiscal promise, in hand just at the time when the Ad Hoc Joint Committee on Educational Television was completing its task in March 1951, allowed this temporary group of collaborators to take a more permanent step, described here by the individual who was soon to become their executive director, Ralph Steetle.

STEETLE: Arthur Adams was the president of the American Council on Education—former submarine captain, salty New Hampshire man, with an ability to bring about connections between organizations.

For example, the American Council might have one position, the NEA another, land grant still another. But somehow, under the stimulation of the American Council on Education, a common position respecting all of the differences could be achieved. So, that "architecture" from the *Ad Hoc* JCET into the *permanent* JCET took place on one afternoon in the American Council on Education conference room.

Telford Taylor, who is the counsel for the JCET, often leaves the room, and goes to the phone and checks with the FCC. And the individual objectives of those individual agencies are hammered out in skillful fashion under the guidance of Arthur Adams—under the pressure of [the feeling that] something is about to happen. The Ad Hoc JCET has been successful. Can we now stand success? Can we move into the next steps? It is proposed that these assignments would be tentative. Can these reservations be made final?

There is a JCET formed, the channels are available, the promise of funds is there. All this takes place in the conference room of the American Council on Education in one afternoon.

~

The following day the FCC came out with its Third Order and Report, which suggested that 209 channels be reserved for noncommercial educational use.

In what cities and towns did the FCC propose to allocate reserved channels? The "freeze" on new applications was still in effect, and 108 duly licensed commercial TV stations already were on the air and scarcely could be disenfranchised.

One version of how the table of allocations was first drawn up comes from Keith Tyler.

TYLER: The commission adopted some rules which had been suggested by their staff about where educational channels should be provided.

They provided that there must be an educational channel in every metropolitan area [according to census definitions] and, in addition, in places which were not metropolitan areas but which were prominent educational centers. And it was proposed that if there were VHF channels presently unallocated, that these be given first of all to the educational stations, but with a real reverence for grandfathering. In communities where the commercial broadcasters had been alert and had already taken up the VHF channels that were allocated geographically, then the educational channels would have to be UHF.

This did some interesting things. Ohio, for example, had very alert broadcasters; every one of the VHF channels was already allocated. So every educational channel in Ohio had to be a UHF channel, which at that time was quite undesirable.

~

This also is the explanation for UHF reserved channels in both New York City and Los Angeles. In each of these cities, seven channels had already been taken up. Therefore, the only alternative at that time seemed to be that the reserved channel would have to be UHF.

TYLER: So with these rules, Belmont Farley and I one night had a census report that showed all the metropolitan areas, and we had some material from the American Council on Education showing where the universities and educational centers were. Then we proceeded to suggest to the commission—they wanted this work done; it was routine from their point of view—where all these channels would be located.

We went through the United States, state by state and community by community, and allocated these channels. We may have missed two or three, but, after all, it was a long night.

Ralph Steetle Takes On A Challenge

Ralph Steetle, initially hired to be the associate director of the permanent JCET under Dick Hull, suddenly found himself in charge when Hull returned to Iowa to supervise more closely what was then going on at WOI-TV. Steetle explains.

STEETLE: Dick, besides being a fine practitioner, was a good foreseer of the future. And part of the problem of the future—but it was happening immediately—was that we were talking about winning channels upon which we'd build stations. One of the major arguments against us by others would be, "What are you going to program them with? You don't have the funds." So one of our first answers was, "We'll produce programs and exchange programs." So his return to Ames was to begin to develop programs.

~

Steetle's term as executive director of the JCET began with the period between the FCC's Third Report in 1951 and its Sixth Report in 1952. He is the best person to explain what went on during that year.

STEETLE: What the commission did in the Third Report was to say, "Well, we've had persuasive testimony, and this testimony provides us with enough evidence to tentatively set aside 209 frequencies. There must be a clear and immediate response on the part of the educational establishment if these frequencies are to be held. Meanwhile, there is a year for this response to be heard."

So my job, in a nutshell, was to take the Third Report and change it from tentative to actual. And the Sixth Report [1952] made it actual.

What we had to do in those 209 communities, and later others, was to make a way for those communities to speak to the commission about their particular channel. This meant a lot of mail, a lot of telephoning, a lot of visiting, a lot of consulting.

It also meant the beginning of a lot of fighting. In some places there would be enough difficulty that it was hard to get a statement in time. We claimed successfully that the JCET was an umbrella organization which had a stake in every proposed reservation. We would, in our own name submit a sworn statement to a channel. Or, if interest was late in arriving, we would enter that statement late under the name of the JCET using that president, that superintendent.

Throughout that Sixth Report, the JCET is built into all of the positions, marshalling all of the arguments, signing the statements if there was no one else to sign. The notary public upstairs at the American Council must have notarized my signature I don't know how many times!

But we really were the advocates. We were the force. And the commission, thank goodness, recognized this.

We began with 209 communities. This was the target. We said, after the Sixth Report, that our percentage was very good because out of the 209 spots we won 242! Those additional channel reservations were added during the process.

~

In April of 1952 when the commission finally came out with its Sixth Report and Order, reserving 242 channels for education, obviously there was cause for celebration—particularly on the part of those whose efforts had been so crucial to this outcome.

TYLER: On that fateful day when the release came out, I happened to be in Washington with Kenneth Bartlett and Frieda Hennock. We celebrated in the Raleigh Hotel, which was across the street from the post office [building] where the commission had its offices, by having a big lunch, with all the appropriate libations!

Hyman Goldin of the FCC staff was asked to describe what he thought was the feeling among the commissioners once the struggle was over.

GOLDIN: The commission—those who supported it, and the majority did, actually—felt relieved primarily. And also, they then took credit for having made the decision. It was that kind of feeling that they had been bailed out, and now they had something to boast about to Congress.

Those who argued from time to time that they were completely dominated by the commercial industry could at least point to the fact that they had saved some frequencies for the educators.

~

Virtue had triumphed, at least for the time being. Had it not triumphed, we would probably not have anything like public television today.

10

Suddenly We Have the Channels—Now What?

After petitioning their government since the mid-thirties to provide reserved space for educational radio and television, those who shared "The Dream" suddenly found themselves challenged by an accomplished fact. On April 11, 1952, the FCC said, "Go ahead and show us what you can do. Here are reserved television channels on which you can now build noncommercial TV stations in 242 communities. The next moves are up to you—and they'd better be made soon."

In the middle of all of this, was Ralph Steetle—the same Ralph Steetle who was an eyewitness to the dedication of the country's first educational TV station, KUHT Houston in 1953. Ralph Steetle, the quiet strategist in Washington, who involved everyone he could in the campaign to secure the reservations, would now employ the same approach to get stations on the air.

STEETLE: The Sixth Report really was the first charter that you could work on. The channels were located in specific places, all of the support around those channels was listed and printed...and the task now—if the first time was a *paper* hearing—was to move into a *people* hearing. What you had to do was to take those genuinely reserved channels and make enough of a show so that they would not be held to be "lying fallow," that there would be *shown use.*

~

April 1952 must have been an exciting month. The historic Sixth Report was issued on April 11. The Ohio State Institute for Education by Radio in Columbus was held the following week, and a national conference involving many of the same people was staged at the Pennsylvania State University on April 21 to 24. Sacramento's John

Crabbe was a member of the Ohio State Institute staff that spring.

CRABBE: As far as the institute itself was concerned, it really didn't have too much direct impact because it was so quick. Nobody had a chance to know what was going on at that point—although that was the time we had "Kukla, Fran, and Ollie" there. They had a ball with that whole business of what this new thing was going to be for these educators getting those television stations.

We took off directly from Columbus the day the institute closed and went out to State College [to participate in the Penn State conference].

Planning the Penn State Conference, 1952

Art Hungerford, who was enlisted to be assistant director of that conference under Carroll Newsom, associate commissioner of higher education for the State of New York, recalled clearly the purpose of the meeting.

HUNGERFORD: [It was] to energize the educational community.

My mission, in effect, was to tell the educators that it wasn't too tough.

~

The conference's advisory committee included men whose names have become even more influential in years since:

Dr. Milton Eisenhower, president of the Pennsylvania State University, brother of General Dwight D. Eisenhower (later elected president of the United States); Rev. Theodore Hesburgh, long-time president of the University of Notre Dame; Dr. Armand Hunter, pioneer in the use of television for educational purposes in Philadelphia, later at Michigan State, whom we recognize as one of public television's "parents"; Dr. Francis Keppel, one-time U.S. commissioner of education; George Probst, pioneer educational radio professional (best known as producer of the "University of Chicago Round Table," one whose work behind the scenes counted greatly in the effort to reserve TV channels for education); Mark Shinnerer, superintendent of schools, Cleveland, Ohio; and Ralph Steetle of the Joint Council on Educational Television. Dr. Hunter recalled the event.

HUNTER: That was an interesting conference in the sense that we were examining some of the potentials that we hoped to achieve by moving actively now into this new communications medium. You had people there from top echelons of university administration, and you had the educational broadcasters—those with radio and some with TV experience—and you had some commercial people there who were interested in public affairs and educational broadcasting from a commercial standpoint.

It was an exploratory type of conference. There were some disagreements and some differences of opinion that obviously would be generated with that mix of interests and experience and personnel.

~

Among the citizen leaders present was Raymond Wittcoff from St. Louis.

WITTCOFF: The meeting was hosted by Milton Eisenhower, whose brother was going to be running for president that year. The Pennsylvania meeting was attended by people representing the various organizations and institutions in the country whose role in this would have to be crucial if anything were to occur.

What I found out, of course, was that there were all kinds of people around the United States who had been thinking of these things for a long time, that they had had the same ideas, that all that was necessary was for them to get together and discover that they had come to these conclusions independently, and that there was really substantial support from some wonderful people who were prepared to get this job done.

~

Fund for Adult Education Vice President "Bill" Griffiths comments on the significance of Carroll Newsom as organizer and director of the conference.

Penn State Univ. Photo/Graphics

Newsom and Hungerford: Carroll Newsom (left), busy with his responsibilities for the New York State Board of Education, found time to direct the ETV Conference at Penn State. He was assisted by Arthur Hungerford (to his left). Both men played key leadership roles in the growth of educational television.

GRIFFITHS: He had a very important role and one that possibly isn't too well recognized. I think that Carroll was the—how shall I say—contributor in subtle and low-key ways, who through his own prestige with the New York State Board of Education and coupled with his very demanding duties there, nevertheless managed to take primary responsibility for bringing off the Penn State Conference. I think doing that would entitle anybody to an important place in history.

One of the interesting things about this to me was somehow ETV and its potential was not something you could so much sell as you discovered who had religion and who didn't. It was unaccountable.

Take, for example—well, take Kimpton at [the University of] Chicago. Certainly in the early stages I think he thought, "God save us from this."

But Ray Olpin at the University of Utah, "Well, of course you have to have it; how can you possibly run a modern university without educational television!"

John Millis at Western Reserve was one of those that I think had religion, and he was at the Penn State Conference.

I remember saying to Millis, " Do you feel that the presence of this new medium is forcing a redefinition of the mission of the university in the community?"

The answer, "Forcing a redefinition? Forcing a definition!"

~

Could Arthur Adams have had a similar thought in mind when he agreed to preside at the conference and tagged Steetle to help organize it? Steetle ruminated on the role of the American Council in this planning.

STEETLE: The American Council on Education is a kind of a holding company for higher education, both public and private. It also has an interest in education all through the levels, but primarily higher education. It has been accustomed in its years to address policy issues of education.

So to get the American Council interested, we had to be thinking of the policy implications of [television] for higher education: does this become a part of your public service obligations? Does this become an arm of your extension? What is the role of teaching?

The American Council thought that maybe the heart of this issue was: What are the programs? What are we talking about here in substance? So this [Penn State] "Program Institute" talked a great deal, not only about the how-to's but about programs themselves. And we brought in program people, both from the commercial and educational worlds. We talked about teaching by television. We talked about program structure. All experiences were grist for that particular mill.

~

Steetle's ability to distinguish between value and cost is reflected in his recollection years later of a pre-conference conversation with the president of the American Council on Education.

STEETLE: As Arthur Adams and I were riding along the road to Penn State for the opening of this conference, he turned to me and said, "Ralph, how is it going to come out? What do you think?" And I said, "I think it will fly, if we don't start with how much. This will paralyze people.

"How much is something that you handle as a matter of course, if you know how much for what. So if we can start this conference with what [television's] values are, what's to be achieved here, and then be realistic about costs—but if you start with costs, this thing will fall on its face." So we were able to keep costs in proportion.

CRABBE: Two things emerged from the Penn State Conference, in my memory. One was, that was the first time that any of us knew about Jack White. He came down from Cleveland and told us all about his telecourses that he had been doing up there.

That's where we really began to think about what the dickens we were going to *do* with these things...and Jack had already been doing them.

First Involvement of Jack White in ETV

John F. White—nearly always called "Jack"—was at that time a vice president at Western Reserve University. Among his other administrative duties, he watched over some telecourses broadcast over the local Scripps-Howard commercial television station, WEWS.

WHITE: It started with a half hour each Sunday afternoon to showcase the university and its activities, later extended to a full hour. We began early in 1951. Could even be '50, but I know '51. By the second term in 1951, [they] gave us first a half hour, then it became an hour each morning at the ripe old time of eight or nine for the teaching of courses.

We developed a combination television-and-correspondence course, and naturally gave credit for some of those.[1]

They asked us at Reserve if we wouldn't come down [to Penn State] and do a demonstration. The producer of all these things was the head of the drama department at Reserve, a fellow by the name of Barkley Leatham. Barkley was the artistic schemer in all of this.

We went down and set up a set. Art Hungerford handled the camera work that day. We took a psychologist—I think his name was Elroy Stromberg—and we did a fifteen or twenty minute cut-down version of what a telecourse was like. Then the combination of Barkley from the point of view of production and direction, Stromberg the teacher, and I from the administrative point of view, served as a panel and took questions and discussed how we put it together and how it worked.

CRABBE: The other fascinating part about that conference—in my memory—was, that was the time that Kay Kyser was going to run educational broadcasting in this country!

The "Kontributions" of Kay Kyser

Kay Kyser, for many years, was the leader of one of the most popular dance orchestras in the country, and as such had presided over a popular network TV program, Kay Kyser's "Kollege of Musical Knowledge." On

---

[1] White subsequently managed WQED Pittsburgh, then was president of PBS's predecessor, NET, for ten years.

Kay Kyser, speaking to an NBC studio audience prior to a 1938 broadcast of "Kay Kyser's Kollege of Musical Knowledge."

the program, the band leader wore an academic cap and gown.

CRABBE: He kind of dominated that meeting, and as a matter of fact, he rubbed some people the wrong way before he got through. He was a very charming guy, and I think he was dead serious. I don't think anybody should have laughed at it at all. But it did get to be kind of funny, because he was going to have Shakespeare taught with a chorus line. That's the way it was going to be. "You've got to have entertainment, guy. Education's got to be entertaining. If you don't make it entertaining it's not gonna go nowhere."

So to have this fellow turn up—if I were a pure academician coming to Penn State to find out how I'm going to use television, to have this guy try to tell me might not go too well.

~

Kay Kyser attended the Penn State Conference because he was the unofficial communications adviser to President Gordon Gray of the University of North Carolina. Kyser had enjoyed excellent financial management during his many days as a band leader and was, according to those on the scene at the time, a very wealthy man who had retired to Chapel Hill. He was very devoted to the University of North Carolina and he had considerable experience in television. When President Gray was invited to the Penn State Conference, he brought Kyser along.

HUNGERFORD: He was a clown! He really made the meeting fun.

~

Hungerford also arranged for Philadelphia's expert in school television, Martha

Gable, to put on a demonstration at the conference—under something less than ideal circumstances, according to Miss Gable's recollection.

GABLE: I was ushered into this huge armory...cement floors and space. They said, "Here are two cameras."

And I said, "Who's going to run them?"

They said, " These two students."

I said, "Have you ever seen a television camera before?"

They said, "No."

A person from Penn State said, " Tell them how to run it."

In twenty-four hours I had to put on a program for these ninety college presidents. There was one RCA man with a switcher table sitting there, and nothing was wired together or anything. And I said, "Get that thing wired up so these men can learn to handle this."

The program we took up there was called " The World At Your Door," because I thought the college presidents might find this interesting. I had an Indonesian physician, and an Indonesian girl who danced, and an Indonesian artist. But I needed some flats to put things on. They came down with some flats and we pinned up the art work and we got our space mapped out, and we went through the program.

I remember Keith Tyler walked in. He looked at all this and said, "How in God's name are you going to get a program together by tomorrow?"

I said, "Only by the grace of God."

So, we put it together...the little dancer and this physician and the artist. It worked well enough so they got the idea. They sat there watching what we were doing and watching the pictures on the screen.

~

Hungerford also recalls a similar episode.

HUNGERFORD: We had invited Bob Banner to come to the conference because he was producing " The Fred Waring Show," which was one of the better television shows at the time. Our idea was to give the participants a rough idea of what this kind of production cost and how they did it.

He was a very humble and wonderful young man. He told us all. And then this joker at the back of the room got up and said, "If I've come all the way from Wisconsin to hear how commercial television programs are produced, I'm leaving!" And I think he went out of the room.

By jingo, we just faded into the woodwork. We were just shocked, because Banner was a wonderful person and doing this as a favor to us. It was a terrible thing.

McCarty Loses His Temper

Thirty years after this episode, when Wisconsin's Harold McCarty was interviewed, he was asked about the Penn State Conference.

McCARTY: Unfortunately my memory of this is blurred by an absolutely inexcusable act on my own part. I'm ashamed almost to relate the incident.

The opening session was a demonstration by a representative from the Fred Waring organization, intended as entertainment and revelation, I suppose, of the intricacies and difficulties of broadcast production.

This angered me just inexcusably...I mean *my* conduct was inexcusable...because it seemed to me that here we were, gathered to think about educational goals, and it was totally unrealistic to bring in for comparison, costs of commercial production.

I rose to protest, and I raised my voice so that I could be heard, and [CHUCKLE] you know, the theory is that you shout and then you get mad, or you stamp your foot and you get irritated. And I shouted and I got mad, and I shouted louder and got madder. And I ended up uttering some inane protest about the irrelevance of all these cost figures at the start of an educational conference, and I stormed out of the room—in protest! Idiotic thing to do! Childish!

One good friend followed me out [LAUGHTER] and in comforting me said, "I understand how you feel, Mac." And the next morning several others confessed that they felt the same way, but felt that it would be a discourtesy to the president of Pennsylvania State College, the host for the conference, to leave the meeting. And it was.

So, on the way over to the morning session I got in stride with Milton Eisenhower and expressed my regrets. And felt foolish thereafter.

Well, I got the reputation for being a kind of firebrand, and for sounding off, and there were times when I did it for provocation—but that wasn't one of the times. I should have kept my mouth shut.

But it was particularly unfortunate, coming at the opening session, where we were primed to set some high goals and to be a little idealistic.

~

Despite such episodes, the Penn State Conference did evoke a considerable amount of thought and discussion, and became a model for participants to re-stage in their own communities. Philosopher-historian-writer Robert Blakely summarized it:

BLAKELY: The conference itself was a job of salesmanship. It was also an educative job because lots of people came and learned things.

Robert J. Blakely

~

John Crabbe's reflections probably are typical of many of the educational radio types who attended.

CRABBE: A lot of us walked into that thing without any real knowledge or understanding of what was supposed to happen. But I think the significant part about that state college meeting was that coming as it did, right after the FCC's Sixth Report, it caused a lot of people to sit down and do a lot of thinking about "Okay, fellas, what are we gonna do now? We got what we asked for, we fought the battle...and by George, we're going to have to put our money where our mouth is."

At least, it did that for me, because I remember going back from that and doing a lot of thinking.

Penn State marker: Evidence of the Penn State Conference is provided by this marker on the lawn of the Nittany Lion Inn, reminding the passers-by that "Plans were made here at Penn State that led to national educational television broadcasting." Present at the dedication of the boulder were John Grant, manager of Penn State's WPSX-TV; Marlowe Froke, who later became

Penn State Univ. Photo/Graphics

its manager, and Bruce Christensen, president of PBS, the Public Broadcasting Service.

~

FCC Chairman Paul Walker told those at the conference that time would be of the essence.

HUNGERFORD: Walker gave us one year. He said, "Look, these channels have been reserved for one year, and if you fellows don't do something about it, the commercial boys are going to want them."

CRABBE: He was saying, "You've got to prove to us that what you said you were going to do with this will happen." Because as a matter of fact, while there was no time table or threatened cutoff, it was pretty darn clear that unless you activated a channel that was reserved for your community, you could stand to lose it.

Of course, that changed later. Now, in 1981, those stars on those things, you couldn't knock 'em off with a cannon. [2]

~

How did that change come about in the next year or two? It was largely because of the influence of C. Scott Fletcher in his role as president of the Ford Foundation's Fund for Adult Education.

---

[2] The "stars" Crabbe refers to are the asterisks on the FCC table of channel allocations which denote specific channels reserved for noncommercial use.

11

The Right Man at the Right Time

C. Scott Fletcher's influence on the beginnings of public television in America began well before the FCC's decision to reserve TV channels for education in April 1952. In fact, that FCC decision was affected positively by Fletcher's activities, some of which occurred even before he became president of the Ford Foundation's Fund for Adult Education in the spring of 1951.

Hy Goldin, a key member of the FCC staff during those years, verifies that the idea of reserving channels was at first not at all secure, despite the constant salvos of Commissioner Frieda Hennock and the urging of FCC Chairman Paul Walker and others.

GOLDIN: Nobody felt very optimistic about it, to say the least. It was obviously very uncertain.

The thing that changed the whole thing was that the Ford Foundation came into the battle. After the Ford Foundation came in, then it was set. There was no further question.

~

After obtaining the crucial initial grants to JCET from the Fund for Adult Education, Fletcher borrowed Robert B. Hudson from the University of Illinois and made him a part-time "consultant in mass communications" to gather information about how ready communities were across the country to activate educational TV stations.

HUDSON: It was decided first of all that we needed to know how many of these communities might pick up these channels. The fund didn't want to do this on its own so they made a grant to the American Council on Education to make this survey and the American Council then hired me to do it.

So I spent a good many months traveling the country. I visited, I think, sixty places and

recommended that thirty-four of them were ready to take action on stations. And sure enough, within the year, twenty of them had done it and others were on the verge.

~

About the same time, according to Fletcher, there were other evidences of eagerness to get started—especially if Ford would provide funds.

FLETCHER: Early in February, after the foundation had been announced publicly, Paul Hoffman received personal letters from the presidents of both Harvard University and the Massachusetts Institute of Technology. The first, from Harvard, requested $4 million to set up an educational television station. The one from MIT requested $5 million to set up an educational television station. A third request from the National Association of Educational Broadcasters was for $4 million to establish a network of ETV stations which would be responsible to the NAEB.

When Paul Hoffman called me to his office and told me about these three grant requests, he said, "If this goes on we won't have any money for anyone else, either in this country or overseas, and it has to cease immediately. I'm going to suggest to the trustees, therefore, that all requests for grants covering educational television and educational radio be submitted to your office for investigation and either rejection or tentative acceptance until they can be submitted to your board of directors."

This is enough to indicate how, by unforeseen circumstances, I had no other alternative than to take on the assignment—which pleased me immensely!

I had told Hoffman, Hutchins, and Chester Davis in the beginning that I was primarily interested in liberal adult education—but as a unique aspect of liberal adult education, as far as history was concerned, I wanted to devote a tremendous amount of time to this new communications opportunity that was now racing along.

Fletcher Gambles On ETV

In later years, many observers have commented on Fletcher's willingness to put so much emphasis on a new and substantially untried medium.

HULL: The fact that he'd bank a brand new uncertain foundation for adult education on educational television—unknown, untried—with one station on the air, and that not typical of what would be, I thought was—you know, he's a real gambler.

~

Fletcher was asked about this willingness to take risks, especially in view of the fact that apparently there was no broadly-based public clamor for such a development.

FLETCHER: No clamor at all. As a matter of fact, the chairman of the Federal Communications Commission, Paul Walker, was horrified that the educational community [as a whole] was just looking at it as if it was a dead butterfly in the middle of the road!

The question you just asked me is precisely what Henry Ford II asked me one day at a luncheon. I was sitting next to him, and he said to me, "Aren't you taking on something too big, not only for the Fund for Adult Education but for the Ford Foundation itself?"

I said, "I don't think so. I am sure we will find a way to stop these requests for unusually large grants, then take a sufficient time to decide how we should approach the entire subject."

And he said, "I'll be very interested to learn the results of your investigation."

~

Fletcher lost no time in proceeding with his investigation. The survey conducted by Hudson—and in parts of the country by Ralph Steetle—was one part of this. Conference with those in the field was another part. Art Hungerford, then associated with the JCET, describes one such conference.

HUNGERFORD: When Scotty makes up his mind to do something, it gets done. I'll never forget a meeting I went out to in Pasadena. It was very early in the game. I guess I was at JCET. I went out there, and we sat there—Hudson and a whole bunch of us, and we talked. What are we going to do about this television thing now? What was going to happen? It must have been right after this Penn State Conference.

Scotty wasn't even there, but we did the best we could. We went ahead and had a nice lunch at that hotel. We came back, and Scotty came in.

He said, "I've got to get a plane to New York now to see the Ford people. I'm so glad you fellows came, and here's what I heard you say." I don't know how he heard us, he wasn't even there!

"The first thing we've got to do," Scotty said, "we've got to educate some TV people, give them education in education. Got to get some television people and give them an educational background. Then we've got to have something that we can interchange programs with, and we've got to have about fifty stations."

And the fifth thing he mentioned was the National Citizens' Committee. "Got to have people that are going to rush around and help raise money."

"I'm awful glad you said all these things; I agree with you, and I'm taking this and I'm going to New York and we're going to do it!"

It's a slight exaggeration, but not much.

I think it was incredible, but when you know Scotty, you understand that this could happen. He can sell anything if he really believes in it, and he believed in it!

~

Hungerford's artistically exaggerated version is strikingly similar to Fletcher's own version of what he thought was needed.

FLETCHER: The first obvious roadblock to be overcome was to set aside a certain number of channels which would be earmarked for educational purposes only.

Number two was to stimulate local interests, namely, universities, public schools, and in certain large cities, private local foundations to apply to the FCC to construct and equip stations.

And the third one of the major objectives of the Fund for Adult Education with respect to television was to create a national program and exchange center.

~

Fletcher told how his board of directors spent whole days inquiring into and gaining a better understanding of the challenge they were about to embrace.

FLETCHER: In order to give the board a better idea of what was in the minds of the FCC commissioners, we invited Paul Walker, the chairman of the FCC at that time, to attend a board meeting.

After listening to Chairman Walker's thinking, I told them of a plan which seemed absolutely essential because of the lack of interest which was being shown by educators throughout the entire country. In many instances in large cities we would not have an institution of higher learning or a school board be the licensee but a local foundation created by local citizens and operated by them.

~

Thus he and his staff recommended two major grants. One was to the JCET for $326,400 over a three-year period to strengthen all that they were doing with the endorsement of the seven national education agencies. The other was $350,000 to a new organization called the National Citizen's Committee for Educational Television. This latter group had as co-chairmen Dr. Milton Eisenhower and Marion Folsom, treasurer of Eastman Kodak, both of whom had been on Fletcher's board when he ran the Committee for Economic Development. It included prominent business leaders in cities throughout the country.

Formation of the National Citizens' Committee

FLETCHER: This National Citizens' Committee would perform three major functions. One, hire a group of promotion and development men who had had experience in raising money and clinching deals of various kinds. Second, they were to issue a monthly and sometimes weekly news magazine to bring everyone in the field up to date on the latest developments. Thirdly, they would employ another group of individuals and associations of all kinds in order to enlist the support of at least 100 national organizations and associations of all types to publicly back and support the development of educational television as quickly as possible and in as many centers as would cover the country reasonably well.

I was quite severely criticized by several people in the field of education for bringing in a group of outside people who were what might be termed in business language "hard-hitting sales types."

The reason I did this was because the educational fraternity, and also the key people who were running educational broadcasting stations, were completely cold if not icy toward the idea of investing money in an educational television station because they knew full well how much more money it cost to make television programs and to transmit them than it did radio.

I can now say in retrospect that this was a wise move. I'm sorry the educators felt I was making a mistake, but I'm glad to be able to say to them, "You were wrong," and today I think they would agree with me.

Fletcher held a number of conversations with FCC Chairman Walker during these months and after. He was bothered by the so-called "year of grace" announcement.

FLETCHER: These channels would not be granted unless the FCC had good evidence that a sufficient number of educators and business and community leaders in larger cities were dedicated to carry on this program. They therefore announced that these channels would be available for one year, but at the end of one year, if the FCC were not satisfied with the response from education, they would go to commercial television.

A Formal Dinner for the Entire FCC

FLETCHER: Immediately following Walker's public announcement concerning the one year of grace, I decided that I would like to have a dinner with every member of the FCC present in order to make a proposal to them concerning the year of grace which had hurt and delayed the general situation rather than helping it. People were saying, "Why apply for a license if the FCC should decide not to allocate channels to educational television? Why go to that expense? Why go to all that trouble?"

The dinner was arranged. The FCC commissioners were the guests of the Fund for Adult Education, and we stipulated that we would not appear unless it was a full commission who could give a unanimous vote on what we proposed.

~

Fletcher was obviously a man who acted forthrightly upon his convictions, a man who was not intimidated by power figures. Indeed, he wielded his own power to influence them.

FLETCHER: We outlined to all the commissioners roughly what I have just told you, except I think it was presented more concisely and I hope more enthusiastically and perhaps more intelligently than I have done on this tape which I don't like doing anyway. I hate making tapes!

The commissioners asked a lot of questions. They were intelligent questions, and they seemed quite surprised and sometimes extremely well pleased with the answers.

When we were slowing up on the questions and answers, I suggested to the chairman that we leave the room and let them have their own decision, and that the fund would guarantee the financing of thirty stations and the program setup, and this would be done by grants and work by the three organizations, FAE, JCET,

Paul Walker, FCC Chairman, listening to Dr. Charles E. Friley, president of Iowa State University.

and NCCET. Excuse the alphabetical way of doing things, but it's an American custom, which is another thing I don't like.

We left the room. A short time later, we were told to return. Chairman Walker, with a few rather interesting and cheerful remarks, said, "Mr. Fletcher, I'm pleased to advise you that the commissioners have agreed unanimously to not announce the year of grace but with your guarantees we will wait through the year of grace. I will still keep emphasizing it in the hopes that it will encourage others."

I pleaded with him not to say anything about the year of grace any more until the year of grace terminated in their formal vote. He told me I could go ahead and arrange another national conference one or two days after the end of the year of grace, at which time we would be able to sail over smooth waters and hopefully arrive in a harbor which would give us thirty stations and a program center.

Immediately after the dinner meeting in Washington, D.C., both JCET and NCCET marched vigorously ahead, and with no word being announced about the year of grace continuing. It was just hushed up.

This Fellow Fletcher -
As Seen By Others

By all accounts, it was clear that the establishment of noncommercial educational television in America had a new and forceful leader, a man with considerable organizational and business experience and a man deeply dedicated to the proposition that the benefits of this new medium should be assured for every person in the nation.

Who was he and where did he come from? Several of the founders of public television have given their points of view.

HULL: He [Fletcher] was an unusual man with a special kind of personal energy level, kind of a dynamic radiation. I'm not talking about charisma—more like you're in a high tension electrical field. You know, you can feel it [as] you walk through some transmitters. So he had the effect of making people feel uneasy in his presence, and of motivating people.

He was always blunt, and direct, and 100 percent honest as far as I could see, a man of great vigor and high intelligence, and extremely well connected politically.

The current generation has no knowledge and cares less about why public broadcasting came into being, but he and the NAEB are the factors there—period. And neither one without the other.

CASE: He had a sense of mission, and he was being a missionary. Often one was prepared to welcome him, but there are moments when a missionary is *not* the most welcome visitor in the world. You've got this and that to do, and you've seen him before, and you know what he's going to say. There were times when you felt like dodging this fellow, but you couldn't, and then you admired him for his persistence, and finally had to recognize that what he was saying made sense and you had to do something about it.

WITTCOFF: Scotty was marvelous. He was not characteristic of a typical foundation bureaucrat.

It was my impression over the years that too often the typical educational administrator put in a foundation role was a person who sort of reacted to what was brought to him, making judgments about what was worth giving money to and what isn't worth giving money to. These people were like good bankers.

Scotty was cast in a different mold. Scotty was a great salesman. Scotty was energetic and hard-driving, and he really was out to make this thing go. And his enthusiasm was contagious. I found him a delight to work with. He was fun to know, and all my memories are good.

~

Jack White—who didn't get to know Fletcher during the early years of ETV—nevertheless captured the Fletcher spirit in comparing him with G.W. "Bill" Griffiths, who was Fletcher's second-in-command at the Fund for Adult Education.

WHITE: They were both charmers, almost the opposite in personality. Bill Griffiths was the quiet, solid, systematic, organized guy who was, if anything almost like a father confessor you'd go to for counsel, whereas running into Scotty was like walking into a den of bears or something. Things were jumping all over and you had to be moving quickly yourself or you were going to get eaten up. He was full of enthusiasm, full of ideas. It was pretty tough getting Scotty to settle down to a single idea for five minutes, but he was a cheerleader for the movement.

~

Frank Schooley, an early president of the National Association of Educational Broadcasters and member of the first board of directors of the Corporation for Public Broadcasting, confirmed the nature of the Fletcher-Griffiths partnership.

SCHOOLEY: Certainly you wouldn't say that Bill Griffiths was the outgoing guy that Scotty Fletcher was, but I knew Bill Griffiths real well, maybe as well or better than [I did] Scotty. He was always appreciative of the things that we got done. He was a very thorough man, and I think he helped make up Scotty's mind on many a case that Scotty would have been unable to decide alone.

~

Griffiths clearly was an excellent balance wheel to Fletcher's rapidly ticking pendulum. He had worked with Fletcher at Encyclopedia Britannica Films. Then, at the Fund for Adult Education, he had further opportunities almost daily to observe this human dynamo in action.

GRIFFITHS: I remember Parker Wheatley once in Boston saying to me, after not having seen [Scotty] for awhile, "Are you still hanging onto that rocket?"

And I said, "Parker, that's not a rocket, that's a guided missile."

Well, I remember both things. Scotty was a rocket, had enormous compulsive energy, but he was always willing at least to listen to input from others. You never felt as a staff member that you were inhibited from saying what you had to say, or disagreeing. We used to disagree. Not that you would carry the day, but you always felt that no matter what his immediate reaction might be, Scotty would do a double- take on things and your arrow wouldn't have necessarily gone into the bushes. It might at least have nicked the target a bit.

He was often rather deceptive in that respect. I would sometimes run into this person or that person in the field from various organizations that we were dealing with, with whom there might have been a bit of a run-in with Scotty, when Scotty might even have dressed the fellow down a bit or removed a couple of layers of his ego. And he would come to me rather downcast, and I would say, "Well, dear friend, congratulations. You've got it made. Tomorrow you'll get anything you want!" [CHUCKLE] So this is again, I think, a feature of this trait of doing double-takes on things. I think that some of the initial reaction was occasionally a bit of protective coloration while the whole thing was deliberated more fully.

I think one of the fine things about Scotty—and there were a very great many of them—was that he never tossed his staff to the wolves in the sense of letting them handle the tough ones. I think he had a sense of the stages where he should rightfully carry the ball, and he did.

~

Fletcher's ancestors had founded a college in Australia and had devoted themselves to the cause of education almost like missionaries. Fletcher's energetic and sincere efforts in the earliest days of public television seemed motivated by his desire to emulate his family predecessors. He was compelled to contribute to society, to do something for people.

GRIFFITHS: I think that's true, but I also think that's true of everything that Scotty touched. It didn't just have to be this. I think that he himself would recognize that if he was a member of a campfire group, his performance with a canoe or with a bow and arrow or with a rifle or whatever, had to be outstanding. He set that standard for himself and in large part I think he did for others, too.

I think [the Fletcher tradition] played a very special role in what he did under the umbrella of education, because this was a return to the family tradition from which, in the eyes of some, he could have been seen to have departed when he left for the commercial world of the Studebaker Corporation. So this was, in a sense, a return to the fold. As president of the fund he was clearly and importantly engaged in an educational pursuit like other Fletchers before him.

But I do think even apart from that, or let's say as an extension of that, Scotty himself had these broad-scale interests in community well-being.

~

Further light is shed on this unusual man by the first person he employed at the Fund for Adult Education, Robert J. Blakely. Blakely has continued his abiding interest in public broadcasting and has become one of its best-qualified historians.

BLAKELY: The Ford Foundation had for many years been a small outfit that fundamentally handled the private philanthropies of Henry Ford I. Then his intended successor, Edsel, died and then I think Mrs. Ford preceded him in death, and then he died, and there was this enormous block of stock coming to the Ford Foundation.

Henry Ford II, who was young in those days and rather insecure, was not really interested in the Ford Foundation at all. He turned to the biggest man in his world—the automobile world—and the biggest man was Paul Hoffman, to accept the presidency of the Ford Foundation.

~

Hoffman had been president of the Studebaker Corporation—an important fact in tracing Scott Fletcher's history—and at the time Ford approached him was the head of the Economic Cooperation Administration, the outcome of The Marshall Plan following World War II. According to Blakely, Hoffman was a great believer in what he called "sub-contracting," or decentralization, a reason why when he took over the Ford Foundation, several subsidiary funds were established.

BLAKELY: There was established quite quickly the Fund for the Advancement of Education and then the Fund for Adult Education. There was the Fund for the Republic, there was Resources for the Future, and there were plans for a special subsidiary fund in the field of mass media [which] didn't work out for some reason.

The Ford Foundation was getting a spate of applications of all kinds, particularly in the field of television, and obviously, since there wasn't a fund for the mass media, they belonged in one of the two funds for education.

The emphasis in those days in the Fund for the Advancement of Education was the training of master teachers. And so they said no, thanks, and so Hoffman came to Scott and said, "Are you interested?"

I don't think it would have mattered much what Paul Hoffman asked Scott Fletcher if he was interested in, Scott Fletcher would have said yes, because he's just that sort of a guy.

But there were particular reasons why Fletcher was interested which go back into Fletcher's own history.

He was born in Australia. His family was a family of educators. It was expected that he would be an educator.

He went to work for an automobile agency when he was seventeen or so. The boss went out to lunch one day and Scott was there and when the boss came back Scott had sold a car. So Scott got advancement there, and he decided to make his business salesmanship. He glorifies in it. He will sell you things that there is no point in selling, things that he doesn't have to sell. It's just his nature.

At any rate, this company was the distributor of Studebaker Corporation, and later on Studebaker took this over, and Scott's talents were recognized and he was moved around, all over. He became a trouble shooter, and he went to China, Korea, Singapore, and he also went to South Africa and Canada and so on. Finally he became head of the advertising and promotion and sales department of Studebaker in South Bend, working under Paul Hoffman.

He would get salesmen together and he would put on shows. At least once he actually hired the Barnum and Bailey Circus. He learned the value of visual presentation. He'd always been interested in gadgets. Somewhere—I think it was in Singapore—he bought a very good German camera and began to take pictures. He used films for promotional purposes to his salesmen.

[When] Paul Hoffman headed China War Relief, Scott was put in charge of money-raising. Later, Paul Hoffman helped start the Committee for Economic Development and Scott went with that. He went around the country and got local committees started in three thousand communities!

The big fear, of course, was that there would be a depression and unemployment after World War II, the same as there was after World War I.

Scott had these business people get together and talk about the situation, report their plans. The reports came in and were added up, and the prediction was there would be no depression, no unemployment after World War II, but, on the contrary, there would be the biggest boom for consumer goods and investment in business that ever had been known. And that turned out to be correct.

When the problem was how to get educational television started, [he went after] local business people, local committees, and that's why there was the National Citizens' Committee for Educational Television to supplement the JCET.

He used films in the China War Relief activity. He used films in the Committee for Economic Development. After World War II, he became president of Encyclopedia Britannica Films.

That was a deficit operation. Scott took charge of it, brought it into the black, increased the number of films, improved the educational quality of the product.

So one strong current in Scott Fletcher's background flowed to audio-visual. Therefore, he was really the guy to go to—as Paul Hoffman said—and Scott Fletcher quotes him often directly, and I quote Scott Fletcher quoting Paul Hoffman, "Make educational television a reality."

It was as simple as that, just a discussion, and Paul Hoffman said, "Make educational television a reality," and I'm sure Scott nodded his head, and that ended that. He did.

~

In a series of conversations at his home in Jensen Beach, Florida in 1981 and 1982, Fletcher documented all that Blakely remembered, and more. Excerpts from his detailed comments during the interview for this book provide additional insight on his views, his own background, heritage, and motivation.

12

Scotty's Own Version of His Story

C. Scott Fletcher is an "unforgettable character" in the development of public television, playing several key roles for nearly twenty years. He is perhaps the most fascinating individual personality of all the founders, and he is a man of colossal achievements. I asked him to tell his story.

FLETCHER: It would be correct for me to say that nearly all of my ancestors were deeply involved in education in various forms: religious, general, youth, and liberal adult education.

My paternal great-grandfather, the Rev. Joseph Fletcher, married Mary Horner, the daughter of my maternal great-grandfather. He was ordained by the Rev. John Wesley, the founder of the Wesleyan, later called the Methodist Church, in England.

The Rev. Joseph Horner Fletcher, the oldest son of Joseph and Mary Horner Fletcher, was sent by sailing ship to New Zealand in 1849 as a Methodist missionary. In 1853 he founded and became the principal of the first Wesleyan college and seminary to be established in Auckland, New Zealand.

Later [he] was recalled to Australia. In 1860, he established and became the principal of Newington College, near Sydney. My grandfather John remained as principal of the college in Auckland until he was forced to close its doors because of the Maori wars.

My father, Michael Scott Fletcher, [was] born at Wesley College, Auckland, May 28, 1868. He graduated from Newington College while his uncle was the principal. He first became a teacher but was then ordained as a Methodist minister and rendered his [pastoral] services in various circuits in New South Wales, Australia. He earned his B.A. and M.A. from Sydney University. Two years later I was born in Sydney, on July 28, 1904.

In 1909, my parents with my sister and me traveled by small steamship from Australia to England. My father earned his degree from Oxford University, and secured his M.A. in Philosophy from London University.

Shortly thereafter, upon returning from England, my father was appointed as the founder and first principal of King's College within the University of Queensland, Australia. And then in 1916 he was persuaded to become the founder and Master [head] of Wesley College within Sydney University, New South Wales, Australia. During this period [he] also earned his Bachelor of Divinity and Doctor of Divinity degrees from the theological college in Melbourne.

Fletcher: Counting on fingers.

~

Scotty Fletcher's father was not his only parent with impressive credentials. His mother also became well-known for her accomplishments.

FLETCHER: During our stay at King's College, mother became extremely involved with arts and crafts, which ultimately made her quite famous throughout eastern Australia. She started with woodcarving and eventually graduated to brass objects. Finally she specialized in wooden jewel boxes, which were covered with pewter sheets with heraldic designs beaten into relief, for which she won many national prizes.

In the mid-thirties mother was elected president of the Queensland Arts and Crafts Society and traveled the state giving lectures and radio talks at the larger towns on the great craftsmen of earlier years.

So, you see, Michael and Winifred Fletcher handed down to their children appreciation of the arts and many other traits such as the education of people of all types, and love of animals, and the joy derived from true beauty.

Entering the Automobile Business

FLETCHER: I entered the automobile business in 1922 and graduated from Sydney University in 1926 with a diploma for Economics and Commerce.

In late 1923, my father decided to accept a position as professor of philosophy at the University of Queensland, which he held from 1923 to 1946. He died at the age seventy-nine.

I want to make the point that without remembering those facts at that time, I followed in my father's footsteps when I accepted the position as president of the Fund for Adult Education.

So it seems very clear to me, at least, that the genes I inherited from my ancestors gave me no other choice than to become a missionary and an adult educator.

~

I asked Fletcher how he became interested in photography and films and audio-visuals.

FLETCHER: With your permission I would like to add the word "theater" to those others.

Going to the theater and opera during my teens and later became a routine similar to that of attending church. The same applied to motion picture theaters. Both art forms have always fascinated me.

The first time I realized the power of photography was while I was advertising manager of the Studebaker Corporation of Australia in 1927 and 1928. Then in the mid-thirties, when I was general sales manager for the Studebaker Corporation of America in South Bend, stage shows in addition to motion pictures were used repeatedly to introduce new models and for dealer meetings of all kinds. In other words, films became for me an essential tool. It is very difficult to describe in words some of the things which can be done so easily by means of sound film.

~

What capabilities were developed as a result of those early years in the automobile business?

FLETCHER: Well, let's start with overseas. My main task was to learn to understand the peoples living in other countries, and to win their confidence.

In such far away and strange lands, there is no one to hold one's hand, and one has to make one's own decisions and face the consequences. Those are required responsibilities for all types of missionaries. I was only twenty-seven when we arrived in the Orient. I was regarded with a considerable amount of curiosity.

One has to learn how to adjust oneself to all types of people in new situations—and as we continue this tape, you will find that new situations cropped up with monotonous regularity!

Raising $7 Million for United China Relief

Partly because of his experience in the Orient and partly because his chief at Studebaker, Paul Hoffman, had become war-time president of United China Relief, Fletcher was invited to become its vice-president in charge of fund raising. Relaxing in his living room in Jensen Beach, Florida, with his shoes off and reference documents spread on the floor, Scotty told us how he met the challenge of raising $7 million in six months.

Fletcher with Documents on floor.

FLETCHER: Now, you see, we're coming to a new type of experience, fund raising on a giant scale. I had to learn many things. But to sum up very simply, we not only raised the $7 million in six months but in that period we raised $9 million. And here's where we get back to the theater.

Paul Hoffman asked me if I would take over the whole of the New York City effort and bring it into line.

John D. Rockefeller was asked to give, free of charge, Rockefeller Center (the entire cast of the program, particularly the—what do you call them—the Rockettes?) and also the director of all their shows, to help us put it on. This was done primarily in conjunction with a famous opera star, Lawrence Tibbett, and his wife.

Thanks to them, I think, every important star we wanted appeared on that stage. The seats sold at $1,000 for the best, then $750, then $500, and the lowest was $100. We had to appear after the regular show was over; we started at midnight and finished at approximately two o'clock. The theater was absolutely jammed, and we raised an extraordinary sum. With pledges that went on for about another six months, we raised the grand total from the $7 million we originally had to $9 million. And that was big-time fund raising!

Again, notice, we used films, we used the stage. In order to dramatize we had to emphasize, so we used the stage and films for emphasizing the importance of the objective.

Because our people in the field were unable to express themselves intelligently concerning the needs of China, we used motion pictures. All the field people had to do was to arrange a meeting, flip the switch, let the motion picture tell its story, and afterwards organize the local fund-raising committee.

Organizing the Committee on Economic Development

Fletcher's involvement with the Committee on Economic Development following World War II, is another story with its own spectacular aspects.

FLETCHER: The objective was to have a quick change from war production to peace production, and to make sure that there would be no unemployment, except the normal unemployment of people changing jobs immediately after the war.

In order to achieve this, two things were necessary. Number one was to create, community by community in the United States, a committee of enlightened businessmen only—plus enlightened economists and social scientists who would handle the second side of the problem, namely, the preparation of statements of policy which were to be presented to the president and to the Congress.

We recruited a total of 165,000 businessmen, all key men in these 3,000 communities,

who completed their plans for the changeover: new products to go into production immediately after the war ended, new store fronts for retailers, etc.

When we first started, the men whom I had employed to assist in this were booed off many platforms. Businessmen would say, "How can we possibly plan for the sort of things you are talking about? We don't know what the tax situation will be; we don't know anything about the economic conditions of the country after the end of World War II; we can't do it." Our men decided they couldn't tackle the job and were about ready to quit.

So I had to go to the chairman of the board of CED, who was Paul G. Hoffman, and tell him that I needed money immediately in order to prepare—what? First, sound slide films. Second, a series of motion pictures. The businessmen were unable to get up before an audience and talk about the objectives of CED when they didn't really understand them themselves.

After the new films and sound slide films had been prepared, the problem became relatively simple. A [local] chairman was established, he would call meetings, utilize films and film strips, and the answer in most cases was, "Yes, we will go ahead."

So here again, without the use of audio-visual aids, CED would not have been able to do the job, another example of my interest in education, in using films in overcoming objections, making decisions on what had to be done, in the utilization of audio-visual media, which is what television is really all about.

~

As the war ended and the work of the Committee on Economic Development was turned over to the U.S. Chamber of Commerce, Fletcher felt that the time had come for him to leave the automobile business.

FLETCHER: I had really been on leave of absence from Studebaker to do the United China Relief job and also to do this Committee on Economic Development job. Mr. Hoffman wanted me to continue with Studebaker [but] I told [him] that I wanted to go into education, and particularly education connected with the utilization of films and film strips. I said to Hoffman one day that the Encyclopedia Britannica Films would be a good example.

On three separate occasions in a period of about a year and a half, Paul Hoffman offered me additional opportunities to rejoin the Studebaker Corporation. But my love of education and my love for the utilization of films for all kinds of educational and instructional purposes was so strong that I said, " Thank you, Paul, but EBF is my niche."

So Fletcher took on the presidency of Encylopedia Brittanica Films [EBF], and met with considerable success.

FLETCHER: By 1950, Encyclopedia Britannica Films was nicely in the black. The period I spent with Encyclopedia Britannica Films and Encyclopedia Britannica and Great Books of the Western World were the four most happy and constructive years of my life until this point.

EBF's President Gets A Call from Pasadena

It was a total surprise to Fletcher in January 1951 when he received a phone call in Wilmette, Illinois, from Dr. Robert M. Hutchins, calling from Pasadena, California. Fletcher had become a close friend of Hutchins in preceding years.

FLETCHER: He was not an easy man to get to know or be accepted by. I always felt I had to be very direct and frank with him about himself and about some of his ideas.

He was a controversial figure. When he was appointed as the young new president of the University of Chicago, he was referred to in newspaper and magazine articles as "the boy wonder of the educational world." This always amused him, and once he said to me, "Just forgive them, for they know not what they say."

~

Hutchins was calling from the Ford Foundation temporary offices in Pasadena.

FLETCHER: He spoke in his usual cryptic fashion, and said very briefly, "Scotty, Paul Hoffman and Chester Davis and I would very much like to visit with you at our offices in the Huntington Hotel in Pasadena, in order to tell you about what we are doing to launch the Ford Foundation and to place a proposal before you for your consideration."

Two days later, after checking in at the Huntington Hotel, I asked for Paul Hoffman's room number. The clerk said, "He and his two partners are not in a room in this hotel; they're occupying a private cottage across the bridge. I'll have someone show you where they are located."

When I entered the room, I was shocked. Here were three truly great men, one sitting in each of three corners facing the wall! And when I came in they all turned around.

I said, "What in hell is going on? I thought this was the Ford Foundation! Don't you have any money? Do you all have to squeeze into one little room like this?"

They all laughed, and Paul Hoffman said, "Now hold it, Scotty. We're waiting for another place to hold our operations, and in the meantime we're saving space and money."

I said, "Well, that seems to me to be a hell of a way to run a foundation, if you don't mind my saying so."

Hoffman said, "Now cut out the nonsense. You first have to have a talk with Bob Hutchins. So you two are excused, and no more funny business."

~

Fletcher, smiling.

Fletcher went into great detail about his conversations with Hutchins, Davis, and Hoffman as they related to him what they hoped he would undertake, namely, the presidency of the Fund for Adult Education, including all responsibility for educational television grants.

FLETCHER: I said to him, "You know my experience in the utilization of audio-visual aids and particularly educational motion pictures. For years I have been involved with utilizing media for many projects, and now I am most interested in the possibilities of hopefully seeing television used for educational purposes, both within and without the schools, in other words, in the home."

Hutchins said, "Yes, I have already studied this matter with George Probst, who as you know heads the radio program called 'The University of Chicago Round Table.' At the present time he is working on this very matter of educational television." He followed up this statement by saying, "I have great hopes that television can become a major factor in educating not only our children, but our adults, in this and other lands."

My reaction was that I had always hoped that communications, and particularly verbal communications and now television communications, could be used for bringing greater understanding between the peoples of the world. I knew whereof I spoke because of my experiences in gaining acceptance from those with whom I had had to do business, in the Orient in particular.

His reaction was exactly the same as mine. He said that he felt this would be a natural avenue to pursue.

His answer pleased me immensely, and I became extremely excited about this opportunity shortly after I arrived in Pasadena.

~

After consulting with his wife, Billie, and William Benton, owner of Encyclopedia Britannica Films, Fletcher accepted the post.

13

Other Founders of ETV

Although C. Scott Fletcher was among the most prominent of those who fostered the growth of public television following the reservation of television channels, he was by no means the only leader of this growing crusade.

Continuing their efforts—now with redoubled energy—were the Dick Hulls, the Ralph Steetles, the Keith Tylers, the Harold McCartys, and others who earlier had begun the efforts to benefit Americans through this new educational medium. In many communities across the nation, men of prestigious reputation and stature became convinced that there were indeed remarkable potentials for good in ETV, difficult as it might be to translate the attractive dream into reality. These, too, are among the visionaries for public television.

To put their efforts into proper perspective, one must keep in mind the three thrusts of the Fund for Adult Education:

—to assure that the channels would remain reserved.

—to develop at least thirty stations as soon as possible.

—to create a method for providing programs for these stations through some kind of national center.

The first of these three objectives, as has been already described, was virtually accomplished within the first few months of Fletcher's presidency of the FAE. The second and third objectives took somewhat longer.

The visionaries participated in *both* the establishment of stations *and* the creation and development of the national program service. Public television was not impressed

from the top or from any single center. It was built by local grassroots leadership collaborating with local leaders from other communities to create whatever national service or aid was desired. Fletcher and the Fund for Adult Education encouraged and materially assisted both efforts.

In the combined recollections of the ETV pioneers interviewed for this book, three community leaders, whom we were unable to interview (because they had passed on), stand head-and-shoulders above the rest: Ralph Lowell of Boston, Edward L. Ryerson of Chicago, and Leland Hazard of Pittsburgh.

There were also many others who caught the glimpse of what television might become if this dream could be fostered. Among them were Darwin Fenner of Merrill Lynch Pierce Fenner and Smith in New Orleans; Mortimer Fleishhacker in San Francisco; and Raymond Wittcoff, a young business leader in St. Louis.

But these three corporate and business leaders, Lowell, Ryerson, and Hazard, are considered to be the most outstanding individuals, who, for several reasons and despite heavy professional burdens and volunteer community leadership responsibilities, rank a step or two above the others.

All three are considered locally to be the fathers of their respective public television stations. All three served on national ETV boards or the National Citizens Committee in early years. But it is the admiration and almost reverence with which they are talked about by so many in the following reminiscences that will reflect the nature of these men and their dedication to " The Dream."

Boston's Ralph Lowell and WGBH

Of the three, Ralph Lowell of the New England Lowells is remembered with the greatest admiration by the greatest number of ETV pioneers. This is in part because he was the father of Boston's WGBH-FM, then of WGBH-TV, and also served for many years (often as chairman) on the board of directors of what started as the Educational Television and Radio Center (ETRC) and subsequently became NET, National Educational Television, "the fourth network." He also played a key role in getting President Lyndon Johnson to encourage the creation of the first Carnegie Commission on Educational Television, which in turn led to the Public Broadcasting Act of 1967 — the landmark legislation that brought about the formation of CPB, PBS, and NPR, and the growth of what is now taken for granted as "public television" and "public radio."

Dr. James Killian, who in 1981 had capped his long tenure at Massachusetts Institute of Technology by holding the office of president emeritus, was an early trustee of WGBH. In 1966 he was named chairman of the first Carnegie Commission on Educational Television. Subsequently he headed the board of directors of the Corporation for Public Broadcasting. Here he recalls the early days of WGBH and in particular, his own impressions of Ralph Lowell.

Ralph Lowell portrait.

KILLIAN: Mr. Lowell was a member of the prominent Lowell family in Boston. I believe at that time he was the senior member of the family. Certainly he was the sole trustee of the Lowell Institute and its funds and had complete authority and responsibility for the way they were used.

He was a banker in part, associated with Boston Safe Deposit and Trust. He became, I think, at one time, president of that and then subsequently chairman of the board. But he was called upon for all kinds of community activities.

The MIT Museum
James R. Killian

Well, anyway, he was a generous, community-minded, social-minded person, and one of the really distinguished Bostonians of that period. He was in art, he was in banking, he was in education, and he was associated with the Boston Symphony. All the great cultural institutions of this area had the benefit of his trustee participation.

He became quite enchanted with the WGBH activity and gave it a great deal of time and attention, and certainly back-stopped the operating people there.

~

Parker Wheatley, the first manager of WGBH-FM and also of WGBH-TV, takes us back to his first meeting with Ralph Lowell in 1946.

WHEATLEY: I went to this bank, [and] was greeted by somebody at the first reception desk, and I said, "I am Major Wheatley." I was in my uniform — I was still in the service.

I was told, "Miss Perkins will be right out and take you in to see Mr. Lowell," and Miss Perkins of the New England Perkinses, God knows how many generations, came out, just a lovely and charming woman.

As we went through another little barrier with the gate open, to the left was an open door, and there sat—[LONG EMOTIONAL PAUSE]—there sat this magnificent old man.

He wasn't that old. He was probably fifty-five or something, I don't know, sixty. But he was—he looked to me like a sea captain. He had a beautifully cropped mustache, perfectly tailored suit. He wore a chain across [his vest], watch on one end, I suppose. I never saw what was in the other pocket, but I did see the Phi Beta Kappa key which he wore proudly. And we talked.

I said, "Are you sure you want a guy like me with a bachelor's degree in philosophy and English from a place most of these great faculty people and scholars have never heard of, Butler University in Indianapolis, Indiana?"

And he said, "Major Wheatley, I think it's better that you don't have a Ph.D. These people are a bunch of prima donnas, and you won't have any jealousy from them with your bachelor's degree. But your experience is the experience that they don't have and you *do* have."

After this one interview, I had a letter—no wasting money with telephone calls—from Mr. Lowell, "If you would like to join us, Major Wheatley, we'd like you to come."

He suggested September 1st, and I replied, "I shall be there," and so it was.

~

Wheatley became the director of the Lowell Institute Cooperative Broadcasting Council, an entity which had just come into being—thanks to the influence of Lowell. Just how this occurred gives us a further glimpse of the Lowell magic, through recollections not only by Wheatley but also by two other parents of public TV who became participants in the WGBH scene shortly after Parker did—Hartford Gunn and David Davis. Davis recalls his impressions of Lowell.

DAVIS: Incredible man. He was one of those people so warm and so normal and friendly, very powerful, but I think so absolutely secure in himself and his roots, he didn't have to put on any show. He could just be a normal nice man.

The roots of that station [WGBH-FM] go to the fact that when some of that Harvard faculty came back from the war, they'd seen mass communications and what it meant, and decided Harvard ought to have a radio station.

And James Bryant Conant[1] did not think Harvard ought to have a radio station—at least by itself—and the secretary of the Harvard Corporation, a man named David Bailey, was asked by Conant to see if something couldn't be done cooperatively.

~

Hartford N. Gunn, who entered the educational broadcasting world about this time, and who eventually was to become the first president of PBS, picks up the story.

GUNN: Dave Bailey said, "Why don't we get Ralph Lowell in? This is a kind of extension activity which is in the tradition of the Lowell Institute."

Hartford N. Gunn

The original Lowell had come over from England with the design of the machines that make cotton cloth in his head, because he wasn't allowed to bring them on paper, and had set up the great milling industry in New England.

He established the Lowell Institute because it was his belief that the soil of New England was so infertile and the limitations of New England so great that it would have to survive on its brain power.

That's poorly said, but essentially what he said was, "We'll have to survive by our brains rather than by our resources since we ain't got many."

~

Bill Griffiths of the Fund for Adult Education recalled a similar account provided to him by Ralph Lowell himself, who seemed always to have been deeply conscious of his family's tradition.

GRIFFITHS: He showed me one day some documents that went way back to the beginning when a progenitor of his had enough foresight to say to himself, "The day is going to come when the center of gravity in American finance and commerce is going to shift. When that day comes, the way in which Boston can hope to leave its stamp on the nation's developing pattern is via the realm of the mind and ideas. I will therefore establish the Lowell Institute."

---

[1] President of Harvard University and strongly oriented toward formal academic study.

GUNN: So he founded the Lowell Institute and set it on this course of serving people of the community who did not have adequate education. The idea was to provide them with the means to get that education, outside of the formal structure but with the assistance of the structure.

WHEATLEY: The Lowell Institute Lectures had been given free to the city of Boston for a hundred years or more. European scholars came to deliver these great lectures. The Boston lecture-goer, who was caricatured sometimes in books about Boston, was a real intelligent, fine citizen. And the Lowell Institute had been responsible for those kinds of great lectures.

They also set up extension courses in which members of faculties, largely Harvard, would teach courses—for which, if you took them long enough, you could get an adjunct in arts degree from Harvard University, if you did well.

And so he was both in the lecture business and in the course business, and he was a loyal son of Harvard.

GUNN: The whole idea of using broadcasting for extension was an idea which Dave Bailey thought would just fit Ralph Lowell and the Lowell Institute perfectly, and it would represent what a modern-day Lowell would do, given the new tools of technology.

So he got ahold of Ralph Lowell, and Lowell recognized the idea as being a valid one and a good one, and they set up a meeting at Conant's house—this must be in, I would say, the late forties—and invited the president of BU [Boston University] and BC [Boston College] and MIT and Tufts, and I think Northeastern, with the idea that this issue of the universities in broadcasting would be discussed.

DAVIS: Bailey knew that probably the single man that could get six college presidents around the same table was Ralph Lowell, because of all of these interlocking directorates, and he was president of the Museum of Fine Arts, he was on the Harvard Corporation, and the Lowell Institute supported night courses at MIT, et cetera.

So the first time those six had ever met together was under Ralph's auspices.

GUNN: Everybody, I guess, thought, "Well, gee, it's a good idea, and maybe we really ought to be doing something here in New England, and if Ralph Lowell is willing to take the leadership and the burden of doing this, we'll come along.

"However, it looks like a big step to establish a station, so why don't we begin with a small step and see if we've got anything to say to the public?"

Hence the decision to form the Lowell Institute Cooperative Broadcasting Council, with Ralph Lowell putting up a major share of the money but each of the universities contributing a little money; to hire a director, who turned out to be Parker Wheatley; and to go forth on commercial radio stations to see if there is indeed something that can be done.

WHEATLEY: It was a two-year experiment. Mr. Conant and Mr. Lowell and I had a meeting one day to figure out what we should call this thing. It didn't even have a name yet.

I suppose Mr. Conant said, "Well, I guess we've got to use the word broadcasting in here." Maybe he said, "council," I don't know. Then I think he said, "We've got to have the Lowell Institute in it." And maybe I tossed in the word "cooperative" or "broadcasting," I'm not sure which word. I had one word in the title. Lowell Institute Cooperative Broadcasting Council. That was it. It was all selected in an hour and a half one day in Mr. Lowell's office.

I was the director. Mr. Lowell didn't have a title, he just called himself a "spearhead."

We were on all the major network stations and we were on at good times, and they all respected us, and they all helped. They thought this was fine. We were treated extremely well.

The faculty were great. Nobody got a nickel; they gave their time. It was very exciting.

And then, because it was a success on commercial stations—not because we were being kicked around but because it was succeeding, the FM station came back [into consideration] because here was the superb instrument for the Boston Symphony Orchestra.

Mr. Judd, the manager, and Mr. Cabot—of the Cabots and the Lowells of Boston, a marvelous man—knew that the great big fortunes were drying out. They were just ceasing to exist, so where were they going to get the money in the future? They were going to have to have more support from the people at large.

GUNN: Parker was set on having his own station, recognizing that the amount of time that the commercial stations would give would be limited, and would be more limited in the future.

So Parker, seeing the handwriting on the wall, really went to work to try to get an FM station. Again, luck stepped in.

It was at a time when Major Armstrong was being frustrated in his development of FM. The Major had some transmitting equipment which he owned, and he went to MIT and said, "I want to give you this equipment on the condition that you go on the air with it."

MIT said, "Whoa, wait, we don't want to get into the radio broadcasting business, we're an engineering school. But we're in this Lowell Institute Cooperative Broadcasting Council, and we'll turn to the director, and see."

WHEATLEY: That is what turned the tide. I don't think they ever would have had the FM station if Major Armstrong hadn't given it to them for nothing.

DAVIS: They got a dollar-a-year lease on the top of Great Blue Hill, which Harvard owned, to put the [antenna] up there, which is the highest spot in the area. There was space in Symphony Hall for a little studio.

GUNN: GBH stands for "Great Blue Hill," not "God Bless Harvard" as some people have been wont to say.

DAVIS: I think this is awfully fascinating, an example of how Ralph Lowell operated.

They [WGBH-FM] really wanted to broadcast the Boston Symphony Orchestra, but they had two problems. First, the musicians' union. They didn't have any money, no conceivable way they were going to pay the players, just going to broadcast them. So, they had the union—and they had the exclusive RCA/NBC contract.

The president of the symphony was Mr. Cabot, the president of the station was Mr. Lowell, and they invited James Caesar Petrillo to have lunch at the Harvard Club.[2]

They described to Mr. Petrillo their ambitions for getting more and better music out to more and more people, and so on, but they really needed permission to get this all started. When I got there in '56 and saw this AFM contract, I couldn't believe my eyes. What it said was to inform the union—national, not the local—one month ahead of time, every month, as to which concert you have decided to broadcast, and that the players have given a waiver, and you automatically have permission to broadcast anything.

Then they had to deal with RCA. Well, the man who was then president of MIT knew General Sarnoff. So he called up his friend, General Sarnoff, and said, "Hey, we're starting this little old radio station up here, General, and we want to put the orchestra on the air."

General Sarnoff said, "I'll take care of that." And the word was passed.

That's a little piece of Ralph Lowell's ability to operate at that level.

The whole origination of that place gave it a structure and a base unique in this country. No other community station went on the air with anything resembling those kinds of auspices.

WHEATLEY: The FM station got started in 1951, and our inaugural, of course was a full-length live concert by the Boston Symphony Orchestra.

GUNN: It was a very interesting evening because present were Mr. Cabot—one of *the* Cabots—who was chairman of the board of the symphony; Ralph Lowell—who was *the* Lowell; and Major Armstrong. We had the Lowells talking to the Cabots to the Major—who was playing God that evening![3]

HUDSON: [Mr. Lowell] took great pride in his FM station in early years. He would walk down the street and friends would stop him and say, "I heard your station last night and I enjoyed it very much." The old gentleman would just beam, and felt a great personal commitment to it. It was a good station.

WHEATLEY: I was asked if we should go ahead with the FM station when there was only a 4-percent ownership of FM sets in Boston, according to Pulse. I said, "Let's go." Within five years, we had 60-percent or more.

~

This growth confirmed the faith and the backing that Ralph Lowell had provided as WGBH-FM came into being, something of a gamble at a time when many were advising against getting into FM at all.

Ralph Lowell's satisfaction and commitment to WGBH-FM made him the obvious target for C. Scott Fletcher as he began to encourage the establishment of educational television stations.

Fletcher's account of his first meeting with Lowell displays another side of the Boston gentleman's nature.

FLETCHER: Very early in 1953 I made a special trip to see Mr. Lowell. With me I had Mr. G.H. Griffiths, whose nickname was "Bill," and who was vice president of the fund.

---

[2] Mr. Petrillo was the renowned Chicago musicians' union head who for years was the feisty and effective national president of the American Federation of Musicans.

---

[3] The allusion here is to a toast proposed by one John Collins Bossidy at a Holy Cross alumni dinner in 1910: "And this is good old Boston/ The home of the bean and the cod/ Where the Lowells talk only to Cabots/ And the Cabots talk only to God!"

When we walked in to meet Mr. Lowell, he greeted us and the first thing we talked about was his radio station and the excellent programs they were producing.

Gradually the conversation moved to educational television. I told him we were in the process of offering grants to organizations such as his that operated a radio station, and asked if he would be interested in considering the establishment of an educational television station in Boston if we were able to give him a grant of $150,000 which would have to be matched by him.

Mr. Lowell was a person who looked exactly like Father Christmas should. He had ruddy cheeks, white mustache something after Arthur Fiedler. He was a jovial person, but he could be a very hard businessman to deal with. He leaned back in his chair, looked at me with his piercing blue eyes, and said, "I've got more trouble than I ever want to have with educational radio. Why in hell should I bother myself and hurt myself mentally and physically by trying to run an educational television station? The answer is NO!"

Well, I didn't know Mr. Lowell very well in those days, but as time went on he became one of my closest friends, and he turned out to be one of the most wonderful human beings I've ever met in my life.

I realized that there was no sense in saying another word to him. After all, he was a Bostonian. He was a *real dyed-in-the-wool* Bostonian. I decided the thing to do was to change the subject, and then, like an Arab, close my tent and silently creep away. That's exactly what Bill Griffiths and I did. [CHUCKLE]

A few months later, I decided to return to Boston and talk with Mr. Lowell again. This time probably he'd just had some very excellent transactions through the bank, because I said to him, "Mr. Lowell, I'd be very grateful if you'd reconsider our offer to make a grant to the Lowell Institute for the establishment of another great educational station in Boston. Won't you consider it?"

And he said, "Well, give me more details."

I won't go into all those details, but the end result was that he said, "I will." So it was a marriage, and one of the happiest marriages that we had in educational television.

~

Another facet of Ralph Lowell is revealed in Hartford Gunn's account of how Lowell managed to interest Boston's Filene family in helping to establish WGBH-TV.

GUNN: As Ralph said, instead of putting a statue on Boston Common, which is what the family originally thought, he said, "Why not give a living memorial?"

So the Filenes made the decision to honor their father with the station.

So with the Lowell Institute money, the Filene money, and the Fund for Adult Education money, WGBH-TV was born in April of '55, the twelfth ETV station.

KILLIAN: Among all of the philanthropic and community activities with which he was associated, I think WGBH became his chief interest. I think Hartford Gunn and later on others were able to cultivate that interest very skillfully and with good results.

~

Eventually we saw the significance of Dr. Killian's last remark, for Ralph Lowell not only "fathered" Boston's WGBH-FM and WGBH-TV but also played several roles in the national educational television picture.

Among these various national roles was his presence on the board of directors of the newly-formed Educational Television and Radio Center in Ann Arbor, Michigan, the first effort to develop a national educational television program service.

CASE: When he was asked to become head of the board of this fledgling organization, he saw it as a chance to spread out, to develop nationally what he was trying to do in Boston.

Thus he came with a certain cachet, and one felt proud to be sitting on a board of which he was chairman. And when he looked most formidable, he could make the most disarming remarks. His sense of humor was never at fault, and he was awfully good company, but one felt a sense of substance there that was unshakable. I think we were very lucky to have him.

~

Denver school superintendent Kenneth Oberholtzer, a member of that board for several terms, and outstanding among the superintendents for his grasp of the instructional potential of public TV, also speaks of Lowell with warmth.

Kenneth Oberholtzer

OBERHOLTZER: Oh, yes, who could forget Ralph! Ralph was from the "old gentleman" school of Boston, of The Lowells. He was the most kindly, friendly man I think I've ever associated with on a board like that. He was generally agreeable, but I always got amused by his tactics which the board tolerated.

He would listen to a discussion for just about so long if he was favorable to that. Then he would say, "Are you ready for a vote, those in favor say 'aye' the ayes have it!" It went just that fast! [BIG CHUCKLE] That's the way he would say it.

We would do that over and over as long as he was chairman of the board. Nobody would laugh about it, but afterwards in private we would talk among ourselves.

I don't think we ever kidded Ralph. He was not the kind of fellow you would kid.

~

Norman Cousins, long-time editor of *The Saturday Review* and widely influential writer and lecturer, also served at various times on that board and obviously enjoyed Lowell.

Norman Cousins

COUSINS: Ralph Lowell was in the great Boston tradition. He was weighty—in every sense! His bulk filled up part of the room and his intellectual capacity took care of the rest!

He was a delight. I'd be a much better public speaker than I am if I could remember half of the stories he told. He never began a meeting without giving us all a good chuckle. And he had integrity and judgement and substance. It was comforting to know that you had someone who knew how to carry a tradition as beautifully as he did—personally, professionally, and socially.

~

Scott Fletcher and fellow Ford Foundation executive James W. Armsey, also were clearly impressed.

FLETCHER: Ralph Lowell was referred to over a period of many years with the utmost sincerity as "Mr. Boston." No man in my memory ever devoted himself more generously to the affairs of a community, from Harvard University on down to small organizations in the Boston area, than Ralph Lowell.

ARMSEY: He was a tower of strength and a man of his word, which I guess the Lowells were known for.

And I wish there were more people who were people of their word today. When he told you he would do something, he would do it.

James Armsey

Chicago's Edward L. Ryerson and WTTW

Just as Lowell was providing the vision and pioneering spirit for educational television in Boston, Edward L. Ryerson, was helping establish public television in Chicago—Channel 11, WTTW. Many, even those who were active in the field at the time, may not realize that Lowell played a role in acquainting Ryerson with the possibilities of an educational television station as a worthy community enterprise.

This behind-the-scenes connection was brought to light during my interview with Newton N. Minow, a Chicago attorney who first became acquainted with public television by watching the station that Ryerson had brought into being in 1955. My interest in Minow was due to the many roles he played in the growth of public television. He served as chairman of the Federal Communications Commission during those critical years when federal funding for ETV first was discussed, he was a strong backer of the groups responsible for the establishment of public stations in New York and Los Angeles, he was a member of the board of WTTW in Chicago, and he was chairman of the board of PBS during its most formative years. Truly a giant among giants!

I met with him in the glass-walled conference room of his law firm atop the First National bank building in Chicago's loop. From there we could see the many TV antennas crowning the slightly-higher Sears Tower nearby.

Here we talked of his activities in public television and his recollections of Edward L. Ryerson.

MINOW: Mr. Ryerson told me the story himself. He was called by his friend in Boston, Mr. Lowell.

He called Mr. Ryerson and said, " There's a new thing, Ed, educational television. If you got a group together, you could get assigned a channel."

Mr. Ryerson didn't know the first thing about it, but if Mr.

Newton N. Minow

Lowell said it was good for Chicago, it was good for Chicago. So he put together a group and applied for Channel 11.

If Mr. Lowell had had a friend in New York and Los Angeles who he would have called along with Mr. Ryerson, the history of educational television certainly could have been very different. If there had been a Mr. Ryerson in New York and in Los Angeles, you wouldn't have had all this trouble.

~

Ralph Steetle of JCET remembers Ryerson as one of the outstanding citizen leaders in the development of what is now public television.

STEETLE: You begin to move into people, as interest grows, and people make the difference. In Chicago, Ryerson was one of the leading people.

One of his early dreams was that television might help to perform the process of informing people about the needs of their neighbors. Chicago was a place where a small

black kid may have never seen the lake. So it grew out of the dreams of a lot of people.

~

As one deeply involved with WTTW from 1955 to 1959, I remember personally the nature of Ryerson's participation and leadership. Ryerson had been the president of Inland Steel. He was a life-long Republican; he'd been chairman of Republican (statewide) financing. He'd been a regent of the University of Chicago, president of the Symphony Association, a patron of the Chicago Art Institute, and one of the finest gentlemen that I ever met. He saw the possibilities of an educational television station for the Chicago community, which he dearly loved and which he had greatly served.

Ryerson and the people who had worked with him did a superb job in defining for the community what the station was going to be—an outlet for, and an extension of the influence and services of all cultural institutions. Ryerson was a highly respected citizen in the community so he got quoted a lot. People raised the question in those days, "How come you're heading this? Isn't this competition for dollars with the University of Chicago and with the Art Institute and the symphony?"

He said, "On the contrary. We're going to get more people drawn into that Art Institute and interested in it as a result of WTTW than we ever would without it."

When Chicago's WTTW moved into its own building and named it after Edward Ryerson, these individuals shared views about the growth of public television. Ryerson is at the right. Next to him is Dr. John W. Taylor, who was WTTW's chief operating officer for two decades. At his right is Chicago's mayor, Richard J. Daley, talking with Larry Frymire, chief of the FCC's Educational Broadcasting branch.

Chalmers ("Chuck") Marquis, who shifted from commercial broadcasting into educational television in Chicago, accomplished that move simply by visiting WTTW's small pre-studio office and announcing, "I want to work for this joint!" He was one of the strongest professionals at WTTW in its early years, became its director of programming, then graduated to key positions in the national scene.

MARQUIS: Edward Ryerson [was] the kind of philanthropist without which you can't have most of the institutions in the community.

APTS Photo

Chalmers H. Marquis

You have to have somebody at the top who is in a powerful business position, who is also of a strong mind and able to run those crazy enterprises we know as non-profit organizations and the screwball boards and stance that they have, almost not able to survive in some instances. If you don't have a strong person at the top like Ryerson, things fall apart.

So he, having felt that the station ought to be the fulfillment of bringing all of the kinds of cultural institutions into the homes, led the station for many years. He was able to make phone calls and have the largest ad agency give us free time for years of a whole staff, give building space [for offices] in bank buildings, give the talents of leadership of all kinds.

And I can tell you now that in many areas of the country they haven't found the Ed Ryerson. There are still places where stations are not wired in at the top.

He could call the governor, he could call the president, he could call the Senate, he could do anything he wanted to, and they respected him. We still don't have that kind of leadership in most areas of public television even today, thirty years after he got into it. That's to the detriment of the system.

~

John Taylor, WTTW's executive director, was another one who could move at the top of the decision-makers' pile and deal with the folks in business and education at the very top. He had been there.

Dr. Taylor had taught every level of school from fourth grade through graduate seminars. He'd taught at Teachers College of Columbia University. He'd been assistant to General Lucius Clay in the German reconstruction period following World War II, setting up the school system in Germany. He'd worked for UNESCO (United Nations Educational, Scientific and Cultural Organization). He'd been president of the University of Louisville. He was no run-of-the-mill educator.

In fact, the best demonstration of that—and I confirmed this in my interview with him—was that at one point when he was the president of the University of Louisville he proposed buying Churchill Downs and leasing it back to the racing interests to generate funding for the University!

He was an enterprising educator—as shown by that Churchill Downs story and a lot of other things. He was particularly concerned at that time about the teacher shortage and very much interested in what he could do about it. He was also interested in the use of the media. He had started some college credit courses on radio while he was at Louisville, and Chicago looked like an interesting community-wide challenge.

But he was interested in community affairs. He had the mien. He always wore a Chesterfield coat and a homburg. He was, to many people, kind of reserved. But there was dignity and respectability, and he gave this to WTTW, which I think was very important.

Along with this element of dignity and respectability, Taylor and Ryerson shared the basic concept of an educational television station as a new institution to strengthen and extend the work of all other educational and cultural institutions in the community. Both shared the dream that television might put education within the reach of more people than had previously been possible.

TAYLOR: Ryerson was absolutely convinced that there was a job that could be done by television that would make things a great deal easier for people who couldn't go to school, and make it a great deal easier for teachers in school because they would have

Dr. John W. Taylor

such a heavy load, and he felt in the end the whole thing could be cheaper. He was a great visionary. He was more interested in education than he was in anything else.

To give you an example: he was a dyed-in-the-wool born Republican, and when Eisenhower came in he offered him the post of Secretary of Commerce, and Ryerson turned it down. He said, "If you'd offered me Health, Education, and Welfare, I'd have taken it.

Ryerson was probably one of the greatest citizens of his generation, so far as public service is concerned, that this town ever saw. I suppose in his era there was nobody in this town that was looked up to more.

I don't think I would have taken the job if I hadn't been convinced of Ryerson's interest.

Pittsburgh's Leland Hazard and WQED

Pittsburgh had a Lowell or Ryerson of its own, but a different personality, in Leland Hazard. Norman Cousins knew him as a member of the board of National Educational Television.

COUSINS: Leland Hazard was a lawyer and business executive for the Pittsburgh Plate Glass Company. And he was a doer. He knew that you got from here to there not by just getting up and walking there, but sometimes by taking the most unimaginable detours.

He was very practiced in the engineering of consent. He knew that in the United States, at least, when you deal with public enterprises of this sort and scope, you need the support of a wide range of people, including your business leaders. But he could speak the language of the artist, of the people who had to dream up these shows, and was respected by all.

Everett Case also knew Hazard as a fellow NET board member.

CASE: Leland had the most sardonic kind of wit. His mind was not only independent but I think his way of looking at things was not the orthodox way. His approach to any problem you were discussing would start not from here but from way out there, and then suddenly develop, and "Yes, yes, that approach is right, that approach makes sense." He was extraordinary. Must have been a very astute lawyer, I would think.

~

Another fellow board member, school superintendent Kenneth Oberholtzer, saw Hazard in another light.

OBERHOLTZER: He had a very sharp mind and also a caustic mind. If there was some opportunity in the meeting where he could burn an idea, he would burn it. If there was somebody that needed criticizing, or [a need for] coming out and saying things that the others weren't quite prepared to say, he would say it. He was valuable in that regard.

He had sort of a leavening effect on a good many of the men who would just say "Yes, we'll do that." But he had questions! I enjoyed him very much.

~

Leland Hazard, the dynamic spirit and practical strategist who founded WQED in Pittsburgh, speaks at the dedication of WQED's building in 1970. Hazard survived several general managers, while supporting and assisting them in the building process necessary for a community-based public television station.

Bob Hudson came to know Hazard not only as an NET board member but also for his leadership in establishing and developing WQED in Pittsburgh.

HUDSON: Mr. Hazard was a very tough-minded man. He had come to Pittsburgh representing some client in opposition to Pittsburgh Plate Glass, [but] the Pittsburgh Glass people were so impressed by him that they immediately hired him. So he moved to Pittsburgh and became vice president and general counsel to Pittsburgh Plate Glass.

He was very active in the Allegheny Conference, which was a blue-chip, blue-stocking thing there in Pittsburgh area that cleaned up Pittsburgh, rebuilt the million dollar triangle down there where the rivers come together, the Golden Triangle. And the Allegheny Conference was interested in cultural things as well. It supported the theater, it supported the symphony, it supported the universities, and so on, and it became interested in educational television.

So it was the Allegheny Conference, with Hazard as chairman of that committee and, of course, some of the Mellon Foundation people like Phil Broughton and Adolph Schmitt and others, who made a go of that.

~

It is said that the Allegheny Conference was the result of a visit to Pittsburgh by Frank Lloyd Wright, the internationally famous architect and designer, not long after the end of World War II. The Mellon interests invited him and took him up to the top of Mount Washington, a promontory with an impressive panoramic view of the city and the confluence of the two rivers. Mellon is said to have asked, "Mr. Wright, what would you recommend we do to improve Pittsburgh?"

And Mr. Wright said, "Burn it."

With that, the Allegheny Conference was formed to recreate the city, a city which by the early 1950s had experienced considerable success in changing not only its image but its attributes.

Jack White described Pittsburgh during 1955-59 when he was there as general manager of WQED.

WHITE: This was the fall of '54 or early '55. They [WQED] were in trouble with the universities, and they were in trouble with the community. They had just not done their P.R. work very well.

They asked me if I wouldn't come down and spend a month reviewing it and serving as a consultant. I agreed to go down for a week.

I went back to Cleveland and wrote what I thought was a helluva good report, which said:

"The baby's got to crawl before it can run, and certainly you've got to grow up and treat universities and public school systems as though they know their business as well as you know yours, and stop belittling, and third, you're not a gift from heaven, you've got to work at this business and develop relations, but if you'll do it and stick with it, it'll go."

About two weeks later, I was in a meeting at Western Reserve and the phone rang. It was Leland Hazard on the other end of the line who said, "White, we've read and re-read your report again and we have concluded that *your* conclusion is absolutely and totally wrong and that the only sound conclusion is to get you to come down and either make this place go or shut it up. Fire everybody and start over again."

I went down by train on a Saturday evening. I was met by a chauffeur who took me to the Duquesne Club and hid me out in the Pittsburgh Plate Glass suite for the night. The next morning I was picked up by another chauffeur and driven out to Ligonier, up in the mountains, a lovely spot. They were doing everything dirty, [but] made it absolutely as attractive as it could be.

And there I walked into a meeting of Leland Hazard, Adolph Schmitt of the Mellon Foundation, Leon Falk of the Falk Foundation (very heavy in steel and everything else down that way), and Jack Ryan of Mine Safety Engineering who was the president while Leland Hazard was chairman of WQED.

I put up every argument I could think of. The important thing was that if I came I was going to be the boss, and I'd report what I had done and wasn't asking permission for anything, and that I might close it in six months or I might not.

When we concluded in the afternoon, they said, "We buy everything you say. There's not a problem you can give us."

~

White asked for a little time, consulted with his wife, and also called his friend, Henry Heald, who had been White's boss at Illinois Tech in Chicago and had just become president of New York University. In view of Heald's subsequent presidency of the Ford Foundation and his influence on the later growth of public television, White's account of Heald's answer is interesting.

WHITE: He said, "Jack, for God's sake, grab it. We're not going to believe what people are telling us about this new thing called educational television until one of us gets in there and gives it a go. You go do it—and if at the end of six months you want to close it, you've got a job at NYU."

I'll never forget going to the president of Western Reserve to say I was leaving to move to Pittsburgh to head this thing. He said, "My God, you're leaving the university to run a popcorn stand!" [LAUGHTER]

~

White's recollections of Hazard and the beginnings of WQED again demonstrate the nature of this unusual gentleman.

WHITE: Leland was a giant of a man. Here was a lawyer, chief general counsel for Pittsburgh Plate Glass—but in a given month he also would have an article in the Harvard alumni magazine having to do with the humanities, and another one over in the field of architecture some place. He was truly "a man for all seasons." He believed in education. His wife, Mary was chairman of the Pittsburgh Board of Education at the same time Leland was doing this.

He was "Mr. Culture" for the city of Pittsburgh, and he didn't cajole, he drove them to a desire for excellence. In those days you had the International Art Festival there, you had a symphony orchestra that was developing, you had an opera company developing, you had Pittsburgh Playhouse developing, and Leland was the heart and soul of that development, and he, as I said, drove everyone.

~

Thus, when Mayor David Lawrence and FCC Commissioner Freida Hennock looked for someone to lead Pittsburgh into educational television, it was natural for them to turn to Leland Hazard.

WHITE: He, with some fear, trepidation, and skepticism, bought in. He agreed to head it up. He organized a board, he went out and raised the money, he put that station on the air. He, at the end of six months, was ready to throw in the towel—but when we got there, he was the man with whom you could dream. The only problem was that his dreams would outreach yours. He was just a magnificent person to work with.

So long as he lived, he became an advocate and determined fighter for quality, and for the greater development of educational or public television in the United States.

~

Another side of Hazard is described by Rhea Sikes, head of school television at WQED and one of the key staff who survived

several cutbacks and moments of serious concern.

SIKES: Leland Hazard was one of the most provocative men I've ever known. I couldn't make up my mind about this man.

Rhea Sikes

He had this beautiful round baby face and a benign expression and I couldn't decide whether he was a Buddha, or who he was!

A brilliant, brilliant man, and absolutely perceptive beyond any man I've ever known. Full of vision. And he knew the political way to work his visions into reality.

He could be ruthless. But he was always ruthless for a point. He had a goal. I think of all the men I've ever known in television, maybe Leland Hazard had the greatest vision.

He talked about what he thought public television should be. For instance, we had done a program on Mexico. I had run a little film on Mexico, and the kids supposedly had been given some pesos to go and buy something. The minute the program was over, I was called to the telephone, and a voice said to me, "What was the meaning of the program, Rhea?" and I told him. "Well, why did you do it?" And I told him. There was a long pause. Then he said, "That was one of the most beautiful programs I've ever seen." And that was the end of the conversation.

I mean, out of nowhere, there was Leland Hazard! But his interest in WQED never deviated. It was his baby. He had the vision, and he was there every second.

I suppose the most vivid experience with Mr. Hazard was at one point in WQED's history at which we were in financial trouble. We had the resignations of all of top management within a couple of weeks, and my understanding is that except for one vote, [the station] would have been done away with by the board. One vote saved it.

And the staff was called into the main studio, and Mr. Hazard appeared, and he announced who were to be the acting administrators among the staff. He told us what a job we had ahead, with no money. Then he said—after a long, dramatic pause, because he was an actor, too— "May the Lord bless you and keep you, may the Lord make His face to shine upon you, and bring you peace." And with that he walked out!

What a man! His wife was a magnificent woman, too, highly educated, highly cultured, beautiful woman. Between the two of them, there was no compromise on quality and standards of taste.

It's too bad every station can't have a Leland Hazard to harass them and also pat them on the back when they do something right.

~

In a somewhat later chapter in the life of WQED—for Leland Hazard was its "father" from its beginning right up to his death—the success of the Jack White years somehow became dissipated and Hazard again was needed. Again there was a search for a new general manager. This time the best candidate appeared to be Donald Taverner, a former national director for the March of Dimes who had gone back to his native state of Maine as director of the alumni association at the state university.

TAVERNER: When I got out there it had been pretty clear that Leland Hazard had been responsible for WQED, its creation, its survival, and its successes. He had really been WQED all the way.

Donald Taverner

So when I went back for further discussion, Leland gave me a list of people that he wanted me to see and visit with in Pittsburgh. He said "Just to get acquainted, so you can get a reaction from them and they get a reaction from you as to things in general."

I had some very, very nice visits with these people and I felt I was well received and we talked about WQED and we talked about Pittsburgh and we talked about Maine and we talked about art and the symphony and many things.

When I got back, I had dinner with Leland and Mary Hazard at their apartment, and then Leland and I got together and talked. Leland said, "Well, we're getting close to the wire on this now, Don." He said, "Before we get down to cases as to whether you're going to be offered or you're going to accept, do you have any questions you'd like to ask?"

I said, "Yes, Mr. Hazard, I have one question."

And he said, "What's that?"

And I said, "Well, how many managers do you think WQED needs?"

He looked up—a little critical look—and he said, "What kind of a fool question is that?"

I said, "It's not a very foolish question, Mr. Hazard."

"Well," he said. "The answer to it is very simple. It's one."

And I said, "Well, who is it to be?"

He said, "If you were offered the job and accepted it, it would be you." Then he said, "With whom have you been speaking?"

I said, "A lot of people in Pittsburgh."

So I said, "Let's talk as if I am to do this job. I'll have to have your confidence, and I'll have to have the freedom of operation. I think the board certainly has every right to guide and to expect, but not to administer."

I said, "I'd like to be assured the board is not going to operate the station" and so forth.

"Well, that makes good sense in any kind of business," and whatnot, and this was it.

It was awfully hard for Leland to pull away from his baby, and from time to time we had to remind him, you know, "Well, now, we're back to two managers?"

"Oh, no we're not," and he would withdraw very gracefully. He was really a fabulous guy.

At the end of a year, Leland and I had some testimony to give, so we went down to Washington, stayed overnight in the old Congressional Hotel there on the hill which is gone now.

And at dinner, I guess it was, Leland raised his glass and he said, "I would like to propose a toast." Leland was an orator, kind of a pontificator, tremendous command of the English language—Churchillian. Well, he raised his glass and he looked at his wine and he twirled it a little bit and he said, "I want to make a toast to the new president of WQED."

And I said, "This new president—who is he?"

He said, "You!"

He was like that. Nothing had been said, you see. The executive committee had met apparently, and we'd been together for days in the meantime, but he had selected that particular moment to do that.

A lot of people found him to be a difficult man, and he could be. One time we were talking and he said, "Don, if you had to indicate my strongest and weakest points, what would they be?"

And I said, "They're one, Leland, to me. Your strongest point is your weakest point and your weakest point is your strongest point." He said, "Well, what's that?"

I said, "You can't stand incompetency, real or imagined. And the real is your strongest point and the imagined is your weakest point."

I had the greatest respect and affection for Leland. We lost him by death here a couple of years ago, but he really was a remarkable man.

~

Ralph Lowell, Edward L. Ryerson, and Leland Hazard—individually and together—demonstrate clearly how men of unusual intelligence and capability saw in this television medium certain potential benefits for humanity and acted on their visions to realize those potentials.

Fortunately for local communities all across this land similar giants arose to take up the cause.

14

The South Rises to The Occasion

Besides the major cities such as Boston, Chicago, and Pittsburgh, other smaller communities were becoming interested in this new kind of television. In the early and middle fifties, dreamers and innovators began to agitate for the creation of what is now called public television.

This was happening in a number of places in the South, apparently for many reasons. Some hoped that television might provide "equal educational opportunity" to students of all ages, races, and economic levels across an entire state. Some even hoped that in this way integration of schools might not be necessary. Some southern states were aware of the comparatively low level of educational quality which was then provided through their traditional schools, and they hoped to raise the quality of teaching at a minimum cost.

Another reason was the receptiveness of the Southern Regional Education Board, a sixteen-state cooperative effort concerned primarily with improving higher education in the South, headed by Dr. John Ivey. SREB became interested in the possibilities inherent in television as an aid to instruction, and Dr. Ivey had heard about another of public television's pioneers, Dr. Kenneth Christiansen.

Christiansen had begun his broadcasting experience in Denver, then moved to Kansas, then South Dakota, then undertook a combination of work on his doctorate at Northwestern University in Evanston. He had practical experience with Judith Waller on NBC's "Ding Dong School" TV series out of Chicago. These experiences were followed by his pioneering efforts in ETV at Stevens College in Columbia, Missouri. Concurrently,

upon the recommendation of Judith Waller, he became the director of speech arts at the National Music Camp in Interlochen, Michigan, for four years, also producing all of their network broadcasts on radio.

John Ivey Recruits Ken Christiansen for SREB

Kenneth Christiansen

CHRISTIANSEN: While I was at National Music Camp one summer I got a call from Atlanta. "This is John Ivey. We have some money for a three-year project in educational television in the sixteen-state area here in the South. You've been recommended to us. We want you to fly down here as soon as you can. We want to have a chance to talk to you."

I didn't have a decent suit to wear to a thing of that kind, so we got in the car and drove to Traverse City and I bought a new suit, got it fitted, and the next night I was on a plane to Atlanta. In a matter of a day, I was there and accepted, and was named project director for the Southern Regional Educational Board.

The project was funded through C. Scott Fletcher and the Fund for Adult Education.

I was there from '53 to '56. [It] was a project to develop educational television, its uses and applications for instructional purposes at the higher education level.

~

Part of Christiansen's reason for taking this three-year appointment must have been admiration for his boss, Dr. John Ivey.

CHRISTIANSEN: Every movement begins with a dreamer. John Ivey was a dreamer. He was a man with a consistent and a persistent dream. I think sometimes he may have had such a consistent point of view about what he wanted to have happen and how it should happen, it may have gotten in the way at certain points. Yet he was very skillful from the legislative point of view. He had the ability to be as folksy as was necessary and as academic as was necessary.

John, of course, was always interested in research, and had that coloration of acceptability in the academic community. And the legislators could say, "We've got the top-notch people working and we need to take their advice." So this was a two-way instrument for John, that I think paid off in terms of his staff. He was colorful because he was controversial... controversial in the sense that his ideas were out front.

[He] looked on the opportunity to use mass media to extend the creative teacher, the unique teacher, and the specialists, by way of television.

The limitation early on, of course, was the fact that there weren't many stations. So I spent a good bit of time in station development, going to legislators, meeting with all of the state school officers and local school boards, because the minute you got a station, you were beyond the higher education concerns. You want, obviously, to include the elementary and high schools. So you became involved in the county education groups, because they would be a support element in the establishment of the station.

The major contact, because of the SREB, was through the higher education [institutions], although there was, in Alabama for instance, a development looking toward a state system, but you were still depending upon Auburn and the University of Alabama, and the University of Alabama in Birmingham, and the Birmingham schools as the locus.

~

Christiansen was asked whether the activities in Washington to secure reserved channels had perhaps encouraged individuals in various institutions to take action.

CHRISTIANSEN: That whole effort in '52 made it easier to plug people into this movement come '53 and thereafter, because they had been a part of an effort to be sure that we had a valuable resource saved for educational purposes.

I think they were almost embarrassed by the term "in perpetuity" [with respect to the chan-nel reservations]. Because it was saying something about how slowly education reacts. They were, in fact, responding to a criticism that education tended to be seven to ten years behind the mainstream of development. And when you've lived with that criticism all your life and then come to a point at which you could almost leap into the present, that was saying to educators, "By golly, we gotta get on the stick this time; this is one place we're really up-front for a change. We've had enough people fight for this thing, and there's enough interest. We've convinced the legislators that this is important, now what are we going to do with it?"

And so the early projects became very important in order to keep the momentum going. The dynamics of wanting to do something was there. The fact that we'd had national commitment—while they were not participating at this point—was still a kind of model emphasis that state legislators could look to and say, "Well, you know, let's keep the states in this. Let's not let all this go to Washington. Let's bring it back where we can have something to say about this, have some influence."

The South really led in the development of stations and getting them on the air, because this impetus of SREB was there to get this happening. But the *uses* by the higher education groups themselves was minimal because the peer group simply didn't want another faculty member in their classrooms. I mean this was often the case.

"Is it going to replace us?" We never really did overcome that argument, it's still the thing.

Problems In Savannah and New Orleans

Christiansen also identified a few contacts he had with community leadership rather than educational institutions.

CHRISTIANSEN: The only effort that I made to get a community involved was in Savannah. But it was just impossible to get a cohesive enough group. They wanted it "community." They didn't want to be involved with the school system. There was a kind of special group that said—as there was in Jacksonville and some of these other places—"My God, if there's anything we don't need it's the anchor and ball-and-chain of the educational institutions or system. Let's have our freedom to make this something that really goes beyond the kind of pedestrian things of education as such."

Cultural—they could see all of these things—Savannah was rebuilding downtown, and they had pride, there was a community spirit. But when they found out what kind of money it would take to do this, and that fund raising was a part of this, that the "tin cup" approach was going to be inevitable, it was a matter of coming up against reality and then turning away.

New Orleans was the same thing. They could sense an immediate rivalry that would come out of Baton Rouge if the state were to get a system.

They wanted to be the flagship station, and the legislators sitting in Baton Rouge wanted the station where *they* were, where *they* resided.

Stalwarts: Graydon Ausmus, John Dunn, Earl Wynn

Several individuals at southern universities stood out in Christiansen's memory. One was Graydon Ausmus, head of broadcasting at the home campus of the University of Alabama, who at one time was president of the National Association of Educational Broadcasters and significantly aided the activation effort in his state.

CHRISTIANSEN: Graydon had a senatorial mien that made him just stand out wherever he was. The voice had a bit of it. It was a colorful— what do I want to say—accent? Deliberate. He staged himself well. Whatever happened, you knew that Graydon was there, stentorian tone and all.

He also had the sense of the spirit of the mission of public television. There wasn't any doubt about that. His great problem was that he was ahead of his own institutional administration. The conflict of interests on his campus was the thing that made it almost impossible for him to have what he wanted.

I remember Graydon for one other thing: his "*ca-mail-lias,*" as he pronounced it. He had all kinds of varieties, and that was his great source of satisfaction. Beautiful things.

~

Another stalwart of the early days, a former NBC broadcasting executive, was John Dunn, head of broadcasting at the University of Oklahoma.

CHRISTIANSEN: John Dunn probably was best remembered for his favorite phrase about audiences in Oklahoma, "There isn't much use to have some of those towers out there, 'cuz there's only jackrabbits and Indians there to listen."

However, in a kind of competition to the Texas idea of bigness, he gloated in the idea that Oklahoma ETV had the tallest tower in Oklahoma City. You always had to go see the tallest tower.

Bricks and mortar, by the way, were an interesting part of this development. We had a brick-and-mortar mentality operating, rather than a service mentality operating.

Bricks and mortar are always something you can point to in a concrete way, and that's not a pun. We didn't need some of those huge facilities in the beginning. You can get a job done without the major emphasis needing to be on bricks and mortar. I think equipment is another matter. But we point with pride to a physical facility, particularly if it can be named after someone as a kind of gift, that they helped in raising funds, a way of getting at a community because you can point to it, you can have your meetings there. We've done this all over the country. But it was problem in the South as well.

Beginnings In North Carolina

Mention of another southern university's interest in embracing television for education, North Carolina, reminded Christiansen of two names. One was Kay Kyser, the band leader and TV producer, who had accompanied the president of the University of North Carolina to the Penn State Conference.

CHRISTIANSEN: Kay Kyser was one of the main supporters. He was the dynamics that got that station on the air.

I think I can say it was both a cross and a godsend. There were people who would look [down] at Kay Kyser, educational groups who couldn't see this kind of influence in their preserve, not recognizing, of course, that this was an individual who was interested in music and musical heritage—and why shouldn't we be talking about that sort of thing?

~

The other name that was recalled by Christiansen was that of Earl Wynn, a stalwart North Carolinian who may have been best known for the leading role he played each summer in an outdoor pageant depicting North Carolina history. His talent for histrionics was evident at other times, also.

He was one of three representatives of the recently unified Consolidated University of North Carolina who attended an early meeting of educational stations held in Ann Arbor, Michigan. Whenever it came time to vote, Earl, and his colleagues, John Young and David M. Davis, each in charge of one of the three campus studios of WUNC-TV, would retire to the hall to caucus on how they would cast their single vote.

Young, who was with WUNC-TV for many years, later served as a program associate for the Educational Television and Radio Center.

Davis got his start in commercial television in Philadelphia and Washington. He helped guide WGBH-TV in its early years, then went on to join the Ford Foundation, and finally gained distinction as executive producer of fine drama for PBS.

DAVIS: In the spring of '54 I was approached by a man named William Carmichael from the University of North Carolina at Chapel Hill. He'd been looking around Washington, D.C., to find people.

I was asked to come down and talk and met Kay Kyser, Gordon Gray, and a guy named Bob Schenkkan. They had a really grandiose plan.

Billy Carmichael, who was the vice president and treasurer of the university, had raised private money in the state of North Carolina to build this elaborate educational television station. And because of the nature of the university, the "greater university" consisted then of three institutions, the University at Chapel Hill, Women's College at Greensboro, and the State College at Raleigh, which was engineering and agriculture. So, because of the politics of it, they had to put equal facilities in each of those three campuses, with a program manager in charge of each. Then they had a central management team which they were putting together.

They recruited me to run the Greensboro operation—2,400 women and me! The central team was Bob Schenkkan [1] and a writer by the name of Dick Burdick, who later went to Philadelphia ETV, and then they had the Wallman brothers, Tom and Frank, who had been writers for Kyser on the "Kollege of Musical Knowledge."

Kyser, whom we first met at the seminal conference at Penn State as the unofficial communications advisor to President Gordon Gray lived next door to President Gray. Kay had had superb financial management in his big days as a band leader and he was a very rich man. He was retired and living in Chapel Hill, and was devoted to the university; that and the Christian Science Church were his life. They all thought

he really could help them and teach them how to put this together.

But then, as usual, things got delayed and we didn't get on the air until about a month after this biennial legislature went into session. We found out that Carmichael's plan all along had been to get it on the air ahead of time, get these wonderful plaudits, and then announce to the legislature, "Here it is, now you have to pay for it."

What in fact happened is really because of Kay's influence. We went on the air with the most terrible program schedule imaginable, all kinds of quiz shows, and charades, and—[CHUCKLE]—you know, variations of this. The Chapel Hill faculty was outraged that this was so lowbrow, and so their support was lost and we went in to the legislature and were given half the money that we asked for, and [then] had an immediate cutback. It was really grim.

Well, part of the problem: Billy died. He had a heart attack. So there really was nobody with his kind of savvy to keep that all going.

Bill Friday was sympathetic and helpful; he was assistant to the president in those days. Bright young Harvard Law School trained guy.

Schenkkan left for Texas, they shut down the central office entirely, and we went into a triumvirate management of the three—one from each place—with the chief engineer running around loose on his own. And the history of triumvirate management, as you may realize, is not replete with success [CHUCKLES].

But we did a few interesting things.

~

ETV in North Carolina recovered from this rocky beginning and began a state-wide service. New Orleans for years has had its community-supported public television station (though not without heroic efforts on the part of many citizen leaders, educators, and a succession of general managers), Oklahoma's state-wide educational television network is now well accepted in that state, and Savannah is served by the highly professional Georgia Public Television Network.

A New Kellogg Center Gives Georgia Its Start

A glimpse of the beginnings in Georgia can be gained from the recollections of Gerard Appy, who in the mid '50s was program director for the Crosley commercial television station in Atlanta. There he helped Dick Van Dyke get his start in television.

---

[1] Schenkkan later became well known for establishing and managing the University of Texas ETV station at Austin, and for aiding the national political efforts which resulted in the Public Broadcasting Act of 1967.

One day Appy read a newspaper account of a $3-million grant which the Kellogg Foundation had awarded to the University of Georgia to build a new type of Center for Continuing Education, which would include an educational television station.

APPY: It was to be one of those places where adults come from all professions, all walks of life, for short courses or seminars.

The concept was that the building itself would be a teaching instrument and that the surroundings were to be such that adults would find it easy and inspirational to learn.

I was interested in the thought that one might be able to use television for purposes other than the extreme commercial hardsell that we were doing [at Crosley], and so this University of Georgia thing seemed particularly attractive.

Gerard Appy

It turned out to be a tremendous experience. I like to think that I got more "continuing education" than anyone who came to the center in its first few years.

~

Appy worked under an innovator in continuing education who subsequently brought into being some additional Georgia enterprises dedicated to informal learning after he had created the unique Georgia center.

APPY: Hugh Masters had been with the Kellogg Foundation. He was a most unusual educator, a Texan, a kind of tough guy, but underneath absolutely warm.

He was something of a maverick. He didn't want his communications division at the center to be run like an audio-visual operation. He wanted new things to happen.

Because the center was not yet ready for television, since it hadn't yet been constructed, Masters asked me to help him on all kinds of things, so I had a chance to learn while I was seeing that the center got constructed, and also to do so at the feet of this unusual educator who was sort of breaking the rules right and left.

~

The station licensed to the University of Georgia and operating out of its Center for Continuing Education was delayed in getting on the air because there was the hope that the tower could be located as close to the Atlanta population area as possible. Once on the air, WGTV undertook such unorthodox things as programming a feature motion picture each week—a practice which commercial broadcasters objected to most strongly, even though many were art films or foreign films with English subtitles.

APPY: There was a hearing before the Board of Regents, and the president of the university and I were there. The president was staunch in his support of our right to program that station without interference from commercial broadcasters.

This was kind of a tough stand to take. The regents stuck by the university administration. I'm capsuling here what was a long and very nervous-making experience. But we prevailed. I think that had we not prevailed, the effect for at least several years on educational television stations throughout the country would have been very negative, because there would have been a precedent set. And sometimes those things do affect other localities.

~

Meanwhile, the Georgia State Department of Education was taking the lead in the planning and development of an educational television network to serve the entire state—nine stations licensed to the Department of Education plus the one station licensed to the university.

APPY: During those early years, I was able to make an agreement with the State Department of Education [which handled the in-school offerings] under which the university station, WGTV, handled the evening programming on all of the stations of the state network.

This was a tremendous advantage to the university, which is one of the first land-grant institutions established in the United States, and it prided itself on the notion that its campus was the entire state of Georgia. Therefore, it was logical in that philosophy that they extend the assets of the university and the university activities to people throughout the state, and television was a splendid way to do it.

~

About this same time, another effort to use television in education was undertaken by the Atlanta public schools. Educational radio had proved useful to them under the leadership of a former high school choral director, Haskell Boyter, and he was asked to begin to experiment with telecasts on the

UHF channel allocated to Atlanta, a channel which has been used for this purpose ever since.

In Georgia, then, it was the Atlanta schools and a maverick in adult education at the state university that caught sight of the dream.

In two adjacent states of the South, the beginnings of what is now public television took place in quite different ways—although in each case it was the hope of improving educational opportunity for the state's children and adults which formed the basic motivation. And all three of these states in the southeast in recent years have enjoyed significant and effective public television, despite the halting and primitive manner in which each was begun.

The First State-wide ETV Network: Alabama

Alabama's story centers around Raymond Hurlbert, who began teaching at Woodlawn High School in Birmingham in 1924 at a ten-month salary of $1,250. Six years later when he became a principal his salary was elevated to $1,741 a year, presumably an indication of his ability not only as a teacher but also as an administrator. During these years he also served as president of the Alabama Education Association. His subsequent activities, not only for the school system but in the cause of educational television for Alabama, proved him also to be a near genius at public relations and a very skillful politician.

Hurlbert had never heard of educational television until the summer of 1953 when he got a phone call from the governor of Alabama.

HURLBERT: Governor Gordon Persons was a man whom I had known and had assisted in some of his public responsibilities previously when he was chairman of our Public Service Commission in the state.

Raymond D. Hurlbert

On picking up the phone, he told me who he was and point-blank said, "What do you think of educational television?"

I said—thinking over the matter very quickly, not knowing a thing in the world about it, and no one at that time did—I said, "Gordon, I think it has great potential."

And he said, "Fine, I've just appointed you as a member of the state Educational Television Commission." Which was an honor I didn't understand, but anything the governor would do, in my opinion, was worthy of consideration, and I accepted.

That was the beginning of twenty years of public service in public broadcasting—which, at that time, wasn't so public!

~

I asked Hurlbert if he thought the governor was "a friend of education."

HURLBERT: I would keep it from being profane, but he had very little sympathy with the educational authorities at that time.

But we had worked together and he had confidence in me. He made the statement to me at the time that I was an educator that he knew who would not sell him down the river.

Very soon after that we had a meeting in the governor's office. This was, I believe, in late June of '53, and the five members of the Alabama Educational Television Commission were present. Those people were prominent citizens—except for yours truly—but I represented to Gordon Persons the educational side of the state.

~

The legislation creating and empowering this commission—the first example in the nation of state-wide planning to establish a state-wide educational television network—had resulted from a governor's conference in February 1953, called in response to urging from the state superintendent of schools, the secretary of the Alabama Education Association, and educational broadcasting leaders from the University of Alabama (Graydon Ausmus) and Auburn University (I. O. Brackeen).

The governor himself appeared in support of the idea, possibly because he himself had been in radio broadcasting in previous years.

HURLBERT: Having been in broadcasting himself, he realized what power exists in that medium, and he moved to set this thing up by law.

I might say again that this was all a very nebulous situation, because there were no criteria anywhere that would give very much of a lead or pattern.

~

But with the encouragement and suggestions of Iowa's Dick Hull, North Carolina's Earl Wynn, and Walter Emery and Ralph Steetle of the JCET, the Alabama plan took shape, created by those few in the state who could see the possibilities.

HURLBERT: Many members of the legislature who had been sympathetic were very helpful. And we had Richard Hull come down and speak to the legislative members, which encouraged them to go forward.

Our state at that time was next to the bottom in appropriations for education in the nation, which I would not criticize because you cannot pay out more than you have, and the State of Alabama did not have the financial resources. Consequently, for a state with that restricted amount of money for the purpose of education to appropriate half a million for educational television was almost unbelievable.

Had it been left to the legislature to take it out of its regular expected taxes, it never would have been done. But the governor knew about $500,000 that was in the building commission fund, and the governor had in mind all the time how he thought he was going to finance this project. Consequently, when the time came, by the action of the state building commission, he made this half million available to the Educational Television Commission.

He was chairman of the building commission and I was chairman for the Alabama Educational Television Commission, and we shook hands and we had $500,000!

~

But there was more than mere manipulation involved—a glimpse of a brighter future for the people of Alabama through the use of television to educate.

HURLBERT: The governor said to me in one of our initial conversations, "If we can teach fifteen farmers how to contour plow, why couldn't we teach fifteen thousand with educational television?"

And the other statement was that the urban areas in the state had fine school systems, but the rural systems in Alabama were handicapped because the better qualified teachers gravitated to the urban centers. The schools in the rural areas were not only handicapped for talent but for funds. Many did not have full terms of school each year. Certain counties would start school early in the summer and then turn school out in the fall for cotton picking.

The cry—and the very plausible argument that I presented to members of the legislature and to all of the groups to which I spoke—was that equal opportunity was going to be enhanced in such a way that the people in the poor and deprived areas of the state not only *should* have but they *must* have access to the best that there is, and that every child in Alabama was entitled to the best, no matter where he lived.

~

First on the air was the Channel 7 transmitter atop the highest mountain in Alabama, Mt. Cheaha, in order to secure the greatest possible coverage. Within a few months, the "network" was born with the addition of Channel 10 in the state's largest city, Birmingham, whose school superintendent, Dr. Frazier Banks, was an early proponent of ETV.

Partly through Dr. Banks' leadership, the five public school systems in Jefferson County began to produce instructional materials. So did both of the major universities, Auburn University and the University of Alabama.

HURLBERT: Rudy Bretz was employed by the state commission to start us off in the art of programming for television. He was a recent employee of CBS and a very talented and a very personable person, and did us a great service.

But it was so crude in comparison with what we eventually developed that it would make you feel that if it never got any further than that, we'd have gone out of business.

I remember some of the people in some of the meetings I went to on a national level would say, "You can't do that," but we were already doing it. Some of the programs that we were having for in-school instruction and college credit—actually, we were doing that very thing.

This was discredited on a national level because it wasn't possible to do this in Alabama anyhow, and furthermore "they" didn't have anybody down there to do it, and "they" had three or four in a studio [crew] and everybody knew that you had to have twenty to thirty to forty people in a studio—and we only had three or four.

Sometimes you had to run the camera and then run around in front of the camera and perform, but we were doing it, and we were receiving plaudits from all over the state.

One of our first broadcasts was the inauguration of Governor Folsom, and we had the parade and all of that, and every town in Alabama had its band. And in order to switch over, we missed a band or two and got an awful reaction from those communities.

Here was a brand new baby and they all, everybody, owned it, and they didn't get their band in the parade!

~

Hurlbert also relates how the Birmingham station managed to get on the air with a used transmitter donated by the Storer Broadcasting Company, which also for a time furnished space in their building for the transmitter and space on their tower to locate the antenna.

HURLBERT: So they were as much a party to helping us get started as any one unit or organization in the state.

The proceeding for Channel 2 was next. We wanted it for an area in Andalusia, Alabama, and the NBC authorities wanted it for the Tallahassee area in Florida. So we were in competition with NBC, and this was formidable opposition. We felt like David did with Goliath, but there was no reason why we shouldn't try. So we proceeded to confer with Frieda Hennock, a member of the FCC. She was very sympathetic, only had one vote on that body, but would do what she could in our interest.

~

Hurlbert somewhat cautiously recounted one aspect of the contest for Channel 2, pointing out that the brother of Alabama's governor was General "Slick" Persons, an aide to Dwight D. Eisenhower.

HURLBERT: So we used our connection to explain the matter to General Persons, and General Persons was able to explain the needs of our state to the authorities, and I don't know what authorities or I don't know how, but I do know that on a certain Wednesday morning following the FCC meeting I had an urgent call from Commissioner Frieda Hennock.

I picked up the phone and she said, "This is Frieda Hennock. We've whipped the millionaires!" By that she meant that we had Channel 2 and NBC did not, and I don't know how it came about. I think the Lord was taking care of Alabama, but of course the Lord works through people.

~

Our day-long visit in Raymond Hurlbert's home was one filled with anecdotes about the many different kinds of day-to-day prob-

Raymond Hurlburt's home.

lems which he and his Alabama colleagues faced in developing their network. After a pleasant lunch, Ray revealed even more stories of the resistance he faced, some of it having nothing to do with whether television could really teach.

HURLBERT: All of the guy lines to the tower were on state property except one, and we couldn't fix it to where this particular guy line would do anything but go into a gravel pit off on the side of the road. But the gravel pit belonged to a local farmer.

We went on down to negotiate, and he wanted $2,500 a year as caretaker of the site and he wanted certain other privileges.

The piece of ground I needed was ten feet wide and twenty feet long. I sat there on the porch with this old farmer all day long, and we rocked, and we talked, and we finally wound up the deal. We paid him twenty-five dollars for the piece of ground.

We were building [another] station between Russellville and Florence, in northern Alabama. The county gave us the property, that is, they would buy the property that we designated. You know, not only do you have to fit into the FCC [specifications] but you have to be at a point where you can get the greatest coverage. And so we were locating this at a place called Crooked Oak. It's just a bend in the road there.

We had the deed to the property, and I sent our chief engineer up there to establish the station. He came back shortly and said he couldn't do it.

I said, "What's the matter?"

He said, "Well, the owner won't let me on the property."

There was a big board posted on the side of the property, and it said: "KEEP OUT OR TAKE WHUT CUM," W-h-u-t-c-u-m. And there was a shotgun pellet hole right through the board. And the man met him up there and wouldn't let him on the property. And *we owned* it.

So I went back to the sheriff of that county and told him that we wanted to build a station but this farmer wouldn't let us on the property, even though he had sold it. Later on, the sheriff called me and said they had negotiated. It seems the farmer had some squatters on his property in another area, and if the sheriff would get the squatters off of his property, he'd get off of ours. So the sheriff got the squatters off and we got to have our property.

But you're talking now about the development of nine stations. There's a long process, and each one of them has a story.

~

It took an unusually devoted type of pioneer to get the Alabama network put together, for in addition to establishing each individual station there was the further assortment of problems which come with connecting them into a functioning network. This entailed construction of 2,000 miles of two-way microwave circuits under circumstances less than convenient.

To assure proper operation of a microwave relay link, there must be no obstruction in the line of sight between each microwave transmitter and its receiving unit.

HURLBERT: We had to have shots as great as forty miles. To do this, we would locate on mountaintops and actually pioneer in certain parts of the state where there was no geodetic survey. You wouldn't believe that was true. As a matter of fact, we used to say we had to flush tribes of Indians out of some of the jungle area to get our signal through.

To employ RCA or some other large corporation to go in and make a survey and establish areas and sites is a very expensive deal. They bring in airplanes and take the measurements by instruments and so on. We couldn't do that, so we had our engineers climb up pine trees and shine mirrors in the sunshine in the daytime and make a grid of electric lights and shine them at night so as to get our distances, going from Channel 2 down to Mobile.

Our chief engineer, Mr. Al Renfro, was a talented and skillful man, and he would supervise all this and climb the trees himself.

Then after we got all through, in order to make certain that these microwave sites would actually function on the necessary proficiency level, we employed RCA just to check our work. I think we had to pay about $2,500 for them to just fly over what we had done through the months in the jungle.

When I say jungle, I'm talking about pine forests and hills and swamps and all that kind of thing, which was an arduous task.

Facing day-to-day problems of this sort did not deter Hurlbert and his associates from pursuing their fundamental objective: to bring a higher quality of education to the people of Alabama.

His own evaluation after nearly thirty years of operation of the Alabama Educational Television network sounds a note of pride in achievement.

HURLBERT: I feel that Alabama has reaped a rich reward for its courage in its pioneer effort. I feel that the people who initiated this had no idea of what a tremendous thing they were getting into, nor do I feel that the legislature understood what courage it was going to take to do this kind of a thing.

I think that the courage of the original group in the legislature has been blessed, because of the dedication of the people who have worked with it—and because of the evident higher level of the academic and cultural situation in the state.

South Carolina's Entirely Different Approach

South Carolina's venture into educational television began without any broadcast stations—just cable interconnection.

Henry J. Cauthen, who played a leading role in his state's development of television in education, gives the reasons—reasons which indicate that South Carolina's planning was focused on basic needs to a greater extent than planning in some other places.

CAUTHEN: We took a look at not just what TV could do for public schools, but we said, "What are South Carolina's needs in telecommunications, not just right now, but in the future? Let's try to look down the road a little bit and see what we can see."

If you looked at public schools alone, you were looking at seventy-five courses at a

Henry J. Cauthen

minimum if you were going to have any impact on education. Then, if you were going to have some impact on higher education, you were talking about an equal number.

And we were talking at that time about junior colleges in South Carolina.

We began to dream about all of these kinds of things—medical education, and so forth.

We just added up what it was we wanted to do, and when we got about 10 percent of the way down the page we'd run out of what we could do with a broadcast transmitter. We said, "If we're really going to have some impact"—and South Carolina desperately needed help in education—"then we're going to have to go another route."

So we went to the telephone company, Southern Bell, and said, "Okay, you've got eleven customers"—meaning eleven commercial stations that were there at that time. "If you had eleven hundred, being eleven hundred schools in South Carolina, might you give us a little better rate?"

They were a little taken back by the scope of what we were talking about. But fortunately the head of Southern Bell was a good friend, and he said, "Well, let me go back to our engineering people, and we will really give this thing a hard look."

If Buck Edwards had not been in that position, the great likelihood is that it never would have gotten off the ground, because he had to put his corporate reputation on the line, stick his neck way out to invest substantial funds on a project that could have folded after the first year.

In the first year they took the system to eight different South Carolina cities and then made a commitment to expand it, year after year, on a rate that was one-third of what the commercial rate for that service was at that time.

~

The project did not fold after the first year. For one thing, legislative heads in both the House and Senate were encouraged by Henry Cauthen's father, who was a long-time and trusted friend of many legislators. He had been the lobbyist for the textile industry which represented nearly seventy percent of the industry for the state. Thanks to confidence in the Cauthens as well as the first-year's successful demonstrations, the Legislature approved $175,000 for the second year.

CAUTHEN: We got their enthusiastic support because they knew the need of South Carolina and they could see this as a possible solution to the educational problems of the state.

We never talked about anything other than serving every school in South Carolina. That was our goal, our objective.

The real culmination of it was when we had this meeting of the political leadership at the old Wade Hampton Hotel, got their support, and then said, "Okay, in order to do this thing, the $175,000 you gave us for the second year, that kind of funding is not going to make it happen, and if you're going to do it you need to do it right.

"We need broadcast quality equipment, the best that's available. We need professional staff in engineering, art, production. The quality of the product must be comparable to what people are used to seeing in commercial broadcasting."

Finally Senator [Edgar] Brown said, "Well, it looks like we might get about $500,000. Will that do it?"

And after some thought and soul-searching, I said, "Senator, if we're not going to do it right, let's just don't do it at all. The figure we gave you was the figure it's going to take to do it right."

He said, "Okay, I'll do my best to sell it."

And he did.

~

Cauthen and others enlisted Lynn Kalmbach, a respected educator who had been evaluator of the two-year experiment in the Columbia city schools, to head the

South Carolina's early leadership: Henry J. Cauthen, George Bair (who later headed ETV in North Carolina), and Lynn Kalmbach, South Carolina's first general manager of educational television.

enlarged project as its first general manager, with Cauthen as director of production and engineering.

CAUTHEN: Lynn Kalmbach was another person who stuck his neck way out, just as Buck Edwards had stuck his neck out with the telephone company.

Now, you're talking about the middle of July for a September start. Southern Bell had to intercept the delivery of a large amount of cable that was headed for the west coast. They just stopped it where it was and sent it to South

Carolina. They enlisted everybody they could get from Georgia, Tennessee, and North Carolina. They had white-collar executives climbing poles installing the system. We started partitioning out the studios in this old supermarket building. And when the 5th or 6th of September arrived, we had our first program on the air on schedule.

~

The first year of the state-wide program involved four courses of 160 lessons each, all produced in studios still under construction, and using the then-new technology, videotape, to handle repeat showings.

CAUTHEN: I think there were some educators in the state who thought if they ignored it long enough it might go away. But we had others who were very excited about the development and who worked very hard to make it happen, because you talk about going into a [high school] classroom with 160 lessons in 180 days and taking thirty minutes of a fifty-minute class period, that's a substantial intrusion on a teacher's prerogative. And this was at the secondary level.

We were teaching math, we were teaching science, we were teaching foreign language. We took on, at Lynn Kalmbach's insistence, the toughest things we could take on. They were the places of greatest need. If we proved we could teach in those areas, we could teach anything.

~

The high school service soon was extended by cable to all the counties in the state.

The next step in the South Carolina system's development was to furnish a similar service to all eleven hundred elementary schools. For this task, broadcast stations were a more economically feasible solution than to attempt to draw cable into all of the elementary schools in the state, particularly since many of them were out in the countryside.

Two stations were activated almost simultaneously, one in Charleston, another in Greenville, both assisted by equipment donations from commercial broadcasters. A third station, WRLK, located in Columbia, bears the initials of Lynn Kalmbach, who died just before its dedication.

The comprehensive nature of South Carolina's present system is reflected in another comment from Cauthen.

CAUTHEN: We've got one other innovation that we added along the way. We have located our stations in such a fashion that every home will get close to a city-grade signal, certainly a good Grade A signal, which means that most schools can pick up at least *two* signals.

It gave us six channels of closed circuit [cable] for higher education and secondary education and two channels for elementary education.

~

Even more comprehensive, now that the South Carolina Commission operates its own multi-channel microwave to replace the telephone company's leased system which had served well for nearly seventeen years, is the assortment of microwave facilities to eleven transmitting towers, each of which re-transmits to thirty-six tape-and-delay centers scattered about the state.

CAUTHEN: So that's the basis, these thirty-six tape-and-delay centers, using videocassette type equipment, broadcasting through ITFS transmitters, giving them four channels to serve fifteen to twenty schools. And we could give them real-time television through using one of the fifty-watt channels and feed them if there were a necessity to give them live programming.

And when it's not used for that, we have four channels that can be used for higher education, medical education, business and industrial education, day-care centers, state agency training—just a host of services.

And then we have the standard broadcast system to provide service to elementary schools and to the general public. [2]

~

Cauthen comments on what he believes to be the reason for continuing state support of this many-faceted educational telecommunications system, possibly the most complex system furnishing the greatest array of educational services anywhere in the nation.

CAUTHEN: I think the reason we've been able to get steady and substantial state support has been that we've been service-oriented, that we've had such a broad base of service, from medical education to law enforcement training, training for volunteer fire departments, business and industrial training, our continuing education for various groups.

For instance, over the last few years, 40 percent of the recipients for master's degrees in

---

[2] South Carolina also provides state-wide public radio services from WSCI-FM in Charleston and WLTR-FM in Columbia.

business administration at the University of South Carolina have gotten them through television. And in engineering it's beyond that. It's 40 percent in business administration and 50 percent in engineering.

These people are middle-management types, working on the job in business and industry throughout South Carolina. This means they don't have to disrupt family life, they don't have to disrupt their career, and they can get their advanced degrees.

This is obviously not only a help to them, but it's a great attraction to business and industry. All of the management-training things that industry is finding so necessary right now in this period when they have to increase productivity are available through TV.

Why the necessity for retraining hasn't been recognized earlier I don't know. But that is accelerating even more rapidly, because the knowledge that you learn today in a couple of years is obsolete.

~

And with all of this array of educational opportunities through South Carolina ETV, this agency also furnishes one of the finest *public* television services to the homes of its constituents throughout the state—not only programming from PBS and other national sources, but also local programming produced for South Carolinians from the Columbia center and from three regional production centers in distant areas of the state: Beaufort, Sumter, and Rock Hill.

15

Sprouting From the Grassroots

Many aspects of American life are the result of persuasive and pervasive nation-wide marketing. Others are brought about through requirements of the federal government. Not so in the case of public television. It was not impressed upon us by any dominating force; rather, it grew from our grassroots, as demonstrated by the accounts of local leadership.

More often than not, the seeds from which early educational television stations sprouted were sown by only a very few individuals in a local community. Sometimes through unusual alliances and often with only reluctant cooperation from those with the real power, they managed to put together the pieces to form a new kind of television station—one with no assured long-term means of support.

The recollections of the pioneers of public television in this chapter not only show the idealism and determination, but also the frailty of those seed-sowers, and the diversity of circumstances which they faced in their local communities.

Among the Very First
Was Philadelphia

In Philadelphia, WHYY-TV came into existence partly because the extensive school-TV telecasts on commercial stations were pushed off the air by rapidly growing commercialism. At the same time, there were several citizens on the station's newly-organized board who wanted to head the project. After considerable in-fighting, a movie magnate—who in previous years had been a crony of Darryl Zanuck and Sam Goldwyn

during Hollywood's heyday—took over and presided over the station until his death years later.

Martha Gable of the Philadelphia schools and Bill McCarter, WHYY-TV's first program director, [1] recalled those days.

GABLE: On television we had "Operation Classroom" at WCAU and "Operation Blackboard" at WPTZ and "WFIL Schoolhouse" at WFIL. They gave us usually either fifteen or thirty-minute programs.

This went on for some time. Eventually we had twelve full-time radio and TV teachers on our staff. This was in '49, '50, '51, when the FCC freeze was still on.

Well, then the networks co-opted the daytime, you see, on the local station. So all but WFIL said, "We're sorry but we'll have to drop the instructional programs, because actually that isn't our job." WFIL kept us on the air, radio and television, all the way up to 1968.

But Walter Biddle Saul, a very respected and well-known attorney in Philadelphia, was the president of our Board of Education. He realized that we ought to have educational television and the only way we were going to get it was to get a public station. So they started negotiating to get Channel 35, which was a UHF station, and they got it.

But we had some very strong in-fighting among board members as to who was going to head that thing up. Mr. William Goldman, who was a theater magnate in this city, and Judge Leo Weinrott, a judge of the Common Pleas

---

[1] The same Bill McCarter later headed WETA in Washington, D.C., and WTTW in Chicago. During TV's beginnings in Philadelphia, he had produced and directed the "University of the Air" project for Walter Annenberg's WFIL-TV, which received one of the first Peabody Awards.

court, both had taken the initiative. They got a community group together. Lawrence LaPage, who was head of the Franklin Institute, was the chairman of that group.

McCARTER: Lawrence LaPage was an urbane electronics inventor to the manner born, Bill Goldman was a streetwise theater magnate, two most unlikely partners who nevertheless meshed beautifully.

Bill Goldman came out of the wild and exciting early days of Hollywood and was a natural communications entrepreneur. With the split between the studios and the theater chains, he took the Goldman theater chain nationwide and created a movie empire.

But both Goldman and LaPage instinctively saw the real promise of television, and this unlikely pair gave birth to the ETV enterprise in Philadelphia.

~

But there was another contestant for the leadership position.

GABLE: Leo Weinrott thought television was the greatest. [He] kept talking this thing up and talking this up until they got sick and tired of listening to him because he was like that. But he was a good-hearted guy and he knew what was happening—but he didn't have the political clout of Bill Goldman.

Bill Goldman was a theater man. He sued the Shuberts, one of the big theater chains. He sued them because they wouldn't allow their movies to be shown at any theaters except their theaters in Philadelphia. He sued them and won $2 million—became a millionaire overnight. Then he had political clout, and he contributed to all the political campaigns. He rehabilitated the mayor's office—refurbished it. He did all kinds of things. He was only five feet tall, but let me tell you, Bill Goldman had a big stick!

Finally one day he just said, "Look, I'm tired of fooling around with this, Leo, I'm taking over." And Leo got up and stomped out of the room and they didn't speak to each other after that. But Bill Goldman got this thing through. He had the political know-how and clout and money and everything to get it. And that's how we got Channel 35 on the air.

And then we went after Channel 12.

~

Because in those days a UHF channel such as 35 was not receivable on most TV sets without a converter, WHYY's leadership yearned for a VHF channel in order to serve the very large population in the Philadelphia and Wilmington area. They got their chance when a commercial operator on

Channel 12 in Wilmington (Delaware's only TV channel) gave up and literally turned his license back to the FCC. After prolonged litigation and seemingly endless proceedings before the FCC involving a great assortment of applicants, WHYY Incorporated finally won the grant after promising always to maintain a studio in Wilmington as well as in Philadelphia.

Seattle Under Loren Stone

In Seattle—as in Philadelphia and elsewhere—activation of a noncommercial educational station required strong leadership on the part of several individuals who had never worked together before.

Seattle's story involves a university vice president with a special interest in communications, a broadcast-sales executive fed up with commercialism, some school people hoping for improvements in education, and a rich lady who owned a powerful commercial TV enterprise and wanted to help.

Loren Stone had spent twenty-three frustrating years in commercial radio, when in early 1950 he broke his leg skiing and had eight weeks to contemplate his successful yet unsatisfying career. Two years later he faced up to his personal situation.

STONE: I said to myself, "Gee, there must be some better way of making a living. This is really getting to me."

We were living about eighteen miles out of Bremerton on a beautiful spot on Hood Canal, looking right across into the Olympic mountains, right on the waterfront, and we had a boat, and it was fabulous country. So I

Loren Stone

just made up my mind I was going to take about three months and do absolutely nothing, and try to recover my sanity, and then find some other way to function.

Educational television had been developing but I had paid no attention to it. But Milo Ryan was a professor at the School of Communications, as it was then called. My old school of Journalism had been developed into a school of communications at the University of Washington. Milo and I were very great friends—but anyhow, Milo had called Dick's attention to the fact that I was not presently employed.

~

Dick Everest was a vice president of the University of Washington who had been acting president for a short period of time. He had been largely responsible for putting together the School of Communications. Prior to that he had been a small-town newspaper publisher and one-time administrative assistant to Washington's then-governor, Arthur Langley. During these activities, Dick Everest and Loren Stone had become acquainted.

The county superintendent of schools had begun to see instructional television as something of value, but because of a state requirement for pre-budgeting, was encountering difficulty in developing a consortium of schools to encourage activation of reserved Channel 9. They had approached Everest, believing that the university would have greater flexibility in hiring, that a station could provide training opportunities in the School of Communications, and that the great University of Washington with its traditional interest in communications should be in on the endeavor.

STONE: So, one day, I get a call from Dick Everest at the university.

"Loren, we've got an application in for a television station. I don't know anything about television. When are you going to be in town?"

This was two or three weeks before Christmas. I said, "Dick, I don't have any plans to come over."

"Well, I'm in no hurry," he said, "but the next time you're in town, come on in. I'd like to talk to you and see if I can get some ideas. I don't know what this is all about." This would have been in late '53.

The day after Christmas I saw in the paper where the university had been awarded a construction permit for an educational television station. So the next day I called Dick up and I said, "Well, it looks to me like you *do* have a problem. Suppose I come in on Monday."

He said, "That'll be fine."

So I went on in and we started talking, and gosh, pretty soon I discovered he was trying to talk to me about being manager of this station. And I said, "No, Dick, I'm not interested. I spent twenty-three years in the broadcasting business and the stress of it has gotten to me and I'm just not interested. I'm going to find some other better way to make a living. To heck with it."

"Loren," he said, "you don't understand this. Here, take all of this material."

I said, "You know I don't know anything about television."

"Well," he said, "you take this stuff home and look it over. You might change your mind."

Well, I did take it home. I did change my mind. It looked fascinating and interesting and challenging.

~

Stone described with characteristic forthrightness another element in the move toward activation of Seattle's Channel 9.

Seattle's initial benefactors and promoters: Left to right, Mrs. Henry Owen of the University of Washington Board of Regents, Mrs. Mary Skelton, president of the PTA for the state of Washington, and Mrs. Scott Bullitt, owner of one of the Pacific northwest's leading commercial broadcasting enterprises. KING radio and KING-TV. The equipment in front of the unidentified gentleman, who represents the Seattle School Board, is part of a substantial amount donated by KING-TV to the new educational station, about to go on the air at the University of Washington, KCTS-TV.

STONE: We had a woman in our community, Mrs. Scott Bullitt, who owned a commercial radio and a commercial television station. I don't think she was at that time on the Board of Regents of the university but she later was. She was a very public-spirited sort of a gal, but she was also a very sharp gal.

She was really canny. She realized that the educational channel allocated to Seattle had better be used for educational purposes or it was going to be commercialized and competitive with them, so she undertook to develop some interest in an educational television facility.

One of her very closest friends and the wife of one of Mrs. Bullitt's executives was a strong member and the only woman member, I guess, of the Seattle school board, Mrs. Henry Owen. Mrs. Bullitt, Mrs. Owen, and Mrs. Bullitt's director of community services got together and they began trying to pull people in. They put on a meeting and I think they had Ralph Steetle out that early.

~

Steetle recounted the same circumstances.

STEETLE: Seattle was one of the areas where a helpful commercial broadcaster made a difference. Mrs. Bullitt, who is one of the fine leaders in northwest commercial broadcasting, helped us in Portland and also was a tower of strength up there [in Seattle]. The combination of a university responsibility with community participation, the university becoming the licensee, was achieved perhaps in its own northwest style in Seattle. It has worked very well.

STONE: Betty Evans, Mrs. Bullitt's community service gal, had started telecourses from the university on the commercial station, and they'd been doing some public relations programs for the Seattle schools, so they began to get a group together.

They first began to pull in school superintendents and school board members to take a look at this thing, and they developed quite a little interest.

This had all occurred prior to my involvement at all. This was all past history at the time I came into the thing.

~

Stone signed on as general manager of the Seattle ETV station in mid-February 1954, and soon discovered that Mrs. Bullitt's station people at KING-TV, in good faith, had done a considerable amount of advance planning, including employing a consultant whose studies projected that the station could be operated on a budget of $168,000 a year. One reason Stone probably was not entirely comfortable with this pre-planning was that during earlier years when he had managed KIRO radio, he saw Mrs. Bullitt's KING as his greatest competitor, and one does not always accept the judgment of one's competitor.

At the same time, however, he could not be displeased with Mrs. Bullitt's offer of an old transmitter and some studio cameras which KING-TV was replacing.

Another ironic situation developed for Stone, who had been in sales and management for the most part, when he traveled to Pasadena to respond to the offer of a matching grant of $150,000 from Scott Fletcher's Fund for Adult Education.

STONE: This was my first experience in grantsmanship and it wasn't a very happy one really, I guess, for me. They had been urging us to [apply], and when I get down there, all of a sudden you find yourself in a position of a supplicant.

This irritated me because I wasn't used to it. Growing up in commercial broadcasting, you went out and you did your own things and you weren't beholden to anybody and you weren't looking for grants and handouts and this sort of stuff.

But anyhow, they were willing to accept the equipment that Mrs. Bullitt was giving us [as matching grant credit]. We finally came to terms and we got our whole $150,000 out of the Fund for Adult Education.

~

With the starting capital in hand or promised, Stone applied his persuasiveness and business acumen to the problem of operating funds.

STONE: The Seattle schools had decided they could pay one dollar per student per year on their enrollments.[2] Their enrollment at the time was sixty-five thousand students, so they said okay, they'd put up sixty-five thousand. So the university said, we'll match that.

Then the group in the county schools figured they could gather together about fifty thousand dollars, so this would make about $180,000.

---

[2] This was a formula commonly used among ETV stations and schools to establish payment for instructional programs to be used in the classrooms.

Then Seattle University decided they wanted to come in, or were invited in, and Seattle Pacific College, and the Seattle Public Library decided they could come in for one thousand dollars, so this was going to provide our operating funds.

~

The transmitter donated by KING-TV was built to operate on Channel 5, but the instructor in broadcasting at the Edison Technical School, a vocational unit of the Seattle school system, developed a class project with some of his students and completely rebuilt the transmitter so that it would operate on Channel 9.

STONE: This was quite a feat for kids to do, and it was a tremendous training experience.

We had a tower erected on their building and the transmitter was housed in their building. They were on fairly high ground in Seattle, so for a number of years, 1954 to 1965, we operated from that site with that relatively low-power transmitter and relatively low antenna height.

~

The university, meanwhile, furnished the fledgling station with space for office and studios—such as it was.

STONE: They had been buying up some property adjacent to the campus, and they had some old buildings that we used.

We started out with studios in a small building that had belonged to the Hillel Foundation, the Jewish student group. We had to carry our scenery across the street, a rather busy street,

and up a hill aways and into the basement of one of the other buildings on campus where we had some storage area.

Our offices were in an old candy factory that the university had bought, an old wooden building behind the Hillel building.

So we started out in pretty meager circumstances.

~

Before the station got on the air, however, Stone and his small staff of associates were presented with an unexpected problem—or, in his words, "challenge."

STONE: I didn't choose to call these things "problems"; I chose to call them "challenges." I would say to my people when they came to me with problems, "Gee, you got a problem? Be glad you've got a problem. If there weren't problems we smart people would all be out of work. Let's call them challenges. Let's go." Because, you know, that's what we were there for—to take care of these things.

~

But after gathering all of the necessary equipment and starting down the final six weeks before their planned air date of December 7, 1954, an event occurred which was not part of the plan.

STONE: I came in on a Friday morning, and gee, everything was in terrible shape. We'd had a fire and burned up most of our equipment in this building we were going into!

KCTS-TV photo: John Boor

Seattle Fire: In 1954, six weeks before its planned on-air date, Seattle's KCTS-TV suffered a fire which damaged these racks of equipment. Fast work by RCA made replacement possible. Thanks to engineering director John Boor and other skillful technicians, Loren Stone's determination to make KCTS-TV's previously announced starting date (December 7) was fulfilled —but it was touch and go for six weeks!

WGBH Educational Foundation

Boston Fire: Seven years later, in 1961, Boston's WGBH-TV was entirely burned out of its original studios and offices in a remodeled roller-skating rink across the street from MIT. But its mobile unit with cameras had been parked outside the building, thus could be used as temporary facilities. Hundreds of in-school videotapes were handed down fire ladders to save them for broadcasts to classrooms in four states.

The fire apparently started from 110 volt wiring that the buildings and grounds people were putting into this building that they were remodeling for us. They had been using BX conduit and it hadn't been grounded properly—that's what the fire department finally decided. You know, that stuff glows like the element of a range if it isn't properly grounded.

I can't now remember, but it must have been a dozen major items of brand new equipment that went up in this thing. It didn't hit the cameras, because they were out in the studio, but the racks in the control room went. It was just a shambles. And we were six weeks from air date!

Well, we got ahold of the local RCA guy and he came out. By three o'clock that Friday, Camden time, he had RCA Camden on the phone with a complete list of everything we had lost. At ten o'clock Monday morning, a truck rolled up in front of our place with every item but one that we'd lost in that fire!

This was RCA to the rescue, and we never forgot that.

Having been in the broadcasting business where time schedules mean something, we had set ourselves a date, and we said, by golly, we're going to keep it, and we did. We made our December 6th date—or December 7th it was—Pearl Harbor anniversary, 1954.

John Crabbe Puts Sacramento and Stockton Together

In quite a few communities, institutions or groups nominally in competition with each other were brought together to assure the activation of a noncommercial television channel to serve their area.

In California, John Crabbe became the coordinator of two separate efforts, one in Stockton and another in nearby Sacramento.

CRABBE: There were two reservations in the area, Channel 42 reserved for Stockton and Channel 6 in Sacramento.

I had had nothing to do, really, with the Channel 6 thing. There had been activity, led by a guy by the name of Dick Kieswetter, who was in a suburban school district in the north Sacramento area. He'd been very active and had done a good job.

I then started to organize some kind of a group in Stockton in support of Channel 42. Of course, UHF was such a weird beast, nobody really knew what it was all about, so that I used as my focal point in Stockton the local school district. They had a superintendent who was

positive and understanding and wanted to take the leadership and did.

We formed a community group called the Delta-Sierra Educational Television Corporation. It was pretty broadly represented; it involved the college, the school district, and community people. And I guess the best thing to say is, we spun our wheels pretty thoroughly there for quite a time. It was just that you couldn't pull together enough real support to make it go.

As time went on it became apparent that the group in Sacramento independently and the group in Stockton independently were just not going to make it. So I initiated conversations between the two groups.

The only way out of it that we could see to preserve the identity of the two areas was to form a third corporation out of the other two, and we did. We formed Central California Educational Television, and we took six members of the board from Sacramento and five from Stockton and that preserved the whole thing.

~

Crabbe described the effect of the matching grant offered by the Fund for Adult Education.

CRABBE: Bill Griffiths kept saying "When are you guys going to get off the dime and move? I've got to get rid of the money; what are you doing out there? Why don't you do something?"

In the fall of '57, Bill came out, and he and I holed up in a motel and tried to design some kind of strategy that would blast things loose. We finally decided that our strategy would be—[LAUGHTER] I'll get hung for saying this, probably! In any case, our strategy would be to give a hard deadline. "Unless you guys can raise your half in ninety days, you're going to lose the grant."

That was a calculated risk. I didn't know whether that community could move that fast or not, but I figured with a carrot of a $100,000 out there, we'd find out in a hurry.

So, in the early part of November of '57, the board rose to the challenge. The university freed me; I could still use my office and stuff at the university in Stockton, but I didn't have any campus responsibilities, they just kept me on the payroll. There was a local community college in Stockton; they put me on the staff so that I could have some bucks to keep me going. And I went out and organized the central part of California to raise dollars.

~

Crabbe's wife, Bobbin, a children's theater activist, worked with him.

CRABBE: She counted the money when it came in, and all that kind of stuff. And what I did was to go out to every little town from Turlock on the south to Redding on the north and find somebody who would be the local chairman.

We peddled memberships for ten dollars apiece. I made ninety-three speeches in ninety days before various clubs. I remember one day when there was one at noon, one in the afternoon, and one at night. I just covered that crazy valley.

But it was the local guy or gal, whoever the case might be—PTAs were very helpful. Some other clubs and organizations were very helpful; women's groups were helpful.

I can remember one night I had gone up to Redding, and I was picking up money. I came back from Redding to Red Bluff to Chico to Maysville to Stockton, all the way down and I had fifty thousand dollars in checks and cash that I put under the bed that night. I didn't get back till about midnight.

And we made it, by golly. We met the deadline of March with $115,000, something like that, as I remember it. It was a lot of dollars from that area.

Keith Engar Marshalls the Mormons in Utah

Utah was another place where institutions which normally competed with each other discovered that they had common objectives in this case—although they found it somewhat awkward to work together, at least at first.

Keith Engar, who later was to find himself immersed in educational broadcasting matters at the national level as the first head of the Educational Broadcasting Branch of the Federal Communications Commission, became director of Radio and Television Services for the University of Utah in 1954.

ENGAR: The Fund for Adult Education had made its famous offer of matching funds, and there was intense jealousy in the state over who was going to be the licensee. These were bitter rivalries, really.

Keith Engar

The State Department of Public Instruction, Brigham Young University, the Salt Lake City schools, Utah State University in Logan, and the University of Utah were primary. Then there were other school districts represented by the State School Boards Association. And nobody really trusted anybody very much!

There were a lot of personalities involved. The superintendent of Salt Lake City public schools was a very able man and was able to conciliate things pretty much. They got legislation through the state legislature creating a public television authority for the state of Utah, but the governor, J. Bracken Lee, vetoed it. So things were pretty much in a shambles.

Then, A. Roy Olpin, who was president of the University of Utah—himself a television pioneer with the Bell System Labs—went to the manager of Channel 4 to get matching funds for this $115,000.

He was able to concoct matching funds out of some old equipment that Channel 4 said it would make available.

~

Olpin had been employed as a physicist with Bell System Laboratories. He also had the unusual distinction of having his visage transmitted during one of the first demonstration of live television. As president of the University of Utah, he not only secured the matching funds for the FAE grant but also continued to keep his hand in the growth and development of KUED.

ENGAR: President Olpin hired C. Richard Evans, who had been general manager of Channel 5 in Salt Lake City and then had been over in Hawaii. He was a remarkable man with fine engineering skill and managerial experience as well. He put the station on the air. I was actually program director.

The studios are where they are today [1981], inadequate then and inadequate now, in the basement in what used to be the old cafeteria [of the university]. Ceilings are not high enough. But we went on the air with fine equipment right from the beginning. We had RCA image orthicons and had a fine kinescope recorder—if there was such a thing. So the equipment was splendid, and right from the beginning we had a fine picture and reliable, on Channel 7. Originally it was Channel 2, but commercial interests got in there and it got changed to Channel 7.

~

Engar was asked if he recalled anything about community acceptance or viewer comment in those early days, since this was such a different kind of television from what people were accustomed to.

ENGAR: Our viewership would vary depending upon the kind of programming. We considered it a pretty high rating if we got a two on something.

What we did was to make sure that during the week we'd have a substantial proportion of viewers watch us at least once, and that was the case.

We made one stupid mistake when we first went on the air. We shouldn't have done it. Instead of saying "Channel 7 in Salt Lake City, we said, "Channel 7, *on the campus of the University of Utah*, Salt Lake City. The president wanted us to do that, and it was just the wrong thing to do. The paranoia was rampant.

McCarty's Wisconsin "Laboratory" Shows Promise

A clear example of early interest in educational television arising from the grassroots occurred in Wisconsin—which may not be surprising, since its university began using radio for education as early as 1917. That experimental handmade transmitter, 9XM, later became WHA, which thus has strong arguments to support its claim as "the oldest station in the nation."

It could have been predicted that those who had become accustomed to using radio for educational and informational purposes for more than thirty years would have invited their experts in broadcasting to look into television. This, according to WHA's H. B. McCarty, is exactly what happened.

McCARTY: In the spring of 1952, there was held here on the campus an agricultural conference, and several representatives of the group, one in particular, called up saying could they come over and talk to us about the possibilities of educational television and what the role of the farm organizations might be. Milo Swanton was one of those who had apparently started a discussion with some persons at "Farm and Home Week" a little earlier.

They came over, and as we talked it was clear that there was emerging among the people themselves a desire to do something. So the invitation went out to other groups, not just agricultural—to parent-teacher groups, to librarians, to women's clubs and so on. So in May 1952, a meeting was held here in Madison at which the Wisconsin Citizens' Committee for Educational Television came into being.

We were always proud to be able to say, " This came without stimulation from us." This was not a promotional device by the staff. This emerged and grew and flourished on the basis of individual interest expressed through various organizations.

~

The Board of Regents of the University of Wisconsin responded to this show of interest more promptly than might have been expected. Three months after the May meeting, they formally allocated almost $100,000 for experimentation with ETV.

McCARTY: I'm amused when I look at the figure now: $99,750! This was like a garment reduced from one hundred dollars to ninety-nine dollars and fifty cents. [CHUCKLE] I don't know who I thought would be fooled by such a proposal.

But they allocated that for equipment to establish a "television laboratory." This provided the facilities on which we were able to superimpose the broadcast function two years later, because we had a television laboratory for the express purpose of research in teaching techniques by television, experimentation in various types of programs which were being evaluated and appraised under a graduate research program headed by Bruce Westley of the journalism school.

~

McCarty recalls the circumstances on many university campuses at that time: burgeoning enrollments, not enough classroom space, thousands of students after their experiences during World War II wanting to go to college, and the consequent interest on the part of college administrators in whether TV might provide some answers to their problems.

McCARTY: So they rushed into television, devised courses of instruction, and said to the students, in effect, "Stay home; we'll transmit the educational materials to you by television." With this big push and the realization that something had to be done fast, Houston got on the air first.

That always disappointed me, because I wanted to be the first educational television station [CHUCKLE], but we didn't make it until May 3, 1954.

I said the previous years were exciting ones. These were excitement *plus*, as we tried, with primitive facilities in an old abandoned labora-

Whoever heard of a television studio with a solid load-bearing post in the middle of it? WHA-TV had one in its early years, along with an uneven floor which made for unsteady pictures whenever a camera changed position. Notice the grey drapes, so often seen as backdrops in early educational television.

tory room. I wish I could lead some of the present-day people [in public TV] through that studio!

I remember once when we were in operation, one of the commercial broadcasters here in town visited us. I gave him a tour, took him through our facilities, and we got back out, and he said: "Yeah, but where's your studio?"

I said, "You just walked through it!"

It was formerly the chemical engineering laboratory, and chemicals had been spilled all over the wood floor, and the wood floor had warped, and it was just that wavy, and you'd try to dolly a camera across it and you'd get the camera lens bobbing up and down. And if you weren't careful you'd back into a post that was supporting the ceiling—and not too well, because not long after that the ceiling completely crashed in!

~

McCarty remembered—as do quite a few others, some of whom were young children then and are now almost middle-aged—an early WHA-TV program created and produced under those circumstances and later distributed to other early ETV stations.

McCARTY: The group of people were so enthusiastic and so on fire with the dream of what could be that they put up with all kinds of inconveniences. And when I think of the lack of staging or costuming or properties—you think of all that, and think at the same time: this was the birthplace of "The Friendly Giant."

This came about so quietly. I knew that Bob [Homme] and Ken [Ohst] were up to something, but I was so busy trying to forestall those who wanted to obstruct the whole thing that I didn't get tuned in on some of the early program developments.

The Friendly Giant

All of a sudden, here was this *beautiful* program on the air *daily!* These guys had other full-time jobs, both of them. They were not paid to produce a television program.

This was strictly a personal project. [It] depended so much upon the imagination of the guy who created it [Homme] and his partner [Ohst] and their skill in operating the puppets and doing the voices and creating the illusion of a giant's castle; they did this single-handed. We entered it as soon as we could in the next exhibition of educational television programs at the Ohio State Institute at Columbus—1955, first award! 1956—first award! 1957—first award! 1958—first award!

~

McCarty explains the unusual nature of the program and reflects on the reasons why it could never have been successful commercially—one of which was that it was broadcast just after the evening dinner hour to coincide with the time when young children presumably were about to go to bed.

McCARTY: It was a "sleepy-time program." It had a tempo designed to encourage children to gradually tone down and then ended with a kind of "good night" thing and the moon coming up, just a very distinctive feature. It was so much appreciated by parents of active little children, who by six-thirty or seven in the evening were grateful of any kind of sedative influence [CHUCKLE].

But this made the program totally worthless commercially. When Bob Homme went to New York to see one of our former staff members who was then with one of the networks, he viewed it and said, "Bob, that's beautiful but it's absolutely worthless commercially. You will never get this program on the air on a commercial station because in prime time—seven o'clock in the evening—you can't segment your audience and appeal just to the four-to-six-year olds."

~

While McCarty and his associates were always grateful for substantial listener and viewer interest, in those days it was moral support—not dollars.

McCARTY: In my wildest dreams I never thought that [public] broadcasting could gain such a large share of its budget for operations from the listeners and viewers. I'm just amazed.

I thought that if we were able to get from viewers maybe $10,000 a year, to publish a nice program bulletin, that would be something. Now, when they raise $175,000 to $200,000, it indicates the extent to which the users have come to feel a part in the whole development, and I think that's great.

Taxpayer Referendum Slows Wisconsin's Progress

A substantial struggle was waged in Wisconsin before that state could move ahead to develop a state-wide service.

Shortly after WHA-TV in Madison went on the air in May 1954, the state legislature asked that a study be made of costs and difficulties and needs. This was followed by a state-wide referendum, the wording of which in retrospect seems to have reflected the origin of the concerned group: taxpayer watchdogs.

McCARTY: The referendum came in November of 1954, when very few people in the state had had an opportunity to view an educational television program. Actually, many areas of the state had *no* television coverage whatsoever, of any sort. The *Milwaukee Journal's* WTMJ-TV was covering a substantial area of the state and there was spill over from Minneapolis and St. Paul, but in vast areas in the interior of Wisconsin, you'd say "television" and they'd say, "What's that?"

So it was significant, we thought, that when the referendum votes were counted, only *one county* in the state approved the proposition to establish what was called, according to the referendum wording—and this I thought was loaded—"a state-owned, tax-supported, noncommercial educational television network."

As a matter of fact, the opposition had created an adversary committee and had a paid lobbyist who was stumping the state telling what a great evil this would be. One of the leaders of that group characterized this whole television proposal as "a dangerous tool in the hands of government." I said that "the public school system is a dangerous tool in the hands of government, too; what are you going to do about that? Education is really dangerous. If it's good, it's always a threat to the status quo."

So, the referendum proposal was defeated by a vote of more than two to one—*except* in Dane county, where the people who had had six months of educational television, said, "*Yes,* we'd *like* to see a tax-supported, noncommercial, state-wide network."

When the results of the referendum were announced, I remember a call from a *Milwaukee Journal* reporter, saying, "What's the effect of this?" I said, "This kills educational television in Wisconsin for ten years." Well, again I was too optimistic, because it was more like twenty years before opinion had come around to where it would support plans for the establishment of a state-wide, educational, noncommercial television network.

UHF Frustrates Armand Hunter at Michigan State

Prominent and progressive Michigan State University, early aware of television's potential in education, was confronted with many kinds of problems. All of the channels reserved for noncommercial use in its area were UHF. And in the mid-1950's, while converters were available, almost no homes were equipped to receive UHF channels on their VHF-only sets. Dr. Armand Hunter was recruited from Temple University in Philadelphia to be Michigan State University's director of television development.

HUNTER: Michigan State had had AM and FM radio stations for years, but they were interested in moving into the new educational television medium.

My first effort was an attempt to get a VHF channel dropped into East Lansing, because I was familiar with the fact that the state of the art at that time was VHF. We were not successful in that.

In that interim period, while the freeze was on, we took this time to develop an exhaustive survey of all of the program potential of the various academic departments and colleges of the university.

In the studios which we had put in and equipped on the fifth floor of the engineering building, we produced on closed circuit, recording on kinescope, samples of various types of programs that could be produced within the university and locally by the station and by our staff, for broadcast when we went on the air.

I felt rather proud of our effort and the university at that point, because we really did an exhaustive coverage of the educational programming resources of the entire institution.

~

Lacking for the time being any capability for on-the-air broadcasting by its own station, Michigan State began to distribute these programs over local commercial stations in Detroit and Lansing that had managed to get on the air before the FCC freeze.

HUNTER: Those were years when you were developing new programs, new types of activity in the whole university arena, giving members of the faculty and staff an opportunity to develop their particular educational expertise and to see how effective we could be in getting that into this new kind of educational broadcasting service. From all standpoints, I'd say that was a kind of a fun, exciting, experimental time.

With the kind of facility we developed, with the training program and all, we were able to develop a workshop for NAEB. Many of the educational radio people around the country came here, and had an opportunity to begin work, with studio and camera.

~

One of the many who became involved in such training at that time was Lee Frischknecht, a native of Logan, Utah, who had dabbled in radio during his undergraduate days at Utah State and then had spent two years at a commercial radio station in Idaho Falls, Idaho. Disenchantment with commercial broadcasting led him to go back to school to learn about television with the hope of getting into it. He recalls entering the graduate program at Michigan State about four months prior to the activation of WKAR-TV on UHF Channel 60.

Lee Frischknecht

FRISCHKNECHT: Even before the station went on the air, I was into course work in television production and had been doing booth announcing and that sort of thing on the closed circuit shows we were doing.

Then when the station went on the air, I had completed the first course in the television sequence and so, as I recall, when we put Channel 60 on the air on January fourth or something like that of 1954, I was the boom operator for the dedicatory program, standing up on the platform looking down on Armand Hunter, Frieda Hennock, and all the other big-wigs that had appeared for this magnificent occasion, trying to keep the boom microphone out of the picture and from hitting people on the head. It was a great occasion!

~

Frischknecht—along with others under Armand Hunter's tutelage—moved up quickly.

FRISCHKNECHT: Before the end of the third quarter, the station had been on the air for six months and I had been working all along on production crews as a boom operator, floor manager, staging and lighting crew, and all that stuff. Then they offered me a job as a full-time cameraman, and I probably enjoyed it as much as anything I've ever done in public broadcasting.[3] There was a certain precision required in

---

[3] A significant observation, since after a term as manager of the station at Michigan State, Frischknecht handled station relations for NET, he played a major leadership role in the formation of National Public Radio (NPR) in the early seventies and subsequently was president of NPR for several years prior to our interview in 1981.

the coordination of various elements, and a creative part of it as well, depending on the nature of the program. I really enjoyed being a cameraman, the challenge of it, and we did some fairly interesting programs that required some camera work that was a little more than ordinary.

~

Fairly typical of the bright and eager and intelligent young people in the field in those years, Frischknecht in two months became a floor director and three months later a director. That led him into doing some producing as well as directing.

FRISCHKNECHT: We were doing a tremendous amount of live programming. There wasn't much service from—what was it?—The ETRC in those days,[4] so we had to do a lot of live stuff.

We did a fair number of children's programs for pre-school kids and for elementary-age kids. We had a story lady who told stories every day. These were daily programs right across the board. We had a women's program, an interview program every afternoon of every weekday. We had a daily "Town and Country" that was a farm and home show that I directed for a long time. Then we had a slew of college level telecourses.

The president decreed that there would be telecourses on the air to deal with the enormously expanding enrollments that Michigan State was undergoing at that time, and the faculty were encouraged to participate or assigned as the case may be, but we had a lot of them on the air, most of them in the evening, some during the day as well.

We had three studios running pretty much full blast for a good eight to ten hours a day, just a tremendous amount of *live* programming.

~

Both Hunter and Frischknecht—along with many other ETV pioneers who attended or visited Michigan State during those years or some time later—remember with mixed emotions the unique building which housed all of this activity, a far cry from the typical public television facilities of the 1990's.

HUNTER: During the postwar years the university had set up a big Quonset hut complex—a dining room and [other] facilities for feeding all these returned vets. There was this huge commissary dining room that the university didn't know what to do with, so we moved in there—temporarily.

Well, it became one of those permanently temporary arrangements. A Quonset hut! But there was space for three studios, control rooms, construction facilities for scenery, paint shop, storage, offices, and all the rest. So we really had a rather substantial facility in terms of size that we could and did convert into a television complex.

FRISCHKNECHT: There was nothing but the Quonset roof, and every time it would rain or snow you could hear it, and in the summer it was terribly hot and in the winter it was cold. We couldn't keep it controlled at all. There was no air conditioning at all in those days in those studios.

I remember one day we thought we were going to be very smart and get the vice president for business of the university to come over and do a pitch for the American Red Cross. He was a member of the local board. So we arranged it on one of the hottest days of the summer, turned the studio lights on about three hours before he got there so that by the time he arrived it was just dreadful in the studio.

I told him that we were very sorry it was so hot in the studios but we don't have air conditioning, we hope to remedy that soon.

He sat down at the desk. Of course, they all sat down behind desks in those days, everybody in educational television, everyone else for that matter, with a gray drape behind them. And he did his little pitch.

His response to me, with the sweat streaming down his face, "Oh, it's perfectly cool in here. I don't feel a thing!"

He wasn't going to let me push him into putting air conditioning in the studios. He was too smart for us. It took a few years before we got air in there.

~

The advent of Channel 60, however, did not bring the desired results despite the remarkable program production capabilities which Hunter and his associates had mounted.

HUNTER: There was a very interesting reaction in the community and within the university, a tremendous amount of support and interest in the service and in the station. But then we ran up against the problem: UHF reception!

People made the investments, they bought converters, they put up antennas, and still the reception was a problem.

---

[4] Educational Television and Radio Center.

[5] Los Angeles was second on the air, but after a few months, folded, until KCET was activated much later, in 1964.

The mobile unit of WKAR-TV covered sports including university baseball and even televised commencement exercises as early as 1955—but UHF Channel 60 could not be seen by most families, whose TV sets only received VHF channels.

We had the best transmitter that money could buy. We went on at full power. We had a 1,000 foot tower. Theoretically we could cover most of lower Michigan. We did everything we could with the hardware and the technology that was available. And I'm sorry to say that the big disappointment was in the fact that people just simply could not receive the signal effectively. Consequently their interest tended to decline.

~

Thus, the second noncommercial educational television station in the nation to go on the air and stay on the air—Houston having been the first—faced a troublesome situation.[5]

HUNTER: Okay, so President [John] Hanna— a very intelligent and inspirational educational leader—said, "We can't really provide service to the people this way, so what can we do?"

Well, that time we went back to the UHF issue. And the commission dropped VHF Channel 10 into Parma-Onondaga, Michigan. This is a little hole in the road, down from East Lansing between Jackson and Battle Creek, but they made it commercial!

Again we fought to get that on a reserved basis for education, and the commission denied it. So we entered a competitive hearing for that channel.

"All right, to hell with you, we're going to compete for it! And we'll operate it as an educational station, even if it's on a commercial channel."

So one of the commercial applicants, WILS in Lansing, came to the university, and we joined in what was a joint application, and proceeded to make our case before the commission with the other commercial applicants on the basis of a *shared-time* arrangement. A certain amount of time would be devoted to the commercial station

and its services, and a certain amount would be devoted to the university and its educational services; we would share that channel. And after *four years* of hearings before the commission, we won. So we were the first shared-time operation of this kind in the country.

~

There were those at the time who disagreed with this strategy, yet in retrospect one can understand Michigan State's position.

HUNTER: I think the university at that point said, "I guess at this point in time, half of a VHF loaf is better than a full UHF in terms of visibility, reception, and an opportunity to get the university's educational program resources to the audience."

And when we moved onto that channel we did have audience access and availability.

We were fully aware that we really had more programming resources and more that we'd like to do than we could possibly do under this shared-time arrangement, but we were willing at that time to make this kind of a compromise.

~

For nearly five years—until UHF had improved to the point of practicality—Michigan State did its best with limited hours. And even in 1959, the campaign wasn't over.

HUNTER: When we made the switch back to full-time UHF again, we had to fight the battle for a changed reservation.

We finally got [Channel] 23 reserved for education.

So poor old Michigan State went through a battle to get a VHF which they should have had in the first place and couldn't win it, went on the air with UHF 60 without audience availability, went the other way on a compromise to get some time on a V, and then gradually as the technique and the hardware and the medium developed, went back on a full-time basis with a lower UHF frequency.

We had to fight every foot of the way.

~

Reviewing the Michigan State saga, one can only be impressed by the convictions which must have been held by those in charge regarding the ultimate importance and remarkable potential value of television in education.

Don Taverner Leads
the State of Maine Into ETV

The southern and midwestern states were not the only places where there was concern about improving the quality of education, and consequent interest in this new medium.

At the University of Maine, a red-haired, freckle-faced, corncob pipe-smoking director of development by the name of Donald Taverner got his first educational television assignment.

TAVERNER: I was at a kind of social gathering at the Tarrantine Club, a private men's club in Bangor, one evening. The president of the university at that time, Lloyd Elliot, and a couple of other fellows and myself got around to discussing the fact that Maine was having economic problems and educational problems. This was around 1957 or '58.

Some of the group said, "Do you suppose there's any correlation between the depreciating economic situation in the state of Maine and the mediocre-plus level of education in the state?"

And then I believe it was President Elliot who said, "You know, this new educational television thing, do you suppose that educational television could raise the educational levels of the state, and at the same time if there is a correlation with economics, begin to raise the economic level of the state?"

So he turned to me and said, "Don, why don't you look into that?"

I said, "Sure, why not? By Tuesday I can take care of that." You know, that sort of thing.

So I was charged at that point to see what could be done to investigate educational television.

~

Actually, Taverner and Elliot had been considering possibilities, with encourage-

ment from those already involved with WGBH in Boston and WENH in neighboring Durham, New Hampshire. Taverner persuaded the Ford Foundation to provide $31,000 for a feasibility study, though he reflects that ETV was "not an overpowering thing at that point" since he was heavily involved in developing a two-year medical school for the university at the same time. But "it became overpowering in rather short order."

Jack McBride from Nebraska was engaged as a consultant and professional engineering and legal consultants were retained, and very shortly it was discovered that while only one channel had been reserved for educational use (Channel 10 in Orono, the site of the university's main campus), there were several VHF channels elsewhere in the state as yet unclaimed.

TAVERNER: And so we did the impossible. If we had known how the industry operated and what the thing was all about we wouldn't have dared do it. But we didn't know.

So we walked in naively to the FCC and asked for conversion of these channels from commercial to educational—which, of course, just is not done, or wasn't at that time. But it worked. We got some great help from our Congressional delegation and some other people. And there was not a big battle over it. It became pretty clear that the economic viability of these commercial V channels in these small populated areas was not really there, and education could best be served. So the FCC agreed that this should be done.

~

But Taverner's and Elliot's work had barely begun—and they were both in the midst of many other projects to strengthen higher education in Maine.

TAVERNER: The big challenge came as to how do you convince the people of Maine, a very conservative state, that they ought to spend a million dollars so that the kids could watch television in the schools. Because television had not come to Maine until about 1954, I think it was, it was the Dagmar and Roller Derby era to some degree. It didn't have an image that projected itself into education in the mind of the average citizen.

But at the university we began to talk this through with the dean of education and other people concerned.

Enthusiasm built from really two vantage points. There were those who felt it might save money in education. That was not a philosophy the university subscribed to, but others did. Then there was the enrichment side of it: that the smaller schools in the state who were unable to afford chemistry or physics laboratories in the little high schools, or other specialized courses, could be leveled upwards in educational experience with other larger schools.

We didn't at that early period give much thought to the use of educational television for purposes other than systematic education.

~

The operational plan was to establish a state-wide network of transmitters and to receive a considerable amount of programming from the Eastern Educational Network, which then consisted only of WGBH in Boston and WENH in Durham, New Hampshire. However, "The 21-Inch Classroom" school telecasts from WGBH-TV, supplemented by plans made by the Maine State Department of Education in conjunction with the state departments of other New England states, offered considerable promise.

All of the engineering and legal aspects were brought into a plan to present to the Maine legislature, the objective being to furnish service to the entire state of Maine.

TAVERNER: Lloyd Elliot, as president of the university, and Warren Hill, as commissioner of education, were sometimes as popular as bats at a party picnic down there in the legislature.

First we were met with gales of laughter. "What's that university going to come up with next?" Then the laughter kind of turned to smiles, and then the smiles turned to serious expressions.

~

Prominent among Taverner's colorful recollections were his accounts of key members of the Maine legislature, both friend and foe.

TAVERNER: There was a freshman legislator by the name of T. Tarpey Shelten, who had come out of New York where he had been an advertising man. He fell in love with the state of Maine and came up and decided he was going to raise turkeys and sheep. And he became kind of a gentleman farmer, and ran for the legislature and won. A delightful person.

Tarpey was a whirlwind, a ball of fire. So we gave Tarpey the word as to what we were trying to do, and Tarpey saw it right away. So he sponsored the bill for us. Tarpey made it his whole life in the legislature at that point.

In those days, if you had a friend in the legislature and you were over there visiting and there was an empty seat, you could go in and sit on the floor, you know. There was a fellow there that was not a friend but we became well known to each other in the course of all this, and he was a very conservative guy. "A million dollars in the schools? Bah!"

So he says, "I've got to show you something." And he took me out in the hallway to the corridor between the House and Senate, and he said, "You see that sign up there?"

I said, "Sure I see it, Ben. It says 'The House of Representatives.'"

"I know," he said, "I mean the other sign."

I said, "There is no other sign."

He said, "Oh, yes, there is. That's your problem. That's why you're going to have trouble.

"The other sign there, I can read it as clear as day. It says, 'There ain't *nothin'* worth a million dollars!'"

And that was the thing that we had to battle all the way through on this thing. It was really tough going, trying to lobby that thing through.

~

Taverner and Commissioner of Education Warren Hill spent hours and hours on lobbying, eventually winning over a block of forty Democrats who initially had been dead set against the project, with Tarpey Shelten still beating the bushes and employing his own special kinds of persuasion with his legislative colleagues.

TAVERNER: As it got toward the end of the session, the House began to get together, and finally voted for it, voted the million dollars and the stipulations for the network and so forth and so on.

Then it went to the Senate. Now, we knew the Senate was going to be difficult. And the legislature was winding up its session, and it went right up to the last hour. As I remember, it was two thirty or three in the morning when a senator decided that since this had such popularity over in the House, this was a good way of getting some land that he wanted into a state park. So he pork-barreled a state park provision in with educational television. And the Senate passed it with no great enthusiasm.

But it had to go back to the House, and the House reared up in great anger and disgust. They said, "We came here to give education for the children of Maine, we are talking about educational television, and the Senate pork-barreled the state park which has nothing to do with it into the thing, so we killed it." It died right then and there. That was it. It was all over. The legislature went home and educational television was dead.

But President Elliot of the university and corncob pipe-smoking Don Taverner held a caucus.

TAVERNER: The president said, "What do you think, Don?"

I said, "I don't think we ought to leave it that way. I think we ought to go after it. I'm kind of set back a little bit here, but I'm not discouraged.

"But," I said, "It depends on how much time and how much money that you feel you want me to spend on this against the two-year med school and other things."

He said, "We came with this, let's go with it."

~

Unwilling to hold back the planning which already was going forward, Taverner went down to Augusta to talk to the governor. The governor was John Reed, who had been a fellow student with Taverner at the university.

TAVERNER: I went to see Governor Reed and I said, "We are going to have to have a special session of the legislature."

Reed's attitude was, "Don, you know better than that. That's going to cost sixty to seventy thousand dollars just to get those guys down here to vote a bill which was killed for a million dollars concerning which there was some question."

I said, "Are you against it, John?"

"No, I'm all for it!"

I said, "Then you'd better put your money where your mouth is."

So we kidded around, because we had kinda grown up together, and there were some other things that needed to be done. But he still balked.

Then I started out on my chicken circuit thing again, hitting the PTA's, hitting the AAUW's, what-not, and the governor began to get all kinds of requests and demands for a special session on this poor treatment that had been given the children of Maine.

So John did call the special session, and in less than half a day, it was all cleared and voted.

~

But, as Taverner remarked, "the fun wasn't all over" because the university could not apply for licenses for these now-reserved channels until authorized to do so by the legislature. Under FCC rules, any qualified party desiring such a channel for noncommercial educational purposes could apply.

And during all of the legislative activity, the presidents of the three major private colleges in Maine—Bowdoin, Colby, and Bates—were getting somewhat concerned.

TAVERNER: They pretty well got the idea, "Look, the university is going to have all of the educational channels in the state of Maine. That may be too much concentration of authority or responsibility or power in one spot." If you will, overstating this now, "Here's telecommunications as a state educational system and private education is out of it."

So, without a "thank you ma'am," they fired off a request for a license for Channel 10 in Augusta!

I was not aware of this; probably the university was not aware of this. One thing led to another, and they got it. They got that assignment before we even got the others.

Relations were strained between the president of Bates and the president of the university for some time to come. I don't know if they exchange Christmas cards even yet.

But that was kind of a blow, because we had promised the legislature that we could cover 92 to 96 percent of the children of the state. And the most populated areas of the state, central and southern Maine, were no longer in the picture.

~

Characteristically, Taverner took the bit in his teeth and went to see Hank Stred, who was alumni director at Bates as Taverner had been at the university. As they began to talk, key legislators expressed concern about just how the three private colleges were going to program their channel.

TAVERNER: Aside from their "it's-none-of-your-business" attitude, because these were private colleges, they indicated their interest was very similar to what the university had in mind. Therefore, they would make their station available for in-school programming produced by the state Department of Education or through the university, they would broadcast them but would expect the state Department of Education to pay for the transmission of such programs. So that brought it back in line.

And they moved forward and were on the air before the university stations went on the air—but not much before!

~

The attitude of commercial broadcasters in Maine was described by Taverner as "a mixed bag."

TAVERNER: Horace Hilldruth—the controlling factor in television stations in Portland and in Bangor—having been a governor and having been an ambassador, caught the vision and could see what we were really trying to do. He did not look at it as being something that was competitive to their television concerns, and he backed us all the way.

Some of the other television operations in the state weren't going to come out heavily against motherhood and the American flag, but they gave us quite a lot of passive resistance.

There was never an easy path; none of these things ever are. It was mountain climbing most of the way.

~

Even so, Taverner in later years offered a reasonably objective assessment of what occurred between his struggles of the 1960's and the time of his observations two decades later.

TAVERNER: I think if I went back to a legislator of the 1960 Maine legislature and said, "Do you think we took you?" his answer would be, "No, I don't think you took us. I think you gave the state a tremendous opportunity. It just didn't turn out the way we thought it was going to."

And he might even say—this may be wishful thinking—"I think it turned out better."

There's no question in my mind that the Maine Public Broadcasting Network has raised the cultural and educational levels of the state. And I don't think there's any question that it's helped the economy. The basic things that we talked about at the Tarrantine Club a few years back really happened.

~

Many other stories of early "sprouting from the grassroots" could be told by others who undertook pioneering in other communities, and although the details would differ, the substance would be the same. What is now called public television was brought into being because a few individuals saw a need, caught a glimpse of a dream, and then persevered in doing something about it. The roster of pioneers includes not only community and business leaders but also those who had come to know the television business well enough to qualify as managers of these new stations.

One of the station management teams most highly regarded by their peers during the early decades of ETV not only demonstrated initiative and courage but in so doing built the base upon which one of the most successful public television stations has developed. This team was composed of James Day and Jonathan Rice at San Francisco's KQED.

Of all of the early stations, KQED stood out, in part because its home town is not a typical city. But no station began with less than what KQED had to start with, and few if any other stations showed so clearly the promise of what all of the pioneers referred to as "The Dream." Nor were there many managers and program directors who achieved the reputation which Day and Rice achieved by starting a station from scratch.

16

A Prime Example of the Dream: KQED

By the fall of 1988, in its 34th year, KQED was paying $9 million dollars for a building to house a staff of 325, and planned to spend almost that much again "turning it into a supertech broadcast facility," according to the San Francisco Chronicle.[1] The same story reported the station's annual income as $32 million with a $700,000 surplus, and quoted KQED's manager, Tony Tiano, as describing KQED as "the most-watched of any public TV station in the country."

This opulence presents an interesting contrast with KQED's beginnings. Its first live TV program originated in a pink bathroom in the penthouse above "The Top of the Mark," the famous revolving bar atop the Mark Hopkins Hotel. And after a year on the air, its governing board—facing an $8,000 deficit—was about to vote to give up the whole idea and let the station go dark.

James Day, its first manager, recalled the earliest months.

DAY: We were on the air, as I remember, two days a week and then only for two hours. As I've said many times in PTA speeches, you had to lead a well-disciplined life to find us on the air in those days.

Early Community Leader
Vaughn Seidel

Actually, the move to establish KQED began before either James Day or his program manager, Jonathan Rice, was on the scene. The key figure who took hold of the idea originally was the superintendent of schools in Alameda County, Vaughn Seidel.

RICE: Seidel had enormous imagination and ridiculous courage. He was not a very powerful man but he had heard Frieda Hennock speak and he decided somehow that he was going to make educational television work.

~

Several leaders in the Bay Area Chapter of the American Association of University Women (AAUW) had invited FCC commissioner Frieda Hennock to come out and were talking up the idea in various ways, despite the fact that CBS wanted very badly to have Channel 9. Ralph Steetle of the Joint Council on Educational Television in Washington, D.C., and Bill Griffiths of the Fund for Adult Education, both recalled those events.

STEETLE: If it hadn't been for Vaughn Seidel, I don't believe that the channel could have been held against a very strong attack by CBS. But Vaughn Seidel was one of those tough, political—[with a] small P—minded persons who was able to hold the fort and to begin to gather the troops to raise some funds to make that station a possibly.

If it were not for Vaughn Seidel, there'd not have been a Day and a Rice.

GRIFFITHS: You had this sort of initially inchoate thing with Vaughn Seidel over in Oakland, a superintendent of schools, seeing this as a great vehicle for them, but pretty narrowly based.

Others with exposure in the community, notably Lew Hill at KPFA [the Pacifica Foundation], realized that this was too narrow and this would never do. And the San Francisco Foundation's interest and other cultural enti-

---

[1] "KQED Finds a New Home, Three Times Bigger," by Lloyd Watson in the San Francisco Chronicle, October 28, 1988. Subsequent stories in 1991 reported some problems arising out of the station's "bigness."

ties there were seeing this in broader terms, and gradually coming to the point where what had been a narrowly-based thing became the Bay Area Educational Television Association [BAETA].

Vaughn Seidel again had to behave in a rather statesmanlike fashion, again saying, "I thought it was my baby, but I guess it can't be, really—and so let's all live together happily and let the child grow up to a better future."

~

Jim Day sheds further light on the man who headed KPFA radio and the Pacifica Foundation.

DAY: Lewis Hill, a poet, an intellectual, an interesting man, started the concept of listener-supported radio. He investigated that, out of which he published a book called *The Two Percent Theory*. The theory was that if 2 percent of your listeners would subscribe $10 a year, you could support a radio station.

I believe that Vaughn Seidel or the BAETA group did get the idea of membership support from Pacifica. [BAETA] was a membership organization from the very beginning, but we copied it from KPFA.

The concept of membership was built into BAETA before I joined.

~

In earlier years, just after World War II, Jim Day had worked at the NBC radio station in San Francisco under John Elwood. But Day went off to Japan for two years to help in the reconstruction of Japanese broadcasting, then spent another two years with Radio Free Asia broadcasting short wave from Manila to Communist China.

DAY: When the CIA decided that there was no longer a need for Radio Free Asia because there was an insufficient number of receiving sets in China, they decided to close it down, and I was offered a job with the parent organization, and I was to be in charge of all media.

But when I discovered that the then president, who was a retired general, was to make my own staff appointments for me and was to decide who was going to handle what medium, I quit. I didn't think about the consequences of quitting, I just quit.

I went out to lunch and came back from lunch and got a telephone call from a man who was then assistant to the president of Stanford University. He said, "I'm on the board of something called the Bay Area Educational Television Association. We happen to be meeting right now in the San Francisco Museum, and we're looking for a manager. Your name was suggested and I was asked to call you to see if you would be interested."

I said, "Well, the timing is great because I just quit my job an hour or so ago, and yes, I would be interested."

~

Day admits to some slight interest in ETV prior to that time.

DAY: Governor Warren had called a Governor's Conference [on ETV]. John Elwood from NBC in San Francisco took me to this conference, and that was my introduction to the idea of educational television and probably led me to have an interest in going into it. Though I would say that I went into NBC specifically because of my feeling that radio could be used for mass education. The idea of mass education rather intrigued me. Why, I don't know.

~

Meanwhile, Jonathan Rice—quoted earlier as one of the early professionals in television—decided he had had enough of Klaus Landsberg and KTLA in Los Angeles.

RICE: I was fed up with the pressures of this, and Kit and I decided either to get into education, which we thought was nice and calm, or farming.

We spent a long time looking at avocado farms and grape farms and the desert, and then we talked to a vaguely-related uncle who was a rancher. He asked how much I had to invest, and I thought it was a huge amount of money, and he said, "Well, that would buy you a small place. If you don't mind Kit getting up every morning and cooking pies and potatoes and roasts by five o'clock in the morning, you can probably swing it, but if you have to hire a cook, you couldn't swing it."

So I decided that was out, and started working really hard on educational television.

~

Rice tells of going to dinner with Fred Friendly, then at CBS-TV, who decided not to hire him, and also of an invitation from Rowan Gaither, then president of the Ford Foundation, which Rice passed up. He was offered a job at the University of Iowa for $2,000 a year if he'd pay his own moving expenses ("I had a wife and son and this didn't seem very relevant.") and was refused by Armand Hunter at Michigan State for lack of an advanced degree.

RICE: Meanwhile, the educational television job I wanted most was in San Francisco, because I had loved San Francisco. Worked here. Always wanted to come back. My whole goal in accepting jobs in New York and Los Angeles was to get back here. [2]

By then there was a board. [I] got an appointment to see them, had a marvelous opportunity of meeting every board member separately, and being in a very real sense, all things to all people.

I could tell Robert Miller, who was president or director—or whatever the title then was—of the Academy of Science what we could do about science, and I could tell the librarian what we could do about books, and I could tell Hattie Sloss [vice president of the San Francisco Symphony] what we could do about music.

They asked me if I wanted to be manager, and I said, "No." My skills and experience were not that way at all. I wanted to be program manager.

Day and Rice Meet for the First Time

DAY: The board that interviewed me said that they had interviewed a man named Jon Rice from Los Angeles and they were very impressed with him, thought he was not the kind of person to be the general manager but felt he would make a good program manager.

They did not order me to interview him; they did suggest that I might wish to go to Los Angeles and talk with him.

RICE: So he came down to Los Angeles, probably using about half of the existing budget for the trip, and came to my house in Brentwood for dinner. We got along very well.

He was the exact opposite of me. For most of our association he was terribly shy on a one-to-one basis, but totally at home before three hundred people. He could wrap an audience around his fingers and make them laugh. I was the exact opposite. I was completely at home and manipulative and skilled and comfortable with any two people, and completely frightened of any two hundred.

One of the things Jim couldn't do was to leave a situation. He never knew how to say good-bye. How do you wrap it up?

In this particular case, he came for dinner, and we talked, and we talked, and we talked about everything we could possibly talk about, such as whether he wanted me, and it was two o'clock in the morning!

---

[2] Rice seems to have fulfilled that desire. He began to work for KQED on June 1, 1953 and was still employed by the station nearly forty years later.

Finally I said, "Jim, Kit and I have to go to bed." And that's not the way you usually treat a hopeful new—I mean, by this time this was the job—it was always the job I wanted most in the world.

He did go home—and he hired me.

~

The Rices moved from Los Angeles to San Francisco. Day kept his home in Palo Alto and commuted into the city each day.

RICE: I would pick him up at the railroad station in my station wagon. All existing files and his typewriter were in the back of the station wagon—it being a different day in which you could keep a typewriter in a car.

We would go over to Vaughn Seidel's office and use his telephones or we'd go calling on various friends all over the city.

~

To begin with, the BAETA board envisioned the station primarily as an aid to schools.

RICE: The by-laws at that time insisted on a very heavy majority of school people on the board. This was natural and logical because it had been Seidel's idea, and really Frieda Hennock's idea, that educational television was going to be supported largely by the schools—that they were going to find the services provided by this new medium so enormous that the state colleges and universities as well as the schools would have to support us.

When we arrived, the school superintendent of San Francisco was not on the board and had not believed much in educational broadcasting. That was Herbert Clish.

Clish and Seidel had never gotten along. They were very different people. And it was clear to everyone including Jim and myself that without San Francisco representation we couldn't make it.

Fortunately, another man was on board, a man named Roy Sorenson, the author of several books and a lecturer on the role of boards and how to be a board member. He was extremely skilled at this kind of activity. He worked on Clish and Seidel and persuaded them to work together for the good of this interesting idea, which Clish hadn't thought that interesting. Clish became chairman and Seidel became president, and that worked.

~

Despite this interest on the part of many Bay Area schools, they were not in a position to contribute funds or even to pay for "services."

DAY: Apparently California law is derived from old Spanish law, so we were told, and unless something is specifically permitted, it is not allowed, and the law did not specify television. It took us four or five years to get that law changed.

So we were caught in that peculiar situation, unlike most of the educational stations around the country.

From my point of view, I thought it was a very good thing. It caused Jon and me to think of educational television as *public* television, as a matter of fact, and while it was a little difficult not to have the support of the schools financially, it probably set us off in a somewhat different direction than we might have gone had the school money been available.

Finding the First Funds

Before any programming was possible, however, there had to be facilities and people—and funding.

DAY: The only money available to us was a $60,000 grant from the Rosenberg Foundation, $30,000 of which was payable when we went on the air—which was an unfortunate inducement. We had to have that $30,000 and had almost no choice but to go on the air to get it.

There was $12,000 from the San Francisco Foundation, and that we used to hire me.

That was the only cash available, aside from the Fund for Adult Education equipment grants. Those were matching grants, and we simply shuffled papers fast enough to make it look like money.

RICE: BAETA also made contracts with San Francisco State College and with the University of California [Berkeley] for studio space. Using those contracts and those grants, Jim Day shuffled papers and cards and was able to qualify for the Ford Foundation's going-on-the-air grants.

~

FAE's Bill Griffiths also recalled these negotiations.

GRIFFITHS: KQED was always a special case. One of the features of the fund grants was that we were really flexible in deciding what constituted assets, and what they should be capitalized at, because we were willing to recognize far more than just the total hard cash.

I can still remember the situation in San Francisco when Jim Day and Jonathan Rice and I were trying to decide what fair value to put on a Mexican cock-fight chair that somebody had donated to KQED for the studio equipment!

As a matter of fact, they never did get the full $150,000 because I don't think they ever qualified for the full amount. I think they fell short, but even that was after capitalizing ashtrays, johnny paper, and God knows what else as part of the matching assets.

~

Some who knew Day and Rice at the time later recalled to Jim Day's mind his own comment that because they had a transmitter atop the Mark Hopkins hotel, they proposed including the value of the hotel in their assets.

DAY: That's right, we did try that. We tried everything we could because we lacked cash.

We also lacked a board that could raise cash. It was a board that was made up very heavily of school superintendents, librarians, and museum directors. So it was apparent from the outset what my principal problem would be: how to put enough assets together, how to even put a board together that could raise the assets to get the station on the air.

~

Again the name of Roy Sorenson is mentioned. Just as he was needed earlier to bring school superintendents together, he became advisor to Day on how to put together a board that could and would raise funds.

Jon Rice also recalled Sorenson in this context.

RICE: One of the statements by Sorenson was, "A board member has to *give, get,* or *get out.*" It's a terribly important phrase. [3]

Sorenson pointed out to the rest of us that we had a board made up of people who had either never had to raise funds, like a school superintendent, or people who were spending all of their time raising funds for their own institution—the symphony, or the Academy of Science, but in neither case were their energies or skills or dedication left over for us.

DAY: It was my good fortune that Roy was still alive then and able to help.

He said, "We're going to have to find some people." And he said, "Mortimer Fleischhacker is a leader in this community, the son of a very prominent banker and philanthropist."

---

[3] This advice has also been attributed to others, including Henry Heald, prominent educator and for a time, the president of The Ford Foundation.

We went to Morty Fleischhacker and talked with him, the two of us, and Morty did the predictable thing. "Don't think I want to come on this board and be responsible for raising this money without any help on that board. I don't think I can do it."

And Roy very astutely said, "Morty, if we get five others to come on, will you do it?" And he got a conditional yes. It was one of the smartest moves I've ever seen done in this kind of thing.

~

Five others with fund-raising experience and considerable influence in the community ultimately were recruited, and they—along with Mortimer Fleischhacker—substantially strengthened the capabilities of the KQED board.

Mortimer Fleischhacker Becomes Board Chairman

DAY: Fleischhacker eventually became chairman of that board, a post he held for many years, during which he served a term or two on the board of National Educational Television, the predecessor of PBS. KQED became one of his favorite community interests.

Morty, I think, always felt a little uncomfortable with the educators. He always felt a little uncomfortable with me, I think. I never quite understood why.

And I always felt a little uncomfortable with him, possibly because—as with Ralph Lowell, and the others—the name kind of put you off: the Fleischhacker name, the Fleischhacker Zoo, the Fleischhacker Pool, and so forth.

We were, in a sense, both beginning. He was beginning some of his major roles in civic service in San Francisco, and in a sense, chose KQED as the main one. We were fortunate in that way. Our relationship was always, I think, a good one, even though as I say, we stood maybe in awe of each other.

~

Not long after Day and Rice got together, Jim's former secretary at the Asia Foundation, Ruth Lane, joined them. In addition to her skills in communication, she was a dancer, and also served as music selector for the station for years thereafter.

The fourth employee was Richard O. Moore. In time, Moore produced many superb series for the Educational Television and Radio Center and for NET as well as for KQED locally. Later he served for a time as president of the station.

DAY: Dick, along with Lewis Hill, had founded Pacifica and was manager of KPFA before coming to KQED. I needed someone who understood the membership process, and I hired Dick as our membership director.

Dick had by far the best voice, he had been one of the voices on KPFA, and Dick became our announcer. He set a style which was followed for many, many years, a kind of dignified relaxation, easy going, but you always had the feeling that there was a good deal more behind what Dick was saying.

Dick wasn't satisfied simply to be membership director, and he began to investigate programming.

Fairly early on, he became our director of special projects, and the one that supervised the production of those things we did for the Center.

RICE: The first set of "golden days" at KQED were those first years when we had less then ten employees, [including] Marianne Goldman, Jerry Marens, Liz Heller.

We were not paying well, but there were enormous challenges, and enormous freedom.

~

Both Rice and Day had stories to tell about KQED's earliest equipment. Although interviewed separately, (Rice on April 27, 1981 in San Francisco, Day on October 8, 1981, New York City) their comments fit together as if the dialogue had been planned in advance.

RICE: An arrangement had been made before Jim and I came here with Channel 5, which was KPIX. They had a transmitter on top of the Mark Hopkins Hotel.

DAY: KPIX was the first television station on the air in San Francisco, and like so many early stations, took the first site available. As television grew older and more sophisticated after two or three years, they recognized that the Mark Hopkins Hotel was not going to be high enough, so KPIX moved to a mountain, Twin Peaks. They bought a new transmitter for the mountain site.

It would have been very, very costly to remove their transmitter from the Mark Hopkins Hotel. They would have had to remove bricks from the walls and drop it down the side. It was on the floor above the famous bar.

RICE: They had offered to change that Channel 5 transmitter to Channel 9 and to give it to us at no cost if we paid $50,000 to make the changes, a very heavy log around our neck.

DAY: I always said that I thought it was a very good business deal for both of us. They got rid of the expense of getting rid of the transmitter by giving it to us, and we assumed that expense.

RICE: When we eventually had to move from the Mark Hopkins because it wasn't a good location, it was a major problem for us.

It was almost a disastrous problem, because as the people were taking the tower apart to lower it down the outside of the Mark Hopkins, the tower caught fire, and there were workmen above the fire on the tower. But they put out the fire. We got the equipment down.

The Most Modest of Beginnings

KQED went on the air on June 10, 1954, with a series of previews and a hand-printed scroll which took advantage of Jon Rice's headline-writing ability.

RICE: This scroll was half an hour long and it had to be in very short paragraphs so that it could be read in the very primitive television of those days. There was a maximum of about twenty characters to a line, maybe fifteen, and it went on for several hundred lines, so writing that was really wild.

DAY: In the beginning we had no studios so it was all on film, except for one live program which was me, asking for money, until the audience wrote in and said, "That doesn't make a very exciting show."

The first time we did it from the transmitter on top of the Mark Hopkins Hotel. We borrowed an industrial camera, and we may very well have used the transmitter engineer as the camera person, because I don't recall that we had any engineering staff in those days.

In order to get me in the frame, he had to back up into the men's room of the transmitter house!

RICE: That was "the pink room," which had been a bathroom above the Top of the Mark. Jim did our first series from there: "Kalaidescope," which was KQED's first and longest-running show.

DAY: I guess I said, "Look, folks, I know this isn't very interesting, but if you send money we can put some programs on the air."

Then I began interviewing my friends. After several weeks of this, Jon Rice decided maybe I could use some help—I was running out of friends very quickly—and he assigned his secretary to be my producer. From then on, she went out and sought guests, and that show went on for fifteen years on Monday nights.

I've often said to my students that there's no better way to sustain a show than to be the manager of the station when they can't take you off the air.

Seriously, I do believe that in public television the management ought to be visible. It ought to have a relationship with the audience and not be anonymous, as it is so frequently in commercial TV. I think it was more than a rationalization for keeping my show on the air; I think I really believed that.

~

This Monday night series proved Day to be a skillful interviewer, and Jon Rice's secretary, Win Schmale Murphy, proved to

**James Day and
Eleanor Roosevelt**

be gifted with a sort of sixth sense when it came to finding guests. "Kaleidoscope" brought the small but growing KQED audience in the Bay Area informal chats with well-known persons—Arnold Toynbee, Buster Keaton, Edward Teller, Eleanor Roosevelt.

DAY: My interviewing technique was to sit face to face so I could look into the person's eyes, and I found I was touching Eleanor Roosevelt's knees, and that was a sensation I will never forget.

~

But it also was a spot in the schedule where gambles were taken that boomed into sensational success stories.

RICE: We had a guest on Jim Day's program called T. Mikami. He was a Japanese brush painter, a most interesting gentleman, with an accent, but he was a great teacher.

Now, no program manager in his right mind in those days would have started a series on Japanese Brush Painting, except that Win Schmale Murphy came to me and said, "This guy is great. We really ought to think about it."

DAY: I said, "You know, Win, I lived in Japan for two years and I don't care about Japanese brush painting, and I can't believe that there's any kind of an audience for this sort of thing."

We did the show, mostly characterized by his inability to understand my questions and my inability to understand his answers.

When I finished, she came to me and said, "Gee, that would make a great series."

And I said, "You must be out of your mind. Why would it make a great series?"

And she said, "Because he's cute."

RICE: I had just been arguing with somebody about numbered oil painting, in which blue was number twenty-seven or something, and I saw in this demon-

stration that his Japanese horse had ten strokes—no more, no less. I watched this thing, and I did something that looked like a horse— which I've never been able to do before or since— with ten strokes! Now, my horse didn't look like his horse, but it wasn't much worse.

And I thought, "Ah ha, this is a great improvement over painting by numbers, but has some of the same factors of ease and continuity." So we did Japanese brush painting, and we offered Japanese brush painting kits with some special stone and solid ink and a special brush for $3.50 each.

At the bottom of his column the day before it started, Terence O'Flaherty in the San Francisco Chronicle said something like "If you want to see a really far-out show, look at 'Japanese Brush Painting.'"

We sold seven hundred Japanese brush painting kits after that one show.

DAY: No one had checked to see how many brush painting kits were available. When the orders came in, the number exceeded the supply of brush painting kits in San Francisco, and we were obligated to deliver them, and the ones we needed were in Tokyo.

So Jon, in his characteristic way, got on the telephone and persuaded an airline to fly the brush painting kits to San Francisco from Tokyo in time for our audience, and at no charge because we were obligated to sell them at the price we quoted and we couldn't have shipped them and done that.

James Day with Japanese brush painter T. Mikami

Leo Lichtman photo

Very soon thereafter, the series began to be distributed nationally. We went in the brush painting kit business, began to have our own packaging printed with KQED on it, and so forth.

I was never closely involved in this. Most of the staff was, because there came periods when most of the staff was packing these things!

RICE: Actually we sold forty or fifty thousand for about three times what they cost—which was another source of income. I think that three or 400,000 were sold nationally, perhaps more.

~

The station acquired temporary studios at the John O'Connell Trade School, where Kenneth Neilson was training student engineers. The first schedule was just two days a week, all film or kinescope from "The Center" (ETRC) in Ann Arbor, Michigan, which was just barely getting into operation.

In addition to the poor technical quality offered by kinescope recordings (TV images recorded on motion picture film), the programs themselves often left much to be desired despite their substance. Occasionally, they were unintentionally amusing.

RICE: One of my favorite early-day stories concerns a program on child psychology from the University of Michigan, taught by a Dr. Olson. One of the things that Dr. Olson was always pushing was for freedom for the child to learn creativity.

One day he's talking about creativity, and he has two little children, a boy and a girl. He puts them at easels, and he goes off to the ever-present blackboard to lecture.

After a minute, the little girl comes up to ask him a question. And he doesn't want to answer so he says, "No"—which you could see on camera—and she asks again, and he says "No, go back to your desk," and she goes for a few minutes.

She comes back again, and this time he says *"No!"* and you see his hand going up like this [GESTURES] and you hear a thump! The show goes on, and she doesn't come back, and she fortunately doesn't cry! You can't see anything but the hand; you don't see her falling on her ass. [LAUGHTER]

So, all two of our viewers complained about this treatment, and I complained to Lyle Nelson [of the Center], whom I hadn't yet met but with whom I was having a superb and humorous correspondence. He allowed as how this was not really very good education, but shrugged his shoulders.

The following Christmas I got a very large portrait of Dr. Olson, all framed in glass, saying "To my greatest admirer, thank you," and signed by him!

Nelson had told him that I was such an admirer. [LAUGHTER]

Really? Egg Crate Liner Acoustics?

Not only were the programs primitive—despite the significant participants and subject matter—the studios were likewise. The plant in which KQED operated after a year or so at the O'Connell Trade School was said to have egg crate liners on its walls as acoustical treatment.

RICE: It was an absolute fact. I promoted the egg crates free from various restaurants which served a lot of eggs. [CHUCKLE]

We hand dipped them and glued them onto the walls. Egg crates, yeah. They are really trays, you know. They're in some sort of a box that doesn't have sides. It's like an egg box but it's a tray that holds a dozen, six by six, sort of like papier-mache. And it makes very good soundproofing, but it's very hard to make glue stick because the stuff's so weak the glue simply tears off.

~

Out of studios such as this, though with improved equipment after a few years, came programs by Edward Teller, Linus Pauling, the Griller Quartet, Eric Hoffer, Glen Seaborg, John Dodds, S.I. Hayakawa, to name only a few. All of these subsequently were distributed to other ETV stations.

Locally, Pontiac auto dealer Roger Boas learned how to be an excellent moderator on "Profile Bay Area," which became an on-the-air civic forum. Boas had to relinquish his role when he ran for political office, but eventually he became chief administrative officer in San Francisco. His place on "Profile" was taken by a then-young Republican attorney by the name of Casper Weinberger, who served as Ronald Reagan's financial officer when Reagan was governor of California. Weinberger became secretary of Health Education and Welfare under President Reagan, then served as chief of the federal Bureau of the Budget, and subsequently was named secretary of Defense.

Even so, the station faltered a year after going on the air.

The Board Decides to Give Up!

A crisis developed in the board—which led to further initiatives on the part of both Day and Rice that were eventually to have their effect on all of public television during the years immediately following.

RICE: We were winning brownie points, and we were winning audience, and life was going very well—except that we were broke, and our board of directors decided that we had to go off the air. They didn't see how they could make it work. We had no state money for many, many years, no education money, no federal money either, no tax money of any sort.

DAY: I have forgotten the precise figures, but we were in debt by about $8,000.

It was costing us about $10,000 a month to operate at that point. The board concluded that if we kept going we'd be further and further in debt with no prospect of getting out. So they decided that the only solution was to give up, raise the money to pay off the eight thousand dollar indebtedness and go out of business.

I argued that on the grounds we had some membership support and we would lose even that, we would lose the continuity we had built up, and so forth.

We finally compromised. They agreed to raise the $8,000 provided I raised the ten thousand for the month of June.

This happened in May of 1955, so the month of June we could have four more weeks of life, in which we promised to raise $60,000 which would carry us for six more months. And in that six months, they would organize a blue-ribbon committee to see whether we were economically viable or not. The games we play!

So, in order to raise the ten thousand for June, I had to borrow money. Jon says I borrowed from his mother. He's probably right.

RICE: We borrowed ten thousand from my mother, and [one thousand] from the mother of Liz Heller, who was on the staff, and that was enough to keep us going for those two weeks.

DAY: I also borrowed five thousand from Bob Mullen in Washington[4] which I never called for, but I got Bob to pledge five thousand in case I needed it.

We tried everything we could conceive of to raise that ten thousand. We had a mobile unit, which wasn't serving us very well as a mobile

---

[4] Bob Mullen was head of the National Citizens' Committee for Educational Television, funded by the Fund for Adult Education to assist major cities in activating stations.

unit. Every station has to have a mobile unit with its logo on the side; we got one and couldn't afford to operate it.

When the crisis came, we put it on the street and KGO supplied a small musical group that sat on the roof of the mobile unit and played, and the Junior Chamber of Commerce walked up and down Montgomery Street, the financial district, with tin cups, collecting money. It didn't prove to be very lucrative.

We hired a public relations firm: Gross and Roberts. Leonard Gross was the man I had replaced at NBC so we had been friends over the years. Curtis Roberts I had known less well.

RICE: And with Gross and Roberts, we started an all-out campaign for $65,000 which would get us through that calendar year—in those nice, cheap years!

~

It was in the midst of all this feverish activity that the idea of a fund raising auction was first suggested.

The Birth of the ETV Auction

DAY: Gross and Roberts—essentially Curtis Roberts—had seen this done, I believe, on radio in the San Joaquin Valley for a charitable organization. He thought if it can be done on radio, it can be done on television, and so he told us how we could pull this off. Jon Rice organized it. We ran out of goods before the show ended. We had to solicit merchandise while we were still on the air.

RICE: The biggest single item was an RCA oven, which they then made, a stove oven. The head of the RCA distributor had seen the program, woke up his warehouse in the middle of the night, got 'em to bring it down to us to sell, and it sold for four or five hundred dollars.

The first item we sold was a ham radio, which sold for twice its value.

We called the winning people to arrange delivery, and they said, "Auction? What auction?"

So the auction idea was not mine. I am called the "father of auctions" because I did, over the years, learn how to make it work.

The first one was part of that crisis drive. The crisis drive was absolutely heart-warming. Two things I remember. One was a woman who came down and gave me a check for $15 which she had been saving up for a warm coat. And the other was a kid who came down with his mother with a piggy bank, which they broke on my desk. And it was $2.75, or whatever.

DAY: That, plus the audience, people coming in with hero sandwiches to feed us, is what fed us for years to come, that community response, the feeling that people were out there, that they cared, they wanted to be a part of it, they wanted to play the game with you, is one of the reason the auction continued. It wasn't the money, because the money wasn't that great.

RICE: Our drive was finally topped off by the phenomenal promise of a local foundation, saying if we got $60,000 they would give us the final five thousand and we got sixty-one thousand and they gave us the final five thousand, and KQED was back on the air.

And KQED had established a rapport with the community that was absolutely invaluable! There was never any real comparison by any other station in the country with that, because we had gotten so much publicity and made so much noise in that drive for existence.

~

One of the more amusing sidebar stories of KQED's subsequent auctions developed some years later. It is indicative of the pure fun which KQED viewers enjoyed as auction time came around—at least in earlier years.

DAY: Actress Kim Novak had come to San Francisco, I presume to promote one of her films, and she stayed at The Clift Hotel.

She was in her lavender period where she dressed in lavender, and she insisted that The Clift Hotel buy lavender sheets for her and they did. When she left, The Clift Hotel, having no use for them, gave them to the Junior Chamber of Commerce. Fortunately the Junior Chamber of Commerce remembered our auction and gave them to us. Also I suppose one could say in poor taste, it was also fortunate that they were unlaundered; this made them more valuable for some strange reason.

They were auctioned off, and a young man who had volunteered his services—we didn't know him at the time—had volunteered to work on the floor, and we put him back in the stock room. He came, I guess, to Jon Rice and said, "Even though I am here physically, is it all right if I bid on these sheets?" And Jon said, "So long as the telephone audience has a crack at it, why, yes, you may bid."

He did bid, and my recollection is that he made the winning bid of $250.

The man's name was originally Ernest Beal. He had been a promotion manager for Columbia Records. At this point he had begun a necktie business and was more or less just starting it.

He took the sheets back to his shop that night, made neckties from the sheets he had bought, and donated the neckties to us. Of course, we relished this and went on the air selling Kim Novak neckties to the highest bidder. It was a good enough story to have made a number of newspapers.[5]

It also *made* Mr. Ernest Beal, who by then changed his name to Beal Ernst. His tie company was the Ernst Tie Company, and the publicity that came out of this did a great deal to launch him in his tie-manufacturing career. He became the fourth largest tie manufacturer in America.

~

Day gives Jon Rice credit for the popularity of the auction telecasts.

DAY: Jon had a kind of wild abandon about him that helped that auction enormously.

Now they're programmed by computer. It's a matter of how much you can sell each minute, and for very good reasons.

But they've lost the ingenuous quality that was so attractive in those early years when the audience tuned in partly out of desire to get a bargain, but most of them tuned in because it was one of the few live television programs left on the air where anything could happen and frequently did.

It was a great show until it got predictable.

Good People, Great Freedom, Low Cost

Three factors helped to make KQED interesting in its early years—not counting that it occurred in San Francisco, a city which perhaps was more ready for this sort of a station than any other American city.

First: Day and Rice attracted excellent people. Second: they allowed them maximum freedom. Third: costs were low.

DAY: We were willing to let them take risks with us, which I think is not the case today. We were sought out by highly creative people who wanted to do their thing. We said, "Okay, go ahead and do it, it isn't going to cost too much."

There is one major difference in those days and these days. It was cheaper for us to do a live show than it was to buy something from outside, and that has changed. The costs have skyrocketed. There are many, many instances—

---

[5] According to Bill Griffiths, vice president of the Fund for Adult Education, who bought one of the ties and wore it for years, it was embroidered, "Kim Novak slept here."

[6] Day cited Children's Television Workshop and its production of "Sesame Street" as an exception which has demonstrated the value of spending considerable sums to achieve quality.

not all—where the programming costs have gotten out of hand. More money does not always make a better program. There are programs today that I think are costing more than they need to cost, and they're not providing better television in proportion to the cost of the show.[6]

RICE: We had people to whom we gave enormous freedom. At various times, almost half of our staff had come to us first as volunteers.

Virginia Duncan came to us as a Junior League candidate who said she was willing to sweep floors, and I didn't believe it. She came in in jeans and she swept floors.

We were able to let people like Win Murphy [Rice's secretary] start to produce and direct because stakes were not too heinous and costs were not too high.

Sometimes I think I'm an old man crying for the past, but then I look at the figures and I'm not. Television inflation, I think—and I've had nobody really successfully argue with me—since 1954 or '55 is between eighty and 100 times.

One funny example. One of our longtime successes was "The Scotch Gardener," a lovely heavy-drinking Scotsman named Jim Kerr, who would come in with his truck loaded with enough plants to do two shows. The producer, who had to line up floor men, an assistant director, volunteers, and so forth, helped him set up the show. Then five engineers would be assigned to it, and the producer was also the director. Six people would do two half-hour shows in an hour and a half.

Now, we didn't keep any kind of good records, but the best I can figure, knowing everybody's salaries and looking at our budget in those days, is that each show cost $350.

We taped a one-camera, out-of-the-studio, local gardening show last year (1980) and its cost was $27,500 per half hour!

Now, that means you can't use inexperienced people. You can't afford mistakes.

You can't risk having happen to me one of my favorite defeats, which was putting on a memory expert whom we took off the air after the second show because he couldn't remember his lines! [LAUGHTER]

We could easily afford mistakes, and we could easily correct things, and so we could do the sort of things like trying Japanese brush painting and not have it come as a disaster. We could afford to take gambles, partly because the real money we were "wasting" was *not* $27,500.

~

A further factor which made the early years of KQED what they were was the unique combination of Day and Rice, with their respective capabilities and philoso-

phies. While there were many other station heads who achieved similar success under equally difficult circumstances, present-day executives might learn much from examining this unique pair.

Day recalled a conversation on this topic which occurred between him and the then-chairman of the KQED board several years after Day had left San Francisco for New York. [7]

DAY: He began to probe. What was this peculiar era that he keeps hearing about when I was out there?

He had heard that I was a programming genius, and I said, "Does that imply that I thought up the programs?" And he said, "Yes." And I said, "Well, I can certainly argue against that. I did not. Jon thought up so many of the programs."

As we talked, he concluded—not I—that it was the relationship between Jon and myself that was the basis for the success we enjoyed. And he described that relationship, that I gave Jon fairly free rein in what he did and backed him up in what he did. Jon was the editor and I supplied him with what he needed. That's one idea.

We're quite different kinds of people. One of the things that always amused me about our difference is that when in a technical sense things got all fouled up, a program had to be put together at the last minute, an important element fell through, I would have gone totally to pieces. Jon could have three telephones going at the same time and put it all back together. He had been trained in news; he was a genius at handling those kinds of crises.

But where matters of principle were involved, Jon would go all to pieces and *I* would calm down. If it was a matter of whether we ought to do this or not do it on the basis of the First Amendment, I find myself completely at home there.

Jon would rush to me in certain circumstances and I would rush to him in other circumstances.

On the other hand, we generally agreed upon the direction in which we were going, and I felt it was my obligation and my responsibility to set that direction and say, "Jon, this is what I want KQED to be. You tell me how to do it because I don't know." And so we discussed programming

---

[7] In the mid-seventies, Day was asked to become the head of National Educational Television (NET) in New York, which subsequently merged with WNET, the New York public television station.

that would put us on the road in that direction. And with that, I always gave him a free hand and supported him in what he did.

~

One element of inestimable importance was Day's talent for interpreting the station to its community, both on the air and before groups, including numerous clubs and organizations.

DAY: Yes, at times it was terribly boring. The food was awful; sometimes the audiences were awful.

I've always complained that I would never make a salesman, and yet I love selling an idea. I think I relished going out and selling an idea.

RICE: Jim made a speech to the Junior League, which took a great deal of pull to set up. The Junior League and other people in San Francisco thought the whole idea of ETV was communistic, certainly socialistic. It was not a popular idea. And Jim, with his sense of humor and his wisdom and his skill at public speaking changed the direction of the Junior League in one speech, so that they became very strong supporters of the station.

One of his great lines—in those days of "I Love Lucy"—was that KQED stood for "I love lucidity!"

Jim became "Mr. KQED" to such an extent that this gentleman who was just on the phone and who knew of my association called me "Jim."

It still happens to me periodically. I was "Jim Rice." This is the fascinating thing, that anyone should be that well identified.

He was superb with groups and I was good with individuals. We both rounded off a little so that we could do some of the other thing.

Jim really hated to make decisions. I'm a very impatient type and I hate un-made decisions. With only one of us at the helm, there would have been disaster with un-made or too-quickly-made decisions. Together it was really elegant. We balanced each other in a marvelous way.

Jim was always much more farsighted and much more philosophical. He was much deeper. He examined the why of things much more deeply than I. My skill was in solving a problem and getting something done, with no money and no time, that had impact and a sense of quality.

We were both father figures in a very different way, although one thing had always pleased me. Shortly after we were hired, one of the local newspapers had a story on us, and it said, "Two ruddy, balding, horn-rimmed-glasses-wearing, slightly paunchy five-feet-ten men." We were described exactly alike.

KQED's Jim Day (center) and Jonathan Rice (seated) along with an unidentified cameraman on San Francisco cable car tracks.

Two Different Men
With the Same Dream

From their interview comments, it became clear that the two men, despite personality differences, shared the same dream for their station.

RICE: My real dream for KQED was that we would become what the nation lost when it could no longer have town meetings, that we could be the town meeting for an urban center of enormous size.

DAY: I believe, and so did Jon, in the role that KQED should play in the community. It should be an organic part of the community. It should reflect it, and I suppose in certain cases maybe even give it some sense of the options open to it for future directions.

While space does not allow for even a listing of the constant outpouring of "public affairs programs" which KQED offered, the record shows that the station never backed away from controversy.

DAY: Controversy is an essential path to the truth. You have to have this interplay of ideas to discover the truth. And since there is no truth handed down to you, there's a certain risk in allowing various voices to speak out. Because when they do, you know you're going to get lots of flack from those who don't agree. So I do believe in the First Amendment and the principle of a multiplicity of voices.

~

Both men acknowledged that controversial programming requires a certain amount of courage as well as good judgment. In this respect as in so many others, Day and Rice seem to have complemented each other.

RICE: Our courages were different. He was bravest when he was angry, and I was bravest before I got angry.

~

Did either Day or Rice feel that controversial programming affected community support, either adversely or positively?

RICE: I think, generally speaking, we made more by being brave and honest than we lost. We gained more membership impact and audience support.

I'm glad that we *were* brave, to the extent that it was brave. I like to think of it as being rational. There are places where you really don't know which one you are being. You really don't know until after it's over.

DAY: Certainly in the years I was there I would have to say it was a constructive element in our support, for the simple reason that the one thing we had most to fear was indifference.

We put these highly controversial things on the air, we got a lot of adverse mail, but we also got a lot of checks. And the checks came from people who, in effect, were saying, "I never expected to see this on any television station." So it was almost the element of surprise that provoked the response.

I discovered early on that simply being in favor of educational television was not sufficient motivation to send money. It took more than that. It took that surprise.

It may not have been controversy. It may have been Frank Baxter [who taught Shakespeare on TV] saying, "Wow! That's exciting!" But it took a provocation, not simply general approval, to get that money. And controversy was an element in that, and I do think it was a positive response. Of course we had cases where we had some difficulty, to be sure, but overall it was positive.

It has become a different kind of game for those that followed us. I suppose they would regard it as a game of survival—which is pretty funny, too, since *we* just barely hung on.

~

So did others in other communities. Next to money, the prime need of these early stations was programming. The visionaries of public television saw the need for a national program service—the predecessor of PBS.

17

The Birth of
the First National Program Service

Seeing the sleek and smartly designed contemporary logo of PBS at the end of national programming today, one might never guess how uncertain and primitive were the first days of what now has become a staple of American television. In forty years, a lot has happened.

As the first ETV stations began to go on the air, the obvious and overriding need was for programming. Even among commercial broadcasters in the fifties, no one expected any individual station to generate all of its own programs. Commercially, there were the networks with their seemingly vast resources to which local management could turn. But in educational television, aside from free films, there was little or nothing.

The visionaries for public television realized this need from the start. Each local station dreamed of spectacular and significant programming to come from the capitals of culture to augment and to headline the local station's offerings, which at best could be only modest.

Establishment of a national program center was one of the three stated objectives of C. Scott Fletcher and the Fund for Adult Education as they worked at reservation of channels and establishment of stations.

FLETCHER: My experience in all other activities, both business and non-profit organizations—particularly my activities with Encyclopedia Britannica Films—told me that we would have to have a national center which would produce and exchange programs for ETV stations, similar to the old bicycle-type distribution plan that was originally financed by another foundation to help NAEB in distributing radio tapes. The question was how much when.

~

The records show, however, that even before the Fund for Adult Education had come into being and prior to the conference at Penn State, Raymond Wittcoff in St. Louis had been energized to pursue this idea by George Probst of the University of Chicago.

Wittcoff persuaded the mayor of St. Louis, Joseph Darst, to send letters of invitation to mayors all over the country to come to St. Louis to talk about educational television.

WITTCOFF: I think it was in January of 1952 we had a one-day meeting that was attended by some seventy people who came to our city hall from twenty-eight cities from coast to coast. At that meeting we discovered that we were standing on common ground. We were saying the same thing in the same way, and we came up with the statement that there ought to be a national program service, a national network.

We did not see it as having live connections at that time, though we hoped that one day there could be, but then we were thinking of it principally as a source for programs that would come through on kinescope. This was even before tape.

We rejected the notion of a mere exchange center. This was discussed thoroughly at the meeting, and it was stated as a principle that this should have as *one* function to arrange for stations to exchange the things they produced on kinescopes, but we went beyond that and said that for this to work it would have to be an institution with the resources to create and arrange for the creation of *great* programming.

~

Fletcher and his staff associates asked Bob Hudson to prepare a memorandum indicating the proper nature of such a center.

HUDSON: My family and I were going to vacation on Nantucket in that summer of '52, so we were there for about a month. And while there, I drew up plans for what then became the Educational Television and Radio Center.

The memorandum of November of '52 included sections on administrative policies, program procurement, production, budgets, standards, scheduling of re-runs, distribution, promotion and P.R., research and evaluation, staff structure, space needs, legal questions, relations with other organizations, and the need for outside support. So it kind of covered the waterfront.

~

The third draft of that plan—the result of the efforts of Hudson, Bill Griffiths, and Ann Spinney of FAE and suggestions from numerous outsiders experienced in either education or television—was presented to the FAE board at its next meeting with a request for $3 million.

FLETCHER: The understanding was that the program center would not have funds to buy equipment or for the production of programs themselves, but would use their money for securing programs from other sources—preferably stations—and also from commercial film producers who would follow scripts written by educators in our field who were competent to prepare such scripts.

HUDSON: Fletcher was most adamant on the point that it should have no studios. I think he had been at Encyclopedia Britannica Films long enough to know that a studio tends to condition what happens. Things have to fit that form rather than going out and making your equipment and your staff meet the situations as they are. So he didn't want to get a studio that had to be the dominant central place for all ETV. He wanted it much broader than that.

FLETCHER: I had been questioned by many people about the wisdom of not allowing the center to produce its own programs with its own studio and equipment. My answer was an emphatic "no" to myself, and emphatic "no" to the staff when they asked similar questions, and an emphatic "no" to the board of directors when they asked the same question. I told them that the philosophy of a foundation is basically to invest money as risk capital for experiments which might turn out to be fruitful for the entire population. I doubted very much whether the trustees of the Ford Foundation, who had to approve all our requests for money for whatever project it was, would be likely to approve the expense of setting up a producing organization. Rather, we set up plans for helping to bring into being programs which were then available to

stations, and as other stations produced programs, these were taken to the center and exchanged with other stations. It would be a very small operation in order to at least start things moving.

Our board eventually concluded that it would be comparatively easy for a small program center to make contracts with regular motion picture studios and with the early ETV stations on the air to produce programs which could then be circulated. Obviously the scripts would be written by appropriate people in the center or in the stations, approved by the center executives, and then produced and distributed.

At the same time, we agreed to consider making additional funds available to the center when we had more experience, which would take several years.

The FAE board, after a whole day's discussion, approved the project. But the one question was, "Would it be enough?" Paul Helms, who was then chairman of the board, felt that we should ask for more to begin with, and if the Ford Foundation trustees wished to cut the amount, it would be their prerogative. So we decided to ask for three million.

Three Million for Three Years

Fletcher and Helms took their proposal to a meeting of the board of trustees of the Ford Foundation, answering many questions, pointing out that the amount of three million was really not very much, and that in two years' time they would have a good idea of where other funds might come from as well.

FLETCHER: We particularly thought of corporations which could use precise wording [i.e., on-the-air credits] as approved by the Federal Communications Commission. This would not be classified as advertising but just a recognition of the fact that funds for this program were supplied by that corporation. This procedure worked better than I expected.

~

It may come as a surprise to some that the notion of on-air-credit for furnishing program costs was in the minds of those early planners back in 1952. FAE Vice President Bill Griffiths also recalled this.

GRIFFITHS: It was always known that the center had to be a much bigger and broader thing than an institution such as the fund could properly provide for.

In the very earliest by-laws, one of the aims was enunciated, I think, with the indication that it had to reach out and tap institutional sponsorship on the part of American corporations. And every time I see the credits to Mobil, or Exxon, or IBM, or whatnot, I say, "Ah, there we go!"

Maybe that's coming with too high a price. I don't know.

~

The Ford Foundation trustees approved the FAE's request for three million to finance the Educational Television and Radio Center, the first agency ever to try to bring into being a "national program service" for noncommercial television stations and their viewers.

Even so, according to Scott Fletcher, the hand of Henry Ford II almost torpedoed the entire project.

Henry Ford II
Almost Kills the Whole Project

Most of the this story has been untold all these years. The following is a verbatim transcript of Fletcher's account of what happened following that meeting of the Ford Foundation trustees.

FLETCHER: A few days later, I received a telephone call from one of the senior staff members of the Ford Foundation, who told me that Henry Ford wished to abstain from voting on that project until he had a talk with me.

He said, "Mr. Ford wants to see you next Sunday morning with his brother, Benson Ford, at White Sulphur Springs, where he and his family will be taking a long weekend vacation."

~

Fletcher managed to arrange for a chartered plane to fly him from an engagement in Atlantic City on Saturday to White Sulphur Springs for the Sunday morning appointment.

FLETCHER: I arrived at the hotel on Sunday morning. I called for Henry Ford, who asked me to come up to their suite at ten o'clock.

The first thing he said was that he did not remember my making a recommendation to the board of trustees for $3 million to start a new program exchange center for educational television.

I explained to him that our chairman, Paul Helms, and I had done so, and that since he had left the room for some time, maybe he hadn't heard the report. He indicated that regardless of

whether he had heard it or not, he had learned of it second hand and he thought we were risking too much money in this enterprise.

I went into a reasonably long explanation.

Up to this time, Benson Ford hadn't said a word. He was a very quiet man, but I wondered why he didn't say anything.

Once again, as happened at the board meeting, Henry Ford had to take a long distance call and left for a little while, during which time Benson and I chatted. At one point he said to me, "When Henry comes back, I'll tell him that he was out of the room when most of the report was given, that I was in favor of it and so were the trustees."

When Henry Ford returned, I continued, as he indicated I should. He had many questions, and I explained to him that really when everything was taken into consideration, $3 million was not very much for the Ford Foundation, which had been hounded by the Internal Revenue Service to get rid of their dollars a little faster than they were doing, and that I thought this would help them get along with their problem. He didn't seem to think that was necessary, but nevertheless I emphasized it.

He said, "Well, I don't know why I can't remember it, but I've been told it and I just want you to explain these things to me." Which I did.

Benson still had said nothing.

After some long questions from Ford and my answers, I said, "Well, this is what we recommended, our board has approved it, I understand that the board of trustees of the Ford Foundation approved it, but there were two votes and yours was one which was to hold before voting."

Henry said, "Well, I just don't remember it." At which point Benson said all he said during the whole interview. What he said was, "Well, Henry, I remember every word that Scotty said. I'm positive that you left the room for a long distance telephone call. I don't know how long you were out but it seemed to be quite a while, and when you returned the board in effect had approved. Evidently you decided to withdraw or to make no vote."

Henry Ford then said he'd like to talk to Benson in private for awhile. They left the room, and I was frankly quite nervous.

When they returned, Henry Ford said, "Okay, I will vote for it, but I will vote for it reluctantly. And before too long I'd like to have a further talk with you about this entire matter."

I said, "Are there any other questions?" They said, "No." I decided at that moment the best thing was silence, so I thanked them and bade them adieu, and went back to the pilot, who flew me back to Atlantic City.

About three weeks later, I received a call from Henry Ford's secretary. She asked me if I would please make a date to see him at his New York office during the next week when he would be in the city. We met, and the subject was educational television.

Henry Ford was very quick in coming to what was on his mind. He wanted me to know that he was not happy about the tremendous amounts of money which were being put into the development of educational television in all its various forms. Although he felt we were making great progress, he was worried about how many more millions of dollars would have to be spent in the next several years.

I said, "Well, I don't know, because I can't tell you at the present time how many other sources of income will be forthcoming as a result of the establishment of the program center."

I said, "We've settled the final amount of money for stations. We've settled the final amount of money for other organizations. They're terminal grants for JCET and the National Citizens Committee for Educational Television. We don't have to ask for any more funds for stations. But we do have to have programming. Without programming the whole of the expenditures to date will be ill-spent."

He then asked me if I would consider giving up this whole idea of educational television if he could persuade me to take another position. For example, if he would be willing to consider buying a commercial television station and giving me the position of president with a contract which would keep me in that position until I retired, would I be interested?

This was a complete surprise to me. I was somewhat bewildered, but I knew that I had to give him the facts that were deep inside me.

My reply was, "Henry, I have dedicated myself to advance educational television. I am deeply interested in fostering and spreading liberal adult education by means of educational television."

~

Fletcher related in careful detail how he continued this explanation to Henry Ford II, speaking also in his capacity as a board member of the Fund for the Advancement of Education, describing various research projects which he and that board had approved in an effort to determine the value of televised instruction.

FLETCHER: "Furthermore, Henry, I have given my word to the Federal Communications Commission that I will be on hand to supervise the distribution of funds for more stations and also funds for the establishment of a program

and exchange center, and I've made the same promise to the members of the board of directors of the Fund for Adult Education. I would rather resign and not take any position for some time, certainly not with a commercial broadcasting station."

Henry Ford's response was, in effect, that given all of these circumstances he would forget the whole matter, but he wanted me to know how he felt. Even so, he indicated that he would respect my decision in the matter.

At last the meeting wound up and we said good-bye.

Frank Stanton Also Has Doubts

While developing the concept of the Educational Television and Radio Center, Fletcher withstood the friendly scorn of others. He was faced with an attitude difficult to recall now, when public television seems as though it has been with us always. But forty years ago, many thoughtful people had great misgivings about it.

FLETCHER: One of the first persons we talked to was Dr. Frank Stanton, president of CBS in New York. He had luncheon with us.

It was an interesting luncheon because everybody was sort of looking at me and at Bill Griffiths, who was with me, wondering what these two freaks were trying to do to get started with educational television. [CHUCKLE] It was really a very pleasant luncheon. All sorts of subjects were talked about.

Finally Frank Stanton said to me, "Scotty, I don't think you know what you're getting into. Where are you going to get all the money? You know that programs cost money."

I said, "Frank, I've produced programs and I understand what you are saying, but one of these days we may come along and surprise you with some of the programs we secure, first-rate programs that cost us very much less than some of the programs produced by CBS." At which point everybody at the table roared with laughter.[1]

~

Fletcher then took up the task of establishing a wholly new institution in the annals of broadcasting. His FAE board gave him complete authority to select the initial

---

[1] Fifteen years later, in 1967, when the Public Broadcasting Act creating the Corporation for Public Broacasting was passed by the Congress, Stanton immediately sent a congratulatory telegram to CPB with this message: "Under separate cover I'm sending you a check for $1 million. Good luck!"

"organizing board of directors" to consist of five individuals who would select another five.

He chose Ralph Lowell of Boston, partly because of his deep involvement with WGBH; from higher education, George Stoddard of New York University and formerly president of the University of Illinois; Yale law professor Harold Lasswell, with whom he had become well acquainted through their mutual involvement in adult education films; and Dr. Robert Calkins, dean of the School of Business at Columbia University, who later became president of The Brookings Institution in Washington, D.C. The fifth was Scotty himself. [2]

Their first job was to find a president to head the new program center.

FLETCHER: George Stoddard, in his position as chairman of the board, recommended Dr. Harry Newburn, who was then president of the University of Oregon. Stoddard was very strong on this matter because of Newburn's interest in liberal adult education and the liberal arts. As a result, the board said that he should be the first to be contacted.

I decided to make an immediate trip to Oregon and took Bill Griffiths with me. We spent two days there. Both of us were impressed with Newburn and his wife and his operation at the university.

~

At a special FAE board meeting, Fletcher and Griffiths gave a detailed report on their Oregon visit and strongly recommended that Newburn be appointed as soon as possible.

The Choice of Harry Newburn As President

GRIFFITHS: The fact that such a man was chosen, I think, was an indication of the heavy bias toward formal education that this thing still had. Harry, I think, had distinguished himself as an administrator and a man who was going to stand up and be counted vis-a-vis his role in the teacher's oath thing in Oregon, for example, in which he took what we would call today a strong civil rights stand. I think he professed no prior involvement with mass media particularly, but was primarily an administrator.

You see, things happened so hurriedly you just couldn't sit back and relax and take a lot of time with things.

HUDSON: When Stoddard was dean at Iowa, I think Newburn was there in the School of Education. Then Newburn went eventually to become president of the University of Oregon, and Stoddard had more or less kept in touch with him.

I think Newburn was in trouble at Oregon and was maybe looking for a place to go, and Stoddard recommended him, and the other members of the board went along. They thought the university prestige was a good thing to have, and so he came on.

It was, in many respects, a mistake—although there were some good points to it. He did bring academic status and prestige to it, but he knew nothing at all about the broadcasting business. He looked upon it strictly as an instructional device—which is all right for instructional TV, but for our purposes, for broader purposes of NET, which has now become PBS, it was a very narrow view.

Furthermore, he had been presiding over a faculty and staff of a large university and then came into a little organization where he had six people working for him. And he had a big office and a big chair, and nothing really to do. And he didn't do much, if I may say so. He may have thought a whole lot.

SCHOOLEY: I thought that Newburn was a pretty good choice—at that time. I think after I saw him operate in the center that I might have changed my opinion over the years.

BLAKELY: I think Harry Newburn gets a kind of bum rap when people look back and think about this. The first president of the center had to be an educator, he had to be a *university* educator.

Newburn did run it as though it were a university. He was not imaginative. He didn't know anything about broadcasting.

But Harry Newburn was the type that had to be picked, and there's no reason to believe that if you'd picked another university president, he would have done things fundamentally different or any better.

The center did survive, the center did get these programs out to stations, and these stations did stay on the air.

[2] Those five soon added to the board, Raymond Wittcoff of St. Louis, editor/author/lecturer Norman Cousins, Dick Hull for his experience as a leader in NAEB and educational broadcasting in general, also the highly regarded Denver school superintendent Kenneth Oberholtzer, and Dr. Everett Case, president of Colgate University. Eventually, the board grew to fifteen, and through the years included many of the country's most capable and dedicated civic leaders and educators.

And we should add into this, the accident—the automobile accident that occurred when Harry and his wife were on their way from Oregon to Ann Arbor. There was this terrible accident, and he was badly hurt. He didn't get on the job for months and he wasn't himself for a long time. I knew him back at the University of Iowa and I had the impression that Harry really never did recover from this.

~

Others testified too, to what Bill Griffiths called "an instance of terribly unfortunate timing." Fletcher recalled more of the details.

FLETCHER: He had a bad concussion, some brain damage, and was told by doctors that he could not continue with his work at the university, nor should he take the position as president of the new program and exchange center until he had recovered and the doctor had given him a go-ahead.

As a result, I recommended to the board that we proceed as though we had a president. I would continue as acting president and we would start the wheels rolling, because time was running short and the demand for programs in the field was growing every day.

Newburn took much longer to recover than was expected. It really wasn't for about a year that he was able to take over the reins.

HULL: Newburn insisted on Ann Arbor as a condition of the job, almost, as I recall it. His reasons are obvious to me now; he felt familiar in an educational community and he didn't want to be too far if the boat sank. So he kept up his contacts there.

As for the center itself, I considered it *miserably* run. It was as if he continued to behave like a college president who has all his deans and department heads—there isn't any faculty, and no students! He was very formal. The stuff went in the box, out of the box, instead of calling up Bob Hudson and that sort of thing on the phone.

Now, this was an anomaly, because I've been to many parties at Harry's house; he was the best party-giver on earth, you know, and genial, and great!

But I thought he was a stuffed shirt. And clearly he never understood the medium at all, not at all, and he wouldn't sit still for anybody to explain it.

~

Kenneth Christiansen, who had been actively involved with the Southern Regional Education Board in the encouragement of educational television in the South and who had been recruited by Dr. Newburn—perhaps because his background was in education—analyzed Newburn with a sensitivity that came from understanding the painful dilemmas facing the academician in show business.

CHRISTIANSEN: It was very easy, coming out of the experience that I had been through and my own philosophical commitment, to accept Newburn as the right man at the right time and in the right place, what educational television needed, out of the image of what it had been created for. Remember that the educational community created this. It was supposed to be used for informational, educational, and cultural purposes. That was its charter of existence.

This was easily translatable by Newburn because the character of any university is teaching, research, and services. So this whole orientation into what educational television was presumed to be at that point was a natural for Newburn.

He had academic stature in the U.S. There was just no doubt about his credentials. The arena of education was familiar to him. He had professional leadership in the associations, the land-grant group, the whole thing—the people and the circumstances of education, and commitment and philosophy—he understood that very, very well.

But the creative dimensions that had to be a part of programming and programming development—and when you say "creative" you're beginning to think about time and people and money—commitment to that was not easily sold to him.

He could see transmission of individuals as they were, "the talking face," which is very powerful when you get a Bronowski or a Sagan, for instance. And that was his background, you see. When you've got great teachers, you've got great presenters, and they're fascinating to people. But a mass audience is quite different. Mass appeal as a service has to have diversity and variety, and that means things other than "the talking face."

Everything we did in the early days always had its educational dimension. You had to have the educational part of the program and then you had the other part—the performance side. But the cost of that was hard—and still is hard—for educators to imagine.

~

The necessity for developing programs of inherent educational value which also would appeal to a broader audience of television viewers—a struggle which continues today and probably will continue indefinitely—

was also affected by certain basic tenets on which the Fund for Adult Education was based.

BLAKELY: The fund's basic mission was liberal adult education. Therefore, in their grant to the center, two-thirds, I think, [of funds] should be devoted to programming in the areas of economic affairs, political affairs, world affairs, and the humanities.

This put a good deal of bind on the center. But it did, I think, have the salutary effect of keeping the center's eye on the ball of some programming for the general public on important issues, and not have the gravitational pull toward instructional television only, or a great clutter of special interests that you can have, including sports.

~

Griffiths possessed another perspective on early agonies.

GRIFFITHS: In the desperate straits of the "desert" of programming then, we went to great lengths to find some film that could be used.

It scared the pants off of a lot of us—because, sure, there was one sense in which you had to have something on the tube, and in another sense it was better to have nothing than some of the things you had.

Everyone was buying time. It was a chicken-and-egg thing. You couldn't get stations unless there was some assurance of programming, and you couldn't get the programming until there were some stations, with some exceptions.

~

Gradually, as Newburn came aboard, other key personnel who were to have significant roles in the next few years were put into place.

FLETCHER: The important thing was to see that Newburn had the right program coordinator, and I recommended that he employ Bob Hudson for this position. Bob was a vital factor in directing the center and the programming activities, which were quite complicated to begin with but smoothed out quite rapidly.

Furthermore, I was delighted when Newburn told me that he was bringing Lyle Nelson, who became very involved with the center and stayed with it for several years. He was a great help to Newburn. He knew him well, and he was understanding of Newburn's problems which resulted from the accident.

~

According to many who dealt with the early center, the two men who really managed to make this infant institution function under such difficult circumstances were Lyle Nelson and Bob Hudson. Nelson did indeed understand Dr. Newburn but also quickly grasped the predicament of those programmers in the early stations, and good-naturedly provided a useful buffer between the fledgling national organization and those in the local situations. At the same time, Hudson had come from many years as a shrewd and highly-motivated programmer. His direct assistant, Kenneth Christiansen, offered an evaluation of Hudson that sheds further light on his unique contributions in those early days.

CHRISTIANSEN: Bob Hudson was, again, a unique individual in the right place at the right time. Bob was not all that easy to know, I mean on the surface. It wasn't the handshake and the hearty-fellow-well-met. But Bob was an intellectual.

He had come out of the "Great Books" experiences and a lot of other things which put him in the midst of knowing an awful lot about the academic community in general. So he was our generalissimo, saying, here are the kinds of people we need to be in contact with from the substantive side—which was very much the basis of our existence in program development. He knew who the humanists were. And so on. Because that had been very much a part of his world.

When you got to know Bob, there was a sense of humor that was absolutely delightful! Which a lot of people didn't get to know. They thought he was kind of austere, sometimes remote, maybe an academic dreamer in a sense. But if anybody was able to bring a substantive cohesiveness to what a program service ought to be, he did it.

The thing that he developed early on was a system of program categories, which were not well accepted by the program people of the stations. They found them much too stuffy, much too academic.

Program Categories: The "Astrology Chart"

Hudson himself, in later years, acknowledged the limitations in the system of subject categories for which he and Christiansen got most of the blame from affiliated stations, whose managers referred to them as Hudson's "astrology chart."

HUDSON: Trying to develop the structure of programming at the center caused lots of problems because it really began to set up a bunch of themes and categories for programs that kind of "wagged the dog." We had to kind of force programs that were available into some of these categories. It really didn't represent affirmative planning. It represented a kind of accommodation.

There was lots of input on them from Ryland Crary, who was a professional educator, and from Newburn himself. We certainly were not *for* them, but we drew them up then from the data and presented them to the affiliates—and nobody liked them very much.

CHRISTIANSEN: We sat for painful hours going over this and redefining this. And I remember my first presentation of these was on a flip chart, and you could hear the dull thud land in the midst of all this!

Probably a lot of it was failure in presentation.

~

But Christiansen, with the benefit of hindsight, added a further observation.

CHRISTIANSEN: When I moved my office recently I ran onto those old materials, and I thought: you know, if you could get that as an overlay now, and say "What does our national program service do that has been significant?"

We had the social sciences, the physical sciences, the natural sciences—and I can think of Sagan, "NOVA", and *National Geographic*—there isn't a thing that wasn't in those categories.

I think the point that was missed was that the premises of public broadcasting are to provide materials that are significant and which can make a difference in the lives of people. Bob saw all of that in whole categorization.

It was ahead of its time—financially, probably, as much as anything else—because it would take money to have brought some of those off.

~

Norman Cousins, who was an early member of the center's board, recalled three decades later the euphoria of those times and the high hopes which he and others held for programming in this brand new educational broadcasting medium.

COUSINS: At that time, a strange thing was still alive: a million dollars was still a million dollars. And it was an awesome figure. It's only in the last few years that this is what you pay your plumber.

But when I came into ETV, there was the magnificent, the unbelievable, the very heavy prospect, that here we had a million dollars to spend, building a blackboard for the American people.

When I thought of a blackboard, I wasn't thinking of a formal prop. I was thinking of those things that had to fit into a survival experience. By this time we've grown accustomed to the fact of crisis, and we adjust to things we have no business adjusting to.

I saw ETV as a magnificently-designed instrument which, better than anything else, could tell the American people what they had to know if American history was to come to anything. And we had a million dollars to work with!

~

But Bob Hudson, the professional broadcaster, faced reality, a reality which today's national programmers may find it difficult to imagine.

HUDSON: We had hardly any money. I guess the center, first of all, had a million dollars [a year] to do something with, but never very much.

For exchange programs, we were reimbursing the stations at around $250 or something like that, you know. That hardly paid for the film itself.

BLAKELY: I did a little figuring concerning the number of programs that were produced and distributed [1952-1956], and the total average was $3,500. Actually it wouldn't be that much because a lot of that money went for administrative purposes.

But let's say $3,000 for an hour program. You compare that with program costs today and you see that one of the main reasons that the Educational Television and Radio Center wasn't more effective was simply lack of funds.

There was also the fact that people didn't know how to do it. They were learning how to do it.

~

There were other frustrations, too.

HUDSON: The idea of exchange was certainly democratic and made sense—except, of course, as we started in those days, stations weren't able to produce very much, certainly not very much that was worth circulating.

The next inhibiting factor was that the state-of-the-art in kinescopes was so poor that even the better program looked pretty bad as it was transmitted from a kinescope.[3]

---

[3] Kinescope recording was a process in which super-sensitive motion picture film was exposed to a brilliant and concentrated TV image, frame by frame, with accompanying sound. Transferring an electronic picture to a photochemical medium left much to be desired.

John Boor, director of engineering at KCTS-TV Seattle, works on a 1955-vintage kinescope recorder.

The Role of the Program Associates

John Crabbe was one of those very early program associates.

CRABBE: I went to Ann Arbor in the early summer of 1954 and stayed through the summer of 1955. I was there just a little over a year.

It was a fascinating year, it really was. We had fourteen stations on the air at that time, and there were two basic program associates. I was one and Dick Goggin from NYU was the other.[4]

People thought we had a lot of money to spend on programming and we really didn't. There was a finite level of grant to the organization and it had to be spread.

While the initial grant was for a substantial sum, if you spent it all at once you were going to go out of business. It was that kind of thing.

Part of the reason was that we were committed to supplying about four hours of programming a week. And the supply was so thin you found yourself grabbing for whatever you could get that was at least half-way acceptable.

~

Yet another drawback was the pony-express-type of distribution system called "bicycling." Kinescope prints and films were air-mailed to stations for their use within a period of several days, after which each station was to airmail its films to the next station on the routing. This was to save the cost of making enough prints of each program to send to all stations at once, a worthy objective in itself.

But neither air shipments nor humans are 100 percent reliable. Hudson supplied an example of the breakdowns which too often occurred.

BLAKELY: Kinescope was indispensable. It was the only method by which the local stations could duplicate for exchange. It was very crude, and a good deal of money was spent by the fund for improvements, and the center spent a good deal of money trying to train people to do it.

As rough and as crude and grainy as it all was, it lasted until the videotape recorder came in, and it made possible these exchanges.

~

Moreover, because the center was new and untried it was not the kind of enterprise that normally would encourage highly qualified persons to give up an already good job in either education or television in order to cast their lot with this newly-born outfit in Ann Arbor.

HUDSON: Here was a little organization that lived from year-to-year on grants that were uncertain, so we were not in a position to offer anybody a permanent job, that is, with any kind of tenure. It was a matter of our getting people on leave of absence from someplace or other, mainly from educational institutions.

Some of the people we would most like to have had were in a real sense unavailable because they were running stations, and if you took them away, what would the station do? It made no sense, so we had to turn mainly to university faculty, people in communications or in teaching in the curriculum. But we had some fine people.

---

[4] In addition to John Crabbe and Dick Goggin, Hudson mentioned Glenn Starlin from the University of Oregon, Milo Ryan from the University of Washington, Edward Stasheff and Ed Willis from the University of Michigan, Kenneth Wright from the University of Tennessee. Later came Donley Feddersen from Northwestern University, Bob Hall from the University of Southern California, John Young from North Carolina, and Edwin Cohen from Indiana University—all dedicated to the purposes of the center, even if they were not always comfortable with its operating processes.

HUDSON: We had one situation where films were sent down to Keith Nighbert's station in Memphis [WKNO-TV], and our film distribution man, Alan DeLand, was on the phone nearly every day with Memphis to get those films back. Weeks went by, maybe a month or two, without getting any films returned from Memphis, and they said they'd shipped them and they had records of it.

But then one day, Nighbert opened a closet door under a stairway and found all the films stashed away there. Their shipping boy had kept all the postage money that had been given him for shipping, and had just stashed the films under the stairway!

That relieved tensions somewhat, but it just shows what the hazards of this system were.

~

Jack McBride of Nebraska recalled his first visit to Ann Arbor in 1954 in preparation for KUON-TV's affiliation with the new center, and going to lunch with its president, Dr. Newburn.

McBRIDE: I can remember going out to lunch with him and Bob Hudson, who was brand new, and Ken Yourd, who was legal counsel and business manager. Ken had come from CBS New York after a heart attack.

It came time to pay the check, and Harry said, "I'm taking care of this one fellows, but you guys are on your own." He was watching the nickels even at that time.

They were in an old mansion on Washtenaw Avenue, setting up business and trying to develop programming.

Even in those days, I can remember one makeshift conference room where Bob Hudson had the walls lined with butcher paper categorizing all the content known to man!

Newburn had his office in the living room, and the basement was used for distribution, as I remember. But they welcomed me with open arms because they needed programming badly, and we were coming out with thirty-nine big half hours of programming on film.

Oh, that was a marvelous period, an exciting period. Everybody was pathfinding, and there was but a small group of us. You got them in a small room very easily.

Every station manager was eager to share everything that was going along, good or bad, with everyone else. It was a "one for all and all for one" kind of an attitude that could not last as this became less of a dream and more of an industry, but it was a most exciting time.

CHRISTIANSEN: The movement was small enough that the people involved in it had a quality of the pioneer. They knew there were going to be tough times, knew how to accept some of the adversity and the disappointment and the failure to emerge at an anticipated point.

There was a great sense of camaraderie—if that is the correct word—because meeting in a small room with twelve, fifteen or twenty people there is an identity that is so much different than the identity where you go now and there are 250 or 500 and you don't even know half of the people who are there. You don't know who your partners are in this mission.

The other factor operating in the early days was that we really weren't big enough and important enough to be significant. When you get to be important and significant, then you become a part of the marketplace, whether you want to or not.

While we were small and insignificant, we were a *partner* in the marketplace, doing some of the things that the commercial broadcasters did not have to do. They applauded us. They wanted us there because it took some of the burden of public service and some of the educational things off of their back, which were audience losers for them.

But when you get significant enough to be even a "One" in the rating book, you are now in the marketplace.

There should be a vote of thanks and commendation to the persistence of that group of individuals who never lost sight of or lost enthusiasm for the original mission. Fifteen years is a long time to sustain this against the kinds of thrusts that came from many quarters. We took a long time to establish legitimacy.

~

At that same time, within the group of station managers and also among the members of the board of directors of the center, there was yet another well-defined issue on which there was no clear agreement. Echoes of the same debate can still be heard—and if board member Raymond Wittcoff's evaluation is accurate, may continue to be heard in the future. It is the argument against centralization of authority in any national enterprise and in favor of the essential independence of the local counterpart—in this case, the center versus the stations.

WITTCOFF: This got reinforced by the long-standing fear in this country of putting too much authority in any kind of a national enterprise. This is certainly true in the field of education, where it was believed that any notion of setting up a strong national entity would be against our tradition.

I remember hearing these debates, and it seemed to me that there was something neurotic about it. In fact, I remember one time it occurred to me that we were suffering from a King George complex. The nation, in its infancy, suffered the consequences of a tyrannical British government, and our revolution consisted of rebelling against that kind of thing.

We've gone through life as a nation with this neurosis, growing out of—as neuroses usually do—our early childhood experience; we were neurotic about the notion of a strong center to provide programs. This neurotic condition was so great that the word "national" wasn't even put into the name of the new center that was created! It was called the "Educational Television and Radio Center." The word "national" was left out for that reason.

Now there was really no point in going to the mat and fighting on this issue, because we didn't have the money to implement the larger vision anyway. So my recollection of this thing is that at no point did the board of the center in those early years ever make a judgment that would commit it to one approach versus the other.

Therefore, what happened was that we got off the ground with a vehicle, an institution, that had some lofty commitments but very inadequate resources.

As a consequence of this, in the early years of the movement, I think the programming could best be described if one could visualize a great vista in which there was a flat plain and an occasional peak. The flat plain suggested a kind of mediocre level of production and the occasional peak was an occasionally brilliant thing that got done.

Dissatisfied Affiliates Form A Committee

For any number of reasons—most of them arising from the circumstances here related—the feeling among a growing number of affiliated stations against the center and its president grew. An affiliates' committee was organized after only two years of Newburn's five-year term, and so-called "rump sessions" were often held behind closed doors after the formal sessions arranged by the center.

Fletcher and his board gradually became aware of this, and began to have some misgivings of their own.

FLETCHER: It was now becoming evident that responsible station managers throughout the country were beginning to lose confidence in the reign of Harry Newburn and the national program center. To find out the facts about these accusations, it was decided that Dick Hull should be dispatched on a trip throughout the country to visit selected stations and arrange interviews with key persons in charge. He was accompanied by his wife, Dorothy, who kept all the records.

When Hull returned, his report confirmed the rumors. Newburn would have to be advised of these reports.

Apparently Newburn was aware of the fact that a production center had far more complications than he thought, and also because of his accident he was not functioning as well as he

Rump Sessions, (informal strategy sessions outside the regular meeting) began in 1955. Rump sessions participants: Earl Wynn, WUNC-TV, North Carolina; John Ziegler, WQED Pittsburgh; author Jim Robertson; Howard Johnson, KRMA Denver; John W. Taylor, WTTW Chicago; Loren Stone, KCTS-TV Seattle; and University of Illinois' Frank Schooley.

had hoped. He decided to resign in due course.

HUDSON: Why this little organization survived is an open question. And, believe me, it wouldn't have survived if Newburn had stayed on any longer.

It was one of those situations that just had to come to a head.

I think Newburn was a little slow in seeing how much it had deteriorated. But anyway, after the famous meeting in Biloxi [of all of the affiliates, during which rumors flew], he presented his resignation, just at the end of his five-year contract. He belonged in university administration. He did not belong in educational broadcasting. But I wished him well and I'm just sorry he stayed with us as long as he did.

~

Robert Blakely, who was associated with the Fund for Adult Education during these same years and who, since then, perhaps has spent more time researching the annals of educational television than anyone else, sums up the Newburn era:

BLAKELY: I think that in the early years of the Educational Television and Radio Center, they perhaps did about everything that they were *able* to do, and they *did* keep the idea alive, they *did* keep the institutions alive, and they *did* give the American people a noncommercial broadcasting system.

~

The transition from the Ann Arbor Center to National Educational Television (NET) and the emergence of "the fourth network" during the ten-year reign of a totally different personality—John F. White—is the next step in the growth of public television.

18

The Emergence of Jack White—And Videotape

Dr. Harry Newburn, once described as "the right man at the right time," became the wrong man as time passed and circumstances changed. John F. White, recognized as having the combination of talents and abilities to take up the task which many believed Newburn would have bungled, became indeed the right man to lead noncommercial television through the next difficult period of transition.

White's experience in college administration at Lawrence College and at Illinois Institute of Technology had led him to a vice presidency at Western Reserve University in Cleveland in the early 1950s. There he first became interested in television when Jim Hanrahan, manager of the Scripps-Howard commercial station, WEWS, offered a half hour each Sunday afternoon to showcase Western Reserve and its activities. Subsequently this led to a full hour each weekday morning, during which the university offered courses which were partly TV and partly correspondence.

As a result, when Dr. Arthur Adams and others were planning the Penn State Conference in 1952, they asked Jack White and producer Barkley Leatham to present a demonstration for the benefit of many attendees who were experiencing their first sight of "educational television."

Three years later, those in charge of WQED in Pittsburgh asked him to spend a week there and write a report on what to do about their one-year-old ETV station, and White delivered the report in person, thinking that assignment was completed.

But the Pittsburgh board, headed by Leland Hazard, was so impressed with White that they prevailed upon him to become General Manager of WQED. White gradually turned the station around and moved full steam ahead in developing one of the outstanding community stations in the nation. In that capacity he also became known to other ETV station managers, who quickly sensed his capabilities and elected him to serve on the first Affiliates Committee when it was organized in 1957 to represent the stations' interests with Dr. Newburn.

WHITE: There was great unhappiness, not only at the quality of center programming but at the areas which they elected to treat. They were very rigid. My recollection is that they were pedantic, they were duller than dishwater, and we were all unhappy because the center was not doing for us what it ought to be doing.

The Gathering Storm: Biloxi

The Affiliates Committee proposed—in fact, demanded—that the center arrange to hold a meeting of all affiliates to give them an opportunity to say what they thought should be done. Newburn announced plans for such a meeting to be held at a resort on the shores of the Gulf of Mexico, in Biloxi, Mississippi.

WHITE: You remember [the meeting at] Biloxi was called because the "Indians" were restless, and this was to be a peace-and-light session where we were going to solve everything. The center asked three or four of us to develop papers representing our kind of station—I think there was a university station, a public school station, a small community station, and a large community station—as to what we saw to be the future of educational television for our constituency and the role we saw the center playing in helping us to get there.

White delivered one of those four papers, representing a large community station. His ideas were applauded by many of his colleagues, although some of the school and university licensees differed strongly with his assertion that the community-based station was the station with true independence because it had to pay its way and if it didn't, it was dead. Jack White was almost always provocative, though not always agreed with.

Bill Harley, the representative of the University of Wisconsin's WHA-TV, recounted his Biloxi experience.

HARLEY: What I remember in particular was that it had been a fairly acrimonious meeting. And then I remember one time when Jack White and Harry Newburn walked out into the night together, and I don't know what happened, but I do know that before too long, Harry Newburn was out and Jack White replaced him.

~

White, when asked his recollections of Biloxi, was his usual colorful self.

WHITE: One sad recollection. As you remember, it was dry. You couldn't get a drink anywhere in Mississippi.

But some of us discovered that clear out behind the hotel, off in the corn fields, there was a thatched hut which the hotel operated, and by slipping a buck to the chief bag carrier, you got a pass to go there, and there you could get beer and liquor. So that became a gathering for rump sessions.

I also have to tell you that after dinner one evening, Harry Newburn took me by the arm and said, "Jack, let's take a walk." The two of us left the hotel and walked around the grounds.

He knew that the chairman of my board was Leland Hazard, who was a very critical member of *his* board. He also knew that I knew some of the other directors.

He said, "Jack, the way these meetings are going, the way my relationship is with these stations and my own board, I have concluded that I have got to get out of here."

It needs to be said, too, that he was talking to me not just as an affiliate, but also as a colleague who had come out of academia and had lots of friends back in academia.

And he said, "If you hear of any openings in higher education, I'd be grateful if you'd put in two cents." And of course I said I would. I did, and I could not offer him much comfort because his diagnosis was totally correct—except that the farthest thing from my mind was that I

would be the guy that would sit in his chair when we finally did help him to get out.

But that was the point at which I knew that Harry knew that things were going to change for educational television, and that he was not built in such a way that he could or would lead in that direction. He did believe in what he was doing. He viewed educational television as an extension of university activity, same sort of things, same subject matter.

I almost believe that had Harry been the kind of guy that would have sat around in smoke-filled rooms with us, there would have been a rapprochement and it could have gone differently, but he was so aloof. He didn't even listen to his own board, which was his mistake.

More Thundering: Madison

Not long after the Biloxi meeting, which triggered Newburn's resignation, affiliates were invited to a meeting in Madison, Wisconsin, at which the possibility of moving the center from Ann Arbor to New York was discussed. There may have been some side conversations also regarding the board's inclination toward White as the next president of the center, as suggested by the recollections of James Day of KQED.

DAY: I know during a break in the meeting someone called me aside—it must have been Ray Wittcoff—and said, "You know, we're thinking about who might be the next president." And I said, "I hope it's one of our own, and I would choose Jack White."

I suspect that a number of us were giving that same message to them, but I also think they'd already made up their minds to choose Jack at that point.

~

White's account indicates that "they had already initiated conversations with me, not conclusive conversations" prior to the Madison meeting.

WHITE: My conversations were with Norman Cousins, I think, Everett Case, and Ray Wittcoff. They came to Pittsburgh to see me, and then Madison came shortly after that.

Even in Madison, Leland Hazard and Jack White had no conversation about this negotiation. It was done very cleanly. All Hazard had done was to say to the board, "You have my permission to talk to White."

~

While there seemed to be a strong consensus favoring Jack White as president, the matter of moving the center to New York had few supporters at the Madison meeting.

DAY: The thing I most vividly recall was when Leland Hazard said, "The board's thinking of moving the center to New York," and the meeting exploded! I remember most vividly Harold McCarty getting up and saying, "If the center moved to New York, I can promise you WHA will never carry another one of their programs."

HARLEY: I guess, at least in the Midwest, there was still a strong isolationist trend, and there was a lot of suspicion about "the Big City" and what this might do to the whole movement if the networking center went to New York. Others argued that this was ridiculous, this is the center of all broadcasting for the United States and the news-gathering systems and so on, and therefore this made sense.

SCHOOLEY: I always took the position—and turned out to be wrong—that it ought to stay in Ann Arbor. I just wanted to keep it educationally oriented.

I thought it had been started in Ann Arbor, you could produce shows in Ann Arbor, that New York had no great advantage as a point of origination. But I guess it was just a philosophical difference.

DAY: I remember the speeches about all the evil things that would befall the center when it moved to New York, and I think during a break I said to Wittcoff, "Don't you think we are obligated to warn *The New York Times*, *Harper's*, the Metropolitan Opera, and so forth? [CHUCKLES]

The situation to me was patently absurd, that somehow we'd fall into evil hands if it moved out of the heartland of America.

~

Not all managers felt as Jim Day did. Seattle's Loren Stone had his well-thought-out reasons for objecting.

STONE: I was opposed to the move to New York because I just thought that was going to throw them into this commercial network milieu of programming and of controlling our distribution.

Leland Hazard was there to kind of pacify us on the move to New York that they had decided. At least a substantial part, if not the majority of us, were kind of opposed to this.

Now, I'm certainly not going to say that it wasn't ultimately a good thing in terms of the programs, but it wasn't going in the direction that I felt the whole thing ought to be going.

WHITE: The vote was about ten to one against moving to New York, and moving to New York was the first decision I announced after I was appointed.

There were two other things that faced me when I walked in. What faced me, whether I liked it or not, was that the center's grant from the Ford Foundation was up at the end of that year. I had to write a proposal for a $5 million grant, and I had to justify it all the way, but it was to be a "terminal grant." Ford was getting out of the picture.

I moved in October 1, 1958. At Christmas time I took Joan and the kids to Florida, and we left the children with Joan's parents while we went over and hid out in a motel, and I worked three days from eight o'clock in the morning until eight o'clock at night doing this proposal, which had to be in by the fifteenth of January. That was that.

The second thing was that I did not want even to appear to be playing God. So I committed myself to go to visit and see the leadership and board and the operation of every single educational television station that was on the air. I ran a three-ring circus around the country for the next nine months.

But I believe that visiting had more to do with the progress that you and Bob and the rest of us were able to accomplish over the next several years than any other move, because they knew we knew them.

That eroded as the years went on—but we were in it together, if you will. And I think that move did work.

It was all the more important because when I got to those towns, I had to justify the announcement that, "This institution is moving to New York, and we're going to move this next summer." When I got to stations and the shot was called and I justified it and explained it, I never had a single criticism on that trip.

We opened offices in New York the first of April, and then we moved all of ourselves by the first of July when we all got our kids out of school, and we were in operation by fall.

~

Norman Cousins, always an enthusiastic and willing board member, described accurately the spirit of late 1958 and all of 1959.

COUSINS: I was chairman of a committee to go to the Ford Foundation, not just to inform them that Jack White was our choice, but to get their support for a considerable escalation in which Jack White would be front and center.

The Ford people liked Jack White. His coming into the picture led to an immediate hike in the budget, so that Jack was able to take his concept of national programming and move very rapidly because of this enlarged support. The meetings that we had at the Ford Foundation turned out very well indeed.

That was when NET went big time. We moved out of Ann Arbor, set up national headquarters, Jack White with this national support concept came on, the Ford Foundation gave increased support, and we did have a tremendous spurt.

Jim Armsey Enters the Picture at Ford

One reason for the "spurt" was a new man on the educational television assignment within the Ford Foundation, just as that particular portfolio was transferred from the Fund for Adult Education to the foundation proper.

James W. Armsey shared with Ford Foundation president Henry Heald and with Jack White an enthusiasm for what noncommercial educational television might become in America. Over most of the next decade, Armsey was responsible for about $100 million worth of grants, the purpose of which was to encourage this development.

ARMSEY: My primary concern, because it became my initial assignment, was the development of a group of noncommercial television stations and the provision of a high quality programming service for the stations to use. I was interested not primarily in the structure or the structures that surrounded those things, although I had to be concerned with them, but in the product and the use of the product.

Heald and I agreed on it because it was something he wanted me to do and it was something that I rather wanted to do.

We pretty much agreed that the center ought to expand its activities, become something more than just a central mailing shop for films—kinescopes at that time—and that probably for lots of reasons it ought to move to New York since that's where the principal media so-called were located, where the networks were located, and where most of the production facilities, if they ever got into production, could be readily assembled.

At that time, Heald said—and I see no reason why this should not be known at this time—"I'd like you to go over and run this center when we get moved to New York." I said, in effect, "No, I really don't want to do that. I've watched what the chief executive of an organization has to do,

the kinds of things he has to put up with. I'm not temperamentally suited for it. I want to make the grants and do the kinds of things I'm doing."

I said, "The guy that would be the most useful at this stage in the development of the center would be Jack White."

I'm sure this was no surprise to Heald—either that I suggested it or that he would think of it—because White and I were both on the Illinois Tech staff together. Jack was director of admissions, he was dean of students, and he was dean of development at Illinois Tech during the time that I was there with Heald.

I pointed out to Heald that what was needed at the center at that time was a thick-skinned, eager, ambitious, shrewd promoter. Without denigrating Jack in any way, that's what he was.

It can be fairly said that Jack was more of an operator than an intellectual—and there were plenty of places where an intellectual could get involved in the center operation without cluttering up its management!

~

Armsey recalled how things got done during that period of time with far greater authenticity than those outside of the Ford Foundation. In his opinion, Harry Newburn was out as president of the Educational Television and Radio Center because the foundation said it would no longer fund the operation if Newburn stayed. He also recalled sitting in on a particular conversation between Leland Hazard, a member of the center's board, and Henry Heald, president of the Ford Foundation. Armsey's conviction was that from that point on, White's presidency was assured.

Moreover, his recollection of affairs is that the $5 million grant to the center also was assured once White was appointed and the decision made to move the center to New York. And it was Armsey's task to take Jack White's proposal requesting that $5 million grant—which, Armsey implies, was patterned after "suggestions" from him and Heald—and redraft it for the Ford Foundation board, and then to argue for its approval—which he secured.

WHITE: Shortly after I knew we had the five million bucks, we called another meeting of the affiliates in Houston. That's the occasion on which I announced that I had five million bucks that the paper said was "terminal" but I didn't believe it, and that we were going to "go for broke," that our only hope was to spend these $5 million well and to earn a situation where Ford couldn't afford to say "no," and that set a new spirit for the affiliates and for all of us.

The Coming of Videotape

A few months later—in the spring of 1959—a technical development of major significance added to the excitement. The Ampex Corporation produced its first professional model videotape recorder, an instrument which finally was to overcome the wholly inadequate distribution of programs on cloudy and fuzzy kinescope recordings.

Hartford Gunn, then manager of WGBH-TV in Boston, purchased the first quadruplex videotape recorder available from Ampex and invited Jack White to come up to Boston and "see himself on television." Immediately White saw the possibilities.

WHITE: Videotape! We went to Jim [Armsey] and said, "Look, this is a new development which is not to be avoided. Kinescope contributes extensively to our mediocrity. We've got to step up and be competitive."

~

Armsey's version was that he went to White first.

ARMSEY: Everyone was dissatisfied with kinescope, and we kept hearing rumors in the foundation that some physicists and others on the coast somewhere were working on an arrangement that would put pictures on tape just as they had been able to put sound on tape, and that this would be cheaper and better, more definition in the picture and all sorts of advantages.

We learned subsequently that there was such a thing as videotape, that you could use it, that there were machines that made it possible to have this tape that you could get pictures on, and that you could even have them in color! I'll never forget what a thrill it was around our shop when we kept hearing this and verified it.

We didn't think then in terms of on-the-air broadcasting with tape. We thought of making tapes of programs and circulating those tapes the same way kinescopes had been circulated. I was absolutely insistent that these new stations have these things, that they be as up-to-date at least in their basic equipment as the commercial crowd was.

Lester Nelson [a staff colleague in the Education Division of the Ford Foundation] and I at one point made a trip to California to see the Ampex people. They really threw a big sales pitch at us, big dinner and the whole thing.

People tend to respond when staff members from the Ford Foundation start asking questions, especially if there might be money involved.

One of the interesting sidelights: We had a dinner at the home of the founder of Ampex. "AMPEX" was formed from the initials of his name: Alexander M. Poniatoff, plus "ex" for excellence. Poniatoff was there that night. He was sort of senior advisor, no longer involved directly in the management of the company.

At this dinner, one of their chief salesmen named Charles Black showed up with his wife. The next day, before Lester and I flew back to New York, someone said, "How did you enjoy meeting Shirley Temple?"

And Lester said, "Shirley Temple? Where? Who? What?" So we explained to him that she was Mrs. Black. Mrs. Black sat next to me at dinner and across from Lester, and I never did tell Lester during the dinner that this was Shirley Temple, so he never knew except in retrospect.

We went back to New York and worked up—with Jack and the center and the stations and all of the consultation we needed—a grant request for the foundation trustees. We talked in terms of buying enough machines to supply each of the ETV stations with one, and securing enough tape to provide the center with a lot of it for some period of time. [1]

WHITE: I think that had more to do with the acceptance of public television—educational television—than any other single move we made, because it put us at a quality level where we could stand up and be proud. We didn't have [network] long lines, we had to resort only to recorded image, but we really set a quality.

~

White and his team at the revitalized "center" were off and running. As the Ford Foundation grant of videotape machines was announced in April 1959, White held a conference in Washington in the ballroom of the Mayflower Hotel, inviting more than 100 national organizations to send representatives to hear about this emerging kind of television.

WHITE: That came from the conviction that we had to excite people to work in communities

---

[1] 3M, an early leader in the manufacture of videotape, provided a concurrent grant of videotape, $10,000 worth to each station receiving a machine, and a generous amount for the duplication of programs at the center. Ampex donated five machines to the center to handle duplication of programs for multiple distribution.

clear across this nation. The Junior League people were very instrumental in getting us set up for that one. In several communities they were supporting children's theater and children's programs. They had been very helpful to Fred Rogers [2] and to people all over the country in terms of children.

~

The announcement of the Ford videotape machines grant in the middle of this meeting of national organizations gave considerable impetus—and nationwide press coverage—to the growing importance of ETV. It also created a ripple effect as nearly all of the national organizations alerted their own people in communities across the country to this new kind of television which had recently become available—or would soon become available—in their area.

At this time also, White began to use new terminology, created a few days ahead of the conference in collaboration with Armsey.

WHITE: Two decisions were made before we left Ann Arbor. Jim Armsey was out visiting us, and Fritz Jauch, who had just joined us for our New York offices, had come out to Ann Arbor. We were sitting in Harry's old office, which was mine for six months. We came up with two things.

One, we added the word "national" and made it the *National* Educational Television and Radio Center, NETRC [eventually NET].

Two, we conceived the concept of "the fourth network" and assigned Fritz to go back to New York and develop a paper and rationale.

The Concept of a "Fourth Network"

ARMSEY: One of the histories that somebody did as a Ph.D. thesis attributes to me the origin of the term "the fourth network," that I used that phrase one time when Jack was putting together a speech, and I think that is correct.

My pitch to the foundation trustees was that there were inevitable limitations to what a commercial structure could do—or would do—in providing a high-level broadcast service via television to the American people, and that what the foundation ought to be concerned with, and ought to be concerned with solely, was the provision of a high-quality noncommercial service unlike the service provided by the commercial stations.

I believed that then; I believe it now. We were taking that position long before Newton Minow came up with his "vast wasteland" phrase.

The conclusions of a study we subsequently did on the role of the center was that the center ought to do only those things which the commercial structure could not or would not do.

~

During 1959 and the early 1960s, the organization increasingly identified as "NET" became involved in many projects and activities which never would have come about under its previous leadership. An active station relations department followed up on White's own visits to stations and assisted many in their local problems as it gathered input regarding NET's programs and services.

WHITE: At that juncture we were not just a programming agency. NET in that six to nine month period had become a wet nurse for stations in trouble, and also an assistant in the operating room when new stations were born. We spent a lot of time on these kinds of things.

~

But the objective always was improvement in the quality of programming. Bob Hudson, who had been Newburn's second in command but who had festered under that type of leadership, finally was free to "go for broke."

HUDSON: We worked hard then in 1959, and began to contract with good producers and producing stations. We raised the level of programming and began to acquire good materials from the BBC and other foreign places.

I went to London a number of times, and with Hugh Carlton Green, who was head of BBC at that time, we negotiated a contract with British Equity whereby we could get multiple uses of their programs on noncommercial television over here. That arrangement has stood us in good stead, and probably still does, although I imagine the terms have changed somewhat over the years. But the whole level of programming was coming up.

One of the conditions of the $5 million Ford grant was that a lot of this money go into stations to help them build muscle, so that they could do their own job and also do jobs for national distribution. So a good deal of money flowed through NET into these stations.

Then, of course, they were enterprising and went out and got [production] money on their own. Boston, Chicago, St. Louis for a period of

---

[2] Fred Rogers had been conducting "The Children's Corner" at WQED, which evolved into "Mister Rogers' Neighborhood."

time, San Francisco, Pittsburgh, and maybe one or two others were doing some outstanding programming.

There was learning all the way along the line, the evolution of NET from strictly a program exchange center into a thing that developed in the late sixties: contracting work with producers on staff—no *facilities*, but *producer* on staff—hiring facilities to go out and produce, and then commissioning work, not only with the major producing stations but with independent film people, all of this was evolving as a way of getting good programs.

~

White's interest in securing superb programming, along with the efforts of Bob Hudson and the urging of the Ford Foundation, led to the merger into NET of the Broadcasting Foundation of America. BFA brought with it the capabilities of a veteran international broadcaster, Basil Thornton, former representative of the BBC in North America. Subsequent formation of "Intertel," involving cultural broadcasting entities in the United Kingdom, Canada, and Australia, with NET and Westinghouse Broadcasting as the United States partners, gave birth to many international documentaries aired by all partners.

A few years later, White assumed the leadership in forming the Asian Broadcasting Union and had Bob Hudson undertake a comprehensive survey of program possibilities in the Orient which led to cooperative productions with Far Eastern television companies, including NHK in Japan. The results of these activities became apparent in the kinds of international programs which began to appear on NET affiliated stations across the country.

Not well known, but another evidence of White's leadership and desire to innovate, is the story of the origin of the "Great Debates" by U.S. presidential candidates.

WHITE: I recall meeting [Senator] Chuck Percy in a room at the Hotel Pierre discussing this. He was intrigued and supportive. He set me up to meet his right hand guy, Pete Peterson, who later was to become secretary of Commerce.

[Percy] was heading the campaign committee for the Republicans and he was very intrigued, and Pete Peterson was, and they tried like the dickens. He got me underwriting for a political series, but we never did get the live debates.

NETRC Rescues the JCET

As educational television was coming of age, it began to require significant representation in the nation's capital. But the Joint Council on Educational Television (JCET), which had played such a vital role in the earlier campaign to assure reservation of channels for educational use and the establishment of the first stations, was running out of money—doing their best with severely limited funds.

WHITE: It was Arthur Adams of the American Council on Education who said, "Jack, why don't we call a spade a spade and quit kidding. Why don't you just take it over?"

And it was with the blessing of all the constituents of the Joint Council—including the NAEB—they were all for it. They were all supportive, as was the Ford Foundation.[3]

The main thing it gave us was a Washington base, because [the station relations office] was doing some of those things anyway. David Stewart served as a kind of extension or a Washington arm.

~

All of these activities as well as the gradual improvement in the quality of programming benefitted from the oversight of a remarkable board of directors of NET.

Dr. Everett Case was president of Colgate University during his term as NET board chairman but had been a board member under former chairmen Ralph Lowell and George Stoddard.

CASE: At that time it was a fantastically distinguished board. One was very proud to be able to preside over it. There were journalists like Scotty Reston of the [New York] Times and Norman Cousins of The Saturday Review. There were public servants like Am Houghton, who had been ambassador to France and head of Corning Glass prior to that; Phil Reed, former chairman of General Electric.

---

[3] Arthur Adams, president of the American Council on Education, and an inspiration for JCET, was a longtime friend of Henry Heald, Ford Foundation, president. It is interesting to speculate on the role this friendship played in the move to place the JCET under NET.

Armsey, "an insider," supplies the fact that many of the strongest members of the NET board agreed to serve because Henry Heald had asked them to, obviously a big plus for strengthening Jack White's hand. Those board members, in turn, hoped that Henry Heald's urging might mean that Ford Foundation money would be forthcoming, not only for NET but possibly for their other interests as well.

At times, some station managers expressed a hope that a station manager might be appointed to that board, if only to provide "the station's viewpoint." On the whole, though, they respected the combination of educators and outstanding citizen leaders who constituted Jack White's trustees.

DAY: I think the board that Jack White put together was the best board that public television has ever had, including especially the CPB [Corporation for Public Broadcasting] board.

I think that was part of the success of NET, and I've commended Jack, not only on the quality of the board but the method by which it was arrived at, with the development of a community of thought sometimes two years ahead to find the right person for that board. We have had no example of that anywhere in public television since, to my knowledge.

~

Jim Day was a close friend and at the same time severe critic of Jack White. He provides a balanced assessment of White's leadership style.

DAY: Leadership has been very rare in public television, from the beginning until today. And I would define leadership as the ability to articulate goals.

Much as I used to tease Jack about those semi-annual addresses he made [to affiliates], I now realize—in retrospect—it's one of the few times in the history of public television that it had someone at the helm giving it a sense of direction.

Since then it's had a whole coterie of people at the helm giving it a number of different directions.

And secondly, he energized it. He just put something into it that kept it going. Again, I used to tease him about it and I still would today, because it was a kind of salesman's role, not even a salesman's role, it was a Boy Scout leader's role, or a coach's role. I wish I could characterize it.

It was sort of "Get in there and fight, boys!" I remember somebody saying, "Well, we ought to take the middle of the road," and Jack saying, "The yellow line runs down the middle of the road." That was one of the more courageous things he ever said to the affiliates, because it could have got him into deep difficulty.

Those two things, more than anything else. It was just the sheer energy that he brought to it.

~

Another station manager among those in what might have been called "the inner circle," also a frequent member of the NET Affiliates Committee, WGBH's Hartford Gunn, had similar recollections.

GUNN: His contribution was to provide the confidence and salesmanship which the Ford Foundation needed to put in the major resources which turned it from a small-town game into a big-town game.

Without the move to New York, without the significant upgrading of the programming which only became possible because Ford was willing to back Jack where they weren't willing to back Newburn with millions and millions of dollars—without all of that having come together, I don't think we would have been in a position in 1967 to have made the case to [Senator] Pastore and have Pastore accept it. [4]

And therefore you wouldn't have had CPB, and you wouldn't have had the federal money which then made possible the *next* leap forward, and you wouldn't have had the live network, without which very little if anything would be happening today.

So, Jack was the right person at the right time.

~

Armsey echoes Hartford Gunn's conclusion that it was the confidence which both Henry Heald and Jim Armsey had in White that made things work.

Even so—and without taking any credit from White's capabilities—Armsey remains somewhat concerned about the impression widely held that the Ford Foundation's role in the development of public television was primarily a "responsive" one, whereas he sees it as "mainly an initiatory one." He offered this viewpoint in correspondence subsequent to his interview.

---

[4] Senator John Pastore was chairman of the U.S. Senate subcommittee primarily responsible for the drafting, introduction and passage of the first Public Broadcasting Act, signed by President Lyndon Johnson, in November, 1967.

ARMSEY: Had not Heald become president of the foundation at the time he did, and had I not taken over the television portfolio in the foundation, there would have been no program grants, no videotape recorder grants, no purchase of the New Jersey station, no move to New York of the programming center, and no real monetary incentive for the forces then at work to continue their efforts to expand and stabilize a noncommercial television system. Quite likely, I am prepared to say, no such system would now exist without the [Ford] Foundation; and if one had, it would be far different from what eventually developed.

Beginning the Drift Away from "Education"

Despite all of these achievements, which, in the minds of many, marked the coming of age of what is now called public television, there were those who were troubled by what seemed to be a drifting away from the educational objectives envisioned in earlier days.

HUNTER: Jack had this conviction and commitment to a "fourth network" and a quality production system. This was, in my view, a perception of this medium and its educational and public and cultural functions that was found more in the large metropolitan centers and community stations, which were being staffed by those coming from commercial television, who had the same kind of network perception and concept and quality production backgrounds.

This was at the point in time where those who were identified with the in-school, school-system, educational, university-owned-and-operated stations began to have some concern. Because it was at this point that the program service of the network seemed to be moving away from what they perceived to be their primary educational function and responsibility. And while this was all great, it did not do the job on the local level in terms of the needs of the elementary and secondary schools and of the general adult public as far as educational and informational types of program resources were concerned. They still had to do this on a local production level.

~

Loren Stone, head of the University of Washington's KCTS-TV, articulated effectively the arguments which made the case for what might be termed "The Loyal Opposition."

STONE: As we were getting ready to come into meetings, they [NET] would try to stimulate some participation, would invite certain guys to prepare papers. I prepared a paper one time, and I suppose the thing that pleased me most was the enthusiasm with which Mac McCarty heard it and asked for copies. For him to give that seal of approval pleased me a great deal because I respected him so much.[5]

But I, for the first time, sat down and wrote out and articulated in advance my feeling about the need for these stations to be educationally based, that this was what it was all about, that we ought to derive our support from the educational establishment.

I said such things as, "We may support our symphony orchestras with community contributions, but we do not support our libraries that way. We have to make educational television as important to our communities, as integral a part of the educational facilities of our communities, as our libraries."

Having come out of commercial broadcasting, where we depended on advertising revenue for our income and advertising revenue depended upon the audience we developed in size, and our audience depended upon the popularity of the programs we could devise, I was absolutely set against funding the stations with listener contributions because I felt this would destroy the reason for our being.

I felt that those stations that had to depend on audience contributions would inescapably, whether consciously or unconsciously, strive to get larger audiences because then they would have a larger field of people to tap for money, and they would get into popular and more popular and more popular programs to get larger and larger audiences, and pretty soon you'd not be able to tell them from the commercial stations.

This I developed in this paper and I never lost sight of it and I never quit believing it. I argued for this all the way through. It underlay my concern about NET moving to New York, that we would get away from the educational base. We would get into the competitiveness of a program market in New York where we were trying to be like the other guys.

The "fourth network" concept was abhorrent to me for the same reason. We didn't need a fourth network, because I was just so determined that we had to keep this thing funded by the educational establishment. I felt that if we served them well, they would continue to finance it, and I still—ah, well, I've got some reservations on that now, and maybe we can

---

[5] H.B. McCarty of Wisconsin was a consistent believer in keeping ETV focused on clear educational objectives.

talk about that, too, in a few minutes—what happened to the educational support for television?

~

In the early 1960s, a dichotomy developed between the desire, on one hand, to provide superb cultural programming for general audiences which could not find this sort of offering on commercial stations and on the other hand, the determination to serve the urgent need of elementary and secondary schools to improve the quality and relevancy of classroom instruction and of colleges and universities to serve adult students both on and off campus.

19

TV as a Teaching Aid—For Some

When the FCC was inquiring into education's need for television channels, college presidents and school administrators and their spokespersons testified effectively about their hopes for using TV as an aid in formal education.

In the forty-odd years since then, television's use in schools and colleges has been significant but not widespread or consistent. Why has this medium, often cited as the greatest communications invention since the printing press, not been embraced with greater vigor by those who bear the responsibility for our American educational system?

The question is unfair in some respects, because more than a generation of school children have enjoyed enrichment of their classroom experiences through TV programs. "Sesame Street" and "Mister Rogers" have been invited regularly into millions of homes in hours before and after school with remarkable effects on those child viewers' experiences while in school. Moreover, in many communities, local public television stations continue to devote most of their daytime hours to the transmission of television materials for in-school use.

But such use has not shown the rapidly rising upward curve in recent decades that many of founders of public television had hoped for.

Lack of Educator
Enthusiasm Generally

Why this lack of enthusiasm among educators? A long-time college president and devoted friend of educational television, Dr. Everett Case, has provided a hint.

CASE: I think this illustrates the ambivalence that the educator feels in the face of this new medium.

He must publicly testify to its importance and his concern about it, and sometimes he's dragooned into attending meetings, and so forth, and doing what he can to help. But he doesn't want to stop what he's doing and devote attention to it, to how you tailor an educational program to this new medium.

~

James W. Armsey, a Ford Foundation program officer involved with various uses of television in education, provided another thought.

ARMSEY: An early interest of the Fund [for the Advancement of Education] was in the uses of television to teach. That's the way I put it to distinguish among the uses of what we call educational television. And they continued that.

They had the Hagerstown [Maryland] experiment, and they had this "national program" that Jerry Stoddard bird-dogged and all that stuff, after I had moved out of the education division and worked for the international division for almost five years.

One of the things I did was an almost worldwide exploration of what I chose to call "an inquiry into the uses of instructional technology."

I came to the same conclusion after that exercise that I came to after I reviewed the domestic thing.

The principal deterrent to the use of television and/or other forms of instructional technology in the direct formal educational process is the reluctance of teachers to use it: the fear that it will show how bad they are, the fear that it will replace them, the fear that it may diminish their salaries, the stated concern that it will eliminate the teacher/student personal relationship, a whole batch of things that teachers have been led to believe by schools of education that are essential to the education of the youth or the middle-aged or old-aged or whatever.

And yet there is no question that television, in one form or another, is having more impact on the "education," the informational channel, the general attitude and opinion-formation of people today than any amount of conventional in-class instruction.

Armsey's Conclusion Shared By Others

HURLBERT: I found in the professional associations—well, two fears that the teachers seemed to have. One was that they were afraid that they were going to have a lot more work dumped on top of them, and this was just another gadget that was going to bother them and get in the way. The other was that here was somebody trying to get their job.

GABLE: If only we could get the teacher-training colleges—I think they're doing better now in some places—but there are still an awful lot of teacher training places that don't have any communications [training], don't give them anything at all.

The training of [classroom] teachers to know how to handle [TV] with security and skill was the key to the whole thing.

MACANDREW: Some of the teacher' union enthusiasts felt it would be "just like our board of education to try and make us merely monitors and use the so-called master teacher on television to do the actual instruction. And instead of suddenly getting a decent living wage which we're fighting for, we'll suddenly become those who monitor and keep the children quiet while some guy on the television set does the actual teaching."

Well, of course, this was never a thought at any time. It was to be supportive [to the classroom teacher] that was why "the project" was created.

TAVERNER: This is a *tool* for the classroom teacher. The classroom teacher does not come in and take attendance and then go to the teachers' room and have a smoke while the kids watch television. She has to work with that television set, with the children. Interaction takes place.

I think if I had stayed with it, another effort I could have made would be to require within the school of education at the university and other training institutions, a minimum of six hours in utilization of instructional television—which they never had. So the young teacher coming out of school, one, didn't really understand what this was all about, and, two, [they thought] it could be a threat to her or him.

I was disappointed along with some others that instructional television didn't really take hold the way we wanted it to. I don't want to overkill that, either. It's going on. There is instructional television in the schools of Maine from nine or nine-thirty in the morning until three in the afternoon every school day now.

But the utilization is not as high as it well could be.

WHITE: We started first with [the idea that] the way to make believers was to have them have their hands in it, so we charged school districts twenty-five cents per pupil per year for the support of this thing, and had an amazing positive response. That permitted WQED to mount a hard-core group working with planning committees involving both city and county schools.

WQED in Pittsburgh claims to have been the first educational television station to become a teaching tool in the classroom.

We pretty much limited it to the elementary level, but you started at nine o'clock in the morning and you went right straight through until two o'clock or three o'clock in the afternoon with courses designed by these crews of producers.

They designed an on-going very effective service. That was done at WQED about 1956 or '57. It was off and sailing at that point.

That whole movement seemed to lose steam later, and I'm afraid I think it had to do with the fact that we had the hardware but we never spent the money for the software to put the [proper] kind of production quality in.

I think we could have defeated the ogre they all talked about—classroom resistance. I think we lost the second battle which gets blamed for it, which was resistance, because we lost the first one, which was productions of quality.

~

Jack White often described his view of the range of capabilities and attitudes among classroom teachers. He responded, as follows, to a question concerning teachers who feared television.

WHITE: My impression then, as I recall it, is that that was a relatively small proportion of the group of teachers that were out there. There was another equally small group which used it as a crutch. They just stopped teaching and stopped working themselves, and just used this as a plaything, turned it on and that was a baby-sitter for the kids.

But neither one of those [groups] was our problem. Our problem group was that great big bunch in the middle which just didn't give a damn. They didn't prepare for it, they didn't use it right, and we never got them to do it, and it just went out of existence due to lethargy.

Fear That ITV
Might Replace the Teacher

Rhea Sikes, organizer and for many years director of WQED's in-school services, had a favorite response to those who asked her about whether TV would eventually replace the classroom teacher.

SIKES: I always used to say, "If I were a multi-millionaire, I would give a $10,000 reward to anybody who could identify for me *one teacher* who lost his or her job because of a television set."

I never had that money, and I used to make that challenge without the money—but I've never had anybody tell me of one who did.

It's a facetious fear. There's no truth in it. There is no television system on God's green earth that could do all the teaching that a teacher is expected to do in one day. And I doubt there ever will be.

OBERHOLTZER: Our strategy to overcome some of this was to say, "Now this is not compulsory for you to receive this material by television; it's up to you."

What we did was start out with a few key principals who were very much interested in the television operation. We said to them, "If you want to participate, maybe we can be helpful to you in some way if you have faculty members who want to do it." Well, we started with those few and it expanded to all the schools by that process, so that it was really voluntary. We didn't say "you must" have television. Whether they received particular programs or not was up to the faculty in the school. As a result, I don't know of any that didn't finally participate in it. But it was a gradual process.

We arranged it so that they couldn't just turn on the television set. There was an active participation in the classroom on the part of the children and the teacher.

~

The account by Rhea Sikes of the way in which she and others went about building the in-school program service broadcast by WQED in Pittsburgh parallels much of what Dr. Oberholtzer implies—that the secret of success is involvement of the classroom teacher in assessing needs, in selecting materials, and in evaluating results.

SIKES: In the period of time from '55 to '73 we had grown to serve a tri-state area. I think there were something like three hundred different school districts with a half-million children involved.

My role in that was setting up an organizational structure that I guess had never been done before. I had two basic tenets from the word go: that educators were responsible for the learning that was to take place, and those of us who were trained as television producers and broadcasters were responsible for the way in which that educational content was presented.

So I formed a school curriculum advisory committee of representatives from the various school districts we were serving. They met every month with me, except the month of July, during all those years. This was almost as holy as going to church!

That meeting was important! There was an agenda. They determined the subject areas to be taught, and at what grade levels. They conducted the auditions for teachers and helped choose those teachers. They had subcommittees that did evaluations.

In the last ten years, I sent out a questionnaire to every classroom teacher in January. She evaluated everything that she had watched. She told us what she wanted repeated, what she wanted dropped, and what she would like to see added.

We hand-scored those things in the beginning. We sent out about ten thousand; the first year we got about six thousand back! Then we were saved by the computers and could program that information so that by the [next] meeting of that curriculum committee—which was made up of superintendents and principals and curriculum specialists—they had feedback from all those teachers all over that area.

I think that was the primary key to acceptance and widespread development of educational television through the area. From the beginning, the educators had to make decisions.

~

For a period of three years, the Pittsburgh service was funded by a grant from the Fund for the Advancement of Education of the Ford Foundation.

SIKES: But after three years, we suddenly had to scramble. It became a matter of my approaching the schools and saying, "This is what the committee has decided for the next year and we need your support."

That meant we started eighteen months in advance. And once we were able to bring programming in from other places, then you had to have lead time for getting those programs on the air and letting teachers evaluate them, get feedback in, and making that happen.

Success In Some Places, Not In Others

Rhea Sikes was asked what it was that led certain systems to reach out and make use of this in-school service when other systems did not.

SIKES: If I can make a generalization—they're awfully dangerous; you know I feel that. So with that kind of caveat: *leadership*. The vision of leadership.

If your key school administrators, your building principals, your PTA, if these groups are saying, "This is good and we want our children to use it," and if teachers have been properly prepared and it is explained to them that this is another tool put into their hands to do with as they see fit, then there's no problem.

But if you are in a school system—and there are many, unfortunately—where it seems "the thing to do," and they're told to use it but given no guidance, it's awfully easy *not* to use it. It's one more thing that has to be worried with.

If they've said [to the teachers], "Here it is, use it" and they've never had one opportunity to say "I'd like it," "I need it," "I don't want it," "I wish you'd do so-and-so," then you've immediately imposed something else upon a professional that doesn't need to be imposed there.

But if they feel from the beginning that they are a part of this and that where it goes from here is up to them, that will make a difference.

~

Philadelphia's Martha Gable, who built the in-school television service in that area, agreed.

GABLE: We asked the teachers what subject matters they thought would go well on television. I said, "Where do you need help? What do you need in the classroom to enrich what you have? What resources don't you have in your classroom?" and then let them decide, so that they used it just like you use a book as a resource, or a film or something else. I tried to develop that concept. This was a tool that they had at their command, and it wasn't any different than the other tools so far as their use of it was concerned.

Another thing: the parents were solidly behind it. We sold it to them, too, and brought them in to see things. When they saw the programs, they decided they wanted TV sets for their schools. So the parents, over a period of about three years, bought $100,000 worth of television receivers, because each local home-and-school association wanted their children to have a television set.

Number three: the superintendent was with it. He would talk about it at staff meetings. We'd have demonstrations in staff meetings when all the principals came in. And both Dr. Hoyer and Dr. Wetter were thoroughly behind and promoted it.

Jerry Stoddard's "Large Class" Experiment

By 1957 there had been enough early efforts to begin using television in the classroom that Dr. Alexander J. Stoddard, who by then had joined the Ford Foundation's Fund for the Advancement of Education, proposed a new approach.

GABLE: Jerry wanted us to have a whole lot of children in a room, five days a week, and get their teaching that way. I said, "Dr. Stoddard"—and he had been my former superintendent so I felt that I knew him well enough to really level with him—I said, "Dr. Stoddard, that isn't going to work. The teachers are going to resist you. The parents are going to resist you. They're going to think we have machine-made education." And I said, "If you will let me work it out, I think we'll make this a success."

I said, "What I'd like to do is have a large class three days a week, but the program is only going to be twenty minutes, and the rest of the lesson, the teacher has a quick follow-up, question and answer. The other two days these youngsters are in their regular-size classrooms with their teachers for evaluation and for testing and for whatever."

The classroom teacher was the key person, and then we selected our television teachers very well. We had some great teachers on television and we had some great teachers in the classrooms, because the principals picked the teachers that wanted to do it. So we weren't fighting anything, you see. The way we worked it out, it worked fine. Our results showed that the children *did* learn.

And it was an interesting thing: the classroom teachers that I had doing this and who were successful all got promoted. They're all principals, or heads of departments and what have you, because their excellence just shone out, you see. It was great.

~

The effectiveness of television as a medium to assist in the learning process was tested in many different ways, as many of the visionaries of public television have said.

Out on the great plains of Nebraska, the Stoddard plan was modified into a different pattern, with significant results that in later years led to further uses of TV at the high school and adult levels.

McBRIDE: Nebraska had, and still has, the largest high school correspondence study in the world, and the thought was, why not combine correspondence stuff with television, and instead of working it toward the large school, direct attention to the small school, the rural school, to see if the combination could replace the teacher—or, if there were no teacher in a particular subject, allow that curriculum to include that subject.

That intrigued Jerry Stoddard and the fund, and that's why, for a three-year period, we got funding and were a part of that project, even though all the rest of it was directed to television in large class situations. And we met with some success.

In Wisconsin, another state in which there had long been a commitment to carry educational opportunities to the people of the state wherever they might reside, H.B. McCarty saw other possibilities.

McCARTY: [Television is] a means of extending the other areas and avenues of education. It has the unique capacity to go directly to the users, or those who need services, and reach them where it's most convenient.

I'm impressed with the current offerings in adult education in so many fields, by correspondence, by attendance at short courses, institutes, workshops etc. I think this is one of the most exciting developments in education generally throughout the country.

I had a nephew here last week. He's a dentist in Eau Claire, Wisconsin, down here for a three-day workshop on the relationship between dental problems and the jaw bone. I think he said there were about forty dentists from around the state here, housed at the Edgewater Hotel, not in an educational environment.

The point of all this is that there are so many needs and so many ways of meeting those needs and so many people involved in the whole thing that we jolly well better be sure that the *media—the broadcast media—*are available as instruments or tools of extending that kind of learning.

It's conceivable that a specialist of this kind could be brought in to Madison, say, for three days of special sessions, that this could be televised and made available throughout the state.

From the standpoint of sheer economics, it would be far cheaper to transmit to untold numbers of dentists throughout the state all of these ideas which my nephew found so dynamic and exciting. He had to come to Madison for three days, hire a baby-sitter to sit with their two children at home for three days and three nights. They have expenses—lord, do they have expenses! Staying at the Edgewater Hotel, you pick up the menu and it just scares you.

~

At Michigan State University and also in his professional involvements with university extension and as a counselor to those administering Title VII of the National Defense Education Act [prompted by the Russians' spectacular success in launching their Sputnik satellite], Dr. Armand Hunter developed an understanding of some of the currents flowing in the educational world in mid-century with respect to television.

HUNTER: There was a lot of research and experimentation into how this new medium could be used to carry out certain kinds of educational functions and objectives, and particularly to fill in where local resources were not available to do a job within a particular content area.

Take language instruction at the elementary level. There weren't very many local public schools with elementary language teachers; French and German and Spanish were not a part of the curriculum. So we decided, under Title VII, we could demonstrate that this could be taught at that level and that a program of this nature could be produced and distributed regionally or nationally. We set out to prove that you could teach French at the fourth-grade level. [We] developed a whole program series. We underwrote the research, the development of the program, tested it out. This is when research and evaluation became a part of most of this type of program activity.

It worked! Sure. You *can* teach French at the fourth-grade level. But the schools and colleges and universities said, "Well, sure, you did it for that [French], but you can't teach *Spanish* at the fourth-grade level." So, you do it for Spanish, [too].

"Well, maybe you can do it for French and Spanish, but you can't do it in *German*." So you do it in German. Title VII was underwriting successful projects in teaching French, Spanish, and German at the fourth-grade level.

Then the response was, "Well, it works all right at the fourth-grade level but it can't work at the sixth!" So you do it again for the sixth.

Now this is where, in my opinion, educational institutional community identification is a handicap: this sense of having to do your own. You remember Baxter and his Shakespeare program? [1]

I don't know how many English departments reviewed that program and decided, "Well, it was interesting, but really it didn't have the academic dignity and the status that was necessary," and if they were going to do a program, they'd do it themselves. So many institutions wouldn't use the program, simply because of [their belief in] the particular quality and effectiveness that only *they* could provide through their *local* faculty.

---

[1] Dr. Frank Baxter, a professor at the University of Southern California, became well known for his half-hour lectures on television. They were considered to be unusually interesting and appealing and attracted viewers who previously had no knowledge of or interest in Shakespeare. Initially produced at CBS-TV in Los Angeles, his programs were later broadcast nationwide by many noncommercial and some commercial stations.

You had this kind of thing running throughout a lot of the instructional program development and distribution and testing that was done under Title VII of the National Defense Education Act, so you proved it over and over and over again.

Feelings Among University Faculty

As a university faculty member himself, yet one with considerable experience in all aspects of television, Dr. Hunter described the attitude of the typical university faculty member toward TV instruction.

HUNTER: Their perception of it was that this is something the university administration is putting in to do away with the cost of additional sections, and they said, "Ah ha! Is the administration trying to provide instruction that is going to lead to the elimination of my particular department—or, at least, the loss of a job for a number of my colleagues?"

Then you had the personal response. Most teachers are performers when they are lecturing. They are at the head of the class and on the platform. It's their show. They are in the spotlight and they are in control. And they enjoy the applause or the boos of their student audience. Now they are reduced to sitting there and letting students watch the program, and then commenting about it afterwards.

Or, there is one of the members of their staff who is selected to do this program and *he* is the star, *he* is doing the instruction and they are not. And they are now held up to comparison between their performance and the "star" of the department who is doing it in this new medium with all of the visual resources that aren't available to them in the classroom.

My hunch is that you'd still run into the same kind of concern and problems today.

The Midwest Airborne Project

Dr. Hunter, along with other believers in the power of television as an educational tool, also became involved in a unique demonstration called the Midwest Program on Airborne Television Instruction, or MPATI.

HUNTER: The theory was that if you could raise the antenna height at the transmitting point, you could cover a wider range, so if you could get that antenna up high enough, it would cover a regional area—several states.

So you move from a ground-based tower to an airborne, airplane-type transmission facility.

This was an interim step to satellite transmission.[2]

~

Ohio State's perennial educational researcher, Dr. I. Keith Tyler, also became involved with MPATI.

TYLER: We tried an experiment coming out of LaFayette, Indiana, in which an airplane flew in figure eights and covered the major part of seven states with an airborne signal—two signals, as a matter of fact. They had two channels [of] school television.

I was on the committee that looked over the television teachers that had applied, looked at the kinescopes of these. Judith Waller and I and several others made tentative selections; then we interviewed these people and selected the television teachers.

HUNTER: You could design programs that would be relevant for regional utilization, rather than just local or even statewide. At this point also, the production quality from the local level was a concern, so you did have development of programs for Airborne that were a higher level of quality than you got from most of the local stations. You could put greater dollar resources into personnel and production and design and all the rest of it.

TYLER: Then we had the job of preparing teachers in the classroom to use television. I took a leave from Ohio State, and from May until August I was director of summer workshops for Airborne. We had forty-two workshops going in university centers—Notre Dame, Ohio State, Cleveland, everywhere. We fed them material from the plane which they would discuss, plus their local leader would go on with other activities which we suggested. We developed a handbook for them on all of the materials that would be fed to them by plane.

It still seemed to me to be kind of a screwy idea that you had to depend upon two airplanes flying, even though they had a better record of being up there and giving a signal than any school system did in terms of snow closings. In other words, they were like 98.5 percent of the time on the air, whereas schools didn't have that good a record.

They eventually tried to get support from state departments of education, so they could maintain this. But the trouble with the experiment was that too large a percentage of the budget was simply to keep these six DC-6Bs in the air, money that should have been going into the quality of programming. So that didn't really work.

But what it *did* do was to train school personnel to take television into account, to utilize it, to learn how to do it.

~

Evaluations of what Tyler calls a "screwy" project were mixed. Some educational stations picked up the airborne signals and retransmitted them; others subsequently made good use of some of the programs on tape. Was MPATI a success?

HUNTER: They did the job within the context of the demonstration: technically it's feasible. From the standpoint of program production and improving quality, and a design to meet regional needs and interests, yes.

Again, you had institutional failure to accept this as a resource, preferring either to ignore it or to produce their own local programs. It was a matter, again, of simple non-acceptance on the part of many institutions in utilizing the resource that was made available.

They were excellent productions and they did represent the highest state of the art that was available at that time.

~

Tyler's subsequent evaluation was somewhat more favorable.

TYLER: The state of Ohio, for example, now supports school television very strongly. They give both grants to stations directly to put these on the air, and they give grants to school systems in terms of their usage of them.

This grew out of MPATI, and this is going on in other states in the seven-state region, so I take my hat off to MPATI. It was a valiant effort.

One thing we learned was that a lot of amateurish things were going on. Individual school systems were putting on their own school broadcasting, using their own television teachers, some of them very good but some of them very poor. They were amateurish.

~

Unquestionably, MPATI also demonstrated another fact: that it is possible to produce instructional materials which are useful in many different localities, responding to instructional needs which are similar even though users are widely dispersed

---

[2] The project's ground base was Purdue University, which housed personnel responsible for keeping three DC-6Bs airborne. Dr. John Ivey, former head of the Southern Regional Education Board, became head of MPATI, an experiment funded by The Ford Foundation's Fund for the Advancement of Education.

geographically. Before MPATI, for the most part, each local school system or group of local systems felt it had to produce its own material.

TYLER: They thought they were unique. This is quite true.

Fourth-grade arithmetic in Miami certainly couldn't fit fourth-grade arithmetic in Columbus. This is nonsense, as we ought to have known, because we have such things as textbooks.

If we can have textbooks that serve the whole country, we can have instructional tapes or instructional broadcasts.

Effective Uses of TV for Instruction

Throughout this same period, in many parts of the country and despite foot-dragging by some, educational stations and schools were beginning to demonstrate the effectiveness of television as a learning tool. This was especially the case where local schools were not otherwise in a position to provide adequate instruction in a specific subject area.

OBERHOLTZER: At that time there was a great deal of interest in elementary-school Spanish, and I knew we had very few teachers who were prepared to do it. So our idea was, we would put on this series beamed into the elementary schools, and the teachers in the schools were learning along with the children in the matter of how to speak and write Spanish.

It was interesting to see what happened. We added four or five components to the teaching by television, and every component that we added, you had an increase in results from achievement tests. One of the most interesting results that seemed quite logical was that when the *parents* became involved in looking and learning *along with* those elementary school children, there was a very significant rise in achievement.

Another program that I was very much interested in was the teaching of reading to children before they came into school—before the first grade, or kindergarten, even. So we developed a series of programs that were beamed to mothers of pre-school children who, together with their children, viewed the program and then went ahead with the development of the learning.

We did develop secondary-school programs, especially for summer school. A good many children, instead of coming to a regular summer school, would take the courses by television.

Then they all had to take examinations to establish their credit, but a great many of them did.

We taught driver training by TV in the schools. We were told that it isn't desirable to get parents together with their progeny and teach them driver training, but we did.

One of the stipulations was that mom or dad had to look at the series on television together with the child. We developed printed program materials along with that. Then we had, at the conclusion, an actual driver testing as they do in school. They had to be able to drive the car. It worked out quite well.

One of the difficulties in high school was that you could only have four or five kids at most together with a driver. You never could fill the demand in the high schools that way except to have a large number of teachers. This way, we had one television teacher, and the volunteer teachers were the parents. It was, we thought, a very fine way of expanding, with a minimum of cost to all, that type of instruction.

MACANDREW: From certainly the days of World War I, the elementary-school teacher has been told that at least one half hour in the course of the week should be called "Current Events," and there was a useful little paper called "Current Events," but not every teacher was able to get it in. Not every teacher was equally able or had the time to put together, for ten- or eleven-year-old children, what happened in the world in the last week.

Now, all of a sudden, came a program for children called "Places In the News." The vocabulary was that which a child of eleven or twelve could comprehend. Difficult terms were either not used or they were put in the most common terms. And along with that came pictures.

I remember when "Places In the News" did a program about Alaska. Now, how many New York City children in the public schools had ever been to Alaska? Or were looking forward to going to Alaska?

We were able to get the United States senator from Alaska to come up to New York City and come to this little television studio and sit down with four children and the host, Jerry Silverstein. He brought with him pictures, he brought with him film—and suddenly, there is Alaska! And it's Alaska being told by the senior senator all the way from Alaska.

Now, wouldn't it be wonderful if that senator and his films and his pictures could go into every single classroom? Obviously, he couldn't. But by going once to a television studio and putting on this program, he had brought Alaska as it is, authentically, into the classroom, where the qualified teacher can then pick it up, and in a follow-up period after the broadcast, excite the children about Alaska so they would go to the library and read about it.

~

Macandrew recalled an entirely different use of television to respond to another educational need.

MACANDREW: Kindergarten teachers across the area were told, "When your children come in for an afternoon session, let them start by having half an hour of "Fun At One." This was an amazing program because it suddenly gathered ratings never dreamed of. The reason was that home viewers were absolutely delighted to discover this program. So in addition to kindergarten teachers and their classes in schools, we had a great many home viewers, where mothers with a three- or four-year-old child tuned in faithfully every day at one o'clock, after the child's lunch and before the afternoon nap, for the youngsters, and they saw those nice ladies on "Fun At One."

I recall a totally unknown but very talented young man named Jim Henson who brought a couple of his Muppets and appeared on "Fun At One."

HURLBERT: When we started our Alabama Educational Television Commission operation way back, we used the Laubach system of teaching reading. We had an instructor here in Birmingham, a black woman, who was a teacher, with whom I worked very closely. And we set up a training program for reading in this area using the Laubach system. She was so effective we had groups meeting in churches—here, there, and everywhere—tuning in on the television program.

~

Several ETV stations became involved in the effort to reduce illiteracy, realizing that even in the poorest homes there almost always was a television set. One of the earliest of these projects was undertaken by Martha Gable through the Philadelphia schools.

GABLE: "Operation Alphabet" was for illiterates. One of the members of my staff, Alex Sheflin, did "Operation Alphabet. He was a very good teacher and a real intellectual Ph.D., but he also could relate to the common man.

This went on at six o'clock in the morning so that working people could get it before they went to work. We had manuals for listening.

This was shipped all over the country. It even went to Hawaii. All kinds of people wanted this thing. It was on kinescope, and it wasn't very

good quality, but it came through enough.

And he had such devoted people [watching]; they would write him letters, and you could see they were struggling with the English language.

We were very proud of that. Some people who were polished English experts didn't think it was what it should be. I don't know what they thought it should be, but let me tell you, it worked! The people learned!

A woman came into my office one day and she said, "I can't tell you how grateful I am for "Operation Alphabet." My husband is a very good-looking man. He dresses well but he can't get a job above a certain level because he can't read or write." And when they discovered this they would keep him at a low level. Otherwise he would go on up the ladder because he had personality, and so on. She said, "This is opening up whole new careers to him."

We had this kind of thing happening over and over again. Same way with immigrants. They learned, you see, so they could go on and help themselves.

~

As the typical station manager or school director became more aware of what was going on in other school systems, other communities, two factors became clear:

One: there was a similarity in educational needs, the areas of instruction where most school systems were not able to meet the challenge with ordinary methods. These included science, " The New Math," and elementary foreign languages.

Two: no one station or group of school systems could quite marshall the financial resources to mount the kind of high quality instructional television materials which everyone desired.

McBRIDE: Up to this point, there had been very little exchange of educational television programming. The kinescope wasn't terribly reliable, and not every station had one. Each station, however close or far, had to start from scratch and develop and originate and produce and bear the costs of fourth-grade arithmetic, or whatever the subject was. Fifty miles down the road there might be another doing exactly the same thing.

It was right in this general period, also, when there was a magnificent breakthrough: Ampex startled the world by announcing the availability of videotape. What in the world was that?

I well recall the thrill and the joy of the Ford Foundation gift, through NET, which resulted one day, at each of our doorsteps, in the delivery of an Ampex videotape recorder.

Videotape Opens the Possibility of Exchange

Probably no other single technological development was as important in so many ways to the use of television in education—both broadcast and non-broadcast—as the advent of videotape. Just as the videocassette recorder now enables families to view TV materials at a time most convenient, the earlier availability of professional videotape recording equipment encouraged exchange of TV materials among ETV stations. Soon semi-professional equipment became available to school systems for similar sharing, as well as to be used merely to record instructional materials off the air and play them back in classrooms at most convenient or appropriate times.

The story of the Ford Foundation's grant of videotape recorders to all ETV stations, described in a previous chapter, was just the first step. The full impact of this technological advance in education was not generally appreciated for a decade thereafter, even though the exchange of instructional TV broadcast materials was greatly facilitated sooner.

Recognizing this new potential for exchange, the U.S. Office of Education made a grant from Title VII of the National Defense Education Act to Nebraska's Jack McBride and Dr. Wesley C. Meierhenry of the University of Nebraska's College of Education to undertake a year-long research project on the feasibility of instructional television exchange. With the coming of videotape, the way was clear for McBride and Meierhenry to initiate several proposals hitherto impractical but now well worth consideration.

McBRIDE: What we did was to develop a plan and a set of recommendations. That report we co-authored was widely distributed. It called, in effect, for the development of a national and several regional instructional television libraries, something that had not existed before, where everybody wouldn't have to produce the same program. Instead, you could acquire the rights to a quality program and arrange for duplicates to be made, and arrange for this to be libraried or arrange to have this leased.

After that year's study, the [U.S.] Office of Education did make several grants. One was to NET to establish a National Instructional Television Library, one was to the Eastern Educational Network for a regional development in the New England area, and the third was to Nebraska for a Great Plains Regional Instructional Television Library. Each of those, for a period of three to four years, received seed funding from the National Defense Education Act to test out different activities and to try and make these things develop.

~

In the shakedown resulting from a few years' experience, NET's library was shunted to Indiana University where it became the Agency for Instructional Television (AIT), and the Nebraska experiment broadened to become the Great Plains *National* Instructional Television Library.

McBRIDE: That really has been a very successful thing. It opened the door for a quantum improvement in the local station program schedule because it made available ever so many more quality programs than previously had been available.

You could concentrate many more dollars on fewer local productions, so local production improved as did your acquisitions.

~

Rhea Sikes recalled what it was like as these developments were taking place.

SIKES: About 1960, when most of us in the Northeast had at least one videotape machine, [we] began to speculate on the feasibility of exchanging taped programs among ourselves, programs of all types but particularly in the instructional area, simply because at that point there were six or seven of us doing elementary science. Which was ridiculous. If there was one elementary science series—if our committees said it was acceptable—why couldn't we all use the same series, and turn those minimal amounts of money that we had into the development of others?

We developed an evaluation system and a distribution system. In the beginning it was by tape, we had no interconnect [live network], but it worked. And if our committee [in Pittsburgh] saw an outstanding series from Boston—I think of "All About You," a health series for first graders. We needed that series, and it was a good series for that day and time, our educators were enthusiastic, our kids were. Okay, that relieved them of having to invest monies in that, and they could turn to something else.

~

The next logical step was cooperative production, and the instructional people in the regional Eastern Educational Network were ready and willing to try it.

SIKES: One phase of that Office of Education Title VII grant of ours, which was different from the others, was that we were supposed to do a cooperative production among the affiliates.

At that time, "The New Math" was hovering on the horizon, and there wasn't a teacher in God's green earth that knew what "The New Math" was! Except the professors who were designing it. So that seemed to be the subject area.

It was eventually produced in the studios of WETA in Washington and it was used by members throughout that network the following year. But it showed that a group of people *could* come together and agree on a need that was common to an entire region and that such a series *could* be produced. I think we learned a lot doing that. I think there were some heartaches and headaches and some problems as well as some victories.

~

From the vantage point of the 1990s, with consortiums undertaking production together on a regular basis, these accounts may seem primitive. But to those who pioneered, such projects as those described were high-water marks in the turbulent current of educational television's formative years.

The Small VCR Gives Teachers Control

In the early 1980s, those earlier professionals had thoughts about what the future might bring. For example, how did individuals like Rhea Sikes and Martha Gable view the introduction of small videotape recorders for use in schools? Clearly they welcomed this new capability to record broadcasts off the air and store and use them at times most convenient for classroom teachers.

SIKES: I think it is absolutely essential that schools use these [instructional] programs to the ultimate advantage, to have the availability to use [them] when *they need* them rather than when they are available in the broadcast schedule. But I know, still to date, the least expensive way for them to get those programs is to take them off the air, and have their own libraries, and then play them when *they* best can use them.

GABLE: Sooner or later we're going to have in the schools what they have in some of the college libraries. The teacher, the professor, says, "Go look at tape number thirty-five." He pushes a button and thirty-five comes up, he

looks at it at a terminal, you see, just like he uses a book out of the library.

Eventually this has got to happen.[3]

I just hope we have the vision and brains to see it coming and take hold of it before somebody else does, and it gets out of the hands of the educators. This is something the schools ought to be doing.

~

Gable also was one of the first to envision the possibilities in the use of a small television camera in combination with a videotape recorder, a pattern sometimes referred to as "micro-teaching." She was employing this technology in an innovative manner before it was widely available, foreshadowing procedures which today are becoming more commonplace. Even so, her imaginative application is worthy of notice.

GABLE: I took a course from Professor Dwight Allen at Stanford, where a teacher would do a five-minute lesson and then observe herself to see how she looked. I came back and I said, "Look, we're going to do this for children."

The youngsters would come on each day with a fifteen minute show. They had news, they had sports, they had weather, and they had school announcements. Four children would do these things and they would take their turn. Those children would come to school dressed up with ties, and the youngsters looked so nice. They got their own graphics. The principal gave us a room where we could have a studio and put everything in there. They'd get a little tape recorder or something to put some music in as background; they decided that. These were all elementary school children, mind you. Then I said, "We're going to record it and let these children see what they're doing."

I watched them, and it was so funny. One youngster said, "I didn't know they could see me chewing gum."

One youngster said, "I say runnin' and walkin' and that ain't right." [CHUCKLE] And then they watched, and you'd be surprised. In about a month, the diction of these children improved considerably. I couldn't get over it. They really took pride in what they were doing, and they saw their own errors.

I really feel that a lot of the values and potentials have been overlooked, that nobody has really pointed these things out, especially this business of transferring the micro-teaching technique to the micro-learning for children.

---

[3] By 1992, there were many places where this was happening.

Difficulties At the College Level

Will higher education ever embrace the use of television in education? Some institutions use it liberally to take the teaching resources of the campus to those distant learners who cannot attend classes on campus, and there have been many efforts to offer course work by television in conjunction with a correspondence-study element in much the same fashion as Britain's "Open University." Some have been very successful; others have not. Whatever efforts have been undertaken in more recent years, the observations of several of the founders of public television are worth consideration.

SIKES: When you get into college courses, you are talking about such a variety. You're talking about closed circuit on campus, emanating from that campus. You're talking about programs in which a part of the instruction is taken at home by television and there are work kits and then the student may or may not go to campus for a periodic seminar. You're talking about courses for credit versus courses that some colleges in the same town will recognize for credit and others won't.

It's growing, though, and I think maybe it has a greater future than K through twelve—simply because the population is getting older. We know from the demographics that people are going to move three or four times during their lifetime, have three or four jobs, and they're going to need job training. We know that industry is beginning to rely very heavily on video education.

The older one grows and the more mature one becomes, the more self-motivated one is, and therefore it is an individual responsibility rather than a classroom responsibility under the expertise of an instructor.

It may be that during the decade of the eighties, educators in institutions of higher learning will really give more attention than they ever have in the past to what might be done to help them provide quality learning experiences for adults in the most economic fashion.

~

Lee Frischknecht offered another slant on the degree of readiness of university faculty to flirt with TV. At the time of our visit, in 1981, he was part of the management team at KAET in Phoenix and was living in Tempe, Arizona. He recalls some of his experiences of twenty years ago with Michigan State faculty members.

FRISCHKNECHT: It's interesting to look back on what has happened to a lot of the faculty members I worked with when I was producing and directing and later on as program manager.

I watched over the years what's happened to those people who came out of those departments to teach those courses on television. By and large, they were people who were young and eager and willing to take the risk of doing this television thing. And a very large number of them ended up being department heads and deans and directors of departments. Which I think was kind of an interesting result and commentary on the kinds of people who were attracted to new things as they were to this new technology.

~

Loren Stone of the University of Washington station expressed his dissatisfaction with some of his faculty friends in higher education.

STONE: I had any number of lecturers when I was in college who read the same doggone lecture notes they'd been reading for twenty years. They hadn't changed it one iota. There was no reason in the world they couldn't have canned that and put it on film or tape and had that run, and spent all of their time counseling students.

This is what I kept trying to urge—but oh, gee, you know, I was not out of education, I didn't have a Ph.D., I didn't know these things, I had come from the outside, and most of these people wouldn't listen.

Some of the chairmen of departments were that sort of classroom lecturers, and they were afraid to have anyone outside see how bad they were. I know one of our deans—I went over one time and watched his history class. He was the worst lecturer I ever saw. He never looked up from his notes; he read every word of his lecture with absolutely no expression. He could never have gone on television and made a good presentation and dared let anybody see it.

~

Here and there across the country, a university president or extension dean caught a glimpse of the potential. At the University of Nebraska, for example, Jack McBride recalls the unusually strong support he enjoyed from two of that institution's presidents.

McBride first spoke about Clifford Hardin, the first president of the University of Nebraska who was called upon to consider educational television.

MCBRIDE: Very supportive. We were able to have a good relationship with him. He, coming out of an extension background and a land-grant philosophy, realized that this was another important way a land-grant institution should serve the people.

We found him quite supportive, and really one of the founding fathers of that which developed here in Nebraska, so much so that a few years back, we had our Nebraskans for public television statewide lay organization give him a distinguished service award for his extensive contribution in developing public television in this state.

He was a member of the first ETV Commission and served well over those years as we built the [statewide] network, and he later moved from that to become secretary of [the Department of] Agriculture in the Nixon administration.

Woody Varner is another one, very important to us. We had an extremely close relationship with him.

It was because of his interest in using distant teaching of college credit courses that led us to develop, first, the State University of Nebraska [SUN], and from that evolved the University of Mid-America and the receipt of about six years of major funding, first from the Office of Education and then the new National Institute of Education, as this country's premiere development of open learning. That really all generated as the result of Woody Varner's initial interest in using the Nebraska network for distance teaching.

~

Dr. John Taylor, long-time head of Chicago's WTTW who spent his entire professional life in education tells of his efforts to generate interest in the Chicago area.

Taylor himself saw the possibilities, and in the mid-fifties established "TV College" in cooperation with the Chicago community colleges, a remarkably successful effort to teach the first two years of college courses by television, the basic courses necessary to secure the associate in arts degree.

TAYLOR: When we had the first television graduates here, our friend Al Eurich, who was still then the vice president of the Fund for the Advancement of Education, came out and delivered the commencement address.

It gave people confidence in themselves. If they could do it by television, some of them went on to the campus. If they didn't [go to the campus to continue], if they finished the TV work and received their A.A. degree, then they went to another institution to go and finish their bachelor's degree.

We had a student in his early twenties graduate with an A.A. degree, and his mother and father graduated with him. They had all done it by television. That's the kind of thing that makes you know it's worthwhile.

And it's still going on. We have what in the Chicago community college system is now called "Chicago City-Wide College." It offers, in practically every branch library, any of the courses that have been offered or are still being offered on television, *on tape*. So you can go there at your own convenience and sit down and put on the earphones at a tape machine and take a course in whatever they have to offer, and then when you're through, you take the examination. If you bust the examination, you can take it again—until you make it.

~

The Chicago "TV College" project led the way followed by a number of other community colleges across the country.

But Taylor tells ruefully of earlier efforts to strike a spark at the renowned University of Chicago. At one time he even joined with Fred Friendly, functioning as a Ford Foundation consultant, to induce faculty at that institution to consider teaching by television.

TAYLOR: We sat down with key members of the law school faculty. Mr. Friendly said, "I've been out to the law school at Stanford and I'm going to the law school at Yale or Harvard, one or the other, and I'm coming to you. And I'm saying that the Ford Foundation will put up the money for the absolute best one in the faculty to teach whatever course he wants. You—all three—agree that you'll credit the thing, that your students take it."

They just laughed at him. They said, "There's nobody that knows more about courts than we do; nobody knows more about this branch or that, why should we let some nut from these other institutions do it?"

I really think it's basically an insecurity on the part of the teachers that some guy is going to become the Number One professor in this, that, or the other field, and it isn't what he wants.

Of course, the arguments that they put up—most of them won't admit it. Like they did out here at the University of Chicago, most of them give you all the other arguments about "You can't do proper teaching without one-on-one. We lecture, of course, but we have discussion groups and we have all these things."

Well, Friendly said, "You can have discussion groups on this, too. Let them listen to the lectures and then have your discussion groups."

"We don't want it!"

I just think you can analyze it from A to Z but it comes straight down to basic insecurity: "my job."

"Sesame Street" Shows the Way to Success

A new approach to "instructional" television was introduced when Joan Ganz Cooney put together the initial concept of "Sesame Street." It is safe to assert that no project—either used in the classroom or for home viewing—ever has accomplished more "instruction" than this single idea, which quickly mushroomed into what is now a worldwide phenomenon.

To begin with, the purpose of "Sesame Street" was to provide pre-school children, particularly those in disadvantaged families, with some help before they started school. But it soon outgrew this purpose. It became a staple in the diet of children's programs during late afternoon hours and was programmed for in-school use by public television stations across the country.

School superintendent Kenneth Oberholtzer recalls the day Joan Ganz Cooney brought her idea to the board of directors of National Education Television.

OBERHOLTZER: She presented her idea before the board. Well, it was a different structure than had been conceived for most of television instruction up to that time. This was more informal, a play atmosphere for children, a use of individual actors who could portray parts to show development and a psychology of learning which was less formal altogether than the typical instructional program produced by the stations.

There was considerable discussion within the board. I had some doubts, frankly, about it at the time. But I think the vote was unanimous to go ahead when it came finally to a decision to do it, and I'm thankful that it was, because the doubts were dispelled once it got on the air and got going.

Can "Instruction" Be "Entertaining" ?

"Sesame Street" seemed to defy the notion which had grown up in early days of educational television that programs either had to be for instruction or for general informational-cultural home viewing, that the audiences were different. Rhea Sikes was asked how she accounted for this dichotomy.

SIKES: It was started by a very capable social scientist, Ray Carpenter, at Penn State University. Ray had done a great deal of work with primates; I think that's where he made his national mark as an anthropologist, behaviorist, I suppose.

But somehow he got interested in educational television, and I assume in order to do his analysis of this medium and its potential for use for the general public, he decided they had to codify the activities. That's the scientific thing to do. He very conveniently codified programming that was developed to be used as a part of a school curriculum as "ITV" and then all the rest of the noncommercial programming was "ETV" —educational television.

The minute this happened, I really was horrified. One cold winter day a little plane landed at Penn State and Ray and I were both on it and we shared a cab in to the campus, and he asked me if I had seen his article on this. I'm afraid I let Ray know how I felt about it. I think it was a very bad mistake.

I can see why scientists would want to codify, but in the codifying you set up a dichotomy which it took us years—and we're still working—to break down.

I think we were interested in bringing information of all kinds at all levels and all spectrums of the human condition in an entertaining way—and by entertaining I mean in an arresting, attention-getting, thought-provoking way—to the general public. And it didn't make any difference to me whether that program went at nine o'clock in the morning for fifth graders or it went at nine o'clock at night for adults. It still had a purpose for going.

The reason that a big division grew larger and larger was mostly a financial one, because the schools were expected to support the so-called ITV programming, and then the general public and other benefactors were supposed to support the programming which was not designed specifically for school use. And I think that's where it grew and became more and more separated.

Had there been more money for so-called ITV, I am sure there would have been fewer "talking faces."

~

Sikes also concluded that the way in which one approaches the design of a program differs, depending upon the likely viewers.

SIKES: In general programming, you could start with an idea or identify a need, and then research it, and then approach it in any way you wanted to.

But [in ITV] you had a bunch of youngsters meeting in classrooms, and you had to develop a creative way of making course materials available to them that had been prescribed by another agency.

~

Nebraska's Jack McBride offered a further clarification.

MCBRIDE: We decided at the outset that we would have a dual-program philosophy. We would produce both instructional programming, whose primary audience was students at all levels, "educational television," if you will—and also, we would produce informational, educational, cultural, public affairs, and children's programming for a target audience in the home. And we've always maintained that dual responsibility and dual interest, even after the coinage of the term "public television."

~

We return to Ohio State's perennial observer of American education and a prominent researcher in the field of educational TV for a few summary comments which hopefully may shed additional light on the elements necessary if television is ultimately to be embraced by educators as a proper and powerful teaching tool.

TYLER: I have two points that I want to make, and they are very closely related.

The first point is that people who go into a new field very often exaggerate the claims for what can be done [with] the new invention or new development.

This was very true of the Ford Foundation when it came to television in its early days; they thought it would solve most of the problems that education was facing because of the limited number of teachers and the burgeoning number of students. They were not really interested in accompanying their experiments with research. They felt the results would be obvious, so why bother to spend money for research.

Later, after these various experiments were over, they came out with some pamphlets which *did* point out the fact they had made unwarranted or exaggerated claims. But this was after the fact.

~

It is only fair to state that the Ford Foundation was not alone in this. Dr. Tyler's first assertion described accurately the activities of many early enthusiasts.

TYLER: The other point is this: It should have been obvious from the beginning that any one means of learning is not as good as a combination.

To expect people to educate themselves by reading in the loneliness of their own rooms is not very realistic—although some people do manage to achieve some sort of education by reading alone.

In the same way, people who were pushing educational television in its early days felt that it *alone* would accomplish great things, that we would have the great lectures and the great teachers on television, and just by sitting in front of the set and listening to them and watching them, we would learn and increase our education.

Actually, we found that this is not terribly effective, though it does have value. In some cases, where a person is ready for that experience and needs what the man [or woman] is bringing, it may be very helpful.

But in general, we know that there has to be in most cases *mediation* of a person between the educational medium and the learner. If it's books, you usually have a teacher who gets you to answer questions about it or write papers about it, or do things of that sort whereby you digest the material.

With television it's the same way. Some person is needed who can prepare you for the experience and follow up afterwards to relate this experience to what you already know or what you already have learned, so that it becomes a meaningful experience.

Indeed, I would say that the best way of learning if you have your druthers would be to have skilled teachers and a variety of media: television, including videocassette recording; radio, including audio recordings; films, books, pamphlets, all sorts of materials. And indeed, let us not forget the community itself where children can go out and interview people, get data from which to draw inferences, and the like.

Learning is not a simple process and it isn't a matter of simply being exposed.

Science has made possible a great many things. And advocates are likely to say that because science makes this possible, therefore they will come true. This is not the actual case.

I heard recently a lecture by the head of Battell Memorial Institute, a big research foundation here in Columbus [Ohio]. He was talking about the fact that they get all kinds of inventions and ideas thrown their way. Let's say two thousand. They examine them and maybe seven hundred are promising. They come out with maybe twenty that work.

The point I'm making is that all these were good ideas, technically feasible, but they didn't fit the real world in which we live.

This, I think, is something for us to remember who are in the field of communications, especially television. There is the human animal and there is the nature of habit, and all of these are mitigating influences, and just because a thing is possible doesn't mean it's going to happen.

~

Many of public television's visionaries assert that greater progress might have been made, in both instructional uses of the medium and in informational-cultural programming, if far more substantial funding had been available. The notion of federal assistance had been put forward in the earliest days of noncommercial broadcasting, but in all probability had seemed unfeasible because of the traditional attitude against federal aid to education in general.

That notion of federal assistance became more than a tentative idea as the public began to respond positively to programs broadcast by the early noncommercial television stations. But many years would pass, and some highly placed persuasive leadership would be necessary, before any help would come from Congress.

20

First Steps Toward Federal Assistance

For nearly a decade after the reservation of television channels for noncommercial educational use, there was no federal effort to determine how these stations were to be funded. All such efforts were state and local, community by community.

But the idea of federal assistance had been broached as early as the mid-1950s by Leonard Marks, the communications attorney who was counsel—many times unpaid-to the National Association of Educational Broadcasters.

MARKS: The suggestion came about during an informal meeting of the NAEB Board of Directors. Everybody there was downcast because their institutions did not have adequate funds to proceed and develop the television spectrum.

And I said that I thought because it was an educational institution, we could follow the precedent of legislation adopted in the early days in the land-grant colleges where the federal government provided the necessary funds to get these institutions started—seed money. I saw no reason why that parallel couldn't be applied to this technology, because these stations were educational institutions the same as land-grant colleges.

Some of the people felt that it would be improper because then the government would have a voice in determining the programming. And I said we'd have nothing to lose by attempting to try, and I would attempt to sell Lyndon Johnson and some of the people in the Congress, House and Senate side, on the theory of it. And they said, "Go ahead and try," so I did.

I found that Senator Johnson was very interested in the idea. He wasted no time. He took me over to Senator Warren Magnuson, who at that time was involved on the Interstate and Foreign Commerce Committee, and aides to Lyndon Johnson and I drew up a bill.

We gave it to Magnuson to introduce. He didn't change a word. He just put his name on it, introduced it, and then that began the process for federal assistance.

~

But what Marks called "the process for federal assistance" took awhile. It did not pass the first time around, or the second. Magnuson kept introducing it in each succeeding session of the Congress, with the strategic help of Senator John Pastore and legislative assistant Nicholas Zapple in the Senate and Oren Harris in the House, urged on by the National Association of Educational Broadcasters and the Joint Council on Educational Television.

Probably one reason for the reluctance of the Congress to approve such assistance was the time-honored argument that education in America should always be locally controlled and therefore locally funded. The federal government, some felt, should stay out of local education. Another concern was that if federal dollars were involved, eventually they would somehow influence programming.

But the Educational Television Facilities bill was so drafted that none of its funds could be used to support program operations. Its advocates pointed out that it was an *incentive* bill; it provided *matching* funds for the purchase of television *equipment* by noncommercial educational stations, making it considerably easier for educational institutions and community licensees to get new stations built and on the air with the best professional equipment.

Long-time FCC Commissioner Rosel Hyde relates that first effort.

HYDE: I recall that when Fred Ford was chairman [of FCC], the Magnuson proposal was made, and hearings were held on it before the Senate committee, and the FCC was asked to submit comments, as they always are on matters changing the law that they administer. This is regular procedure.

The majority of the commissioners took the position that whether or not there should be matching grants was a matter of policy which would be better left to the Congress. The commission didn't feel it was in a position to advise.

I dissented to this statement and submitted a statement of my own in which I took the position that the commission, as the licensing authority, *was* in a position by reason of its experience and its licensing function to offer advice. And my advice was that the provision of funds for stations which would operate from a different economic basis from that of advertiser-supported television would give a new dimension, provide a new kind of diversity, and I strongly favored the proposal.

Chairman Minow Differs With Colleagues

But it was not until Newton N. Minow became chairman of the Federal Communications Commission in 1961 that movers and shakers in Washington became aware of the need to assist the growth of this new kind of television, which the FCC had authorized nearly a decade before. Minow's interest in television as an aid to education had begun much earlier.

MINOW: The first time I saw a television set I was totally convinced this was one of the most important inventions of all time.

I was still in college, but I had served in the war in the army in India, and I had been deeply impressed by the power of film as an educational and training device in the army. We used to have movies at night; we were outdoors. When the lights went on in the trucks to take us back to the barracks, I found thousands of Indians who had come in to see the movies. I was immediately thunderstruck by the implications of all this for education.

When I finished my education and started living in Chicago, I became aware of *educational* television for the first time because our Channel 11, WTTW, was one of the early stations. And I became involved, and my wife became involved right at the start in trying to help support the work of WTTW.

Minow testifying

Of course, what I knew was really what I saw in Chicago; I wasn't aware as much of what was happening in other places.

In Chicago, our educational television station was closely associated with the public school system and the community college system.

My own feeling was that the programs were singularly unappealing. It was usually a grey professor giving a grey lecture in front of a grey drape and the result was not attractive to a large audience. But I felt that in time this "sleeping giant" could be brought to life and could become a major national force.

~

Minow recalls that on the first day he was presiding at the commissioners' meeting, in March of 1961, one of the items on the agenda was the draft of testimony the FCC was to give to Congress on that year's legislation sponsored by Warren Magnuson in the Senate, and Oren Harris in the House to put some money for the first time into educational television through matching grants for facilities. As Rosel Hyde recalled at an earlier time, the commissioners felt this was properly a matter for the Congress to decide and that the FCC should not take a stand, one way or the other.

MINOW: I said, "No." I said, "I think our job here, under the law, is to advance the public interest—and I think the FCC should say that."

So I think the first time I appeared as chairman it was in a role where I read the majority statement of the commission and then read a dissenting statement of my own, saying that I felt that the legislation was desirable and that I felt that the FCC should support it.

That was sort of a signal to the view I held: that our job there was to be more than a referee. It was to be an advocate, and to do what we could to advance educational television.

~

Where Rosel Hyde had sown the seed, Newton Minow forced its growth. And by 1961-62, more and more constituents of the congressmen across the land were asking for assistance for their fledgling ETV stations. Finally, in 1962, the Educational Television Facilities Act became law. And Leonard Marks, who had initiated the notion nearly ten years before, was among those at the White House when President John F. Kennedy signed it into law.

MARKS: One of the greatest moments of my professional life: I was invited to the signing, and Kennedy gave the pen to Senator Magnuson and said, "This is your bill."

And Magnuson turned to me and said, "No, this is Leonard Marks' bill," and he gave *me* the pen.

Other Friends at the FCC

Veteran communications attorney Marcus Cohn, partner with Leonard Marks—and like Leonard, a former staff member of FCC and a shrewd observer of the Washington scene—has frequently paid tribute to the two chairmen of the FCC who gave their support to this history-making legislation.

COHN: I've always had a tremendous affection for Rosel. He knows the general direction that broadcasting ought to have as its goal, but he wasn't tough, he wasn't dynamic, he didn't inspire.

I recognize him to be a very, very devout religious person, a person who is considerate with society, where society is and where it's going. He has spent his entire life really devoting himself to helping society. You have to bear in mind also that Rosel came up from the ranks at the commission. As I recall, he was a file clerk or something at the very beginning, and then step after step after step went through the legal department and then finally became a commissioner and finally became chairman.

It would have been of such great help had he been tougher, had he been more ruthless.

Newt had all those qualifications that Rosel had—a great big heart, great big concern about society, a dedication to the public—but Newt was bright and tough, and that's what's needed at the commission.

It's not sufficient simply to have good people, because good people don't necessarily accomplish results. What we need in administrative agencies are good and dedicated people who can be tough when necessary, can be very articulate when necessary, and indeed can almost be ruthless if necessary.

~

A comparison of Minow with Frieda Hennock is offered in the comments of Hyman Goldin, who served at the commission under several administrations.

GOLDIN: Newton's interesting in comparison with Frieda [Hennock]. Newton was the second Jewish commissioner on the commission, and they both were lawyers, both came from big cities.

Newton was far more sophisticated than Frieda. Frieda was first generation. Newton, you know, was a different stripe. Newton was very skillful in his public relations. He was extraordinarily good at Congress. He never shouted and ranted and raved as Frieda did. He had the congressional hearings in his palm all throughout his tenure.

And he was always receptive to new ideas. He basically was not for program regulation; he was for program diversity through the growth of UHF, he hoped, and then he saw educational broadcasting as a possibility.

He obviously met with a lot of people. And one of them, somewhere along the line, said to him, "You know, wouldn't it be a great idea to have a special unit in the FCC devoted to educational broadcasting?" And he thought that was great.

~

Chairman Minow was looking for a way to demonstrate that he intended to follow through on his convictions about the desirability of the FCC encouraging the growth of noncommercial stations.

The Educational Broadcasting Branch

MINOW: To telegraph to the broadcasting community that we meant it, we established a separate bureau in the agency to help educational broadcasters. That continued for many years.

I wanted somebody [to head it] who knew something about it and who had confidence of the educational broadcasting community. Curiously enough, if you did that today, people would say, "That probably is a conflict of interest." But I think that's one of the things that has gone sour. You should have people in those jobs who know something, and the only ones who know something are the ones who have had some experience.

~

Hy Goldin watched over the Educational Broadcasting Branch as part of his assortment of responsibilities.

GOLDIN: It was formed in the latter part of '61, and without a very specific idea except that [it] would be a kind of lobbyist for the educators within the commission, at least to acquaint the commission with what was going on in the field, and also have a place where educators could talk [to the FCC] about their problems.

It was kind of a limited enterprise. Keith Engar was the first person I hired, and we had only him and a secretary basically. And that was what the Educational Broadcasting Branch remained throughout its tenure.

ENGAR: There was a generally favorable disposition toward educational television on the part of the commissioners, but on the part of the staff, there needed to be a real education job done.

They set it up so that I had a chance to visit and spend time briefing the persons in the Broadcast Bureau. And I was able to eat in the executive lunch room; this gave me further chance outside the Broadcast Bureau to talk to people about educational broadcasting. I found a surprising degree of naiveté in the commission on what educational broadcasting was all about.

Hy Goldin was a great human being. He even let me share his office, which he regretted because it was awkward for him, but I felt it was important that the Educational Broadcasting Branch have sufficient prestige so I let him do it, and he put in a temporary divider, blessed guy. He was just fully supportive.

I will say I had a great deal of respect for the commission and the people on the staff. They were conscientious, they were professionals, they were out to do the best job they could.

GOLDIN: To influence policy in the FCC you have to be very knowledgeable about the institutional arrangements and the people who work those arrangements, who work the system within the commission.

The people whom I hired—Keith Engar and Larry Frymire and Bob Hilliard—never got into that part of it.[1] I remained the one who was in that part, and they were essentially people who were liaison with the educators rather than people who shaped policy within the FCC.

There was great cooperation between our Educational Broadcasting Branch and the processing unit in the Broadcast Bureau. That worked out fine.

~

Despite Chairman Minow's initial enthusiasm for educational television, he discovered that ETV was, at that time, not nearly so widespread as he had assumed.

MINOW: After I got into it and started studying it, I became aware of my own ignorance. I found out, for example, that in 1961 there was no educational television station in New York, or in Los Angeles, or in Cleveland, or in Baltimore, or in a dozen other major American cities. I thought everybody was like Chicago!

President Kennedy, who came to the presidency from Boston, thought—having lived in Boston—everyone had a station like WGBH.

So, imagine my surprise when I found what a small part of the nation was covered by educational television. There was none in Washington at that time!

I concluded the first thing we had to do was to get some major cities to have stations, and I felt that it was crucial we get a station in New York and in Los Angeles, because that's where most of the production of television was. I felt that we had to do that.

I also felt that the only future for educational television on a national basis was to open up UHF, because the VHF channels were basically gone, and if you were going to have a national system, UHF was the only answer.

---

[1] Frymire and Hilliard were subsequent heads of the FCC's Educational Broadcasting Branch of the Broadcast Bureau.

Overcoming the Curse of a UHF Channel

In the middle years of the twentieth century, TV receivers in the hands of the public were incapable of receiving UHF channels. Only those who purchased converters could watch the few noncommercial UHF stations that had courageously gone on the air. So in cities awarded only a UHF reserved channel, there was minimal incentive to activate a station, and three-fourths of the channels reserved for noncommercial use were UHF.

GOLDIN: Newton, however, came in fresh and believed that something could be done about UHF. And there were many, many meetings with the staff and many meetings on the hill.

A compromise was worked out by the FCC people and by industry people and by that Association of Maximum Service Telecasters. They finally persuaded Newton that that was his only hope.

So the All-Channel Bill requirement was that all TV receivers would have to be able to receive both V and U.

That was kind of radical at the time. I think it's one of the few times—certainly the first time—that the FCC dealt with receivers, and one of the few bills where Congress required the industry to do something like this. The industry was recalcitrant at the beginning, but they were brought around because RCA was involved and thus they began to accept the bill on the grounds that greater evil might take place.

After eight years, UHF was still struggling but nobody ever thought of going back.

MINOW: All of that happened in '62, a big year for educational television. That meant that: one, some money was going in to build stations; two, it meant that UHF would be much more attractive with people having UHF receivers in their homes, though we knew it would take a decade for that to occur.

And then, of course, we got involved with the New York situation, which is a different subject.

~

Minow was right. Proponents of educational television were psychologically heartened and materially assisted by the passage of the Educational Television Facilities Act and the All-Channel Receiver legislation—not only by these enactments but by these indications of a rising tide of interest and support for this new kind of television.

Even so, it would be five years before even the phrase "public television" would become known—years in which many more stations would come on the air and those on the air would become stronger, years in which National Educational Television (NET) would provide greatly improved programming but also would generate greater dissatisfaction among restless affiliates, years in which a distinguished national commission would be funded by the Carnegie Corporation and encouraged by President Lyndon B. Johnson to show the full promise of noncommercial television.

These developments would be necessary before public television, as it is known today, could come into being as a result of the Public Broadcasting Act in 1967.

21

The Late Bloomers:
New York, Washington, Los Angeles

Because New York, Washington, and Los Angeles were places where commercial television had developed early, all of the VHF channels in those cities had been occupied by the time the FCC acted to reserve at least one TV channel in each of 242 communities for noncommercial educational use. Thus the channel reserved for ETV in each of those major communities was UHF. So during those years when no home TV set was built to receive UHF, what were leaders to do who were convinced of the value of educational television and yearning to bring it to these major communities?

In New York, the Metropolitan Educational Television Association (META) was formed to do what it could. In Washington, much was accomplished through cooperation with commercial stations before the commercial demands on their daytime hours drove away the in-school telecasts. In Los Angeles, one man built a television station which nobody could receive. When he pulled out, the channel went dead, until ten years later.

Several of public television's founders recall each of these developments, demonstrating again the dedication to the cause manifested in these cities.

Members of The Ford Foundation's Fund for Adult Education under Scotty Fletcher and Bill Griffiths were concerned about all three situations.

META, the Earliest Effort
in New York City

GRIFFITHS: The role in New York, thanks again to the UHF curse, was largely to keep something alive—something we talked about with the Metropolitan Educational Television Association known as META, which was a pretty impressive cluster of interested institutions with nowhere to go, really.

That was Art Hungerford's baby, with quarters in the Carnegie building over on the East River.

HUNGERFORD: In this situation with no access to a channel, the only thing we could really do [was] to build a studio and try to develop some programs which could find space on commercial stations pending the time when the UHF station might be practical [because] there might be some sets out.

The pattern I saw anyway was that we would have a studio which the constituent organizations who could not afford one of their own would use to package their programs, and then we would agree to send them live or by whatever means to the stations.

The first thing we wanted to do was in-school programs, the next thing we wanted to do was high school programs, the next thing we wanted to do was college programs, and then way down the list eventually, cultural and informational, plus production work for the Educational Television and Radio Center.

~

Subsequently, Allen Brown, previously president of Hobart College, was imported to head the operation, and he brought in Richard Heffner, who had been one of Brown's students at Columbia University. This change in administration led to some differences in approach which were not altogether successful. Although air time was acquired on commercial station WPIX from eleven o'clock to noon weekdays, and some satisfactory programs were produced, both for schools and for the center, the board was not a fund-raising board and things began to look bad at META.

HUNGERFORD: I'll never forget a meeting with [Alvin] Eurich [vice president of Fund for the Advancement of Education of the Ford Foundation] and [Joseph] Eisman [Ford Foundation attorney]. It was simply, "How do we bury META in a nice way, so that it can make way for a different organization that will have more financing backing from the big shots in New York?"

~

The in-school programming produced at META and aired on WPIX was taken over by the State Department of Education and continued on WPIX under James Macandrew.

Maneuvering to Buy A VHF Channel

About the time of the demise of META, Jack White was bringing NET to New York. He and his board-indeed, most everyone in the field—anguished over the lack of a station in New York.

WHITE: I knew we had to have one. I went to see two people: Frank Stanton [CBS] and Frank Marks, who was head of engineering for ABC. It was Stanton who said, "Jack, there is a station which can be had here, and it's Channel 13." He advised me how to go about it. That was, to get a broker and get an estimate of what it was going to go for, so that I had something to work with.

~

Stanton introduced White to broadcast station broker Howard Stark, whose investigation showed that Channel 13, though allocated to New Jersey, was indeed available—for a price—probably about $4 million.

WHITE: My first call was to George Stoddard. He was a member of my NET board but also was vice chancellor of New York University. I said, "George, who do I have to see to start working on a station for this town?"

He said, "You've got to go to see Arthur Houghton. He heads Steuben Glass, he's very active at Lincoln Center, also at the Metropolitan. He's interested in things cultural. I think that's where you start."

So George called Arthur, and he said he'd be glad to see me, and the result of that half hour was, "I'm with you. I'll work with you, Jack, but I'm not your leadership. You've got to go see John Rockefeller." So he made a date for me to see John Rockefeller.

Now it needs to be said that in the meantime, Henry Heald had moved from NYU to be president of the Ford Foundation, and I knew I had to have resources so I had him all built in. I went to see John Rockefeller. John Rockefeller said, "I'm with you, great idea, we're going to make this thing work—but I'm not you're leadership." He said, "You've got to see Robert Moses."

I recall that day I had to fly immediately afterwards to Cincinnati and said I'd call Moses when I got back. I didn't have a chance. I was at the station in Cincinnati, a phone call came through. It was Robert Moses calling me. He had to see me!

So the next day when I got back from Cincinnati I went out to Randall's Island, where his headquarters were, and sat down, and—what an afternoon! He had huge maps. "Now this is where we're going to put it, and we'll condemn this property and put it right here."

I said, "Now wait a minute, Mr. Moses. Let's not worry about real estate quite yet. I've got to buy a channel first." I said, "When I'm ready to talk about real estate, we'll be back."

So I got myself extricated there, went back to Mr. Rockefeller and said, "John, some day that may be great, but right now that's the wrong way to go. I think you and I ought to go over to see Henry Heald at the Ford Foundation, because we've got to have their support." So I made a date, and Mr. Rockefeller and I went over to see Henry. After outlining it all as though it was strange, Henry said, "What's this station going to cost?" And I said, "Well, our broker estimates $4 million." He said, "All right, John, the Ford Foundation will put up two million if you will go out and raise the other two." Rockefeller said, "You're on, Henry."

~

The Ford Foundation's Jim Armsey was playing a role in all of this, too, as well as on subsequent occasions as the price for Channel 13 escalated.

ARMSEY: Everybody agreed we had to have a VHF station in New York so we started trying to see what we could do about that.

There were a lot of people running in and out of the office. Heald and I had interminable and numerous meetings with these characters who would come in and say "We're doing this and here's the problem and can you do this?" and we kept saying, "You do that; we'll do this."

What one must remember about foundations—and especially the Ford Foundation the way it was functioning in those days—was that what we had was money and what we could provide was money. Now, money would provide the convincer with leverage to get other people to do things because they thought that later on in their interest they could get some money, too. But it was money that talked there, and that was what we had, and we were ready to move.

I convinced Heald that all this made sense and that there simply had to be a station to take care of that New York area.

~

In the conversation between Heald and Rockefeller, it was agreed that another individual whom Jack White should see was Devereux Josephs.

WHITE: They made a date for me to see Dev, who again gave me the same line, "I'm with you, I'll work, but I'm not your leadership."

Between the two of us, we came up with the name of Howard Shepard, who was just at that time retiring as chairman of First National City Bank. He didn't have all this commitment all around town to Lincoln Center and everything else so he was fairly flexible. Dev [Josephs] made a date to see Howard, and Howard said, "Sounds intriguing as hell. I'm with you."

So Howard became chairman, and Dev Josephs, John Rockefeller, Arthur Houghton, George Stoddard, and Jack White started out on the business of raising the money. We didn't have a line of publicity; we didn't put out any word to anybody. In about seven weeks, we had raised the money. Not one single foundation or corporation we called on said, "No." Every single one put in.

The three networks had pledged half a million dollars each. The two independent stations, Metromedia and the *Daily News* station, had pledged $250,000 each.

We had begun our negotiations, we were in hot sessions and all three networks had announced it, when the word came through on a phone call that ABC didn't intend to give a half million dollars; they were only going to give $250,000.

Well, we actually had an air check of Leonard Goldenson himself on radio announcing they pledged a half million dollars, but that did no good.

So I went to Frank Stanton. Frank said, "All right, let's go to see Bobby Sarnoff." He said, "I'll tell you right now, if either one of the networks puts up a half million dollars, we'll fulfill our pledge, Jack." But he said, "Let's go. I'll help you with Bobby."

An Assist from Newton Minow

At about this point in the negotiations, FCC Chairman Newton Minow read a front page story in the *New York Times* about a group made up of foundations and educational broadcasters who were trying to buy Channel 13.

MINOW: I read that on my way to work one morning. And I called our staff in and I said, "How can we help them achieve that? We've got to get an educational TV station in New York."

They said, "There really isn't any way you can help that. The owners can sell it to whomever they please."

And I said, "Yeah, but we'd have to approve the transfer and we have the right to disapprove it."

They said, "Yeah, but you can't disapprove it just arbitrarily, you have to have a reason. And you can't disapprove it because you think another buyer would be better." A specific provision in the law which would have given us that power had been taken away by Congress.

So I said, "Well, that's not good enough. We're not going to see that station go to another commercial buyer." I said, "If there were seven printing presses in New York—only seven—we would not say that all seven should be used exclusively in commerce; we would say that one should be used for education. And one of those seven TV channels in New York has got to be set aside for education."

I said, "The commission made a mistake when it made its table of allocations in not designating a VHF channel for New York." Similarly, it made the same mistake in Los Angeles, and we had to correct that somehow. So I said, "How do we correct that mistake?"

And they said, "Well, you'd have to go through a rule-making [which] would take forever and everybody would be fighting about it."

Just around that time, I let word go out that we would not—*not*—approve a transfer unless it was to a noncommercial buyer. And the owner of the station heard about it. I think it was Mr. [Eli] Landau. And he called me up.

He said, "Is it true that you're opposed to the sale of this station to a commercial buyer?"

I said, "Yes, sir, it's true. It will be approved over my dead body. As far as I'm concerned, we're going to get a noncommercial station in there, one way or another. I don't know how yet, but I'm going to be very straight with you. I'm going to oppose any transfer to another commercial licensee. Nothing against *you*, this is just—I'm telling you, this is what is going to be."

~

Minow and his associates then set about the task of figuring out how to accomplish this. They drew up a proposal for rule-making affecting *any city* where there were seven VHF channels—which thereby included Los Angeles—providing that in such cases, one of the V's would be reassigned. Most of the commissioners felt this would be an inappropriate rule.

So Minow sought out FCC veteran Rosel Hyde.

MINOW: I went in to see Rosel and said, "You've been around here a long time. How do I get this done?"

Rosel said, "You can't do it the way you're doing it." But he said, "I'll support you if you'll make it into an *inquiry* rather than a *rule-making*." Which is a less formal procedure. He said, "You'll send out the same message, and I'll go with you on that."

I didn't even know the difference between an inquiry and a rule-making; it made no difference to me. I said, "Fine." So that's what we did, and we put together all seven commissioners for an inquiry.

At that point, the group trying to buy a Channel 13 took heart. They got some more money, I think, and there was one wild weekend where I sent Ted Myers up to New Jersey, where he actually got in the middle of it to explain all the regulatory problems.

Eventually a deal was made, and Channel 13 was sold to what is now WNET.

~

Jack White and Frank Stanton did meet with Robert Sarnoff, who is reported to have said he was "damn sick and tired of ABC riding for two-fers. If they only give 250, we're only giving 250." That left Jack White and friends with a loss of $750,000 within just a week of final agreement on the sale. Moreover, by that time the price had also risen to $ 6 million. Nevertheless, according to White, verbal agreement was reached "about four o'clock one morning" with contracts written on a Saturday and on into Saturday night, since delivery was called for on Sunday.

WHITE: Two o'clock in the morning we finally finished the job and it was there to be signed. And Dev Josephs said, "I can't do it. John Rockefeller is in Tokyo and Arthur Houghton is overseas some place. Those are the two men who can give this million which we are short. I haven't got the million to give you, and I can't speak for them."

So I said, "Gentlemen, I will sign the contract."

I got home to Tuxedo Park about four o'clock in the morning. At eight o'clock in the morning I was at Henry Heald's house.

I said, "Henry, I want you to know I've just committed a million dollars of your money." That's just about what our NET grant reserves were at the time.

And he said, "What the hell else were you going to do? God bless. Go ahead."

Negotiations With New Jersey's Governor Meyner

There's more to the story. Once the necessary applications for the transfer were filed with the FCC, New Jersey's Governor Robert Meyner began to object to the granting of the State of New Jersey's only VHF channel to a New York station.

WHITE: I went to see the governor several times, trying to arrive at compromises, and was not doing very well because he really felt that he should block this whole thing.

I remember being with him one day in his office and he said, "Jack, the trouble with you fellows from New York is whenever you think of New Jersey you think of pigpens, swamps, and Joisey City."

Well, I resisted and did *not* say, "You're right."

~

Shrewdly, White brought Norman Cousins, an NET board member, into the act.

COUSINS: New Jersey had every right to this, and the business people of New Jersey were very logical in bringing pressure on the state legislature and the governor to hold onto it. The challenge, of course, was to find some way of getting them to surrender this very natural right.

I was given that assignment of negotiation with Bob Meyner, for whom I can't have too much praise. He was remarkable, because he had an obligation not to turn down logical arguments to keep the station in New Jersey. On the other hand, he recognized that the people of New Jersey would benefit, along with the people of New York and Connecticut or wherever the channel might reach.

I suppose I was asked to negotiate with him because the governor and I had been good friends; we'd been tennis partners. And the agreement actually was reached on a tennis court!

Once he was convinced that this was something that had to be done and that there was a way of reassuring New Jersey—there was a formula that we worked out which would assure New Jersey of ample time on the air, and that [the governor] would be on the board—after that, I had the job of persuading some of the people in New Jersey myself. It would have been awkward for him to do that.

Since I was born in New Jersey, I had a strong feeling for the state. I was not entirely an alien. I understood their problems.

I must say that I made promises in good faith that have not been kept. The main promise that was made was that New Jersey was not giving up its franchise without getting something in return, something of great value, not just access to programming but a very active presence in that decision.

~

New Jersey was promised that a studio would be maintained in New Jersey, that their governor would be on the board of the station, that there would be a reasonable, fair, and proper proportion of time allocated to New Jersey's needs. WNET did not live up to these early assurances to the degree anticipated at the outset.

COUSINS: Now in fairness to [Channel] 13 [it] sees itself more as a national flagship station than it does as a local vehicle.

It's just one of those things where you had an unnatural situation to begin with and an unnatural arrangement had to be made to deal with that original unnatural situation, and at some point the unnaturalness had to recede and give way to something that makes sense in its own terms. But in doing so, we have to recognize that some people have been hurt along the way.

I've been called "the father of Channel 13." Actually, I was sort of a John Alden to it. Bob Meyner was really the father. He really made it possible.

~

After a long conference on a Sunday at the governor's mansion, Norman Cousins telephoned Jack White, who was in the midst of a State Department assignment at the U.S. Embassy in Bad Godesburg, West Germany.

WHITE: It was about six o'clock German time, which means about twelve o'clock here, and they arrived at a compromise position.

Norman called me in Bad Godesburg to check it out. I recall the embassy staff took a telephone with a long extension cord on it and pulled an elevator to that floor of the embassy, opened the door and put the telephone in on the floor of the elevator, and I sat on the floor of that elevator and talked to Norman Cousins in the governor's mansion and said, "Great! Buy the compromise. Go!" So that's the way we got 13.

The Special Circumstances In Washington, D.C.

The nation's capital just *had* to have an educational television station. Everyone agreed on that. But in the unique commu-nity that is Washington, how could this be brought about—particularly with the disadvantage of a reserved UHF channel which TV sets in those days could not receive?

TAVERNER: Washington is not a Pittsburgh. It has no major industry at all. It has no major foundation interested in the area that we're concerned with—local foundations, but they're not very extensive. It is not a state, so there is no state support for it. In most states there is some state support that finds its way into public broadcasting. District of Columbia is not a state and they don't have anything that would compare to this, so there is no money there.

Washington [was] different from any other station because the city is different from any other city. It's a transitory town. People don't *live* in Washington. The only people that stay in Washington are those that have a disease called "Potomac Fever." Others pass in and out.

So in the early days of WETA they really had to depend on gifts of the well-to-do individuals. There was never enough and it was always pretty close.

~

Gertrude Broderick, whose recollections went back to the days before there were any ETV channels, knew Washington over many years.

BRODERICK: There isn't a closely knit community spirit here that you find in other communities. And there is a degree of sophistication, if you want to call it that, which—oh, brushes things off as if they were non-existent, or at least unimportant.

I recall the early days of WETA. They were poor as church mice, you know. They didn't have a pot to cook in. This has been an uphill pull for them all the time, but here again so much depends on leadership.

Always there was Elizabeth Campbell. She was there, and never for a moment dodged the responsibility she really didn't have to accept, but she did. And thanks to her, the station has flourished.

The Saga of Elizabeth Campbell - and Friends

Described by the *Washington Post* in 1989 as "WETA's Grand Dame," Elizabeth Campbell achieved such distinction through her constant efforts to improve education through the use of television going back as early as the mid-1950s, before she and other key leaders managed to get WETA on the air in 1961.

Taught by her mother to play both piano and viola and to sing, she went with her two sisters and three brothers to Boston in 1929 to accept the Music Federation of America's award as "Most Musical Family in America."

At twenty-five, she had earned a master's degree at Columbia and had become dean of the Moravian College for Women in Bethlehem, Pennsylvania, later was appointed dean of Mary Baldwin College in Staunton, Virginia.

CAMPBELL: But I didn't know anything about the public school until I married and came to Arlington, Virginia, and we had two children who had to go to public school, and I became aware of the inadequacies of the schools. That is really the reason that I began to work first with the PTAs, and then later [as a member of] an elected school board.

Mrs. Elizabeth Campbell

The schools in Virginia were near the bottom of the list if you were going to talk about teachers' salaries and offerings within the schools themselves, because in Virginia the *public* schools were started quite late. There had been very good *private* schools, but the public schools were for the blacks and poor whites. So Virginia had a large number of very good private schools, but public education hadn't caught up.

I was always looking for some way in which to improve our schools with a minimum of tax money because, although Arlington was a wealthy county, it needed a great deal more than we could get. And I had heard that in Pittsburgh—this was 1957—they had a television program.

At the same time, the Greater Washington Educational Television Association [GWETA], which had been formed in 1953, needed someone to be president of the organization. Mr. Willard Kiplinger, the editor of the Kiplinger letters, who was a member of their board, had learned about me through publicity in the Washington papers and through some of my friends, and he suggested that I might come and be president of this organization.

So I accepted the presidency in 1957. [1]

On the White House lawn, Mrs. Elizabeth Campbell of WETA, with Willard Kiplinger

The organization had fumbled for about a year in trying to put on so-called cultural programs using materials from the cultural institutions in Washington, and using commercial stations in a very unsuccessful way because they didn't have the money to put on really good programs. They didn't have the know-how.

And I realized that the real need in this area was for help for the public schools. I knew I could get the support of the schools because I had run twice for election to the school board. I was known. And I believed very firmly, as I believe today, that the television medium is one of the strongest teaching mediums, and I've resented having it used just for commercial purposes.

~

Elizabeth Campbell went to Pittsburgh to learn what Rhea Sikes and others were doing at WQED. She was impressed.

CAMPBELL: I came back and went to see personally all of the eleven school superintendents in the Washington metropolitan area. I asked three questions. One: What subject in your elementary school is giving you the most problem as far as teaching is concerned? Second: What is the reason for this? Third: Do you think that television could help?

~

It took her the better part of a year to see each of these men, most of whom identified science as their problem area. Through a friend at the National Academy of Sciences she was able to secure a small grant from the Ford Foundation to hold a workshop involving local educators and those who were developing in-school programming in Pittsburgh.

CAMPBELL: I still feel that the approach that we made is the best approach that has ever been made, because we worked with representatives from every school system that was involved, and they met regularly; they talked very openly about what their school problems were, what was needed, and then there was a consensus in regard to the program. And that's the way they did this one. And they called it "Time for Science."

~

One of Washington's commercial stations furnished camera facilities for auditioning possible TV teachers, and each of the stations had indicated that when the science program was ready, they would provide air time. Meanwhile, Elizabeth Campbell was securing sufficient funding from the Meyer Foundation and the Old Dominion Foundation to mount two programs per week for the eight months of the school year.

CAMPBELL: Then we took our programs to the commercial stations, and every station manager turned us down! This was in July, before we were supposed to go on the air the first of October.

~

Undaunted, she enlisted the help of Father Daniel Power of Georgetown University, a strong and supportive member of the GWETA board, who worked out an arrangement with Channel 5 to provide half an hour each day, five days per week, allowing for the two programs to be repeated plus an enrichment program on the fifth day—but this would cost GWETA $30,000.

She phoned the Meyer Foundation executive with a request for an additional $30,000.

CAMPBELL: I was told, "Mrs. Campbell, I've never before asked the foundation for *more* money."

So I said, "Will you see if you can get $30,000, because if we don't have it, we can't do the program at all, and we're ready to go." And I said, "Is Mrs. Meyer in town?"

And he said, "No, she's at her summer home, but you know that Mrs. Meyer doesn't have anything to do with foundation grants." He said, "I know she's interested in the program."

And I said, "Well, I know that, but I would like to know how interested she is."

So I called Mrs. Meyer at Mount Kisco and she said, "Elizabeth, I do not have anything to say about the foundation grants, but I do hope you can get the money."

And I said, "Well, I do, too, because we've spent an awful lot of time and we're ready to go."

I was getting ready to leave for Europe. About three days later I got a telephone call from the Meyer Foundation saying that we had the money.

~

So, in the fall of 1958, "Time for Science" was transmitted by Channel 5 into classrooms all over the Washington area, thus providing a demonstration of what television might be able to do for education.

CAMPBELL: We had to let the public know what television could do before we could hope to get any kind of support to get a station on the air.

The PTAs provided the television sets in every fifth- and sixth-grade classroom and these same PTAs were supporting the program with viewers.

Children at Page Elementary school in Arlington County, Virginia, appear to be so fascinated with the WETA program on children's literature that they didn't notice the photographer who took this picture.

Arlington (VA) Schools photo

We had telephone calls from parents and grandparents who watched the same programs that their children were seeing over the commercial station. This helped to build a very wide community support. If we had not built that kind of support, we never could have gone on the air with our own station.

When we finally did go on the air, people were willing to buy UHF converters because these same people had supported us in the past. The PTAs bought converters for the sets in schools, the families bought converters for their homes, and the people who had been involved felt very much a part of it. It was *their* station. I think that this is something we have been able to keep in a very real way, even now, through the years. I think people have a real feeling that this is their station.

~

Elizabeth Campbell's claim seemed, at least in the late 1980s, to be verified by the record of contributors to the station. Of those who regularly were watching WETA by the early eighties 25 percent were sending cash contributions regularly to help support the station. At that time, this was said to be the highest percentage of contributing viewers of any UHF educational station in the country.

When WETA went on the air in 1961, all of their operating funds came from the area school systems: $150,000 to provide school telecasts from 9 a.m. to 3:30 p.m., five days a week.

I don't quite know but we will have to do something."

Then I remembered that National Educational Television had a service and that the expense of the service was dependent upon the number of hours and the audience we would expect to have, and the final figure was $8,200. We didn't have $8,200.

I said to my husband, "Is there any foundation that you can think of that I haven't asked for money?"

And he said, "What about Phil Stern?" Phil-again, a friend—had been the editor of an Arlington newspaper, and I knew that there was a Stern Foundation. So I telephoned Phil.

"Well, yes, Mrs. Campbell," he said, "There is a foundation. The board is meeting at my house"—and I don't remember whether it was that afternoon or the next day in the afternoon—"but if you will come and present your case, I will be glad to put you on the agenda."

So I remember very well driving in to Washington, to F street, and parking and going to his home and coming in before his board and asking for $8,200 and coming out with it.

That paid for two hours, five nights a week, over a period of—I think—eight months.

And, of course, that was on tape. It was sent down by train or plane, and I can remember several times driving over to the airport to pick up the tape that hadn't come in and we had it on our schedule.

When you look back over it, it's hard to realize what has happened to the whole industry since that day. That was really a hand-to-mouth kind of operation.

CAMPBELL: When I was asked by the board how we were going to get the community to watch us when we didn't have any community programs, I said, "Well,

Pictured at a promotional exhibit in July 1961, Mrs. Campbell and William Dalton (at extreme right), then president of the National Cable TV Association, with three FCC Commissioners: John S. Cross (at extreme left), Robert E. Lee (at Mrs. Campbell's right), and T.A.M. Craven. All were strong proponents for the Washington, D.C. station and for UHF.

There is so much more to tell about WETA's early struggles and turmoil, far more than can be included here—including the roles played by Willard Kiplinger, Max Kampelman, the Ford Foundation, FCC Commissioners Robert E. Lee and Newton Minow, and others who helped to build the educational-public television enterprise in the nation's capital into what it is today. Studios and offices moved from one place to another, and policy shifted.

What was significant was the determination of citizens and the creative ideas they brought to the creation of educational television—in Washington, as well as New York and Los Angeles. Visionary leaders saw that television could bring real benefits to the American public.

An Oil Millionaire's Dream In L.A.

The Los Angeles story proves the same point—even though educational television in that community experienced a unique and aborted start in the form of UHF station KTHE.

John Crabbe, who in 1953 had been busy in Stockton and Sacramento, was among the few who could recall aspects of the second noncommercial station to go on the air—and the only one to go off.

CRABBE: The thing was the product of one man's interest: Captain Allen Hancock, who was on the board of trustees of the University of Southern California.

The captain got enchanted with the notion of putting a television station on the air at USC, and he was able to do it. He had all the resources needed.

~

The Ford Foundation's Vice President of the Fund for Adult Education, G.W. "Bill" Griffiths, was also aware of this interest.

GRIFFITHS: Here was Hancock, with all the dough that stemmed from his father's discovery of oil in the La Brea tar pits.

Hancock had these two overriding notions that mankind in the twentieth century faced two major problems: food and communications. Food might be solved in the sea and communications would be enormously aided by television, ergo, his grants for food research at USC and his attempt to buy a station.

CRABBE: He just literally built a television station, and the university was charged with the responsibility of staffing it and operating it, though he put up money toward the operation, for that matter, as part of his contribution or endowment or whatever it was, out of the foundation itself.

It was kind of crazy, because nobody knew what they were going to do with it. There was just absolutely no commitment to what the station was there for. The university administration, frankly, was not terribly enchanted with the idea of having it. They were frightened of it, because I think they could see the possibility that foundation support might diminish and then the university would be faced with trying to support the thing. It was just put together backwards, that's all.

~

James L. Loper, deeply involved during the 1960s and 1970s in the activation and then management of KCET, Los Angeles' current public television station, probably was a party to more of the subsequent stories about Hancock's effort than anyone, given his long association with the communications department at USC.

James L. Loper

LOPER: It went on the air roughly, as I gather, at the beginning of the school year in 1953 and lasted for about nine months to the end of that school year, in 1954.

Mr. Hancock, as I understand it, saw this as an adjunct not only to a telecommunications program at USC but as a cultural outlet. In fact, one of the rooms in the Hancock Foundation building which still exists is a re-creation of the living room in the mansion in which he grew up, and it is told, at least, that he participated in playing string quartets in this living room that became part of the programming of the station in the beginning.

~

Arthur Hungerford, who visited KTHE for the JCET, recalled hearing a similar account.

HUNGERFORD: He had taken his home that used to be on that strip where they discovered oil, and he had put it into this USC building. And he and his other two or three chamber-music people used to meet there, like they were in his mother's living room, and they would play. So when this television thing came along, he thought this would be a great idea, you know, to try to help.

It was a UHF station; nobody could receive it, but that didn't matter.

GRIFFITHS: There may be a lesson here. It may be the only operation, the only one I ever knew, that got blessed by a cardinal!

That hasn't any business in this story, but I can't help myself. That was the most lavish spread of a catered dinner I have ever seen in my life—the opening ceremonies for KTHE. And that's where his eminence, the cardinal, gave his blessing. The food just kept coming and coming and coming.

LOPER: Hancock saw to it that his man, William Sener who married his niece, was named to head the station and also was the chairman of the telecommunications department at USC, and the station was, as I understand it, in conjunction with the telecommunications department.

CRABBE: I don't know where Bill Sener came from. Just all of a sudden, there was a Bill Sener running KTHE in Los Angeles. And Bill, for whatever reasons I don't know, didn't communicate with the educational community. He didn't talk to the schools, or—well, in fact, talk to anybody, basically. He just ran that thing.

~

Another perspective was offered by KQED's Jonathan Rice.

RICE: I was living in Los Angeles, and looked briefly into the USC [station] and met Allen Hancock's son-in-law, whose name was Bill Sener. And I didn't find what he was doing very exciting and he didn't find me very exciting.

Probably less than a year later, Jim Day and I went down to see them, as one of the very few educational television stations on the air.

We went into this vast building. We had to ring; the front door was locked. The janitor let us in and we walked down these long waxed halls and the janitor waxed our footsteps out behind us and we thought we were going to oblivion!

We met Sener and talked a little about his plans. They weren't relevant to what we were trying to do. He was doing programs to get funding called "Know Your Long Beach" and "Know Your Girl Scouts," and he had a chamber music program on the air in which Hancock was one of the musicians, and that didn't interest us very much.

GRIFFITHS: I think Bill was effective in larger ways. Bill had political ties at the state level. I think he was partly responsible for Governor Warren's being at the Sacramento conference [on ETV] in '54 or '55 or so. Bill was on the national scene in certain respects too; he knew several congressmen and he was one of, I would say, the quiet operators who was effective in various ways.

CRABBE: In the meantime, Bill had married the captain's daughter, I'm pretty sure. Some people say it was his niece but I think it was his daughter. And the last I heard, Bill wound up in Santa Maria, running a belt-line railroad that the captain had up there.

That's really all of the story I know, but I know that it was a very strange chapter in public television in California, believe me.

LOPER: There were a number of stories, accurate or not, that were told about the station, one I remember being told by the educators who were trying to become involved in the station, or the station trying to become involved with them.

I remember one particular story where they had asked several hundred teachers and school administrators to come to USC to the studios. It was evidently a night when it was pouring rain, and they got there and they were completely locked out. Evidently no one had remembered that they had extended an invitation to all these people. That was one of the ways the whole educational community was turned off about the whole thing.

The major problem with that particular operation was that there were simply no UHF sets in southern California or anywhere else at that point, and that there simply was nobody to watch the station.

Toward the end of that particular school year, '53 to '54, there had been a falling out between Captain Hancock and the University of Southern California, and he withdrew all of his support from USC including the television station. And the station then, as a result of no support, went off the air.

For years the antenna sat rusting away down in a kind of back yard of the Hancock building. I think there had always been some hope that they would try to put it back on the air. The studios and office space became the basis for the teaching element of the department of telecommunications.

I think from time to time there had always been efforts to link KCET with that particular operation, and yet, we have just looked at every conceivable way where there might have been some connection and there really is none whatsoever.

~

Thus, America's second noncommercial educational television station, KTHE, became the only such station ever to go off the air—for many understandable reasons—chiefly, perhaps, because its time had not yet come.

Later Moves Toward Activation of KCET

Ten years later, however, the time arrived. Educators and certain key citizens became aware of what had happened in New York. Newton Minow, while chairman of the FCC, had put through the inquiry which signaled his interest in the activation of a noncommercial channel for southern California. Jim Armsey of the Ford Foundation began to be encouraging. Moreover, in 1964 to 1965, Los Angeles was experiencing enormous interest in culture and the arts.

LOPER: Within a period of about four months the music center was dedicated, which was the first time we had a central focus for cultural activities, KCET went on the air, and the Los Angeles County Art Museum opened. I don't think ever in the history of one city has so much in the way of cultural explosion happened within such a very short period of time. It was clearly the right time to put this kind of station on the air.

~

It was the right time for other reasons. Loper and others who already were involved in creating programs from the resources of Los Angeles educational and cultural institutions for release on commercial stations were already experienced in program production. So also were those actively interested in telecasts for in-school use, who already were occupying daytime hours on commercial stations but felt uneasy about retaining extensive time on the air for such purposes.

Urged on by those at National Educational Television who were eager to enjoy the benefits of a Southern California producing center as well as an outlet for NET programming, a small group of skillful strategists had begun to develop the base upon which KCET ultimately was built.

LOPER: There had been a group formed called the Committee for Educational Television, by two advertising men, Winter Horton and Ed Flynn. They were attempting to rally the educational community around them, and they contacted me in the position I had [at Cal State]. They had several meetings, including bringing Jim Day down from San Francisco to talk about what educational television could do.

That group finally got off the ground when they attracted Rose Blythe Kemp into it. She then, in turn, in her position at Cal Tech, got Lee DuBridge interested in this whole business.

She knew that Glenn Seaborg, who was a close friend of DuBridge's, was on the board of National Educational Television. My understanding was that she arranged for Seaborg to talk to DuBridge to enlist his support and interest.

While some of us had the vision of the fact that Los Angeles needed a public television or an educational television station, Dr. DuBridge served essentially as the catalyst for making it work. I have never since underestimated the ability of people to create things entirely out of whole cloth if the idea is right, particularly if you have an absolutely untarnished and unblemished reputation that you can lend to a project, which he did, and with great enthusiasm he made this whole thing work.

Lee DuBridge Becomes The Godfather

Lee DuBridge, at that time president of California Institute of Technology and highly regarded both professionally and personally as one of the nation's top scientist-educators, offered his own recollections.

DuBRIDGE: It must have been 1961 or so when Rose Blythe, who worked at Cal Tech in our public relations office and sort of managed what few things we did in the radio-television field in those days, came to me one time and said this was going on, and they wanted me to have a part in it, partly to get the Cal Tech name and partly to attract other people.

Dr. Lee DuBridge

I said, "I don't know anything about television. I have never been a television watcher, and have just never paid much attention to the ins and outs of either radio or television." I said, "You've got the wrong guy."

But she said, "Well, talk to these people." So they came out and talked, and told about what educational television was. They were doing some school broadcasting even then, but they thought it was time to have a separate educational station devoted entirely to educational programs.

Well, the question was, how do you finance that? They said, "We're sure that if we have a separate educational channel, the schools will contract with us for daytime classroom programs, and this will give us operating funds to pay for an office and transmitter and so on, and then we'll have to raise private funds for the rest of it."

This sounded pretty scary to me at the time, because nobody had heard of educational television, and who was going to give some money to something he hadn't heard of? I said, "All the people who are interested in education are working for the colleges around here."

Well, I don't know all of the items that came into it, but they finally persuaded me to be a member of the board, and then we started selecting other people and soon we had a board organized, and then went on from there.

We tried to get people in prominent business positions. Many of them were friends of mine, or people I knew about. Many of them were suggested by Loper and others. But we knew that unless you had the business community leaders involved, we wouldn't have the credibility that would be needed. That's where Elden Smith came in as a great source of strength.

LOPER: Elden Smith was at that time the chairman of the executive committee of Security Bank, later to become Security Pacific National Bank. He was amenable to this and to the concept of this kind of television because his bank had sponsored the first telecast from the Hollywood Bowl on Channel 9, KHJ-TV, and he then had developed a feeling as a result of that program that there was a market for this kind of television in Los Angeles. So he came to the project with great enthusiasm after being enlisted by Lee.

Largely because of Lee DuBridge's contacts, other prominent business leaders became interested in this and took a gamble. If this was something that he was interested in, then they should be interested as well, [not only] Elden Smith of Security Bank, but also the [heads of] Bank of America, the Southern California Gas Company, and on down the line. I think the only entertainment figure that expressed some interest was Jack Wrather. He was one of the first people to come on board, and he supported it with contributions.

~

Smith soon was asked to be president of the board, with DuBridge as its chairman, which combined a top business leader and the best-known president of an institution of higher education. Similarly, city and county school superintendents were members of the board, with Loper, Horton, and Blythe as strategists and advisors.

Perhaps the largest question facing this group was whether to try to secure a VHF channel or to go with UHF reserved Channel 28.

At this time, Los Angeles shared with the rest of the nation this dilemma: effectively, there wasn't anything but the VHF channels 2 to 13. Even after all receivers were designed to tune in UHF channels as well, many viewers had not made the conversion in their own minds.

DuBRIDGE: People are so in the habit of clicking in to 3, or 5, or 9, or 2, or whatever, instead of having to get that knob and....

Somebody went to Ed Pauley [a major oil company executive] for some help and, talking about Channel 28, he said, "Where do you find that?" Well, that's on Channel 28.

"Oh," he said, "that's where you've gotta turn that god-damned knob!" [LAUGHTER] He used some much stronger words than that! But this was the attitude of many people.

~

Thus, as the Los Angeles dreamers and strategists laid their plans, they were obliged to consider the possibility of securing a VHF channel instead of the difficult-to-find Channel 28. And thereby hangs yet another tale.

Another Assist from Newton Minow

MINOW: John Kluge, head of Metromedia, called me up. He said, "I want to buy a station in Los Angeles, and I'm dickering on it, and my lawyers tell me that I might run into trouble because you've got an inquiry out, saying that you want to change one of those stations to an educational station."

To tell you the truth, I had forgotten about it. But he reminded me, and I said, "Yes, that's right."

He said, "I'll tell you what I'd like to do. You tell me if this makes sense to you." The government operated a lot more informally then than it does now!

He said, "If I could get the other VHF stations to put up some money as they did in New York to buy one of the stations for the educational broadcasters, would you then feel differently about approving a station that *we* bought in Los Angeles as a commercial buy?"

I said, "Yes, I would—and it's obviously to your advantage as well, because you'll only have six commercial stations in the market as well as a noncommercial. You'll have one less competitor in the market going after advertising."

He said, "You understand the business. Do you have any objection if I go to the others?"

I said "That's fine with me. All I care about is that we get an educational station."

But then the man that ran the educational station board in Los Angeles called me up. I don't place his name at the moment; he was a banker. He said, "This is a little too rich for our blood. Even though we'd prefer to have a V, and even if all of the stations helped us, we still would be short X dollars, and unlike New York, we don't think we can raise it."

I said, "I think you're making a mistake because you'll never get another chance to buy a V."

And he said, "Well, we think we can go with U." And I was torn.

Here I was, just having gotten the All-Channel Bill passed, torn between two desires: to make the UHF thing work, and the loss of a V. I said, "It's got to be your decision. If I were you, I'd go with a V but I'm not going to fight with you."

Well, they decided to go with the U. And I suppose, in the long run, people will differ about the wisdom or lack of wisdom in that decision.

LOPER: I still think the decision was probably correct to get something on the air and reasonably well-financed at that point. It's a handicap that we have had to live with throughout the years, although I must say that in the last years that has diminished very substantially and I would say that virtually at this point there's almost no difference.

~

What sparked the imagination of outstanding and very busy people like those in New York, Washington, and Los Angeles and motivated them to devote so much time and effort to the establishment of these stations? Doubtless there were many factors. Lee DuBridge touched on one of them.

DuBRIDGE: The story that Jim and the others told me about the almost complete lack of cultural-educational-artistic programs on commercial TV impressed me. That's the reason I had never listened to it, [CHUCKLE] because I was not interested in the kinds of things they were putting on.

And, the idea to have programs devoted to music, to science, to the arts, I guess, just appealed to my inner nature to get something on television that would get into a lot of homes and be something more than the lowest common denominator of public tastes and appeal to the higher levels of public taste. Even though it was a minority of the total population and Nielsen ratings would be small, still there was a big demand for it.

You know, when you think of the total number of people that can and do go to a symphony concert every year, and think that *one* TV program can reach many times the number of people that go to the Los Angeles Symphony *all year*, this gets impressive.

~

Watching the highly professional programs produced for PBS national distribution in the 1990s by KCET in Los Angeles, WETA in Washington, and WNET in New York, one finds it difficult to imagine how uncertain were the beginnings of these great stations.

A partnership of television professionals, along with business and community leaders, overcame apparently insurmountable obstacles thirty years ago.

The new challenges of the 1990s call for a reawakening of that sort of leadership.

22

The Natives Are Getting Restless Again

Public television grew from so many different roots that it is no wonder its early years were characterized by diversity within its unifying dream of "something better" for the American television-viewing family. "Better" was defined in different terms by different people, and because each station was brought into being by local leaders in order to serve local communities, every station was somewhat different from every other station. No outside source was going to tell any local board of directors or local station manager what to put on the air.

Reasons for Discontent

The early lack of the sort of superb programming that everyone dreamed of—the kind that frequently is seen on PBS today—generated frustration on the part of local stations. That frustration was expressed by criticizing whatever national agency might be striving to develop such programming at the time.

A dilemma caused further frustration: no one had sufficient operating funds; at the same time, the stations did not want to be beholden to or controlled by any major benefactor. Utah's Keith Engar recalls the situation.

ENGAR: We were all hungry for money, and also kind of frustrated that we were a creature of the Ford Foundation.

I can remember all of us trying to butter-up Jim Armsey so that we could get our program grant or whatever, and this was an uncomfortable thing. Not that Mr. Armsey wasn't a fine person, but—you know, it was just a terrible situation to be in. I think there was a general sense of unease.

But actually, when you think of it, how remarkable this coalition was, how politically effective it was. You had public school stations, you had stations licensed to universities, you had stations licensed to public authorities, and you had these metropolitan nonprofit corporations in the larger communities.

This astonishing coalition had amazing political clout throughout the United States, because, by and large the *establishments* in each of these communities were behind the [public] television stations or they never would have got off the ground.

McBRIDE: I think there are two fundamental problems which existed then and continue to this day to exist.

One is that of under-funding, which motivates a number of activities, thoughts, and emotions. Public television has, from day one, been under-funded and still is grossly under-funded.

The second is the diversity of types of stations, which is both a tremendous blessing and also a tremendous problem. With distinctly different types of licensees, who have every shade of objective and mission, it's inevitable that no one organization—nor one administration of that organization—can satisfy all of those people.

That's what happened, I think, as far as Jack White at NET was concerned in his tenure. At some point there, he started to feel criticism, some of which may have been justified and some which may not have been justified, but justified to different degrees by different people because they're coming from different perspectives.

You can't please everybody all of the time. That's what it comes down to.

~

Gerard Appy first observed these circumstances while heading the University of Georgia's station and later as NET staff.

APPY: There was an increasing level of discontent among the stations. Part of it was because most of the stations were users but not producers, and they were as discontented with the slow growth in quality as anyone. Most of them were not able to do a great deal locally. As a result, they depended tremendously upon what NET distributed, and a lot of it didn't measure up to what they would like to have had.

Then there was also the fact that for many stations, NET seemed to go out of its way to treat sensitive issues, and to treat them in some cases in a liberal manner. I don't know that this was NET so much as it was that much of the production was coming from communities that probably were more liberal than some of those parts of the United States which may have been more conservative than the community-type stations.

At any rate, there were a number of programs that many stations thought they were being forced—because of a paucity of programs—to run; or, if they chose not to run it, they became socially castigated by those people who heard about it being available and felt that they were unduly censoring the nationally-available material.

In retrospect, I don't think there were too many NET programs that were recklessly done in that regard.

It was not always comfortable. I had a lot of phone calls on certain programs. Most of them, if they were put on today, would be considered so bland nobody would protest. But it was a factor, and some of the stations felt much more strongly about it.

A good many station managers, I must say, were as much concerned with preserving their tenure, if they had it, or their situation within the educational structure, as they were with being broadcasters leading the crusade to provide the public with a new and necessary and valuable service. Or, at least, they were torn between those two desires. And it was very distressing to some of them to be the focus or even the peripheral attention of controversy.

As a member of the Affiliates' Committee, I was involved in those kinds of discussions at the time when there was a pretty lively dialogue going on. I can remember some violent arguments, all by men of good will but with quite differing opinions in many cases.

~

Michigan State's Lee Frischknecht, during his time on the NET staff, experienced similar expressions of dissatisfaction from stations.

FRISCHKNECHT: Some of them had very difficult times with some of the NET programs in two areas.

One was material in the cultural area which was deemed to be offensive to some people in the audience as a result of profanity or nudity or anything verging on that. Some stations just had a devil of a time dealing with it. Others felt that they *would* have a tough time dealing with it, whether in fact they were or not. I don't think there were ever very many situations where stations had trouble with those programs—but there were *enough* times and there were *enough* people who were very vocal about it in their letters to NET and in their comments in affiliates' meetings that it whipped up a considerable amount of ferment.

The same thing was true in public affairs programs. Controversial issues were covered by NET from time to time and not always as fairly as they might have been. Some programs appeared to be slanted one way or another.

Every once in a while we would come out with something like "Banks and the Poor" in which banks came off looking as if they were ripping off poor people—which they probably were. Yet you couldn't say that on the air without alienating a very strong constituency. A lot of community stations had bankers on their boards, and there was a lot of pressure from that sort of thing that fell back on station management.

The funding squeeze was coming on, too. The development-underwriting thing didn't work well enough. There was not enough money generated, partly because of the very real reaction of potential underwriters to the fact that the industry still had not developed a national audience.

~

Bill McCarter knew about those conditions. Before he took on his station management career in Washington and then in Chicago, he was a development officer at NET serving with Warren Kraetzer, vice president for development.

McCarter talked about the problems faced in finding underwriters.

Difficulties Faced With Underwriting

McCARTER: It was very difficult in those days because the audiences really were small compared to what we've got today and no interconnection and no color!

Warren and I and some other people spent an awful lot of time at that. We knew there was a market but it was still very hard to sell because you had to cross over between a very high-level public relations motive and a community contribution of sorts.

I remember one particular presentation we made to AT&T. It was very difficult. They never did really join in those early days, and they've never been heavy up till now. But those were the early beginnings of trying to move beyond just a one-source finance base and bring in the private sector.

~

The concept of underwriting—by which is meant giving a credit to the enterprise which has provided funding to make a specific program possible—was established very early in consultation with the Federal Communications Commission. Ralph Steetle, who was at the time the head of the Joint Council on Educational Television in Washington, provided the facts about the justification for underwriting credits.

STEETLE: We raised this before the FCC in those Third Report sessions. There are certain programs, we said, that are commercially-sponsored but that educational television must have. And the commission said, "How's that? How's that?"

And we said, "Well, the political conventions, now sponsored by Westinghouse. We should have them." So the commission puzzled about this and decided we could carry them without the commercials. We said, "Yeah, but on the background is a big screen that says WESTINGHOUSE. We can't erase that."

So the commission said, "Oh, well, okay, I guess then, that you may show incidental things such as that."

Then the commission got to thinking, "Here are all these people providing programs; maybe they're *sneaking in* programs." So the commission, in another part [of the FCC rules] wrote, in effect, if you accept program support, you must name the donor. So the whole underwriting business grew out of attempting to carry the national conventions.

I used to think that one could define this fairly closely, that if an educational producer defined a need and set forth a program idea to do it, and then he went to somebody with money and said, "Say, I've got this idea, can you support this?" And the guy said, "Yes, I can." That was the best use of underwriting. If, however, the educational producer went to Ford or Westinghouse and said, "Say, what are you interested in? I've got these production facilities, I've got this network." That is the same as selling—that is totally not acceptable.

So, it depends upon where the initiative arises, where the initiative stays—and unless you can tread that thin line, you're in real danger.

~

That danger loomed large in the mind of Seattle's Loren Stone, the former commer-

cial broadcaster in charge of the University of Washington's educational television station.

STONE: I had grown up with a rate card, and as far as I could see, [Warren Kraetzer] just had a poor rate card put together, but he had a rate card. He was just going out peddling my station with a rate card, and I was darned if I was going to have him do that.

The minute we begin to rely on underwriting we begin to find more popular programs, because the underwriters aren't putting in their money for the love of it.

This is the thing that kills us, because the underwriter wants a bigger audience, and you get a bigger audience, put on more popular programs, and pretty soon we're not doing what we ought to be doing at all. If we rely on underwriting, pretty soon we are doing the same things the commercial stations are.

~

Another reason some NET affiliates had misgivings about underwriting was recalled by Kenneth Christiansen from his years as manager of the University of Florida's WUFT.

CHRISTIANSEN: The bonus in the long run was on the side of developing new sources, better quality, and diversity of programming. Where it impacted us on the local level was the criticism we got from the commercial broadcaster.

He sometimes felt that because we had gotten those dollars somewhere along the line, they really should have been available in the marketplace, that there should have been sponsorship at the [commercial] network level. Then the programming would have come to him, and now it was in competition with him. And I must say, that was not an unusual circumstance.

The local press wouldn't carry our schedules. There were several years before WUFT schedules were carried. It was never mentioned in a news story; we were never identified by call letters in the early years. "A local television station" was the only identity we had.

I went down several times and would talk to the ownership about this, and say, "You know, it doesn't make much sense." And the management and the publisher always gave me the same answer: "Macy's doesn't advertise Gimbel's."

My response to him, in a good-natured way, was to say, "You're paying us a compliment far above what we deserve. We are not in competition. We are a different kind of service. We don't take one subscriber away from you. So it's not Macy's and Gimbel's. We are really partners in this community, standing for the same thing: a better-informed community. We'll make it a better community—a better place for you to live and have your paper, and certainly a better place for television to have *its* place."

But it took a change in ownership before that ever changed here.

~

Yet another complication faced by those who pioneered in seeking underwriting for national noncommercial programs is remembered by Don Taverner from his days at WQED in Pittsburgh.

TAVERNER: Here we sat in Pittsburgh with these big corporations—Westinghouse, Gulf, U.S. Steel. At least twenty out of the top 100 would have been right in Pittsburgh. So we were getting money from them for grants to do [local] programming, and we worked desperately to freeze NET out.

This matter never really was a serious problem, because we got some pretty good understandings with NET on it. All that we ever asked was that if their director of development or whoever was going to come in, we'd like to know they were there. That generally worked very well.

In any event, at this time the chairman of our [WQED] board was Howard Kaltenborn, who was a vice president of Westinghouse. I got a call from Howard's secretary saying, "Howard has someone in here he wants you to meet and wants to know if you're all tied up or could you come downtown."

I said, "I'll come down." I knew what was up. So I went down and went in and here was Howard with a big grin, and Kraetzer, or McCarter, or Winter Horton, I don't remember who it was. I guess it was Warren.

Anyway, poor Warren! He didn't do this subversively, you know. Somehow he got in there, but he hadn't realized that the guy he was giving the pitch to was the chairman of the board of WQED! [LAUGHTER]

So then we all went out and had coffee together.

How Long Might The Ford Foundation Help?

The effort to find underwriting during the early 1960s was an effort to develop a new source of funding for national programming. Until then, the Ford Foundation had been by far the largest source of support for NET. But as the grants grew larger and larger and costs escalated, various people began to sense that the foundation could not continue this escalation forever.

One such observer was Boston's Hartford Gunn.

GUNN: I knew that by nature most foundations are "beginners" but they're never "enders." They begin enterprises. "Enders" isn't right, but they're not "continuers." They start things and then expect somebody to pick them up.

And I had a prophetic—pathetic, maybe, but certainly prophetic—conversation with Jack White—and you'll see why it was pathetic as well as prophetic—in Cambridge. I remember very clearly, it was somewhere around Brattle Square, and we were walking along, and I said, "Jack, I have a feeling that Ford is not always going to be with us."

Jack was saying, "No, it's a marriage and it will go on. They're so deeply involved and committed that they can't get out."

But I was convinced of two things. Ford, by nature, was not to be counted on as a permanent ongoing source of funding. The other thing I was convinced of was that we had come to the end of what we could reasonably expect any foundation to do, yet the amount of money required to go the next ten, fifty, hundred miles plus, was enormous.

~

The concern over future funding had led Jack White to propose, well along in his tenure as NET president, that the Ford Foundation consider an endowment for NET.

WHITE: Our budget was only a million and a half when we started, and it was a five-year-grant for $5 million that I was applying for [in 1959].

Long before the five years were up, we'd spent the $5 million, but long before we'd spent it, you'd had the grants for videotape recorders. We also got a commitment from them to a step-up for us so that we could improve our programming.

But they then came and said, "Look, Jack, this is going from bad to worse, buddy. We've got to get some pattern that makes some sense. Let's take the long term view and arrive at a conclusion as to what our level of support should be."

We took three months or so, and we did a fully documented proposal on what Ford should do, [and that was] to give us an endowment, I think of $500 million. We then had a fall-back position at $200 million. That was the lowest figure we gave them. And we had it all spelled out that if they really wanted out—that they were so committed they couldn't without besmirching themselves walk away from us—this was the best way to do it.

Ford Foundation's Jim Armsey also remembered.

ARMSEY: There was no way the foundation could have provided enough money to endow a "fourth network." There was no way that NET, as it existed then or as it exists now in a different form and with a different name, could rely upon one source of money to sustain itself. It had to have income from multiple sources: corporate, governmental, individual, foundation, otherwise.

We were never able to get NET, or indeed any other organization, to face up to that fact, because the people who were running these organizations wanted to do what the organization was set to do and not divert their energy to fundraising, either because they didn't want to raise money or because money was too hard to raise. Fund raising is a difficult job. So it was never in the cards that NET would be endowed.

The figure tossed around in those days was $100 million. Well, the foundation could have supplied NET with $100 million, but if it had done that, it would have had tremendous pressure to supply other agencies of equal merit with similar amounts of money or more. It could not have done them all, and it would have been absolutely impossible to make reasonable judgements among them. And if it had done so, it would have so depleted its own resources to do a variety of other things that it wouldn't have made sense.

~

But there remained the question of how long and to what extent the foundation should or would support NET—an extremely critical question to every one of the stations which depended so heavily on NET for their major programming as well as for many associated services.

Scottsdale: No Meeting of Minds!

Apparently as part of an effort to create a clear and reasonable scenario for Ford's future support, Armsey invited station representatives (but no one from NET) to a meeting in Scottsdale, Arizona, in December 1962—a meeting which is recalled with some discomfort by several who attended.

CHRISTIANSEN: The thing I remember most about the Scottsdale meeting was the disaster in the negotiations.

I think that the foundation—and Jim Armsey, particularly—was looking for some kind of direction: what next steps the foundation ought to take, what level of support. Ought there to be a motivating principle in the foundation effort as there was in their international efforts, for in-

stance, which meant setting a target year and diminishing participation—which has the nurture in it that you need, to know that you can be sustained by time enough to look forward to how you're going to meet the full level of sustaining your operation without outside help? I call it the weaning process.

I'm trying to recall some of the circumstances, but I think there was some misguided leadership that emerged. There was a feeling that what needed to be done was to place an ultimatum before Jim Armsey, based on the premise that they put so much money into it, he and the Ford Foundation are not going to back away from this baby now, and let's go and lay it on at the level that we think we really need, and be sure to get it, and let's stand united on this.

As I recall, I was chairman of the Affiliates Committee at that point. And Jim was not meeting with us in our closed portion of our meetings, and I and somebody else had to go and present the recommendation to him in [a] separate audience—although he had been meeting with us lately at some point.

And the outcome of the meeting [with Armsey] was very certain after the first couple of sentences in the presentation. It was not going across. The Ford Foundation was not about to be told what it should do.

CRABBE: I remember the meeting. It was—what was going to happen to NET? Really, what should the foundation's role be with reference to the future of NET. And I do remember that we urged the foundation to stay with [us]—not necessarily NET in particular but public television—for as long as it possibly could.

The premise was that short of other substantial resources to which the whole thing could look for support, the foundation at that point probably represented the only one that could be dependable for a period of time, at least. "And don't cut us short on that."

We did say this. We said it loud and clear: "Whether it's your fault or not—and we're not saying that it would be your fault—but if in fact the ball was dropped, you'd get the blame. So cover your tracks, guys."

I remember that being said very loud, and I remember Jim Armsey hearing that one.

McBRIDE: It was very obvious that NET personnel were excluded. And it was very obvious, as I recall, that Armsey was under some pressure himself within the foundation, because of the internal study that was going on. It was also—to me—very obvious that his mind was pretty well made up early on.

I think the same thing happened at the Scottsdale meeting that happens in any meeting of the representatives of the television stations: every shade of opinion was expressed.

In a situation like that, when we are unable to speak with one voice, those who are seeking information are able to read from that what they want to read. I think that's what happened there to a certain extent.

~

An important decision affecting educational television in America was about to be made. The entire movement was becoming much larger and therefore much more costly than any foundation could afford to support indefinitely, yet no other funding source then on the horizon could provide the funds which NET and the stations needed to fulfill their increasingly obvious potential. Because the rapidly growing number of stations across the country depended more and more upon NET for their audience-building programs—the blockbusters of that day—the future growth and significance of this new movement hung in the balance.

Nearly twenty years later, Lee Frischknecht—reflecting on his past experience of several years as major liaison between the stations and NET—looked back to that historic moment.

FRISCHKNECHT: I think that Ford came out of the meeting with the message that they wanted to get—that programming was the important thing and the only thing that NET ought to be concerned with, that high quality programming was what they ought to be engaged in. And anything else was so secondary—promotion, field services, engineering, planning, audience research—that those things ought to be severely restricted in favor of putting money in programming.

Well, the station managers, wrestling with all of these problems, not just programming—while it obviously is the key to it all—had grown accustomed to getting certain services from NET in these other areas, limited though they were.

So bad feeling developed. And somehow or other, I think many of the station people felt that it was really Jack White's fault, or NET's fault, that a lot of services like station relations were going to be done away with.

So when those changes were made, on the other end of the stick, Jack White felt also that the stations had let him down at Scottsdale by saying it was okay to do away with station relations and cut back promotion and cut back all these other things that NET had been doing.

I think that Scottsdale meeting was sort of the watershed toward the beginning of the end [of NET], because neither group trusted the other

thereafter as much as they had before, and things began to deteriorate.

Armsey's own recollection of the Scottsdale meeting and his role within the foundation at the time sheds more light on the circumstances.

ARMSEY: My principal recollection is that it was a nasty event of some kind. We were constantly trying to point out that the foundation could not be relied upon to provide enough money to do everything that all of the stations and NET wanted to do, and that there needed to be indigenous support, local support, community support, built around the stations themselves; and that NET must eventually find some source other than the foundation for its resources, or the preponderance of those resources.

Now, the stations and the center [NET] were ambivalent, as agencies and people often are. On the one hand, they both resented any kind of control that the foundation exercised over its grants. At the same time they wanted more money. The foundation staff members were confronted with the integrity of the grant-making system, which was something like this.

The proposals made to the trustees of the Ford Foundation were written by the staff members themselves. I wrote all of the material that made the case for the center [NET] and for the stations, and I had to be convinced that I had a case, and I had to deal with the negatives as well as the positives and then balance those out and make a case for the positives on balance.

It was a mistake, because it was inaccurate and untruthful, to say that everything was rosy. You had to point out some of the warts as well as the rest. But I tried always to make the case in a positive way, on balance, to get money for the stations and for the center.

In order to do that, I had to present a fairly clear and accurate picture of what the money would be spent for. In order to present that picture, I had to get some idea from the center and the stations, when they made their requests, of what they had in mind, what they intended to do, what kinds of plans they had, how they intended to carry them out, above and beyond what the foundation could supply. In order to do that, I had to ask a lot of pointed questions. I had to gather a lot of specific information. I had to inspire a lot of thinking that they either didn't want to do or weren't capable of doing—and in many cases, they simply weren't capable of doing it. There were a lot of fairly mediocre people in the educational television picture at that time. There still are.

Having done all that—having made the case, having made the presentation, secured the trustees' approval for the grants—I was charged with the responsibility of monitoring those grants, reporting back on a regular basis that what we had promised was going to happen was, in fact, happening. That's why I kept trying to emphasize to some of the people involved in the thing who simply refused to recognize that as a requirement. They refused to recognize it—from the very bottom of the structure to the very top, including Jack White and Everett Case and Norman Cousins and the whole batch. They thought, on the NET board, that all they had to do was to go over and say a nice word to Henry Heald and everything would be all right. That was simply not the case.

As I recall, I went to this Scottsdale meeting with the intent of trying to get some sort of consensus that could be presented, and all I heard was a lot of complaints. "You're sticking your nose too much in our business." "It's none of your business what we do, but at the same time, give us more money."

This position I considered totally unreasonable. I considered it unreasonable on the part of Hartford Gunn, who at that time was an articulate spokesman; [of] Schwarzwalder, who was a madman; and [of] Jack White, who had all kinds of pressures from his board and thought he had a back-door entrance to Henry Heald for all the money he wanted any time he wanted it, that dealing with me was a pro-forma thing and that Fritz [Jauch] could write up a proposal and we'd put it in the file and he'd get the money. It didn't work that way.

~

The Ford Foundation's assessments did have a significant effect on the future of NET.

The Ford Foundation Makes Its Move

GUNN: The foundation felt that we weren't going far enough fast enough—and Jim Armsey, if you're listening [CHUCKLE]—I think this may be where you intervened and said to Jack, "You've got to put some more pizazz into your programming, and drop the other ancillary things. Jack, you've got to concentrate on programming and you gotta get a big programmer."

WHITE: The conclusion [of the foundation] was that, number one, it could not justify an endowment where they had no control over expenditures from then on in; number two, that the time had come for educational television to grow up and that stations were going to have to take care of themselves and if there was any more activation somebody else was going to have to do it; and three, we should get the hell out of radio and just become a television programming entity. Period.

At the outset they said no children's programming, no station relations, no development. You don't have to take money from anybody else, and we will give you $5 million each year. [1]

That was the announcement that we made some time in '64. And that was when I had to do two things. The toughest job I ever had was to go back and tell half of my staff that they were out of jobs. The other was to employ a new professional staff, because that was part of the prescription that we were given.

A Different Brand of Professionals At NET

GUNN: They got Bill Kobin from ABC, and Bill made *his* contribution. In the process we lost something but we gained something. These are always "win-some-and-lose-some" situations.

With Bill, I think we made another leap forward. Certainly Bill toughened up a lot of the public affairs approaches. In the process, he lost the support of the stations, certainly the major producing stations, because he tended to feel that they didn't have the capacity and they really weren't worth bringing along. At least, that was the impression he left, and we were dealing with impressions, and this was an environment that he was setting for all of us, and it was one we didn't like.

APPY: There were a number of what we later came to call "advocacy journalists" hired as producers. At that time, on the part of Kobin and these producers, there was a degree of incredulity that the stations could or should have the attitudes that they had about some of the muckraking programming that they thought appropriate and the positions that producers were going to take.

But they did turn out programs that raised a lot of hell.

GUNN: We weren't upset by the topic they were dealing with, but there seemed to be a little looseness with the way in which they were working with the truth, as best one sees truth, or the facts as best one could ascertain the facts.

I think good reporters always start with a hypothesis, but they're willing to adjust their final writing or their final documentary to the facts as they are, not as they wish they were. I think there was a little looseness in that area.

Charges and counter-charges would fly, and producers would say that the stations are just responding to the conservative members of their board, and the stations would say that the

[1] Other sources recall that amount as $6 million.

producers are not being fair and not being balanced, and there is a little truth on both sides. It was creating a tension, which was further exacerbated by the loss of interest on the part of the big stations because they were increasingly being cut out of production. Rather than being brought along, they were being shunted to one side.

~

NET's president, Jack White, years later expressed his own view of why "the natives never were anything but restless."

WHITE: While I am not at all close to public television now in 1981, the few times I do bump into friends in the field, they're having *precisely, exactly* the same situation now. They will never get away from it.

You must remember: Number one, we had that commitment to do public affairs programming; number two, the sixties were very troublesome years. You had everything from Vietnam to Cuba to you-name-it. Number three, if educational or public television was to have any place at all, it was to strike those strictures that affected commercial television and call spades spades.

Now, when you said that, the large community stations almost to a man were totally supportive. The small institutionally-based stations, where you had state legislatures or you had public school systems and also those in the Deep South and elsewhere where you were going to treat race relations and other issues that were troublesome, were bound to be negative.

At the same time, what really inverted them was that by that time NET was getting national publicity and national kudos and national advertising, and they were being forced to run programs that they didn't really want to run—not by us but by their publics.

NET, while I was there, refused to forego its leadership role. And we did say, "This is it. You're in charge of your own station, you are the licensee, you do what you think best, but this is the role we must play and the road we think you should follow—but it's up to you." And most of them did.

But that was the cause, and it's the cause today. Remember, "blue language" was another favorite word we used to get about drama. Well, you know, blue language that we were using in those days they use in children's programs in 1981!

~

Lee Frischknecht, one-time director of field services for NET, later lived through very similar dialogues when he was president of National Public Radio. He finally concluded that such debates are bound to be a part of such circumstances.

FRISCHKNECHT: There is going to be, always, a natural separation develop between that national organization and individual units throughout the country, simply by virtue of the fact that somebody is sitting up there being a gatekeeper on what is going to be programmed and when it's going to be programmed and how it's going to be evaluated. Making those kinds of decisions, it is impossible not to alienate people.

But I also recognize that if you're going to have a strong national program service, I don't think there is any other way to do it than with a strong national organization that has the freedom to make that happen.

~

Sacramento's John Crabbe, who spent a year on the staff of the Educational Television and Radio Center before it became NET but who spent far more years as a station manager, held similar convictions, and expressed them from the perspective of a local manager.

CRABBE: I have always felt that a strong network is important. That is to say, I think that NET—or whoever—should listen to what the stations have to say about what they think their program interests and needs are. But somebody's got to make the final decision as to what's going to be done and what's going to be distributed. And democracy is great, up to a point—but, son-of-a-gun, it's got to stop somewhere!

I never did get caught up in all that imbroglio that went on about NET ramming things down our throats, or all of the program decisions being made east of the Hudson, and all that sort of thing. A lot of people got terribly agitated about that, a majority did by far.

I really never had any particular quarrel with NET. Sure, they did things I didn't particularly like—and if I didn't like them, I didn't carry them. That was my privilege.

Okay, sure, we'd like to have this, we'd like to have that, we think we need this, we think we need that—but when push comes to shove, you guys are there at the frontline and you know what you can do and what you can't do, and I'm convinced you'll do the best by us that you know how. And I think they did. I really fundamentally believe that they did.

~

Although the views expressed here by public television's founders reflect the range of opinions when the national program service was NET and the arguments which raged during the 1960s and 1970s, arguments of similar nature have dogged the footsteps of PBS ever since its inception in 1969. PBS's "lack of objectivity and balance" in public affairs is an issue with a few critics even as this book is being written in the early 1990s, and PBS is marshalling rational arguments for its decisions.

Perhaps one should welcome the fact that "the natives are restless." Conscientious criticism has to be a consequence of the freedom of our American communications media to provide our citizenry with all shades of opinion. In the final analysis, "The People" decide. To help "The People" remain attentive and vigilant has been and continues to be one of the functions of noncommercial broadcasting.

23

NAEB in Crisis and the Return
of Scotty Fletcher

By the mid-sixties, public television's parents and their colleagues were in disarray. NET, following the Ford Foundation's directive attached to its grant, phased out many vital support services which had been available to stations for ten years. The stations grew restive about NET's controversial programming, despite its gradual improvement in quality. And there was more and more uncertainty about future Ford Foundation financial support in the face of increasing operating costs at the local level. Where could they turn for leadership at the national level, and where was all the new money to come from? Might NAEB come to the rescue?

The Primitive Years of NAEB in Illinois

The National Association of Educational Broadcasters, which had accomplished so much in earlier and simpler times, was an old friend to some. Back in the 1950s, its executive director, Harry J. Skornia, overworked himself to encourage those who were trying hard to improve their educational radio stations.

SKORNIA: I was in a room in Gregory Hall [at the University of Illinois], by the grace of L.V. Peterson, whose office it was and who had been asked to move over a little bit so they could put another desk in there.

~

Harry Skornia

Skornia was also responsible for setting up and operating the first "network" for noncommercial radio, the NAEB Tape Network. Programs submitted by member stations were duplicated at Urbana and the copies mailed out to other NAEB members.

SKORNIA: We put that [the tape network] in the back room, which had been a storage room. Dick Rider was the first manager of that.

Boy, the tape recorders were so primitive that sometimes they didn't record and sometimes the tape would break and sometimes they'd be de-magnetized in shipping and sometimes there would be foul-ups in the post office.

The university mail room would mess us up and [tapes] would still be there the next day, and—oh, boy, I tell you, the frustrations that we had to put up with!

~

In addition to his duties as head of a rapidly growing organization devoted principally in those days to radio, Skornia traveled the country to encourage those considering educational television.

SKORNIA: I would usually go in at an early stage when some "crackpot," as some would call them, was thinking of ETV. And I would work with them at that stage and advise them and meet them and meet people and assure them and talk about structure and things like that.

Then, if they got organized and they wanted to hold an orientation meeting and said, "Hey, we've got a lot of questions we'd like to ask you," then I would come back again and do that.

But I never got really very close, and very, very rarely did I meet with a whole board. I was not the front man who would come in like the JCET or NCCET and operate with boards in that sense. I met with very few boards. It was more a humble role, more behind the scenes.

~

Skornia was almost a one-man show in those days.

SKORNIA: I was so cotton-pickin' busy traveling. I was so short-handed staff-wise, and still had a [tape radio] network to run. I was so preoccupied between trips getting back to cover what there was.

We didn't get an associate director for years, didn't have anybody to cover the office except a secretary, that I usually didn't have the time to go into depth that some of these other guys could. I must say, I walked out many a time wishing I could stay another day or another week, but I'd have to get back.

Rivalry Develops: Radio Folks vs. TV Folks

Many NAEB members—principally *radio* members—were familiar, therefore, with Skornia's efforts and those of Harold Hill and Bob Underwood and others who had served the member stations as well as they could, given the circumstances.

However, within the NAEB by the middle 1960s were many newcomers—principally *television* members—with no such acquaintance with the organization who saw a need for a far more aggressive and capable "trade organization" than NAEB had been able to mount, especially now that NET was going out of that business.

William Harley, who as NAEB president moved the association's offices to Washington, D.C., recalled the mid-1960s.

HARLEY: There was a rivalry between the old hands, the radio people who had been in this business for a long time, and these newcomers—these upstarts that thought they knew so much about the application of broadcasting to education. The two did not mix too well. And you had a situation in which you had managers of radio stations with a total budget of maybe $50,000 a year being on a board of directors [of NAEB] with people who were operating something that had a budget of $3 million. That kind of imbalance made for some difficulties.

There was a movement among some of the ETV managers to pull out of NAEB and start their own organization, because they felt they were being somewhat held down by being in the larger context of association with radio and instructional concerns.

APPY: With NET getting out of the station-representation business, the kind of thing that trade associations usually do, they had no spokesman that they were comfortable with to take up that cudgel in Washington, nor was there any money available, at least visible, at the moment to do that.

So there became the huge question on the part of the affiliates: "Shall we create a new organization or shall we do this station representation function within the NAEB?"

The Affiliates' Committee of NET was the body automatically in place at that time, and that was a fascinating experience because the six of us on the committee were quite diverse.

We cogitated, we argued, we thought, and we came to the unanimous conclusion that NAEB had demonstrated such lack of effective leadership that the thought of depending upon NAEB to take our money—and we knew we were going to have to recommend that the stations put up a pretty good sizable budget in order to set up representation in Washington—the idea of doing that through the NAEB was not a palatable one. And we recommended to the stations that a separate organization be set up.

A number of the people who had been over the years more closely associated with the NAEB—Dick Hull, I remember, and Bob Schenkkan—felt very strongly that we would be wiser to create our trade association *within* NAEB.

After great debate, the Affiliates Committee was rebuffed [by the stations]. We were told to go negotiate with NAEB and get a deal that would insure that the interests of the television stations would be protected, but that it would be done under the blanket of NAEB. And a board was elected by the stations to establish what later became the Educational Television Stations division of NAEB.

That board then set about the task of trying to figure out who should head up this wonderful organization. We wanted to have a president who would be a nationally-known figure—and, of course, we had no money! We had to anticipate that we would go to the stations and get them to pay dues—a very distressing thing for many of them, for the big stations might have to pay several thousands of dollars. And the small stations, how many would sign up? We had no notion. It was going to be a major sales job.

It was a very iffy time. There was a great question whether ETS would ever get off the ground. We cast about for all kinds of names [of persons to head the effort]. Of course, most of the names we talked about would certainly have expected to be paid something rather substantial. Finally, among the names suggested was that of Scotty Fletcher.

The Recruiting of Scotty Fletcher

As Fletcher recalled it, he received a long-distance telephone call at his Florida home from Dick Hull.

FLETCHER: He didn't tell me much on the telephone. He merely said, "I want to advise you in simple language that the ETV station managers and NAEB are in a dreadful tangle with one another. The situation is so serious that the station managers want to break away from NAEB to form their own separate association."

I said, "Well, that is pretty serious."

He said, "In my own judgment it is so serious that I wonder if you would be kind enough to fly up to Columbus, Ohio, and meet with Bill Harley, president of NAEB, and Robert Schenkkan, the station manager in Austin, Texas, who is proposed to be the new chairman of the new organization, when and if it is formed."

"This *is* bad new. Yes, I'll be glad to come up. Tell me where and when."

We met at the motel in which I was staying in Columbus. The first time we met the main topic of conversation was a description of the chaos which eventuated in Milwaukee when, in effect, the station managers with one voice said, "We want to leave NAEB and form a corporation or association of our own." It took practically all morning to explain all the reasons for this by all three men—the Schenkkan version, the Harley version, and the Hull version. They didn't agree. Obviously, there would be no quick solution to this particular problem.

I said, "I'll be very frank with you. The first statement I will make is that if ETS at this stage in history tries to break away from NAEB and start a new association of their own, they will, in effect, be committing suicide."

They looked a little aghast, and I said, "Yes, I'm serious. I would not under any circumstances be interested in heading any new national organization if it were not affiliated with or connected with NAEB. I made that statement, I said to them, "without knowing all the facts."

The afternoon was spent in getting to all the whys and wherefores. They were in confusion, *I* was in confusion, and I said, "Let's sleep on this and I'll sort it out and tell you what I recommend tomorrow."

The next morning Hull as spokesman said, "The main purpose of talking to you is to invite you to become president of ETS as a division of NAEB. What you might want to do in the future is to reconsider making it a separate operation, divorced from NAEB."

I said, "The answer to that question is no, I would not be interested unless you agree right now that should I agree to become president, I would continue the operations of ETS as a division of NAEB."

"Then the second question is, would you be interested in coming to Washington for a long period of time in order to help us achieve this?"

My answer was no. I was very frank about it, and they were disappointed. I could see that by the way they looked at one another.

Hull then said, "We are facing a major crisis. On March 18, the affiliates will be having their regular meeting in New York City, and at that time we have to announce what our plans are for the future."

Dick Hull pleaded with me to agree to come up for "just a few months" to help them get over the hurdle of the New York meeting, and then spell out what should be done from then on.

So eventually I said, "Dick, I will agree to come to Washington provided the doctors give permission for Mrs. Fletcher to travel at this particular time, and see you through the first hurdle—which is the meeting in New York City—and then to spend one or two months after that and help you arrive at the next decision.

"You're talking, Dick, about major decisions about the future of educational television as it applies to the entire United States. You people have a definite responsibility—every station manager should realize he has—a definite responsibility to the people of the United States of America, not to just a few station managers who are always fighting with both NAEB and NET."

The rest of the day was spent in listing the problems to be solved, in a fashion which would start with the worst problem and end with the lesser problem. In my own mind, I decided that most of them were not problems but just general gripes.

So, hearing the whole story, I said to him, "Dick, you called me in the first instance. I will call you from Miami in two days' time and let you know whether I can come to Washington immediately. It will all depend on Mrs. Fletcher's health and what the doctors recommend." I shook hands with them all and left.

APPY: Scotty was in semi-retirement at an age when he didn't like retirement. He might be interested in taking on one more adventure in that field which he had helped to spawn.

HARLEY: I think one of the reasons that he gave it consideration was that he was still smarting under the fact that the Fund for Adult Education had been dissolved, and he really wanted to get back into the national picture. He still felt he had the strength and vigor to do something important.

We said, "You bet you have; come and join us."

FLETCHER: On March 17 there was a board meeting of ETS as a division of NAEB. I was introduced to all the members, and they were told that I had tentatively agreed to become the chief executive officer of ETS until the New York meeting was over and the recommendations made at that meeting were put into effect.

The following day, Bob Schenkkan chaired the Affiliates meeting in New York, which was packed. After his opening remarks he gave a brief report on the various actions which had been taken by the ETS board of directors on the previous day, then asked Dick Hull to introduce me.

Hull, the senior and most respected educational broadcaster in the country, spoke with fervor about my accomplishments and his confidence in my judgement. He realized that the new managers had never met me, but handled the situation skillfully without boring the many old-timers who were present. His introduction evoked a standing ovation, which was most helpful to me and I was grateful.

I had decided to be extremely frank. I stressed the reasons why a decision to abandon NAEB at this stage would prove a panacea rather than a cure for their problems. The desirable alternative, I explained, would be to operate as a division of NAEB with the distinct understanding that all ETS membership fees would be used exclusively for ETS affairs.

Next I outlined a program of positive goals, all of which had to be given preferential treatment during the next six to twelve months.

My major goals for ETS—and that also meant NAEB—were to make ETS a strong, united, and viable organization which must win and hold the respect and the genuine financial and moral support of state governors and legislators, of U.S. senators and congressmen, the FCC, the Department of HEW, and finally, members of national organizations, philanthropic institutions such as the Ford Foundation and others, and finally, the president of the United States.

APPY: Scotty got up and gave one of those Fletcher speeches which went on interminably but was full of fire and enthusiasm. Though he didn't know most of the players any more or any of the politics, he had a kind of sense of the dramatic and he was a pretty good salesman and I remember at the end of his address, Jim Robertson from KCET got up and said, "Okay, I'm with you from our station in Los Angeles. We'll put up the $4,000 we have to put up." And a few others followed suit.

~

Fletcher persuaded Gerard Appy, then manager of the University of Georgia station and a member of the Affiliates' Committee of NET and also the new ETS board of directors, to negotiate a six-month part-time leave to act as ETS vice president.

Start-up Days of the ETS Division of NAEB

APPY: It was a frantic six months. We put ourselves together some office space adjacent to NAEB. We tried to cope with what we considered to be the extreme lethargy in the major institution, NAEB.

As it turned out, my job was to sell the stations on joining up. Within a short time we had $100,000 pledged which was more than I ever thought we'd get that soon. It later became many thousands more, up in the $180,000 bracket, but it was enough to start.

Scotty was looking toward a new world. He figured the way to do this was to get a conference in which, for the first time, there had to be *two* people from each station, the station manager and also the board chairman or lay head.

He recognized that station managers in many instance really didn't have much clout. This may have been a blow to us as station managers, but it was quite visibly true. He also recognized that the chief lay people—the chairmen of boards at the local level or presidents of universities or the chief state school officer or the politically-appointed chairman of a state commission, who were the titular heads of these stations—really in most instances didn't know what was going on in public television. In some instances, they were not even readily accessible to the station manager.

~

Fletcher had learned this from a succession of personal interviews he undertook with key leaders in Washington who themselves were acquainted with what was going on in the educational television field, including members of the FCC and NAEB's attorney and long time friend of educational broadcasting, Leonard Marks. Then he called on Tom Clemens at the U.S. Office of Education.

FLETCHER: "Tom, the only way to begin, from my experience, is to have a national conference on the long-range financing of educational television stations [with] two representatives from each station present at the meeting in order to work out how we can have an act passed by Congress which will be similar to the one that was recently passed concerning educational television facilities—which means bricks and mortar—but now I'm not talking about hardware, I'm talking about software: programming!

I would guarantee that we would have two key persons from each and every station, otherwise there would be no conference, if we can get approximately $70,000 from HEW to fund and operate it."

~

Concurrent with the filing of an application for such a grant, Fletcher and his associates at ETS sent a letter to all ETV stations, addressed this time to the chairman of each board, which according to Fletcher included the following statement.

FLETCHER: "This conference will not be held unless, except for illness, every station is represented by the chairman of the board of the station—be it a university, school, state operation, or whatever—and this must be guaranteed by each station, at which time we will agree to pay your transportation, hotel, and miscellaneous expenses—so that the trip to Washington for three days will not cost you anything, except for what you want for personal reasons."

The letter ended by saying, "Please give us your reply by return mail so that we can complete arrangements for securing a grant for this purpose from an appropriate source."

~

Frederick Breitenfeld, later of Maryland ETV, and Philadelphia's WHYY-TV, had been drafted by ETS to assist with the proposed conference. His recollections leave no doubt that ETS had picked the right leader in Scotty Fletcher.

Frederick Breitenfeld

BREITENFELD: Scotty realized we needed federal funds. So what he then did was to say, "How do we get federal interest? Well, we get federal interest by going to the White House. With whom do you go to the White House? You go to the White House with the people back home who are the movers and shakers. Who are they? Well, in many cases, they are on the boards or the very chairmen of these licensees."

So he was the first to try to bring together the chairmen of the boards of local stations.

A remarkable number of station managers called or wrote and said, "Not on your tintype. I'm not giving you the name of my chairman, and I want you to stay the hell out of here if you're going to go to my board. They hired *me*.

I'm their boy. They gave *me* responsibility to deal with you, all you national types, so you ain't gettin' names of anybody."

Well, it wasn't long before Scotty just went to the FCC and found out who the board members were. But interestingly enough, the managers— the "professionals"—were shocked in 1964 that somebody should say, "Would you mind sending us the name of your chairman?" It was a fascinating little phenomenon which gave evidence of the feisty nature of the managers in those days. They were a gutsy bunch.

~

HEW finally came through with the grant and the conference was held December 7 and 8, 1964. Every station was represented by two or more people, the local board chairman or his representative and the station manager. The event generated considerable enthusiasm, not only among those representing the station but among many government officials including senators and congressmen who attended parts of the sessions.

The First Conference on Long-Range Financing

BREITENFELD: The conference had one thing going for it, and that was Scott's doing: Class! Francis Koeppel, the U.S. Commissioner of Education, gave an address—which I was asked to write, which I did, and he never read it, and I don't know where it is, and I would estimate that it was no good—but I thought I was a famous ghost writer there for a week. Koeppel came, other wheels came. This was all Scotty's doing.

What came out of it was just the report Scotty had in mind. To some of the veterans, it seemed apparent that Scotty had this thing so well in hand that the conclusion of this group would be: one, educational television is important to this country; two, it needs a greater backing and by that we mean financial support; three, something's gotta be done; four, we want a White House commission. And one, two, three, four, they came out.

Scotty sent a series of position papers to the participants, but he chose those papers with the care of a sorcerer. The papers that he used as background papers were class items, intelligently written.

He told me once, "Never hold a meeting when you don't already know what the outcome has got to be. Don't just sit around and say, "I wonder where we're going." A valuable lesson.

He also taught me: "Most people are stupid. And the stupider they are, the nicer you have to be to them." [LAUGHTER]

But the point is, Scotty made sure that packets were on time, that fourteen papers were carefully selected, that the proper people knew about certain things. Following him around was a wonderful education in how to get major things done. That was his strength, getting things done.

What was important was this galvanizing which Scotty was able to do, this bringing together of human flesh so that superintendent could meet college president and nod, "Yes, this is important," that then we were on our way to go in to the White House and say, "Where is the commission?" That was the outcome of the conference.

~

Indeed it was, keynoted by the position paper read by the Grand Old Man from WGBH-TV in Boston, Ralph Lowell. His station manager, Hartford Gunn, later related the background behind Ralph Lowell's speech.

GUNN: I had begun earlier to think and think about how you could get big money. And the answer kept coming back: the only big money that's bigger than the Ford Foundation is the federal government.

So then the question was: how do you tap it? And we were doing the program with Mrs. [Eleanor] Roosevelt, "Prospects for Mankind," and I had become enormously impressed with Mrs. Roosevelt and her ability to articulate fairly complex issues and her drive and the enormous respect that she engendered in those later years on the part of her listeners and others.

I thought maybe if we were to make Mrs. Roosevelt the chairperson of a commission that would look at American communications, that she, then, could make a recommendation with that commission, that could put federal support under public broadcasting.

We had already achieved the Educational Television Facilities Act, which proved that it was possible to get federal money. So it was clear that we could get the federal government involved. At that time, it had been made clear to us that the federal government should never get involved in supporting programming, never get involved in the operating side. But we needed some mechanism to get the attention of the president and the Congress, and it seemed to me that a commission, headed by Mrs. Roosevelt, would be an appropriate way to do that.

~

Gunn took his notion to Newton Minow, then chairman of the Federal Communications Commission. Minow felt it was a good idea but that it would be inappropriate for the federal regulating agency to take on such a project.

GUNN: I went back to Boston, obviously discouraged. I told David Ives, my director of development, "David, we've struck out. I don't know where else to turn if the chairman of the FCC won't step up and do it. There's no real solution."

It was shortly thereafter that the call came from Scotty to have the meeting in Washington to get about this whole process of trying to get greater support for educational television. And Ralph Lowell was invited, and Lowell called up David and me and said, "Hey, fellas, I need a speech. You guys write it."

It really was David's idea. He said, "Hartford, why don't we pick up on your idea of a commission?"

So I said, "Well, let's propose a presidential commission." It was becoming very fashionable to have presidential commissions; I guess it was [President] Kennedy who had started a number of commissions to look at different things.

So between David and myself, with David doing most of the writing and with my structuring the thing, we wrote the speech for Ralph Lowell in which he called for a presidential commission to be established, and Lowell floated this idea before the group when they met in Washington.

Scotty, to his credit, leaped on it and said, "That's a good thing!"

FLETCHER: The most important decision of the conference was that the president of the United States should be asked if he would create a special commission to investigate the needs of educational television as quickly as possible.

After the conferees had voted unanimously to proceed with the commission idea, Mr. Lowell was asked if he would chair a committee to approach the president and ask him if he would cooperate in this venture. Lowell agreed, provided—he said—"I must rely on you to select the names of the committee because I know so few people outside of Boston. As you know," he continued, "I don't travel at all except during my vacation, which is by ship or train. I never fly."

~

Fletcher, in consultation with others, prepared a list of names of individuals to serve on such a committee. He wisely included both Republicans and Democrats, leading educators, business men "and other people of significance" from various parts of the country.

GUNN: They were invited to Boston—because we couldn't get Ralph Lowell on the train again!

I remember the meeting in our little conference room.

FLETCHER: All ten members of the committee were present. A draft of a letter to be sent to the president was presented to them, which had been prepared by Hartford Gunn and myself. We were also present at the meeting.

After considerable discussion and the usual type of fly-specking which goes on in any operation of this type, we emerged with a letter which was satisfactory to everyone. It was mailed to the president, but only after we had decided what type of commission we wanted—a presidential commission or private commission to be financed by private funds.

My friends in the Committee for Economic Development's research department in Washington, D.C. urged me to make it a private commission with private funds, because otherwise the cost of handling this matter would be taken out of the president's own funds and this would mean he would appoint the staff, and this possibly could cause problems. We gave him his choice.

It took a long time to be able to have every member of the committee sign the original letter. Unfortunately, Marion Folsom, who was a member of that committee, happened to be in New Zealand at that time attending a peace conference, and because I insisted that every signature be a legitimate signature, we had to wait until we got his signature from New Zealand. Having done all that, and having done some special survey work, we actually mailed the letter to the president, and he held it for some time.

Eventually, on June 9, 1965, Douglass Cater, special assistant to the president on educational matters, wrote to Mr. Lowell, and some of the paragraphs read as follows: [READING]

"The president has asked me to thank you for your letter and proposal. As you know I have had many discussions with Mr. Scott Fletcher on this matter. I am hopeful that in the very near future arrangements can be worked out which will provide for a suitable inquiry into the subject which you suggest. The president wishes me to inform you that he will be prepared to communicate directly on this matter at that time. Signed, Douglass Cater, special assistant to President Johnson."

The Road to Carnegie I

During the interim, Hartford Gunn had been continuing his efforts to follow up on the committee meeting in Boston.

GUNN: I was still convinced that the presidential thing was doable, but that the president might look for an excuse not to do it, and he could use the fact that he didn't have money to fund the commission. We knew it was going to be expensive to do a year's study and to do it right. I estimated it was going to cost $250,000. It cost $500,000, by the way. But I estimated $250,000 as a minimum it was going to cost.

I was determined to cut away every excuse, and I thought if we could go to him with money in hand and say, "Mr. President, we have the beginnings of a commission and we have the money; what we need is your blessing." I thought that stripped away everything.

So we went out to find some money.

The first thought was Ford, because Ford had been and was the definitive great benefactor of this system. But I rejected it as fast as I thought about it, because I felt that Ford would have a conflict of interest—that if the president were to take us up on this, it would look as if Ford was trying to buy its way out, and I didn't want to let Ford off the hook.

Carnegie was the next largest foundation that I knew of, and we did know Arthur Singer. Art had been at MIT. He was a good friend of David Ives, and for some reason I remembered David saying that Art Singer had gone to the Carnegie Corporation.

So I called David, David got to Art Singer, and Art said, "I'll set up a meeting for you, and you and Hartford can come down and make the case."

John Gardner was then the president of the Carnegie Corporation and Alan Pifer was the vice president. And John Gardner, Alan Pifer, Art Singer, David Ives, and myself went to the big Carnegie board room, which must seat fifty or sixty people, and we were just a few of us at the end of this huge table. They brought in some lunch.

I ate none of the lunch. I began a conversation, and I just talked constantly for about an hour, beginning with a little bit of history of public television, how it had been sustained and how it had gotten to a point now where it was just beginning to show that it could be a significant force, but it really was never going to go any further unless it could now develop quality programming and a live network and become something approaching the commercial networks in terms of its capacity, and that we had the interest of people like Ralph Lowell and Scotty Fletcher and Milton Eisenhower and Leland Hazard, there was a nucleus of people there that were committed, that were willing to get in and push this thing along.

I told them of my experience with Newton Minow and the FCC and our feeling that the president might be the only way to go, and that it would take something at that level to bring it off.

I can remember John Gardner sitting there, listening and taking it all in. He then asked a question. He said, "How much do you think it would cost?"

I said, "About $250,000." As I mentioned a moment ago, I was off one hundred percent! [LAUGHTER] It would end up costing $500,000. And he said, "All right, let me get back to you." I should have known then that we were a long way home when he asked that question.

~

From other sources it is now known that Arthur Singer had already suggested to John Gardner that Carnegie might consider sponsoring such a commission, and that the idea apparently was looked upon favorably by Gardner fairly early in the game. Gunn's presentation in the Carnegie board room was recalled by Singer as "magnificent" and "valuable as reenforcement."

What Hartford Gunn also did not know was that at that moment, behind the scenes, Lyndon Johnson was trying to persuade John Gardner to join his cabinet as secretary of Health, Education and Welfare. Gardner likely conducted his own soundings, got the impression that while President Johnson might not wish to set up a commission himself, he might not be averse to finding some other way to help.

GUNN: I can't remember how we reported this all to Scotty, but Scotty was beginning to make inquiries through Doug Cater, President Johnson's man at the White House in charge of the education area. It probably was Doug who was the middleman with John Gardner on the whole thing being involved with the president. So, anyway, by serendipity, the whole cast of characters were all working behind the scenes. Scotty was going to the right person: Cater. I was going to the right person: Gardner.

It then became clear from Scotty's inquiries with Cater that the president was not going to do the commission, on the advice of Leonard Marks. But at this point I felt there was enough momentum going, and everybody was feeling kind of sad for us.

I went back to Gardner, and I asked Gardner and Art Singer, "Wouldn't it be possible for Carnegie itself to sponsor this commission?" I cited the fact that they had funded James Bryant Conant to do a study on the American high school, as a Carnegie function.

They said, "Yeah, we could do that, we could make the grant to ourselves. We did it once before and we can do it again."

~

Fletcher, meanwhile, had accepted the urgings of the ETS and NAEB boards that he continue to command this campaign. Believing that the Ford Foundation as a funding source was at least entitled to the courtesy of an invitation, he had lunch with his old associate from fund days, Dr. Clarence Faust, who by that time was head of the education division of the Ford Foundation.

FLETCHER: When I explained what we had done and what we proposed to do in the future, I asked Faust if he thought the Ford Foundation would be interested. His answer was a very emphatic, "No, I don't think so."

Later, I heard on a confidential basis that the Carnegie Corporation might be interested. I checked with one or two intimate friends who had dealt with the Carnegie Corporation in the past. Miss Sarah Blanding, president of Vassar College and a charter member of our FAE [Fund for Adult Education] board for ten years, told me she knew Alan Pifer quite well. He was acting president while John Gardner was in Washington. I called Pifer for an appointment.

My meeting with Pifer was extremely pleasant, and during our conversation he called in an executive associate of the corporation, Mr. Arthur Singer, who then became the liaison man with me from that point on.

The next day I received a call from Art Singer. He suggested that as quickly as possible we submit a proposal to the Carnegie Corporation and "give the usual type of information with which you must be very familiar from your experience with the Ford Foundation. We want all the facts, reasons, the background, the president's approval of the idea, and we will pick it up from there."

In the meantime, I called Ralph Lowell long distance, and also Hartford Gunn, and explained to them that it would be unwise to make any suggestions to the Carnegie Corporation unless requested to do so concerning anyone who might be selected as a member of the commission.

~

During all of these going-ons, Leonard Marks played a crucial role, though it was not well known or understood at the time. We need to remember that Marks had been the Johnsons' attorney handling their commercial broadcasting properties in Texas and that he was known for his long association with and assistance to NAEB.

MARKS: I was in the government at the time. I had become director of the United States Information Agency in 1965, and I separated from the law firm—completely severed my relationship with the *commercial* process—but I kept up my relationship with individuals because I felt that the efforts of the educational community were lagging and anything I could do to help them I could certainly legitimately do in that role.

Again, it was the old story of money. The institutions were never able to command the resources that were really needed to fully develop the spectrum.

So Doug Cater and I—Doug Cater was assistant to the president—got together and talked to Alan Pifer of the Carnegie Corporation, who Doug knew. I never really had much to do with those discussions. But we pointed out that if a commission were created, the imprimatur of the president—not a government commission, a *private* commission—if Carnegie would provide the funds for it and they did an in-depth study, their findings would have a tremendous effect upon the Congress, on other foundations, and upon the business community. And we got an informal commitment that they would put up, I believe, a million dollars for that study. [1]

President Johnson signed a letter which we prepared, endorsing the concept, and the commission was appointed, and money was appropriated.

Finding A Proper Chairman

Who, then, would be an appropriate individual to head such an important commission? Who would be satisfactory to Carnegie, to the stations, to President Johnson?

Hartford Gunn, as usual, was thinking ahead.

GUNN: We had to have an individual like a Conant to stand up and give this thing legitimacy in the same way that Conant provided the legitimacy of the study of the American high schools in American education.

So we went to Professor Jerrold Zacharias, the physicist at MIT. Art Singer and Zacharias were friends. They talked it over and I think it was Zacharias who said, "Why not Jim Killian?"

Jim was then the president of MIT, and [Zacharias] said, "Jim is scheduled to retire, and he's much too active a person, too active a mind to retire totally. He's going to continue his

association with MIT but he'd have time to do this." So Zacharias was commissioned to sound Killian out.

And Killian said, "Well, I don't know." But Killian said he'd think about it. Either David or Art Singer got back to me, and we tried this out on Scotty, I guess, and he thought that was a good idea.

Certainly Singer had cleared it with Gardner, who thought "Yes, this is right, it's another Conant." They had picked Conant off just as he was retiring as president of Harvard, and here is the retiring chairman of MIT. And not only that but he was a man with scientific knowledge in the communications field; it all kind of came together. He had been Eisenhower's science advisor, so lord knows, he knew his way around government, and he had all of the prestige, and he could talk to people in the networks, he could get the information—nobody was going to withhold information from him. And he was also on the board of the CIA.

~

According to Singer, who played a key role at this time, there was initially some sentiment for Conant to be chairman, but others feared he might focus on instructional television. Stephen White, then a CBS producer, who subsequently became chief of staff for the commission, argued that the group should instead be principally concerned with the "public" programming. To counter the Conant suggestion, he proposed Killian's name. Singer took that nomination to Gardner, and for all the reasons enumerated by Hartford Gunn, Killian was an excellent choice.

KILLIAN: The first I heard about any association that I might have with such a commission was when I ran into John Gardner's ultimate successor, who became president of Carnegie when John left: Alan Pifer.

I was in England, and he came up to me in the dining room of the Athenaeum Club in London and said, "I understand that there's a chance that you will chair a commission sponsored by the Carnegie Corporation." I told him that was the first I'd heard about it, and it was. He was somewhat taken aback.

But later on, John Gardner was in touch with me and finally asked me if I would chair such a commission. He left it to me to help shape the membership if I undertook the chairmanship.

I came back and had long talks with Lowell and with Hartford Gunn, and they brought real pressure on me to take this assignment and that was persuasive, because I respected both of them and I knew that they would be helpful.

---

[1] Marks' recollection of the amount was incorrect. Carnegie agreed to provide half a million dollars.

GUNN: One night I was home. My apartment was on the fifth floor at 100 Memorial Drive. That apartment house is owned by John Hancock but it's on MIT land—a 100 year lease or something—and the condition of the lease was that they make the penthouse available to MIT. And when Killian moved out of the president's house, he had moved into the penthouse at 100 Memorial Drive.

So I was at home one night, the phone rang, and Killian says, "Can you come upstairs? I want to talk to you about this proposed Carnegie Commission." So I just walked out into the hall, got in the elevator, and went up to the penthouse. And there was Dr. Killian, at home! And Jim said, "Come in, sit down."

He said, "Zacharias has told me about this Carnegie Commission. I've got a lot of things I could do in retirement, and I'm only concerned that I do something that will have some real value." He said, "I do not want to do a study that's going to go on the library shelf. The government is littered with those, we just don't need another. I've got a lot of things I'd like to do with my time—the time that remains—and I want to be productive."

My job was to assure him that we would all get behind this thing and make this go, and that it would not go on the shelf. For whatever reason—probably other people, too, worked on him—he was persuaded to take it on.

And that really was that, because once you had the Gardner-Cater combination, and now Gardner was moving to Washington and Alan Pifer, who fortunately had been in there that day, was taking over the Carnegie Corporation—they all knew Killian, and the "old-boy" network was at work. They had total confidence in Killian and his ability to do it.

~

At long last, there was going to be convened a gilt-edged group of powerful and influential people under the chairmanship of a man whose credentials and reputation for integrity were impeccable, to take a hard and comprehensive look at the state of educational television and the potentials it might hold for the future.

Just how they were brought together, how they proceeded with their assignment, and the subsequent congressional response which their report and recommendations comprise the rest of the story told by the TeleVisionaries.

24

Carnegie Maps Out A Whole New Era

The first challenge facing Dr. James R. Killian as the newly-named chairman of an as yet unnamed national commission was to help determine the individuals who would share this monumental task with him.

KILLIAN: John Gardner had persuaded me—and I was not wholly willing at first. I sat down with Alan Pifer and we put together the names of a committee.

It included importantly, DuBridge, who was then president of Cal Tech. It included Ed Land of Polaroid, who had been my close associate in a study in 1954. It included one man who was suggested by President Johnson, and that was the man [J.C. Kellam] who was running his television station in Austin; otherwise Johnson took no part in the selection of the commission.

[Kellam] proved to be very helpful, and in no way did he deliberately complicate our assignment at all. There was some concern at first that he was "the president's man" and was there to serve the president's interests, but he never gave any indication. We also had Joseph McConnell, the former president of NBC who had left NBC and gone with the Reynolds Aluminum Company. He had had a lot of special television experience.

Then we had a distinguished musician, the pianist Rudolph Serkin.

One evening we were meeting at Endicott House, a place that MIT has had that was given to it, a former palatial residence of Wendell Endicott.

It was a June evening and the flowers were all in bloom and it was beautiful. We asked Serkin if he would play for the group, and he said, "I have to practice every day anyway, I'll be glad to play." So he gave a concert for the commission that evening, which was very memorable.

~

From comments made during interviews with others, the makeup of the first Carnegie Commission on Educational Television was helpfully influenced by several other friends of ETV. Among them was Leonard Marks.

MARKS: There were several people on that commission whom the president felt were knowledgeable and who could help considerably. I think particularly of J.C. Kellam, who had been the manager of radio and television for the LBJ family from the time they went into the business, a fine man who worked hard and long in the industry and had a feeling that education, public television, could be important.

Another one was John Hayes, who was head of the *Washington Post* radio and television stations. Subsequently he was appointed by LBJ as ambassador to Switzerland. He served as chairman of Radio Free Europe, Radio Liberty, for several years before his death.

Another one...I believe Oveta Culp Hobby was on that commission, she being from Texas, former secretary of HEW and a person whom LBJ knew and felt could carry a lot of weight if she became convinced.

~

Killian also relied on Hartford Gunn. Like Leonard Marks, Gunn saw the desirability of pleasing President Johnson.

GUNN: I told Killian that to prevent this from going on the shelf—which was Killian's worry, that it would be an inconsequential study, or dust-gatherer—I said, "We've somehow got to keep the president involved." He agreed that somehow the president had to be close enough to this thing without appearing to be close to it, that he would have full confidence in the recommendations so they would automatically have his approval when they came forth, so the end was to be pre-determined when you went in.

I didn't know what the solution was, but somehow we had to keep the president in there, so that when the recommendations came out, we wouldn't be fighting with the administration but the administration would feel that they had been substantively involved.

The solution that got worked out—and I don't know who worked it out; Doug Cater, I guess—was to get two people on that commission. One was the manager of the LBJ station, and the other was the head of the *Washington Post* stations in Washington.

And then all other names that went on that commission were cleared with Doug as the president's overseer. This was essential to get the whole thing together.

KILLIAN: It was a first-rate group. Oveta Culp Hobby came on, never missed a meeting. She was really attentive to it. And [Robert] Saudek was a commercial producer who had had considerable experience producing programs for television. We had [James B.] Conant, of course, president of Harvard, and we had the president of the University of Illinois, David Henry.

~

Other members of the commission were author Ralph Ellison; Franklin Patterson, president of Hampshire College; Terry Sanford, former governor of North Carolina, and Leonard Woodcock, vice president of the United Automobile Workers of America.

Hyman H. Goldin, who earlier became one of the TeleVisionaries during his years at the FCC, at this point was suggested to Arthur Singer by Scotty Fletcher as a possible staff person for the commission. Singer tentatively hired him and sent him on to Killian. Goldin, also, was impressed with the individuals chosen to serve on the commission.

GOLDIN: They had everybody who mattered in terms of selling the report. It was really a first-rate commission, one of the outstanding commissions, I think, of all time.

Stephen White and Hyman Goldin As Staff

KILLIAN: I think the first person to come aboard as a staff member was Stephen White.

Steve had worked with Zacharias on a revolutionary program for science teaching in high schools and in the production of educational movies as a part of a curriculum that was developed for high school teaching, in which the best scientists in the country were making motion pictures. He also had produced programs for CBS, television programs.

I remember at our first meeting, which was in the board room of the Carnegie Corporation in New York, Stephen White undertook to tell this group of people, inexperienced in television, what television was all about.

Goldin had a great deal of experience with all the legal and regulatory, technical, and financial aspects of television, so he was an extremely important resource for the commission.

GOLDIN: Steve White is by far the ablest person I have worked with in terms of educational broadcasting. He's not well-appreciated and not that well-known by the educational community. He came out of commercial broadcasting, originally a newspaper man. He has a personality that not everyone can get along with, but he's extremely able.

Stephen White

Steve could write very well. But beyond being able to write, he had a very good grasp of what he thought educational broadcasting should be about.

It's a pity to underestimate the importance of Steve White in the work of the Carnegie Commission. I believe that he was by far the most creative person in that work. And Steve White and I got along very well—fortunately—because if we hadn't, there wouldn't have been any study. There just was nobody else there, basically.

Although he was more conservative than I was in some ways, we both agreed on some basics. But the Carnegie thing was done to a very large degree by the interrelationship of Killian and the two of us. Killian was excellent, really not a person that you easily liked. He's not a warm, outgoing sort of person and he can stare you down hard. He has a background of board of directors of AT&T and General Motors and that sort of thing, although he comes from a small South Carolina town, and he wasn't an engineer to start with.

But he was a person who was greatly gifted in managerial skills. He had fine judgment. He just knew how to deal with people at the topmost level, and the commission was purely top level.

FLETCHER: The very first time the members of the commission all met one another was in January 1966. To that dinner meeting were invited Mr. Ralph Lowell of Boston; Mr. William Harley, president of the National Association of Educational Broadcasters, and myself.

First there was a cocktail party, at which time we met every member of the commission and the staff. After dinner Dr. Killian first called on Ralph Lowell to say a few words.

Ralph Lowell does not enjoy public speaking. He avoids it whenever he can, so what he says is right to the point. This time he went a little overboard and expanded quite enthusiastically about what had happened to educational television up to the present and how he was looking forward to further expansion and improvement after the commission had completed its task and their recommendations were placed into action.

Next, Harley gave a brief history of the development of educational television, and I filled in with the developments which led up to the appointment of the Carnegie Commission and the interest which President Johnson had shown in educational television, and particularly his enthusiastic approval of the idea of the formation of this commission.

We three then left and the Carnegie Commission went to work.

DuBridge Describes Beginning Efforts

DuBRIDGE: The first thing was to spend the first one or maybe two meetings just getting briefed by people in the television business, and in education, and culture, and so on about how such a system might operate, what NET was doing, where they would like to go if they could afford it, some of the opportunities that might arise in the world of entertainment, music, culture, art, education, public affairs, and so on. We were briefed by a lot of different people that had different approaches to it. And by people who talked about the funding of it.

One person who talked to us, I remember, gave an impassioned plea: Don't go to the federal government, you'll be a captive and a slave to the federal government if you let them in on this.

Seldom has there been assembled as distinguished a group to contemplate a concern in American society as the first Carnegie Commission on Educational Television, shown here with their staff. Chairman James R. Killian, Jr., is front row, center.

This was a feeling many of us had. We all agreed that the federal government was a last resort. If we could see any other way to get adequate financing, we would be glad to take it.

~

DuBridge served as chairman of a subcommittee on financing, one of five or six subcommittees delegated to work on specific segments of the larger topic.

DuBRIDGE: Hyman Goldin's the one that really gathered together the information about the financial status of all the stations then operating in the country, about NET, about what it would cost to mount, first, a substantial increase in the number of stations; second, a quantum jump in the quality of their programming, and what the budget ought to be for a going ETV system.

And, you know, the figures got kind of big!

They look smaller now, but they looked awfully big then. The whole commission argued about this. Our committee reported every now and then, and we were coming more and more to the feeling that the federal government was the only hope for a viable, really national, ETV system.

At many of our meetings there would be many people who said, "Aw, you're leading us down the golden pathway and we'll be sunk. It ain't the thing to do." Yet the more we explored other alternatives, the more people came around to saying, "I guess it's the only hope, but, we must set it up in such a way that we're not under the thumb of Congress or the president."

DuBridge remembered the emergence of the notion of a separate nongovernmental body that could be a buffer between the politicians and the ETV community. Selection of a name for this body brought further debate.

Separating "Instructional" from "Public"

DuBRIDGE: Should we go on with the name "educational TV?" Should we call it the Corporation for Educational Television? That was the first idea. And gradually more and more people —not including me at first—said, "Educational is giving the wrong impression to people. They just think of classroom instruction and teachers writing on blackboards. We are losing potential audience by the very name. We ought to have a name that would reflect the fact that this is not classroom teaching. They are cultural programs in the very broadest sense of the word."

At first, I said, "Look, educational television *has* a name. People know what it means."

And they said, "That's the trouble, they don't— or, if they think they do, they have the wrong idea as to what we're thinking about." And I had to agree. So we called our report: "Public Television"—not "Educational Television."

~

At the time there was quite a lot of discussion of this point outside of the commission as well as within it. One reason was that the proposed new label seemed to set aside rather than to include instructional television, when many of ETV's leaders were doing their best to establish it as an aid to formal education at all levels.

One such leader was Nebraska's Jack McBride.

McBRIDE: They opted not to address any of the *educational* television aspects.

I can remember being in a Boston ballroom, one of a number of people who had been invited to come in and testify, and part of my pitch was the continuing importance of *educational* television: "Please don't exclude it."

But they understandably chose to say, "That's the responsiblity of another study."

~

South Carolina's Henry J. Cauthen felt deeply about this point also.

CAUTHEN: My concern was that to continue to get state support—and, in my belief, federal support—education was the base from which we had to operate, and that if we were going to move into something called "public broadcasting," it would eventually lead—in the perception of some people—to either something frivolous or something that was competitive with commercial broadcasting, and certainly something not as basic and not as necessary as education. I felt like there would always be a strong base of support for education, but I was not at all sure there would be a strong base of support for something called "public broadcasting."

~

Cauthen wrote to Dr. Killian about what he felt was a most serious concern.

CAUTHEN: I call it my deathbed letter.

I had gone into the hospital for a gall bladder operation, and I was quite convinced I wasn't going to survive it. The night before the operation, already under some degree of sedative—I probably would never have written it otherwise—I wrote a rather strong letter to Dr. Killian about my concerns, about the direction the commission was going and the naming of public broadcasting; was this not turning its back on education?

I got a very nice letter back from Dr. Killian saying essentially that education was such a broad issue and an area that they really didn't have time to concentrate on, so that would be a subject of another study at another day perhaps, which never really materialized.

~

As for the origin of the term "public broadcasting," New York City's M.S. Novik, long-time head of municipally-owned WNYC, believes that he coined it twenty-five years earlier in a piece he wrote for WNYC's program bulletin.

NOVIK: The reason that I always used the word "public" was because I had to explain what kind of a station we were. And it's in here, in one of the editorials.

I came up with the term "we are a public broadcasting station."

When Novik is gone, history will record that the term "public broadcasting" meant a helluva lot more to me than it means to many of the kids, young men, and older men who are now running public stations, because of this whole struggle [with] the concept.

~

In any event, the term adopted by the first Carnegie Commission has stuck, and is even defended now and then by individuals who are outspoken proponents of education in both its formal and informal modes. One such defender is Norman Cousins.

COUSINS: I think one of the best things that ever happened in the history of this movement was changing the name from "educational television" to "public television."

If the Carnegie Commission had done nothing else except to come up with that name, all its effort, I think, would have been justified.

Periodically we would struggle with the name of ETV. It was misleading in the first place. And while we were concerned with classroom TV and while we did have that unit set up to take care of it, you were still dealing with quality programming. So their people came up with the idea of "noncommercial television," or something else that had a "non" on the front of it.

Well, there are those of us in this world who have higher aspirations than to be a "non-something." I've never relished particularly being a "nonfiction author."

The term "public" was positive. It put the American people in the saddle. It was *their* television show.

"Public" was just right. It was noncommercial in its connotations without using the word "non." It was just one of those simple things that makes everyone say, "Why hadn't we thought of that before?"

~

On the policy issue of whether or not to include instructional television in the study, there were conflicting views within the commission and its staff.

GOLDIN: I felt that from a political standpoint, if we came out without having dealt with the instructional broadcasting part, I was fearful that we wouldn't be able to sell the rest of it. And I argued that strenuously. But I was overruled on that. And of the people who were very strongly anti-instruction, one of them was Conant. He was very much into that, changing American education at the time. And he had nothing but contempt for all that had gone into instructional broadcasting.

And nobody else [on the commission] had anything good to say for instructional broadcasting. I'm not sure it was quite that bad, but the commission compromised in a sense. We said, "Well, that's a large issue all of its own and so we will propose another commission," et cetera, et cetera. And that other commission never did anything of significance. But that was the way we got off the hook.

Probing, Inside and Out, for Ideas

The commission and its staff reached out in many directions for information and recommendations. The Arthur D. Little consulting firm studied the economics of the problem. Papers were commissioned from Professor Albert G. Hill on technical aspects and J.C.R. Licklider on future uses of television as an instrument for education. Under the supervision of staff member Greg Harney, borrowed from WGBH-TV, almost every existing ETV station in the country was visited. Others examined noncommercial television enterprises abroad. Killian went to Japan, Goldin to the BBC and to Italy and Germany.

KILLIAN: We had a mass of material. We held a series of meetings in various parts of the country, inviting many people to give us their wisdom. I remember a long meeting with Frank Stanton [president of CBS], who was one of our really enthusiastic supporters. I remember our sessions in Chicago where Edward L. Ryerson spent a lot of time with us. He was head of their ETV station board, one of the leading citizens of Chicago, head of the symphony—he was the Ralph Lowell of Chicago. He made contributions that were helpful.

~

Goldin describes the intellectual rigor of the deliberations and cites another issue with which the staff grappled.

GOLDIN: We had long discussions. These monthly meetings with commissioners would last a couple of days, and they were at places such as Endicott House in Dedham where you could get away from things.

These were very busy people who were spending the time doing nothing but thinking very seriously about this field. And they were all very active. A great deal of thinking went on in those meetings.

One conflict on policy was basically between DuBridge and the staff. DuBridge was very strongly for NET and for the structure as he found it. And Steve and I were very strongly anti-network.

~

DuBridge at the time was a member of the board of NET as well as a member of the Carnegie Commission, not a comfortable position in which to find oneself since the NET board and its president, John F. White, naturally felt they should be the entity to carry forward the work they already had accomplished during the preceding ten years.

Dr. Everett Case was chairman of the NET board at that time.

CASE: We responded very favorably when Scotty [Fletcher] and others—Jim Killian, who was one of my trustees at the Sloan Foundation, and our friend Alan Pifer at the Carnegie Corporation—talked with us and we were all for it: let's have an investigation. This would be great.

We felt that our board, while we were centered in New York, was representative of the entire nation and of the stations and of national concern. Therefore, we felt that if the Carnegie Commission report should produce the authorization for a commission for public broadcasting, that as its operating arm, NET was there, in place and qualified, the only one that was existent that could be used and had great potentialities for that purpose.

While there was some apprehension that this might not be true, because Washington did not like New York-centered agencies, we decided that we had to play it on the assumption that we had every confidence that we would be so designated. That's what we did.

~

Meanwhile, back in the Carnegie Commission's staff discussions, a wholly different philosophy was crystallizing.

GOLDIN: I had been strongly anti-network in the FCC. I had been part of the [commercial] network investigations in 1956. So Steve and I were protagonists of the idea of getting rid of networking.

Steve came to it as a journalist who believed in the newspaper as an institution which is locally produced. I came to it in terms of my social policy, in terms of the structure of industry, my anti-monopoly view. And we reenforced each other.

Steve carried it even farther than I could in terms of the implications of what that meant in terms of what we finally sold to the Carnegie Commission. But we were very strongly anti-network.

DuBridge argued very strongly to retain that NET structure. He felt that was academic, you know, you weren't building from where you were. And there were many heated discussions on that point.

CASE: We consulted DuBridge on what the commission was likely to recommend and what was likely to transpire.

I know of no more honest person intellectually than Lee DuBridge, intellectually and every other way, too—but his answer was reassuring. I think he would now say it shouldn't have been.

There was beginning to be cause for apprehension in the fact that so many members of the commission courteously listened but didn't seem very much impressed with NET as the agency for carrying out this mandate.

GOLDIN: We went at that for a long time. We sold it finally. We sold Killian on our approach generally. And we finally won on that.

The Inevitable Problem: Financing

DuBRIDGE: We were terribly anxious to get away from the annual budget congressional appropriation. And I guess the only thing we could think of was the excise tax, as in Britain.

GOLDIN: We went around and about on how it was going to be financed, and we charted out all the possibilities. It was clear that each one had disadvantages. And we felt that the least objectionable was the excise tax. After all, excise taxes were part of the financing of the Korean war, for example. They had been on TV sets, and only recently had been taken off TV sets, so we had that precedent.

The only one who was in favor of doing it by taxing commercial broadcasters was McConnell. McConnell had been bounced by NBC. I think he wanted to get back at them. He was never terribly interested in the study. He came along and he was gentle and supportive, but he basically was not terribly interested. It was simply that at that point he came alive in terms of putting it to the [commercial] broadcasters!

KILLIAN: He [McConnell] felt that the commercial stations ought to pay the cost because they were getting the benefit of a free use of a great national resource, and that they had an obligation to finance it.

It was a very interesting position for him to take, having been in the commercial field.

~

The commission tried to find out the likelihood of the administration and the Congress endorsing the notion of a tax on television sets. Inquiry was made through Douglass Cater at the White House.

GOLDIN: He said hands off on the excise tax. They threw us to the wolves on that one. They said, "If you can sell it...."

Killian and I went to see the House Ways and Means Committee chairman and we saw the chief Treasury expert on taxes, general counsel of the Treasury Department. They were very polite to us. We talked to [Senator] Pastore and others. They were all polite to us but we didn't get any support. It was not doable as far as they were concerned.

We had been arguing very strenuously against governmental appropriation. We were trying to figure out a way in which there would be no supervision, and that just isn't doable in our system—and probably shouldn't be.

~

Goldin continues and offers a better understanding of the immensity of the financing dilemma.

GOLDIN: Up to this point, there had been no federal money for programming, [although] there had been money for instructional work in the Office of Education and in the Facilities Act. So the issue for us was, how do you get programming money without it seeming to be programming money?

The excise tax was only going to bring in a small part of what we thought was required, ultimately $100 million, we said. But there were $200 or $300 million that had to be for running the stations and for reconstructing the stations.

We saw it in two steps. The excise tax would go directly to the corporation, but the money for the Office of Education had to go through Congress—through the appropriations channel—while we were arguing that not a penny of program money can come through the appropriations channel.

At the same time we set up what we called an operations fund that was going to go to the Office of Education—and was the largest sum actually—and that they would pass it through to the stations for "operations," which really was programming.

When that came out, the Office of Education said, "Nothing doing! We're not going to be involved." Gardner turned us down at that point.

So they left us with nothing, basically, because the Congress did not adopt the excise tax. HEW was still fiddling around with the facilities bill, and there was public broadcasting hanging on a limb.

~

So the notion of creating a nongovernmental corporation to receive whatever funds could be made available and then dispense these funds to program producers gained credence. In retrospect, Goldin—as one of the principal architects of the plan—seemed not so sure of its validity as he once was during its formation.

GOLDIN: The point at which I think we made a serious mistake, maybe it was inevitable, given our point of view, was in terms of our conception of the programming arrangements.

We came up with the idea that the Corporation [for Public Broadcasting] would be nothing but a program contributor. In other words, the corporation would provide funds for program production, mainly to NET and large stations, and we had it all worked out in terms of grants for that.

The idea was that we wanted to prevent NET from taking over the new organization; we wanted to avoid the example of commercial broadcasting. So the idea was that the corporation would fund these programs but would have nothing to do in the way of censorship of the programs, and no one would have a program schedule.

The programs would be sent over the lines—it was assumed that they would have interconnection, first with reduced rates from AT&T—eventually satellite—but that the individual stations could carry them live if they wished to, but if they didn't they would tape them and then play them in terms of developing their own schedule. We were so strong in the view that the local station should reflect local communities' needs and interests, and that *it* should have the power to decide what its scheduling was, rather than having this imposed by a network.

Our idea was that the corporation would have nothing to do with the contents of the programming [or] the quality of the programming once they had provided the funding. They could choose not to fund the same people next time, but they couldn't do anything with the program fare.

It was a newspaper idea basically. It was more radical than newspaper; it was more like an "access" idea.

It was a great idea on paper. The educators never bought it. I don't think the commission ever clearly understood it. Maybe Killian understood it. I'm not sure he did. I don't think anybody else thought about it.

~

Goldin also reflected in later years on the well-known feeling among the stations themselves that they wanted any financial help to come directly to them, with no intermediate bureaucracy.

GOLDIN: If they had their preference, they would have had all the funds go directly to them, all the government funds.

It was afterwards that Hartford Gunn worked up his idea about stations buying programs from PBS. He mentioned it while we were still in the study, but at that point the study was too far along, really, to seriously explore that.

~

But funding and the desirable isolation of the source of funds from programming were not the only looming difficulties facing the Carnegie Commission and its staff as they entered their final weeks of work.

How Does One Define Public Broadcasting?

GOLDIN: One of the areas which we had the most difficulty with, was how do we describe what public broadcasting is going to do?

We tried many passes at that. [Robert] Saudek believed that he understood. You know, he'd been in on the early part [of ETV], he'd done "Omnibus" and he thought he knew what public broadcasting was about. I'll never forget that meeting. Ralph Ellison, who was generally cooperative, took Saudek apart. And we battled. We didn't feel that anybody knew.

We even got a young man who was writing plays at that time. He had written a few plays that had been staged. We had him on in the summer to see if he could develop this. What we wanted to know was what was happening in the avant garde part of the cultural community, the cutting edge. That's what we were struggling for, and Saudek was no help in getting us to the cutting edge. Nobody really was.

We got in Lewis Freedman [producer of the notable TV dramatic series, "Play of the Week," among other significant productions] and we had an interesting session with him. He was very good in some ways, but again was rather traditional. He wasn't at the cutting edge, but he was farther along in that than anybody else we met.

At one point, Steve wouldn't write the section on programming, and I wouldn't do it. And then Killian sat down and wrote a piece on programming. I saw it and I told them I thought it was terrible. And I edited it a little bit but then I gave up.

It was just the cliches, you know; we're going to do the news in depth, we're going to do modern plays, we're going to do old plays, well, that kind of trash you don't need to spend time on. Anybody who understands anything about the problem would start at that point.

And Killian never got beyond that point. We never were able to do anything with that part. We got a lot of flowery language about the hopes and aspirations, but we never succeeded in describing what public broadcasting was really going to do that was worth all the money and effort and time. It was a hope.

My own view is that it's still a hope. But I thought that was an area in which we did the least well. We didn't really succeed on that.

~

Dr. Killian recalled those latter weeks of work.

KILLIAN: We had almost monthly meetings for a period. Of the last two meetings, one was out at Endicott House, where we invited the heads of all the major foundations, like Mac Bundy of Ford, and Alan Pifer of Carnegie, and they had a Rockefeller representative to meet with us, to hear our views, and to get from them their feeling about the possibility of foundation financing.

We then had the concluding meeting out at Los Angeles. That was the time when I visited the station there. And I remember standing at the blackboard for some hours, leading the discussion and writing down the conclusions reached with sufficient unanimity to make them firm, and we put together at that meeting our report.

The writing of the report was done by Steve White, but a lot of the telling conclusions were written by members of the commission itself.

Killian Takes Soundings in Washington

Having framed a text of the report, Killian felt that it should be tried out in advance of its release on some key people in Washington, D.C. He went first to President Lyndon Johnson's education and communication advisor, Douglass Cater, who had encouraged the commission all along, indeed, had helped in the selection of individuals to undertake this significant task.

KILLIAN: We presented the conclusions we had reached. He gave us the names of people in congress that he thought we ought to make contact with, so Lee DuBridge and Franklin Patterson and several other members systematically covered all of these people in congress by going to visit them: [Senator] Magnuson, Magnuson's associate in the Senate, Pastore from Rhode Island, who handled all the action in the Senate.

We went to see the then chairman of the Ways and Means Committee, the great tax expert [Congressman Wilbur Mills]. He welcomed us with open arms and was very helpful. And we covered [other] people in the House.

Ted Kennedy heard about this whole enterprise and got interested in it and said he would like to help. He came up to see me and I had a luncheon in my home for Ted, and got Land and some of us together and we reviewed all of our ideas on funding for Kennedy, and found him supportive. He said, "Well, I would like to go back and arrange a luncheon of members of the Senate to hear your story," and so he did.

We went down, and I guess it was DuBridge and Patterson and I met with twenty-two senators that he brought together to talk about public television. It was in that way that we gained, really, the support of the politicos, the influential people in the Senate.

This was an important lesson for many of us. I'd been on a number of commissions that had brought in good reports and mailed them to members of Congress or other people, and stopped at that point. Unless you really promote and explain and engage the interest of the people who make decisions, a commission of this kind doesn't get very far.

Fortunately we didn't do that. We covered the waterfront with Congress and members of the administration. Had a long session with John Gardner, who was then secretary of HEW.

The one place that we found opposition was in Treasury, where the then-advisor to the treasury on tax matters, a professor in the law school at Harvard, objected to our proposal for the excise tax on television sets. But no kind of tax would have won the approval of that group. But all of the others were very supportive.

And then we arranged a set of meetings with the head of RCA, David Sarnoff. They had a luncheon at which we explained our conclusions. He was skeptical. We did the same at CBS through our contracts with Stanton, and they were very supportive; they went all out to be helpful.

We had the report printed over a weekend through special arrangements we had made with the printer. We delivered copies to a selected group of people. One, for example, was Frank Stanton, who had a chance to read the report before it became published.

We announced a press conference at the auditorium of Rockefeller University in New York with the members of the commission present and a very large contingent from the press. We presented our

story, and I received a telegram from Frank Stanton, who had read the report that we had sent him over the weekend, saying that CBS was prepared to donate $1 million to the Corporation for Public Broadcasting on the day that it was chartered. And we had other pleasant reactions of that kind.

So the report was launched in an atmosphere that was favorable and helpful. And I think within less than four months, the Senate had passed a bill accepting most of the recommendations in the report.

The Heart of the Carnegie Proposal

That ninety-nine page report (with 155 additional pages of tables and supplementary papers) concluded with two especially significant paragraphs:

"If we were to sum up our proposal with all the brevity at our command, we would say that what we recommend is freedom. We seek freedom from the constraints, however necessary in their context, of commercial television. We seek for educational television freedom from the pressures of inadequate funds. We seek for the artist, the technician, the journalist, the scholar, and the public servant freedom to create, freedom to innovate, freedom to be heard in this most far-reaching medium. We seek for the citizen freedom to view, to see programs that the present system, by its incompleteness, denies him.

Dr. Killian, chairman, announced the Carnegie Commission on Educational Television's findings at a January 25, 1967 press conference. Seated (L-R): Commissioners James B. Conant, Lee A. DuBridge, Edwin H. Land and Terry Sanford; second row: Robert Saudek and Leonard Woodcock; third row: Ralph Ellison.

"Because this freedom is its principal burden, we submit our report with confidence: to rally the American people in the name of freedom is to ask no more of them than they have always been willing to provide."[1]

This was a high note on which to end, and a challenge to those who would need to act skillfully if Carnegie I recommendations were to bear fruit in follow-up legislation.

A lot more carefully orchestrated persuasion was mounted during the weeks following the report's release, involving Dr. Killian and other members of the commission as well as leading figures in educational television generally. And much of 1967 was occupied with debate, disagreement, and discussion before the first Public Broadcasting Act was passed by the Congress and sent to President Lyndon B. Johnson for his signature.

---

[1]From *Public Television: A Program for Action*, Harper and Row, 1967, pages 98-99.

25

The Last Mile to Congressional Recognition

It had been a long, hard way from the reservation of television channels for education in 1952, and the establishment of the first ETV station in 1953, to recognition by Congress in November, 1967, of the importance of public television and radio in our American society.

However, once the Carnegie Commission came out with its landmark report and recommendations, those who had pioneered this venture could sense the growing sentiment in many high places supporting some kind of national declaration of support and encouragement.

Encouragement from LBJ

Lyndon Johnson had initially encouraged the establishment of the Carnegie Commission partly because of his high regard for education in general and partly because of the efforts of Douglass Cater, his man for educational affairs, and Cater had kept the president aware of that commission's actions throughout its year of activity.

The following year in his "State of the Union Message," Johnson became the first president to formally recognize and endorse this new educational medium.

In that address he said: "We should develop educational television into a vital public resource...We should insist that the public interest be fully served through the public's airwaves. I will propose these measures to the Ninetieth Congress."

As Robert J. Blakely put it in his excellent book on educational broadcasting's history in America, "Educational television had fi-

nally cut through to the brink of receiving federal aid for program development."[1]

M.S. Novik, with his omnipresent political antennae out, provided us with his version of the reason for LBJ's interest.

NOVIK: The president was exactly like Truman. He was sympathetic to the potentials of mass education, and to challenge the control that—for lack of a better word—"Madison Avenue" had. And this is why a populist like Truman and a populist like Johnson would be the naturals for us, because they basically believed in helping the little people.

~

Illinois' Frank Schooley, who had opportunities from time to time to visit with Doug Cater about public broadcasting, offered another reason for the president's interest.

SCHOOLEY: That's one advantage that Lyndon Johnson had. He had a staff—or at least some members of his staff—who were interested in it and kept up with it and were active. The people who have succeeded Lyndon Johnson haven't had that help from staffers who had that same concern about public broadcasting.

~

William Harley, at that time president of the National Association of Educational Broadcasters, was among those greatly encouraged by the climate in the White House.

HARLEY: The White House took this [report] and ran with it, so to speak. I guess never in the history of our nation has one piece of legislation

---

[1]*"To Serve the Public Interest,"* Robert J. Blakely, Syracuse University Press, page 173.

been pushed through so fast to completion within little less than a year.

I was very much involved in that whole undertaking because obviously our association had a lot at stake here.

It was just really a pleasure to work with Doug Cater. He had a basement office that we would meet in almost every week as the provisions of the Carnegie Commission report were rapidly put into legislative form. Then we had to go through hearings, of course, in both houses, and then try to get it passed.

Heretofore we had nothing but money for equipment to help the states get started in establishing the broadcasting plants, but there was no money for production, for program support, whatsoever. So this was a whole new level of assistance, very important to us.

~

Working closely with Harley was Chalmers H. Marquis, who headed the Educational Television Stations division of the NAEB. His constituent members had the most to gain—or lose—depending upon the nature of the Carnegie Commission recommendations and the resulting legislation. Scotty Fletcher, also still allied with ETS, managed much of the behind-the-scenes liaison with Dr. Killian and the commission during its fourteen months of effort.

MARQUIS: President Johnson picked it up as soon as it came out, and asked his staff to prepare legislation. When the [draft legislation] came out, actually in February, we organized the Second Long Range Conference on Financing in Washington—the laymen and managers again—to study the legislation.

The bill had just come out that weekend. We got an advance copy, I think, printed it up for the conference, along with copies of the Carnegie Commission book, with the object of studying that and endorsing alternatives, which we did.

Endorsement by Fletcher's Second Conference

Following, as always, his mode of operation, Scotty Fletcher knew well ahead of time exactly what needed to come out of that second Washington conference. He employed the same formula as he had done in organizing the first such conference, the one which had recommended the creation of a group such as the Carnegie Commission. Each station had to send not only its manager but a key officer of the licensee to represent the station's board. Again, all participants be-

1967 luncheon in Washington during Second Conference on Long Range Financing. C. Scott Fletcher, second from left; NAEB-ETS president, Jack McBride, at the podium; at the speaker's table to the right of Fletcher are Richard B. Hull and Dr. Everett Case.

came involved in detailed discussion in small groups, whose individual reports to the full body were combined into a statement of endorsement of the Carnegie Commission's recommendations by the entire public television profession.

FLETCHER: The meeting was opened by Dr. James Killian. We had many members of Congress attend certain parts and speak to the conferees.

The main point of the conference was to develop a document to send to President Johnson and to key people in Congress saying, "These are the recommendations, these are the disagreements if any"—and there were none. And everyone approved.

~

In the meantime, efforts were proceeding to hold hearings on the proposed legislation, and Killian and others were preparing to be called—though no date had yet been set, probably owing to the pressure of other legislative business. Hartford Gunn tells the next part of the story.

Fred Friendly's Satellite Plan

GUNN: Fred Friendly had come, in the meantime, to the Ford Foundation, and had assumed the role that Jim Armsey [previously] had as chief honcho of Ford in charge of educational television. And Fred wasn't terribly enthused about federal funding, but he was totally intrigued by the development of satellites.

He had hit upon the idea of getting what he saw to be the enormous profits of the soon-to-be satellite carriers—and the networks, he thought, would have to go to satellites—get a portion of that income diverted to the support of educational television. And he put forth his so-called Ford Satellite Plan—to put up a satellite system and have the profits flow to the support of ETV.

"Let us use our new communications technology...." (I can hear Fred speaking on the subject) "Let's turn it to some real substantive purpose and get it to support this wonderful, poor starving child—educational television!"

And Jim Killian called me up. "Hartford, what the hell are Friendly and Mac Bundy doing!" I'd never heard him so angry.

I said, "Oh, you mean the satellite plan?" I said, "Well, obviously Ford is looking for a way to get out from under and they're reaching for this thing."

And he said, "But the timing! The timing is *terrible!*"

Carnegie was just coming off the press. "The timing is awful," he said. "This is in complete conflict with our report. I think they're doing this deliberately."

I said, "No, I don't think so. From what little I know about Fred Friendly, I don't think he had given a thought to the Carnegie Commission. This is just his dream, and he's got it all written down, and he's got a whole bunch of lawyers and technicians to work on it. Fred just develops these great enthusiasms, right or wrong. Many of them are right, but many of them are wrong. He's gone off on it, and he's sold on it."

Fred is, you know, when he wants to be, one of the ultimate salesmen of the communications industry.

So it was a very tough conversation, because I was trying to convince Jim that I didn't think this was any plot—and he was absolutely convinced that this was some plot to upset the whole Carnegie Commission and ruin it, just at the time the baby was being born. And this is where the "accident" comes in.

Fred persuades Senator Pastore to hold hearings on the satellite proposal, and somehow they expanded the hearings to take up the whole thing! The presentation was broadened. It was a hearing ostensibly on the use of satellites and the Ford Foundation proposal, but Killian was given time to present the Carnegie proposal. And they brought in all the commercial networks and AT&T.

Well, needless to say, the commercial networks and AT&T were absolutely scared out of their minds with Fred Friendly's scheme to force them into satellites and then take all this money and give it to educational television! Neither the phone company nor the commercial networks were very keen on this idea.

So when Jim Killian came in with his suggestion—that there be a corporation and da-de-da and the federal government—oh, great idea! And everybody patted Jim on the back. Everybody was saying, "Go, Jim, get this fellow Friendly off our backs!" They didn't want to have anything to do with that satellite scheme.

Accident? Serendipity? I don't know. Absent the accident, and Fred stumbling in with his plan and getting everybody heated up and the issue focused at the Senate Subcommittee on Communications—and scaring the commercial networks and the telephone company, and getting Jim Killian so angry that he was ready to chew nails and spit them out at Bundy and Friendly—and he was a personal friend of Bundy, former dean at Harvard.

Well, anyway, it is so typical of how our future has been written. If these things hadn't happened, would we be where we are today? Would the country have a public broadcasting system?

Testifying Before Senator Pastore

Lee DuBridge, Ed Land, and Dr. Killian took part in the portion of the Senate hearings relating to the Carnegie recommendations.

DuBRIDGE: Killian pretty well outlined the report: the purposes of public television, the proposed financing arrangements, and so on. And then he turned to Land. And Land gave the most beautiful fifteen-minute talk! It just left everybody flying. He's so eloquent, such a marvelous command of the language, and so deeply probing into the feelings of human beings and the way in which their needs and ambitions and yearnings could be satisfied through a properly-financed public television system.

KILLIAN: [Senator] Pastore had a wonderful television hearing. It was jammed.

Another member of our commission, the head of the automobile workers' union, Leonard Woodcock, spoke at that hearing and announced that they would give their support to the proposed plan. That again was very telling.

So we got rapid action from Congress and the system was brought into being.

~

But Dr. Killian would be the first to acknowledge that a great deal of work was done in Washington before the legislation was passed and signed by the president. And Chuck Marquis was one who was in the midst of that effort, along with NAEB president Bill Harley.

MARQUIS: One of the big hassles was that the people in the Congress didn't watch educational television. WETA, Channel 26, was just getting started and had not really made much of a mark on the community [being UHF].

Bill McCarter came in then as manager of WETA, and he worked wonders with publicity and programming to try and hype the watching of programs. There really couldn't be much support for something they didn't know about.

Bill went so far as to get a mock remote truck. I hope I'm right about this. He got an enormous van which was occasionally used for remotes by putting equipment in it and going out and doing things, although very seldom did they do any remotes. But every day he'd park it up around Capitol Hill and around the White House and various places. It had "WETA Channel 26" painted all over the side in enormous letters.

~

Both Harley and Marquis emphasized the high degree of interest shown by both Senator Warren Magnuson and Senator John Pastore.

HARLEY: They had a somewhat different relationship in the sense that Magnuson was the chairman of the huge committee of the Senate on education—Education and Labor, I think it was called—but there was a subcommittee that did most of the work which was run by Pastore, the Subcommittee on Communications.

I got to know both of them quite well, but particularly Pastore because there were many more hearings of the subcommittee than we had with the whole big committee.

Pastore was a consummate master of using the hearings for his purposes, so he could put into the record what he wanted when he came to presenting whatever the legislation was on the floor of the Senate. He could point to the record [of the hearing] and say, "This testimony was presented" and so on and so on, and he would use that to answer questions.

When you knew what was going on, you did a little point-counterpoint kind of an arrangement back and forth. Otherwise you would say to yourself, "What on earth is he asking that question for? He knows the answer to that very well." But if you knew what he was doing, you would play the game with him. You'd say, "Senator Pastore, I'm glad you asked that question because I want to take this opportunity to say ...such and such."

MARQUIS: We had an enormously good friend in Senator Magnuson, and his staff person whose name was Nick Zapple.

~

Zapple was, indeed, the strategist year after year who arranged details of the hearings and recommended effective procedural steps to the proponents of the act. As the act of 1967 was being written, he succeeded in having included many details which later became of great importance to public broadcasting.

One of his big disappointments, as he admitted in a conversation years later, was that he thought he had the tracks laid to secure for noncommercial broadcasters the *free* use of AT&T's network circuits across the country. Not knowing about his quiet advance work, others met with AT&T and were pleased with the offer of a 50 percent reduction in the normal charges. Zapple was disappointed that his behind-the-scenes work did not come to fruition, through no fault of his.

MARQUIS: The House was not interested at all, basically. We had to work on the House—Congressman Harley Staggers—to get him encouraged to hold hearings. He did, and those hearings became textbooks of public broadcasting.

HARLEY: Torbert McDonald of Massachusetts was very friendly, sometimes surprising in the way he conducted hearings. Torby was very helpful to us. We would always, at the beginning of each legislative term, go in and see him in advance and talk with him—Chuck Marquis and me—about what we hoped to have accomplished within the next legislative session, and he was very understanding, very helpful, very supportive of public television.

MARQUIS: We brought in people from all over the country to help lobby at that point. Finally, by only about nine votes, we passed out of the House the bill that became the Public Broadcasting Act of 1967.

Circumstances On November 7, 1967

As things worked out, the signing of the act by President Lyndon Johnson finally got scheduled—at an appropriate time but not an altogether convenient location.

McBRIDE: The NAEB was having its convention in Denver right at that time, and there was great speculation about what day Lyndon Johnson would sign the Public Television Act into being. I was invited back to the thing, but since at the time I was the president of the NAEB and

Standing behind President Johnson as he signs the Public Broadcasting Act of 1967 are, left to right, Senator John O. Pastore; Alan Pifer, president of the Carnegie Corporation; Dr. James R. Killian; and John W. Gardner, secretary of Health, Education and Welfare.

had responsibilities there, I couldn't leave—along with a number of other people—to go back, and I've never forgiven Lyndon Johnson to this day! [CHUCKLE]

MARQUIS: We thought it would be nice if the president would sign the act and we would televise this from Denver. It would be a first-time feed.

First of all, the Secret Service did come out and check the convention site in Denver. We thought there would be no problem. But President Johnson was in a big hassle with the Congress, so things were a little tense in Washington.

It was also a big civil rights period, the Public Broadcasting Laboratory [a project promoted by Fred Friendly though a part of NET] was the first program on the NET interconnection schedule, and somehow the script got into the hands of our good friend Doug Cater in the White House. They were displeased in the White House to see how the president and the government were being castigated on behalf of civil rights.

So the plans to have the president come to the hotel in Denver were suddenly dropped, and the signing would be, instead, in the White House. So only those folks in Denver who could take an all-night plane and get back to Washington were going to be in on the signing.

~

To make matters a trifle more complicated, the key speaker at the convention at the same hour as the signing ceremony in the White House was Secretary of Defense Robert McNamara. Harley, always a gentle-

man and one conscious of protocol, decided he would stay in Denver to introduce McNamara and send me, the newly-elected chairman of the NAEB Board, to witness the White House ceremony.

HARLEY: We arranged to have an audio line put in that would carry the proceedings directly from the White House to the hotel ballroom in Denver.

MARQUIS: I called and arranged most of it while standing in a phone cubicle in the lobby of the Hilton Hotel in Denver. It cost a dime, I remember, to make the call. I ended up talking to some Marine colonel who was in charge of arrangements, and we talked and talked and talked, and I was up about six o'clock in the morning in the bedroom of the hotel continuing to talk. As I talked to operators back and forth, the phone company vice president and all kinds of fun people were involved in order to get this done.

When it became clear that I really *was* talking to the White House and this was really serious, and the president did approve and wanted to do it, finally on the stage of the grand auditorium of the civic center in Denver, the time came.

And Bill Harley interrupted Secretary McNamara and said, "Thank you, Mr. Secretary, and now, ladies and gentlemen, the President of the United States"—which Bill had always wanted to do all his life, and never had done before.

But, backstage, the phone company man had the cables coming in, and he had no time by that time to make the usual installation. So he clamped wires together. I was over him with a finger, with a cue. He was stretched out on the floor, and I was on my knees, and when I, with a telephone in one hand, heard the cue in Washington, "And now ladies and gentlemen, the President of the United States from East Room of the White House," I cued Harley, who said the same thing at the same time, and then cued the guy who put the wires together on the floor into the p.a. system, and out came: "Good morning. I understand I am being heard in Denver." And nobody could move! If I hung up the phone, he was off the air. And I sat there and just sweat, and the guy on the floor kept holding the wires in place. We stretched out for forty minutes while the thing went on.

It worked fine, and nobody in the audience could see us. We were all backstage. It was hysterical!

~

One of the NAEB's venerable past presidents, Frank Schooley of the University of

Illinois, tells a story of another occurrence that morning, an experience of Dr. Frank Stanton, then president of CBS-TV and a strong supporter of the Carnegie Commission and the resulting legislation.

SCHOOLEY: Stanton was pretty close to President Johnson. Johnson sent him a telegram in his New York office inviting him to the ceremony. Frank flew down to Washington in his plane and got to the White House gate on Pennsylvania Avenue, and they said, "Where is your invitation?" He said, "Back in New York on my desk."

Somebody happened to look out the White House window and see that they were holding up Frank Stanton, so they called the guard and told them to let him in.

But they had already started the ceremony. Frank couldn't break into it—and didn't want to, because it would have been a discourteous thing to do—so he stood in the background, and that's about as far as he got with the ceremony. Then he got in his plane and went back to New York.

~

Upon returning to his New York office Stanton sent $1 million from CBS-TV as the first contribution to the Corporation for Public Broadcasting.

Dr. Killian, who probably thought he had completed his assignment for public broadcasting but later was to head the corporation which his commission had initially recommended, talked with pleasure about November 7, 1967, and all that led up to it.

KILLIAN: It was really a great experience to be a member of that group and to have the kind of enthusiastic participation that we had on the part of a very dedicated group of people.

And President Johnson went all out in support. At the time the Public Broadcasting Act of 1967 was passed, he had a gathering at the White House including all the congressmen who had been involved and the others, and he made a beautiful speech, which Doug Cater doubtless wrote for him, and lent his full support to the effort at that time.

~

Today and perhaps in years to come, there may be those who mark November 7, 1967, as the moment when public broadcasting began. The TeleVisionaries know better—but even they agree that the passage of this Act by the Congress and the endorsement of it by the president of the United States marked the beginning of a new era in American communications—and in American education.

In the reception line at the White House, following his signing of the Public Broadcasting Act in November 1967, President Lyndon B. Johnson welcomes author Jim Robertson as Mrs. Johnson greets Alan Pifer, president of the Carnegie Corporation.

26

The Struggle is Not Over Yet

After those years of conferences and Carnegie I and lobbying and testifying, one might have been excused for feeling that with the passage of the 1967 act, public television finally had arrived.

Not so. In fact, more than two years passed before the provisions of the Public Broadcasting Act of 1967 were fully implemented. Such are the circumstances in the real world.

Communications attorney Leonard Marks remembered.

MARKS: [President Johnson] told Doug Cater and me to find a chairman for CPB. We went through a list of about thirty people whom we thought were well qualified. None of them would take it. I had never had an experience like that before. This was not to be a governmental job. It was to be one that had a certain prestige, great challenge, opportunity to create a whole new field of communication, but the people we went to just did not feel inspired, nor did they feel that the challenge was worthy of their time and effort.

Only at the very end, right before LBJ left the White House, were we able to convince someone whom we thought was capable of taking it on. That was Frank Pace, who had been director of the Budget and who had worked with Lyndon Johnson when he was in the Senate.

~

During this search, Marks himself was asked to consider accepting the chairmanship of CPB. He was just about to leave his post as director of USIA.

MARKS: I wanted to do it, but I must tell you that my wife, whose judgment is pretty good, said, "No, you'll find yourself involved in endless conflicts." Because I was going back into private life, I would be going on the board of other

business corporations, I'd be practicing law, and she said it would take somebody that is either retired or can dedicate their full time to it. So we didn't do that.

~

NAEB's president, Bill Harley, who had met Frank Pace earlier, provided typical assistance.

The Modest Beginnings of CPB

HARLEY: Like any enterprise like this, they didn't have any offices or anything else.

Frank used to use my offices, first of all, because he didn't have any secretarial support. So he would phone from there and get some things typed, and so on, for the first month or so of the Corporation for Public Broadcasting.

~

Chalmers Marquis, vice president of NAEB and head of the Educational Television Stations Division, was even more directly involved in trying to get CPB into action.

MARQUIS: The first battle was to get a board. They didn't get a board for a year.

They only named two people at the outset, and the accusation—which I guess is true—is that they had to go through a long list of people to get two.

Frank Pace, a Democrat, was named chairman, and Milton Eisenhower, a Republican, was named the first other member.

Then they had to lobby for the appropriation. Pace worked very hard at this, based out of New York. He had his young assistant, an attorney named Ward Chamberlin, assigned to this virtually full time. [Nearly two decades later, after much experience at CPB and elsewhere in public broadcasting, Chamberlin became president and general manger of WETA in Washington, D.C.] And we spent many hours together. The first money was not funded until 1969, al-

Hartford Gunn of Boston's WGBH, left, joins three of the men most responsible for creating and establishing the Corporation for Public Broadcasting; Frank Pace, CPB's first president; James Killian, Jr., chairman of the Carnegie Commission on Educational Television; and NAEB-ETS executive consultant, C. Scott Fletcher at the NAEB convention in the fall of 1988.

though Frank Pace was lobbying for money—as we were—to get the thing going in the last year of the Johnson administration.

The original authorization was for one year only, and the first thing we had to do the very next year—before any money had even been appropriated—was to go back to the Congress and ask that the year be changed, another year added.

Torby McDonald by that time was the chairman of the House subcommittee and he added that with rather little fuss and feathers, and Pastore added it in the Senate, and they agreed to it—added one more year with a $9 million authorization. We subsequently got five million.

NET's Worst Fears Become Real

During this same period there was considerable furor aroused concerning the future role of National Educational Television (NET). Partly because of the individual stations' characteristic distrust of any national entity with power, but also because of a number of program releases which gave some stations troubles, NET had not fared well during the deliberations of the Carnegie Commission.

APPY: When the Carnegie recommendations came out, the worst fears of NET were evidenced in the pages of that report.

The report, while it did recommend that NET be preserved, it also said that the distribution of programs should be undertaken by a separate agency as yet undefined. They were thinking that it would be the Corporation for Public Broadcasting; that's what the [Carnegie] report presumed.

As a result, NET found itself—at a time when it had been making great strides in interconnecting the stations, at a time when it had been trying to create a framework for partnership with the stations in the control of interconnection—that Carnegie was recommending a completely different way, and that those efforts which NET had under way were in great peril.

By the time [the NET plan] was getting off the ground, these other thrusts of the Carnegie Commission followed by the Corporation for Public Broadcasting's establishment were in the works. And the Ford Foundation, in the person of Fred Friendly, and the corporation, in its initial framework with Frank Pace and his employee of long standing, Ward Chamberlin, were redesigning the world of public television. And NET was in a position where it was most unlikely to play the role that it wanted.

I remember that Fred Friendly came over to NET one day to talk to a group of us. In effect, he was saying, "Quit worrying about it; you guys are *not* going to be the distribution agency."

Friendly's "Public Broadcasting Laboratory"

Part of the affiliates' discomfort with NET was due to their reaction to a project initiated by Friendly called the "Public Broadcasting Laboratory." It was at first created as an autonomous unit but soon was made a division of NET.

APPY: In actuality, PBL attempted to operate almost autonomously. That created a whole flock of problems, the result of which was not just a general station falling-out with the people who ran PBL but also a perception by the people at PBL that NET itself was encouraging station unrest and that NET itself was threatened by the existence of PBL.

Well, to the suggestion that NET was convincing the stations that PBL was up to no good, there is no truth. Nobody needed to do that. PBL's problem was not so much one of doing bold programming which was uncomfortable for some of the stations, but PBL's biggest problem was that their leadership had no patience with the stations.

Av Westin, who was no doubt a tremendously capable producer, had been brought in by Fred Friendly, who said, "Look, here's $10 million. Now pay no attention to the existing structure. You're going to show them what public television can be all about."

Av said, "I'll try to do that" in whatever way he thought was the best way to do so. He had not taken the time nor did he particularly care to take the time to find out what kind of customer he was dealing with. And at least to a degree, the customer was not just the viewer at home but more likely to be the television station which was the local conduit to reach the viewer.

~

Appy recalled a revealing episode at a meeting of NET affiliates when Westin and his crew were telling the stations what they were planning to do.

APPY: When some of the stations voiced what I suppose could be called parochial concerns, Av at one point said, "Well, you've simply got to remember that you're not running mom-and-pop candy stores any more."

This was not exactly the most diplomatic thing; it set the tone for a relationship that never did really become comfortable.

~

Now the forces lacking confidence in NET included not only many of the station managers and the Carnegie Commission but also the Ford Foundation, which had been NET's principal source of support since its inception.

APPY: The Ford Foundation at that time, I think, was inclined to believe that NET was an organization which probably should pass on its own way, that its time had expired.

This probably was not too surprising. Henry Heald had been responsible primarily for the support of NET over the years; McGeorge Bundy had a different set of interests. [McGeorge Bundy succeeded Heald as president of the Ford Foundation.] And he was excited by Fred Friendly.

And Friendly—like everyone who has come into public broadcasting over the years as a leader—began from a point of view that seemed to say that nothing worth a damn had happened before, and now we're going to show these practitioners in the field how it's really done.

~

Appy was very close to Jack White during this time. White admitted that, despite Friendly's statement in a book he published about this time that Jack White should be regarded as "the first guy on the beach," he was convinced that he was not going to capture the support of McGeorge Bundy because he would never have the complete support of Fred Friendly.

APPY: Well, the friction—both real and imaginary—gave Jack White perhaps the last needed convincing that he wasn't going to be able to pull off those things which he had hoped to pull off, and that it was time for him to make another move. And he went to Cooper Union, and I think was subsequently rather badly treated by the public television industry.

Frank Pace and Ward Chamberlin, who at that time were ensconced as the chief people to deal with at the Corporation for Public Broadcasting, assured Jack that they wanted to use him as a consultant, but to my knowledge he was never called to participate in a committee meeting.

Jack had really built the house that made their future at the Corporation for Public Broadcasting and the present-day status of public television a reality. Otherwise, it might never have happened—at least as effectively and as promptly as it did.

~

David M. Davis, the educational television veteran from North Carolina, Michigan State, and Boston's WGBH-TV, became Fred Friendly's deputy at Ford during this same period. He tells why he felt he should accept the assignment.

DAVIS: I had turned down jobs in New York for fifteen years. I didn't want to work in the city. I loved Boston, a civilized place, everything you'd want artistically, culturally, intellectually.

But the Public Broadcasting Act had just been passed in the fall, they weren't even organized yet, I knew the foundation was going to be central to a drastic reorganization in the system.

And [I wanted] to be on the inside there and be able to have some influence on what Bundy and Friendly might do. I felt I just owed it to the system—to what I'd put my professional life into, really.

Changing Attitudes At the Ford Foundation

Davis offers his version of the marching orders given by McGeorge Bundy to Fred Friendly.

DAVIS: He came in with the express assignment to "make it fly so we can get out. If we get out now, it'll die. We're just too central, too much money, too much power, and the foundation shouldn't stay with anything forever and we're stuck with this."

Fred came in, and despite the immense mistake of the Public Broadcasting Laboratory, he did really teach the trustees what it was going to take before they could see a way out of it.

At its peak, we had ten people including Fred and me and the secretaries giving away $18 million a year or something.

~

So it was that Davis at the Ford Foundation played a critical role in the first formative months of CPB and also of PBS.

DAVIS: Pace had brought along a chap named Ward Chamberlin. Before there was any other staff [for CPB], Ward was the staff, and he borrowed Don Quayle from the Eastern Educational Network to help.

Together we began to work on how we could get long lines [interconnection] going somehow beyond just Sunday night. Then we drafted the early papers on what PBS would be—at the Ford Foundation. Chamberlin at CPB put together a committee of the stations, but the staff work was really being done at my shop.

~

In Washington, Marquis was watching the same set of developments.

MARQUIS: It never went forward the way NET wanted it to. It went away from there very rapidly.

The stations were opposed to having NET in there; the stations wanted to keep control themselves. So a combined group called the Interconnection Management Group or something, six people [station managers] who became known as "The Six Pack," decided what was the court of appeals.

Don Quayle, on behalf of the corporation, was brought in to be the staff for the Six Pack. So there was many a meeting, and decisions were made then as to what programs would be on the interconnection on a day-to-day basis.

The Stations Decide to Form PBS

NET's Gerard Appy summarized the reasons why the stations across the nation shifted their support away from NET and moved to form PBS, the Public Broadcasting Service.

APPY: The stations at that point really saw in the creation of the Corporation for Public Broadcasting and in the legislation creating it, the opportunity for a station organization which would handle all of the distribution. And they found allies in the Ford Foundation and in the Corporation for Public Broadcasting. That is, in essence, how PBS came to be.

The corporation had done an outline of what they thought PBS might be. Convinced by their legal experts that the legislation creating the corporation clearly stated that the corporation was not empowered to operate a network or a distribution system, and not believing that they wanted this to be a province of NET, they sought then to structure a new organization. And many of the station leaders found this desirable.

Did CPB Satisfy the Hopes of its Architects?

There are those who express considerable disappointment in both the stature of the CPB board and the ways in which it conducted itself during the decade of the seventies.

GOLDIN: We took giant steps forward with the Carnegie study, and fortunately it did survive the early Nixon days. But in the process, it partly lost its soul. The appointment of the corporation people, after the initial group which included some of the commissioners, ran downhill. Even [President] Johnson appointed a number of people who were simply hacks.

We had looked upon the corporation as a kind of BBC, or at least the American counterpart, not as being a producer of programs or as a runner of the system, but [as] trustees for a new view, a new approach to public broadcasting.

And that suffered the political fate. Appointees to commissions are people for whom the president has to do something or someone down the line has to do something. And so that didn't work out as we thought.

~

The story of the Corporation for Public Broadcasting and, indeed, the Public Broadcasting Service, goes beyond the time span illuminated by the testimonies of the pioneers that appear in this book. Still, the TeleVisionaries, when they were interviewed in the early 1980's had been able to observe the development of the medium under CPB and PBS for a decade. Their reflections on that decade add perspective to our view of a broadcast system that is taken for granted today.

27

Has Your Dream Been Fulfilled
or Become Lost?

When I asked the founders of public television if their dream had been fulfilled, more than ten years had passed since the establishment of the Corporation for Public Broadcasting and the emergence of PBS as the national program service. Most of these pioneers compared the public TV they were watching in the early 1980s with what they initially had envisioned twenty-five years earlier.

From that perspective, they recalled their earlier dreams, voiced their convictions concerning the strengths and weaknesses of public television, and expressed some opinions about its future.

What Was The Original Dream?

BREITENFELD: What many of us wanted to build was the first national system of broadcasting in which the American tradition of localism was realized.

What we shared were two things, I think. One was the dream of this democratic do-good system that didn't stand a chance but which had a certain fun to it. "There's no way we're going to win this, gang, but isn't it a good battle?"

The other thing we had in common was abject poverty, which tends to pull people together. NET's suggestion that some day we would be interconnected was an absolute pipe dream. Poverty and the excitement of the possible dream gave us joy.

HULL: Somehow I got all steamed up on "everybody should know more." You get that way at a land-grant college or university. In a sense, this whole dream was my church.

Of course there was a drive for recognition and vanity, but I believed rather more naively then that if everybody knew all there is to know,

it would be a great step forward. And out of that whole thing came the notion of the alternative, the choice, in broadcasting.

HUNGERFORD: Coming as I did from NBC, I really thought there should be a BBC eventually, because commercial broadcasting is limited in so many ways with its appeal to mass audiences.

SKORNIA: The potentials of these [broadcast] media are so great. It's as if it were medicine, let's say. Here are tubes capable of carrying life-saving blood. Instead, there's a mixture of beer and Clorox and all kinds of dangerous drugs and everything else there. The perversion is almost too unimaginable. It's as if we designed fine instruments for operating on the brain and here are those guys standing around slicing bread or chopping leather with them.

HURLBERT: It was like a new hope. This was going to give us an opportunity to get to the people with what we felt they needed.

I believed with all my heart and soul that we were going to make the best we had available to everybody, which had never been done!

SIKES: We used to say very proudly that "we are programming television to motivate you to do something else than watching television."

HUNTER: I thought that what we were building was essentially a new educational delivery system. We were going to be dealing with problems of illiteracy; we were going to be dealing with the problems of basic language instruction, with information and with art and with culture and those things—which we could now bring into the homes and into the lives of people who did not have access or opportunity for these things.

What Led Individuals to Respond?

How did it happen that this brand of television, almost unknown in the fifties, attracted certain individuals from both education and from broadcasting?

At least a hint or two can be discerned in the following personal revelations.

CHRISTIANSEN: It's interesting for me to think back to the influences in my own life that led me into the communications field.

It started back in 1925 with a kind of maverick hired hand we had [on the farm] who was not so much interested in working on the farm but in technology. He had an old Mother's Oats box that he wound copper wire around, and had a pair of "cat whiskers" on this. ["Cat whisker" was the term applied to small wires touching a crystal and clamped to a coil in such a way as to tune in whatever radio broadcast transmissions might be audible on headphones.]

And the phenomenon for a youngster to be able to hear music was more than a curiosity. It was just something finally you had to find out about on your own.

And I think the next unusual thing was the fact that in our little old high school in Canby, Minnesota, our superintendent of schools, Myron Smith, had the whole high school listen to Walter Damrosch and the NBC Symphony on its network broadcasts. That rural Minnesota town of 1,800 had someone in its midst who felt strongly that education is more than books and classrooms—that it is culture, providing things that can make a difference in your life—and he felt strongly enough about it so that school was dismissed so that we went to the assembly hall and heard that. And that had a tremendous impression on me.

~

Chuck Marquis learned television production in the early 1950s at both WGN-TV and WBBM-TV in Chicago.

MARQUIS: I was the best diamond commercial director that ever existed for a cheap chain of jewelry stores in Chicago that featured $29.95 diamond rings and up, for credit, a dollar down and a dollar a week. And I could slap those things together like nobody else. It was beautiful. They even built a special lens for me to take a full-screen closeup of the diamond ring—a $29.95 diamond. That's not easy; you have to find it first.

But there it was, on the ring. I had a little motor that turned it, reflecting things, and it was just gorgeous. It would take a long time to set that up; it was between segments of a western movie on Saturday afternoons.

One day I came in as usual two hours before the first commercial in order to do all the set-up on it, and the stage hands were in bad shape. "Something terrible has happened!" I said, "What is that?" They said, "The diamond ring for the commercial is gone. We had it in locked storage and it's gone."

Well, the store was about two blocks away, and I said, "Well, send somebody down and get one, can't be much for $29.95."

They said, "No, you don't understand. That was a $500 ring we used for the commercials!" And I knew then that for a year I'd been shooting commercials with a $500 ring and pricing it at $29.95. I thought I'd go cut my throat.

Shortly thereafter, I was interested in trying WTTW [Chicago's noncommercial educational station].

~

Prior to Jonathan Rice's time at San Francisco's KQED, he produced news programs for KTLA, Paramount's television station in Los Angeles.

RICE: I did "Magazine of the Week," which was a sixty-minute program with pages devoted to sports, animals, fashion, nature, and anything you can think of, both news and features.

I was limited by [an] order that none of those sections could be more than five minutes, because people would lose interest. This drove me crazy in some cases, because I went to great effort to get really superb people of enormous topical interest and I could only have them on for five minutes—even though I cheated occasionally.

My news program was sponsored at the last by Shell, and Shell's slogan then was: "The most powerful gasoline your car could use." And my son watched it with his mother. And when we used to drive around, whenever we passed a Shell gasoline station, Jeff would say, "Look, Daddy, the most powerful gasoline your car could use." And he could barely talk; he was two years old at the time. And I thought, "My god! What an educational tool."

Then, the last assignment I did was political convention coverage. And when I came back to Los Angeles, all of my friends knew more about civics than they had learned in all of their years of school and college.

So I thought, "Good lord! This is really enormously impactful."

Though I had never thought of myself as a teacher, I was a communicator and always wanted people to understand what it was that I was trying to say. So I was excited about this, and it made the idea of educational television much more important to me.

~

Norman Cousins became intrigued with the possibilities of television as an educational tool in an even more unusual way.

COUSINS: I became aware of its possibilities during the Stevenson campaign for the presidency. This was the first time, it seemed to me, that the possibilities of television—not just ETV but all of television—became fully apparent. Also, the need for it became deeply emphatic.

The '52 campaign was not so much a run for the presidency. It was that in its basic sense, but it was really an educational experience for the nation—and Adlai Stevenson regarded it as such. I don't know whether he really felt that he could beat the champ. From the very start he was battling big odds and he meant to win, of course. But I think that he relished the chance to convert the campaign to a classroom for the American people.

I was part of that campaign. I traveled with him, at least some of the time, and spent a great deal of time in Springfield [Illinois] at his request. He would never say how many votes there were in this or that issue, in this place, at this time. In going to the next stop, he would always say, in effect, "What is it we can tell the people that they really ought to hear?"

This sense of the election campaign as a classroom was very real to me. Naturally, as you went along, you kept asking yourself, "How do we make this blackboard visible for the entire nation?" And that was when I first became aware of ETV. I became aware of its possibilities during that campaign. I joined ETV in one role or another not long after that.

~

For various reasons, then, public television's founders were attracted to this completely new kind of "blackboard for the American people"—this elusive hope so well described by E.B. White years later in a letter to the first Carnegie Commission:

"Noncommercial television should address itself to the ideal of excellence, not the idea of acceptability which is what keeps commercial television from climbing the staircase. I think television should be the visual counterpart of the literary essay, should arouse our dreams, satisfy our hunger for beauty, take us on journeys, enable us to participate in events, present great drama and music, explore the sea and the sky and the woods and the hills. It should be our Lyceum, our Chautauqua, our Minsky's,

and our Camelot. It should restate and clarify the social dilemma and the political pickle. Once in a while it does, and you get a quick glimpse of its potential."[1]

No better definition of "The Dream" has ever been written.

Joys, Hopes, and Fears

It should surprise no one that many of the pioneers who created educational television found the programming in the early 1980s to be, in many respects, fulfilling—but at the same time, expressed disappointments and concerns.

KILLIAN: I have the feeling that the American people want public television.

It is performing a service that there's no evidence yet that the commercial stations are willing to perform.

DuBRIDGE: It's gone way beyond what I ever imagined would be possible. I just think it's a miracle—this little enterprise which I never imagined could grow into a very major one.

ARMSEY: It's pretty good. It doesn't do as much as I'd like or everything I'd like, but it does a lot more than at one time I thought it would do or could do.

And it does provide for someone who has the slightest interest in intellectual matters or in cultural or artistic matters an additive and an alternative of considerable significance to the commercial structure.

CAMPBELL: In many ways it has gone beyond my highest dreams. When I look at the fact that people who could never see an opera now know what the Metropolitan Opera has, what opera means, that people who had never seen any kind of ballet except the little bits they have children do in the schools can now see what a beautiful ballet is like.

I was an English teacher in the beginning of my educational career. I would have done anything to have had a presentation of Shakespeare.

And of course, as content for "The MacNeil - Lehrer Report," for "Washington Week in Review," for the kinds of in-depth news that public broadcasting carries, I feel that we are truly educational in a bigger sense than I could ever have thought.

---

[1] "Public Television: A Plan for Action," Harper and Row, 1967, p. 13.

TYLER: Has it fulfilled our expectations? In one sense, it has more than fulfilled them. We never dreamed that there would be this many stations on the air. Well, that was '51 and this is '81.

But still, to have all these self-supporting stations on the air and flourishing indicates to me that this is more than fulfilling its promise, that it has found a niche in the whole battery of communication instruments, and that it is using this position to inform and educate great segments of the American public. It's tremendous.

McCARTER: I truly believe that public broadcasting in many parts of the country is one of the most remarkable accomplishments that this nation has behind it. This is going to come out some time, and they're going to look back and appreciate it.

BREITENFELD: What we have to be proud of is the series of installations that have been built philosophically, physically, financially, from nothing. And together they make up something that America seems to see as a hell of a lot less fragile than it really is.

CHRISTIANSEN: Public television is a community that exists with its own identity wherever you go. When you go out and talk about public television now on the West Coast, it has very much the same meaning that public television has in this community in Florida.

In fact, as we get a lot of people coming into this area, the first thing they want to find out about or get associated with is not the university; the exportable item which they brought with them is an identity with public television.

HARLEY: I can remember when we had great difficulty in getting educational television stations' programs even listed in the newspaper. They were thought to be so inconsequential. Now they have a prominent place in *TV Guide*, in all of the publications.

As you talk with people at luncheons and clubs, there is a great deal of talk about it. "I only listen to the MacNeil - Lehrer Report," or this or that. Of course, just seeing pictures in magazines of what's going on in public broadcasting is a source of satisfaction, that there has been this recognition, that this is now an important and well-established aspect of our society.

SIKES: One has to go out and get away from it—as I have, a little bit—to see what an influence it really is. People's viewing habits are changing. People do appreciate what's coming over public broadcasting. And we have set stan-

Rhea Sikes' retirement home in the shady woods of Washington Island, Wisconsin, where she has been able to "get away from it" and contemplate the effects of early public television.

dards and we have opened doors and we have dared to go down avenues that people never thought about being capitalized upon in television.

I think we have elevated people's interest. And they don't say it. But when they do say, "I don't watch anything now except public broadcasting," that's what they're saying to you. "You have raised my sights. I'm not satisfied with anything less than you."

~

A somewhat different but similarly philosophical comment was offered by the man who arranged many of the initial start-up matching grants awarded by the Fund for Adult Education, its former vice president, G.H."Bill" Griffiths.

GRIFFITHS: On the one hand, I think there have been superb achievements, examples of the very thing that some of us dreamed of. I'm thinking here of some of the great dramatic productions. I'm thinking of some of the coverage of public events. I'm thinking of some of the programs of analysis that public television has made possible. These are things that you hail.

On the other hand, you feel very sad—although I suppose not actually surprised—to see that you are never going to escape from the source of funds swaying what goes on the tube. This, I think, is too bad. I suspect that lots of those involved perhaps regret this too.

It seems to be an instance of the theme that any institution that is out to correct some of the imbalances in society will itself be so marked by the characteristics of that society that there is a very severe limit to what it can hope to accomplish.

~

Maine's Donald Taverner, who established his state's ETV network and went on to be general manager of public television stations in Pittsburgh and in Washington, D.C., also looked at two sides of the situation—as did many others.

From this modest bungalow in Augusta, Maine, Don Taverner took us out to find a fresh Maine lobster and some yellow sweet corn, then cooked us a memorable dinner himself in his own kitchen--after which he lighted his corn-cob pipe and expounded on his public telelvision experiences in Maine and elsewhere.

TAVERNER: If I went back, say to 1958—in there somewhere—and predicted what I hoped public television would do, it has gone way beyond what I would have hoped it could have at that time.

I never really dreamed that we'd be doing Lincoln Center or Wolf Trap, MacNeil-Lehrer Report, so many things that we see, and some of the children's programming that we've seen developed. I think we've been awfully successful, I really do.

Now, on the educational side, no. We have not done what we said we were going to do or we hoped we would do.

It's the corn pudding. It's not the main course at all in the whole thing.

Educational television has never really made it in education. That's the feeling I have. It's a disappointment that I know is shared by a great number. It's working—but not well.

~

As Taverner indicated, scores of other pioneers shared his disappointment. Among them was Washington communications attorney Leonard Marks, who helped to generate President Lyndon Johnson's interest in this field.

MARKS: I want you to know that my original concepts—and, I believe, President Johnson's—have not been fulfilled by the Corporation for Public Broadcasting.

He envisioned it as an adjunct to the educational community and not as a new force, duplicating what commercial television has done.

I just don't think that the performance of the public television stations has been equal to the imagination and the dreams that we had when it was created. The people who became program directors and had responsibility for administering it directed the enterprise into this channel.

We were aware of what the BBC had done and what other countries had done with radio and television to reach into the home and instruct people who couldn't get formal education in four walls, but I haven't heard any efforts come in that direction from CPB. [2]

Rather than being entirely negative, I'd like to point out that the opportunities now are even greater because satellite technology has reached the point where it is available at relatively low cost, and with cable and other means of delivery, there is no reason why the Open University or in-school instruction cannot still be created.

I'm inclined to think that if we're to revive this with any degree of success, it'll have to be in the field in which it was originally intended, as an adjunct and as a part of the educational community.

BREITENFELD: The thing that we didn't do in public broadcasting was to provide *services to humans*, services that commercial broadcasters could *not* provide because they were designed to make money and reach large groups. We went astray from that and went Hollywood.

We never really went at classroom television in a significant way. The reason we didn't, I think, was that American education itself is ailing.

~

A very large factor in the efforts to utilize educational television for instructional purposes was the hesitancy of many in formal education to embrace this new medium.

MINOW: The biggest frustration to me has been that we have not as yet married television with education.

---

[2].Since this time, CPB has initiated efforts to redress the sitution which Mark describes.

McBRIDE: I think one of the largest, if not *the* largest disappointment I would have in the period of time over the fifties, sixties, and seventies, is that we have not been able to really get American education to realize the full potential available to them through the medium of video. It has advanced, but at a snail's pace.

There's so much more that can and should be done, but it's too bad that we haven't been able to find ways to convince the traditionalists, the academicians, the educational administrators of the real potentials that exist for education.

HUNGERFORD: I think the educators thought they were being exploited by people who just really wanted to take their money and then put on opera or something.

There's always been a sort of tension. If the educators were going to use the medium, they wanted to control it. And if they didn't control it, they didn't want to bother with it. It seemed to me that it never focused.

~

John Taylor, who had failed to convince the University of Chicago to utilize television but who subsequently founded the Chicago TV College, believed that as technology allowed the educator somewhat greater control over the use of these new media tools and the prospective student also manipulated the materials at his or her own pace, greater use of technology in education would be inevitable. He believed that the early pattern of accommodating classroom activities to broadcast schedules was one of the problems.

TAYLOR: The teacher doesn't want to be bothered by having to be ready at five after ten in the morning to get this particular thing. She wants to fit it into her own programming, and you can't blame her really. But with the number of channels that you're going to have, with cable TV, discs, and all of this, she can use it like she can a textbook.

You see, what's facing the world is this: what do you do with people whose jobs have been taken away by technology?

Every time the doomsayers have talked about this we've found something for those people to do. And it's going to keep on that way. So why not continue to work at your [educational] technology? You've got to keep providing the means.

Nobody ever thought it was going to be easy, and it still is not going to be easy. But that doesn't mean it shouldn't be done, you shouldn't try.

MACANDREW: To capture the mind and imagination of the average boy or girl, you've got to have more in the front of that classroom than an earnest and perhaps tired man who maybe has an outside job in addition to his teaching to keep his family going, or a weary young woman talking not just to, but at, the children.

I think that all that could be done was done in the early days in instructional television by the pioneers—but I wish that we could have done a better selling job.

CAMPBELL: I think my disappointment lies in the fact that we have never been able to present the great teachers, the exciting scholars, the specifics in education that people would like to have now.

The other thing that has always bothered me is the fact that we have not been able to touch the illiteracy problem in this country. I would like to see something done for them. Here is a medium that all of the people watch all of the time, that could teach, if we just knew how to do it and how to get them there to watch.

COUSINS: I've always felt that one of the great services that public television could provide is a full college course for credit in prime time, where you could make use of the fact that you could get the finest professor in each course in the United States, and thus have the ideal college course, the ideal university curriculum, on public TV, and grant degrees.

This in itself would solve the major problem confronting colleges and universities, namely, sources of support, because I felt you could get at least four or five million people in the United States who could enroll in college courses for credit. And the proceeds of that would mount very sharply and reach substantial figures, and the local college or university would process the materials and do the grading locally and share in half of the income, and thus create, open up, a very substantial source.

But the only way you could do this, as I say, would be if you had more than one channel. You couldn't take the system channels which had to be concerned with the general needs of the population and take your prime time and use it for this purpose.

I suppose we ought to feel lucky enough that we have at least one station in each city. The consummation I'm talking about is devoutly to be wished, but not within the realm of possibility.

LOPER: I think, frankly, there will be a time coming when we might want to retreat—if I can use that term—back into the base from which we came.

The one clear thing that we do in a different manner are these programs which have an educational orientation, and I would certainly classify programs such as "The Ascent of Man" and "Cosmos" and other programs of that type as falling into the heritage of what we have done originally.

That may be the thing ultimately that will differentiate us from all this other maze of communication that is going to take place. If all the predictions come to pass that the home will be the center of activity—probably because we won't be able to afford to go anywhere in a car—then it could well be that [educators] may have to rely upon television to reach the people, and go almost full circle back to what we originally envisioned for these kinds of stations.

Too Preoccupied With Numbers of Viewers?

Along with these concerns over the lack of full use of noncommercial television by the educational community, public television's pioneers repeatedly expressed worries about an apparent tendency in the field to gauge success in terms of audience size.

McCARTY: When education gets into a popularity contest with entertainment, it's dead! We must not let ourselves be trapped into counting viewers and using that as the main criterion of our success. Who is going to attend a lecture when he can go to a Broadway musical revue? Well, a few, yes. But there's no question about the *relative* popularity of some kinds of performance.

"Mac" McCarty hosted us in this lovely home in suburban Madison, Wisconsin, his residence for most of the forty years he spent as head of Wisconsin's educational broadcasting. Long after retirement, his views continued to be inspiring to others.

Boy, I wouldn't want to be in the position of a present-day public television station manager having to deal with that.

Shall I try for the popular and publicly-applauded? Or the truly significant program which will change attitudes and ultimately make us a wiser, better people?

In the long run, if you're going to try to reform the world, you have to do it through ideas—which, in the beginning, were appealing perhaps to just a limited few. But how did the majority get to be the majority? By starting as the minority in the first place and growing and spreading and expanding and developing, and thus altering the previous ratio.

You start with mass audience appeal as the sole criterion for success, and you are stuck. You can't rise above it.

So, in our planning, let's see that somehow we get supported and financed and isolated from the pressures of popularity to be able to do what in the beginning may be limited in appeal but nevertheless significant in the long run.

WHITE: I'm afraid I think that the differences between public television and commercial television have been eroded, and that public television—as I see it—is not much different from commercial television, committed to mass audiences, which is the antithesis of what we were aiming for, where we were looking for the special interests and the fulfillment of special desires and stimulation of new interest.

It's now providing for the public that which they want. No longer are you trying to push people to grow. Rather, you're trying to fulfill their interests just to get them—and hopefully to separate them, I suspect, from some cash.

ARMSEY: One of the problems then and one of the problems in the interim and one of the problems now is the preoccupation with viewer numbers, and the tendency always to imitate the commercial structure in order to get viewers. In my view, that's a mistake.

If the noncommercial structure—or what's now called public broadcasting—can't do something different—and I say it ought to be better but it certainly ought to be different—if it can't be different from what the commercial structure with three networks and a whole variety of individual stations can do, then the noncommercial structure had no reason to exist.

~

Thus a major dilemma faced by every public television manager is how to generate enough income to sustain all the things he and his colleagues want to do without resorting to the same money-chase that has made commercial television what it is. Since the educational community has seen fit to provide only a part of this financial support—a much larger part in some areas than in others—and the federal government through the Corporation for Public Broadcasting provides another part—less than 20 percent on the average—there is the constant effort to solicit viewer support for operations.

But substantial funding is also required for the *production* of programs, which has led to the practice of crediting companies which provide such funds, a practice long accepted by the FCC.

Some of the television pioneers who understand this "underwriting" practice are wary of carrying it too far.

Are Underwriters Becoming Sponsors?

HARLEY: We used to be able to say that we weren't competing with our commercial colleagues for advertising dollars, just for listener interest. And we sold our legislation to the Congress on the basis that this was not a competitive but an alternative service, a complementary service to commercial broadcasting. People perceived that. They understood that. Here was a kind of cafeteria from which people could select things that they couldn't find elsewhere, that would be—well, food for thought, that would be nutritious, would nurture the mind and spirit in a way that commercial people could not do.

I think the present system of using credits with merely mention at the beginning and the end is workable. But actual advertising, I think, is going to be very destructive to the future of the noncommercial system. Well, it won't be noncommercial any more. It'll be just like commercial broadcasting.

I can understand the pressing needs under current circumstances for more and more sources of funds, but we'll completely lose our identity.

~

Veteran FCC Commissioner Rosel Hyde made the same point.

HYDE: I am personally disturbed by suggestions or recommendations to finance public television by getting into the advertising market. I am committed to the proposition that this other service should have a different financial basis. Having a different financial basis would provide a diversity which wouldn't otherwise be available.

It doesn't disturb me too much for public television to say, "This program has been made possible by a grant from Exxon" or the telephone company or W.R. Grace. I think sometimes they put in a little more than would be necessary, perhaps appropriate, but at least they're not making sales pitches for goods or services, which I think would be wrong in principle.

~

Former Ford Foundation executive James Armsey was fearful that underwriting practices may be leading public broadcasters to undertake more and more programs to attract the masses rather than to concentrate on public television's original mission. He added these comments to what he said earlier about the need for public television to be essentially different from commercial television.

ARMSEY: I fear that one way or another the so-called "underwriter" is looking more and more like a "sponsor." I fear for the Philistine-inspired view that somehow public television ought to have a bigger audience, much bigger in terms of numbers, and ought somehow to do the same kinds of things that commercial television is doing. And I fear that pressure to do so will become even greater as cable television extends its coverage around the country.

I hope—but I have no belief that this hope will be fulfilled—that somehow there can be a true alternate service, built on what PBS now does, that will emphasize art, literature, culture, music, dance, and those things that go beyond the ordinary day-to-day activities, the ordinary financial matters, the ordinary concerns that occupy the human animal, that there surely is something beyond the financial, the material, the mundane, that is necessary in the human spirit to sustain some kind of intellectual, cultural, artistic appreciation in life.

COHN: There's no question that public broadcasting is now far more competitive with commercial broadcasting than it used to be. And there is always that temptation to pay extraordinary attention to the ratings.

It's a constant struggle to remember what your goals are, to remember what your responsibilities are, and yet on the other hand to attract the kind of audience you want in terms of quality and numbers.

I get a feeling of a tension, of an envy. How do you get the largest possible audience? Do you do what commercial broadcasters do in order to get it, or do you get this largest possible audience in terms of a selected group of people in a community?

I would much rather have a devoted following of the people that public broadcasting means a great deal to, rather than people who simply turn the tube on and whatever is there they'll watch.

~

The view expressed by Marcus Cohn and shared by others may seem to some to be elitist—a criticism which frequently had been leveled at public television. Audience statistics, however, forestall such criticism.

Is Public TV Really "Elitist"?

APPY: I think it is ironic that we have just now reached a time [1982] when 50 percent or more of television households watch public television regularly, and still we are being accused as much as ever of being "elitist." This can hardly be true if half of the households are watching.

RICE: If we're going to have public funds, then the size of our total audience is obviously something we have to care about. That's why the elitism charges, I think are full of shit. Because if we [at KQED] have 1.1 million viewers, that's 58 percent. That's somebody's funny definition of "elite." If you have more than half, you can't be elite.

COUSINS: I think that there has been a tendency at times to imitate commercial TV and to grab for ratings generally with the sort of thing that they would put on commercial TV.

TAYLOR: I'd like to see them get away from competing with commercial television. I'd like to see them concentrate on local programming. Let the people in the city who are supporting that station realize that it's theirs, and it's there to do whatever job needs being done.

GRIFFITHS: One of the things that I regret about the current enterprise: it's not using TV as a vehicle for the diagnosis and treatment of community problems.

BLAKELY: It shouldn't just be something that offered good things to the American people. It ought to be an instrument that the American people could use for communicating with each other, and help in all sorts of action programs.

DAY: I think that KQED has lost touch with its own community, and I suspect from what I do know that that is true of many stations around the country. I think it's true of WNET in New York.

I have strong feelings about centralizing national production, and part of that feeling is to leave the local station free to concentrate its energies upon being a part of the community instead of playing that game with Mobil: "Can we do something that Mobil will pay for?"

There is one major difference in those days and these days. It was cheaper for us to do a live show than it was to buy something from outside, and that has changed. Costs have sky-rocketed.

RICE: Television inflation, I think—and I've had nobody really successfully argue with me—since 1954 or '55 is between eighty and 100 times.

Where else but on one of San Francisco's hills would one expect to find Jon Rice's home? Here we reveled in his recollections and listened carefully to his observations about what was happening in public TV in the 1980s.

One funny example. One of our longtime successes was "The Scotch Gardener," who was a lovely, heavy-drinking Scotsman named Jim Kerr, who would come in with his truck loaded with enough plants for two shows. The producer helped him set up the show, and was also the director. Six people would do two shows in an hour and a half.

Now, we didn't keep any kind of good records, but the best I can figure, is that each show cost $350. We taped a one-camera, out-of-the-studio, local gardening show last year and its cost was $27,000 per half hour.

We did "The Red Myth" with the Hoover War Library, a reenactment of Russian history, with many actors in costume and a very complex script. I found the budget not long ago. It was $6,500 per program. This was probably 1958, maybe '57. If we wanted to attempt such a thing now, it would definitely be over $500,000 and probably three-quarters of a million, and that's really tragic.

Some of those who turned out programming from primitive studios in the early years seem unconvinced that recent investments in facilities have proved to be prudent, particularly since in some cases they are not heavily used.

HUNGERFORD: I think most of these high-cost producing stations are equipment-happy. Commercial stations would have gotten along in the early days with lots less equipment. Educators have had gold hardware, and I think that's always been one of their problems. They spend too much money on that and not enough on ideas.

~

Others reflected on some of the reasons why local stations find it difficult to originate locally-produced, locally-oriented programming.

MARQUIS: The difference is that most of the stations depend so heavily on the networking services they don't do very many live programs. We [WTTW] did five a night; a typical station today does five a week. That's a loss.

The small station, caught in a cost squeeze, simply lays off people and doesn't do local programming, doesn't do creative scheduling, just takes everything that comes up on the line and they really don't have much choice about that. I'm not knocking the fact that they have to do it. I think it was more fun when there was a lot more different kinds of programming.

It's also true, though, that the audience now has seen much better programs. They aren't willing to settle for variety; they want high quality.

Is Public TV Responding to Needs?

MARQUIS: If I were to look back and advise public television, it would be to learn from our education colleagues. You should be able to have a reason for every single program on the air. It should be attempting to address a *particular need.* And those of us who have been saying that have not been successful.

~

Public television historian Robert Blakely echoed Marquis' emphasis on approaching programming from the viewpoint of a recognized need. He cited "Sesame Street" as an example.

BLAKELY: That was done because people didn't say "What about television?" They said,

"How can we help to educate these deprived kids?" And they set about and produced a program.

If you'd applied that same sort of questioning with the same sort of money to problems on a general-equivalency education in high school, on literacy education, on—I could go on and on —the whole educational picture in the United States would be different, and the whole non-commercial public television situation would be different.

What About the Multi-Channel Future?

Although the TeleVisionaries were interviewed principally for their recollections of the past, many of them—even in the 1980s— could foresee a future filled with many more distribution possibilities than the single-channel broadcast station—the one distribution mode to which they had become accustomed. And in the face of these new technologies, the pioneers did not all wring their hands in desperation.

ARMS: With all the gloom and doom that's being sung nowadays, I think it's realistic to say that educational-public television will survive in some form—with great changes though.

So many don't yet realize that educational television no longer consists of a transmitter and *a* program schedule—that survival in a community means *multiple* distribution modes, *multiple* production modes, *multiple* acquisition modes, and *multiple* financing modes. That seems to me to be a relatively simple survival concept, but it has not penetrated yet.

There are so many more tools now, including satellites. We human beings have a chance to accomplish far more than we did in my day.

It's like the atomic bomb. We can blow ourselves off the face of the earth by the end of the twentieth century, but we can also take those same tools and create a world that's worth living in.

HURLBERT: I have said, in many talks in Alabama, that *television is the most dangerous instrument that has ever been devised by man.* You can do anything you want to do with it. Public opinion is the greatest force on earth, and television can do anything it wants to with public opinion.

I said, "If Mussolini had had this same instrument, he could have made warriors out of babies. It is fantastic what it will do."

Also, it is the most glorious, most vital, most potent force that has ever been devised for getting over the good, the growth, the development. We have been derelict, restraining television from doing what it ought to have been doing.

GABLE: I see the future of education as a network of technology.

When satellite direct-to-home comes and it's going to be pay TV, some of it's going to be porno, some of it's going to be culture, some of it's going to be education. We're going to have a lot of education in the homes.

McBRIDE: I don't believe we have come anywhere near fulfilling the educational/public television potential. It isn't a case of having seen its start and now having seen it at its zenith. I think we're far from the zenith.

Cable is going to have an amazing influence upon this. The home videocassette, the videodisc, possibly satellite-to-home broadcasting, subscription television—all of these things are going to make for ever so many more opportunities. They're going to continue to fractionate an audience. That, to me, says that it's going to be more difficult to continue to sustain the development of public television.

SKORNIA: Well, now, with cable—I'm in a muddle. I don't know how we're going to make out. People have so over-proliferated things that it's going to become an eenie-meenie-miney-moe selection process. I don't know how public broadcasting is going to survive in that mess!

CRABBE: I can't subscribe to the notion that the proliferation of distribution systems is going to hurt open circuit public television. It's going to change the character of open circuit public television, that's what it's going to do. [But] broadcast still remains the most cost-effective means of distribution.

HYDE: I still feel that we will need the delivery of educational material over the air, even though we have these developments on videotape. There are a lot of things where time is of the essence—matters which are valuable because of their timeliness.

Also, there is a certain economy in delivery from the transmitter to the home. It's the least costly way to reach masses of people. And that's perhaps the genius of broadcasting; it has the potential of reaching *everybody*. You can't reach a lot of people with the various apparatus that have been developed, but there's one thing that characterizes broadcasting, distinguishes it from all other forms of communication: it can reach just everybody, no matter where he is or what he is doing.

~

Several of public television's pioneers offered somewhat different interpretations of public television's likely challenges as it moves toward the close of the century.

MINOW: I am not one of those who is discouraged about the future of public television. I think the future is going to be very bright. It's an emerging public institution.

CHRISTIANSEN: It has earned its right to exist. I don't think there's any doubt about that.

We'll have again some tenuous times, some struggles. I hope there will be missionaries there who will rise up and take some of the pummeling and meet the emergencies and the crises that exist, and come through smiling and hopeful.

I think it's been easy in the past decade to develop a sense of disenchantment about a lot of things. It's catching. And it's going to take some zeal and some sustained enthusiasm just to keep a momentum here, worthy of it as an institution in America.

HUDSON: What happens to educational television with the advent of cable coming on strong?

There's even talk in the trades now of what happens to a network in the long run—although I learned long ago never to bet against the networks!

But programming of cable may not necessarily be syndicated. It might go by satellite to cable head-ends around the country which will be offering, in many respects, the kind of programming that we've come to expect from public television.

With that kind of thing going on, with the advent of direct-to-home satellite service, all of us having our little dish in the yard or on the roof, picking up signals from direct satellites—and with talent and production costs rising all the time, and with the advent of videocassette and videodiscs, with your Betamax and your other home entertainment centers where you can buy your programs or lease them and play them at will and then with money sources up for grabs, public, private, and memberships....

What's going to happen to public television?

It raises a lot of questions, my friend. And maybe some of those questions are even tougher than the ones we faced in 1953 and '54.

COUSINS: I don't think that by any means all of the creative possibilities of public television have been exhausted.

I think it's always important to have a certain dissatisfaction with the things you are close to, as the only way of transcending your limitations.

~

Whatever various characteristics were posessed by the TeleVisionaries whose stories make up this book, they displayed one common characteristic when they were asked if they thought their dream had been fulfilled. They all defined "fulfillment"—some more explicitly than others—in philosophical terms.

In his living room behind those huge glass walls, we sat with Armand Hunter and gazed out at snow-covered Colorado mountains while he shared with us, in his kindly yet insistent manner, his convictions about television.

HUNTER: I welcome those tremendous programs in music and the arts and in drama that are now part of public broadcasting services, that are of a network quality that simply could not be matched on any other basis. Those are great and wonderful, and I enjoy them and profit from them. This is a kind of unique service that is not available through traditional commercial network fare—which, in my opinion, has degenerated to the point of idiocy.

But, I still would like to see some of that original dream a part of the total spectrum—the informational resource that fits into the various educational development stages of the individual.

This goes into types of program content that are not just the broad music-art-drama-cultural part of the spectrum, but the more pragmatic, practical, useful. Here is an area of educational need that does not represent a large group but which is very real.

I'm talking now about an educational communications system which covers a range of human needs and interests that are part of the primary learning experience of the individual, not from the cradle to the grave necessarily, but at least somewhere within that total range.

I would like to provide each person with some awareness and understanding of the earth beneath his feet and of the stars and universe above his head, and of the world in which he lives, and of the relationships between individuals, and the society in which he lives, and the world of which he is a part. And within this context, I think that educational communications have a *tremendous* role to play—and that we are not realizing this kind of potential.

So when I say I want this individual to be able to look at the mountains or at the sea or at a tree or at a flower, that there is somewhere within him an opportunity to comprehend, to understand, to see the kinds of relationships, and within all of this context, to realize his own nature and the fulfillment of his nature within the context of the life that God has granted him. I just want the medium to help in that kind of individual growth and development.

McCARTY: I think television more than any other medium is capable of transmitting emotions. Feelings.

I would hope that we could relax sufficiently in our concern for filling the microphone with sound constantly and the camera with movement and dynamic happenings, that we can quietly come to feel those human values. I don't get enough of *feeling* from television. I get information, intelligence—but oh, when you get a person who can communicate something inside, and do it through facial expression and the conveyance of poignant meaning, then we have true understanding.

I don't think television has done its job yet in communicating our finer feelings. After all, this is the way in which people are moved and stimulated to action. Though they may try to act rationally and reasonably and sanely, it's probably some emotional stimulation to which they are responding. And we ought to be sure that these are the finer emotions, not the wild ones stirred by mass demonstrations or wild rantings.

Communication is the very heart of civilization, certainly of democracy. If we don't have good communication, one with another, how can we exist?

We apparently have many in-bred natural animosities, prejudices, and disagreements, but we've got to learn to live together peaceably—and I think we can only do it through communication, of the heart as well as the mind.

The world isn't motivated by ideas so much as feelings. And I would hope that all those who come after would look upon broadcast media as a means of cultivating true understanding and full appreciation of every other human being on the planet.

"To Whom Does the Baton Go Now?"

GUNN: When I came on the scene, it was the Harleys and the Wheatleys and the Schooleys and the Hulls and the McCartys and others who had carried this thing through the Depression years in educational radio, kept the thing alive during that period, and who saw the potential in television and fought the battle along with Frieda Hennock to get those reservations. Obviously, without two or three or four of those men, that would not have happened.

And then there was waiting, the Scotty Fletchers and others to pick up on it and put the resources into that battle that made it possible for those stations to get started and for the original Educational Television and Radio Center to get started—which was essential, you know. Without an exchange of programming you couldn't have cut it.

And so it went, from era to era. We've just been fortunate as you look over the whole period that there were always leaders in the wings, ready to pick this thing up and move it.

To whom does the baton go now?

Who is now going to go in, with all of this new technology, and sort this thing out? And who is going to write the legislation? How are we going to pull this thing into shape?

We very quickly have got to have some new design. Either that or phase out. You can make the case—I would reject it—that we should phase out. I don't see anything in the next ten years that will diminish the importance of public television. I won't take bets after ten years.

A picturesque parking place for our motor home: Ralph Steetle's retirement residence overlooking the Pacific at Waldport, Oregon. The ocean was obscured by light fog, but Ralph's observations about public television were as clear and bright as ever.

STEETLE: I've thought from the beginning, back in 1950, that whatever we invented as a people-serving process ought to be in terms of the needs of those people. It ought *not* to be permanent in structure. Educational television, I thought, ought to be reinvented about every seven years.

My philosophy says that educational television was built upon a developed and then recognized public need. It ought to change as the technology changes. We ought to not become loyal to an approach; we ought to retain a loyalty to a human and a personal need. And we ought not to become so stuck in the technology that we forget what it is for.

So I look at the problems—cable television, direct satellite receiving, all the forms of communications there are—as major opportunities for redefinition, reexploration. Sometimes an organization's best function can be to work itself out of business or into a new one.

Educational television can't be framed under glass as a museum piece. It has to be a worried, striving, fretting force—subject to, and hoping for, change.

I would hope that what you and I have been responsible for helping to bring about would be a sensitive, probing, wondering mechanism, searching for tasks—and willing to change itself in framework and nature to meet the priority tasks of our time, whatever they are. If we determine what they are today, the only thing we're sure of is that they won't be that tomorrow. So I'm not sure that educational television should be a stable force.

I guess your receiving antennae have to be out, and your priorities must be based upon people. The medium is neither the message nor the purpose.

BREITENFELD: The thing that keeps my dreams up, the thing that keeps me optimistic and excited, is the idea that trying to help people with today's electronic machinery is still a good one.

What we're talking about is a different way to use it, a different way to distribute it, and possibly a different way to pay for it. But if I remain a professional educator interested in electronics, I do believe all I have to do is to shift with the times.

Epilogue

I have shared some of the observations of fifty-five pioneers in public television about what happened in the early years, before there was a Public Broadcasting Service (PBS) or a Corporation for Public Broadcasting (CPB). In the decade that has passed since those interviews took place, both commercial and public television have changed dramatically. Can we even begin to imagine what things will be like by the end of the next decade and beyond?

To clarify my understanding and to help shape my conclusions, I went to Washington, D.C. in April 1991 and talked with key people at CPB, PBS, and the Association of America's Public Television Stations (APTS). I wanted to find out what their thoughts were about the state of public television today and what might be expected in the coming years. The commentary which follows contains my observations on what has been happening to public television, some of the challenges it now faces, how it may be better utilized and more strongly supported in the future.

The Situation in 1992

It is not surprising that public television has grown. It may be surprising to some to discover *how much* it has grown.

PBS research figures show that in the fourteen years from 1977 through 1991, the number of American TV households viewing public television during an average week rose from 37 percent to 54 percent. In numbers of viewers, that 1991 audience, in a typical week, was eighty million people.

Public television viewers are very selective. In fact, because not everyone watches public television every week, we can get a better idea of how many households watch public television by looking at *monthly* averages. During the same fourteen year-period, the number increased from 60 percent to nearly 78 percent. Thus, the number of viewers watching

public television in an average month in 1991 was 149.4 million.

Moreover, a separate survey showed that not all children, when given a choice, were watching cartoons on commercial stations. In an average viewing week between October 1990 and September 1991, better than 45 percent of all youngsters aged two through five were watching public TV. That's nearly 6.5 million little kids! The figures drop slightly as the boys and girls get older. Even so, 28 percent of elementary age children watch public TV. Among teenagers, one out of five watched public TV. Altogether, as we entered the decade of the nineties, more than *sixteen million* young Americans between the ages of two and seventeen were regular weekly viewers of public television. These figures represent only home viewing and do not include what children may have watched in school.

Ward Chamberlin talked with me about this when I visited him in his office at WETA in Washington. Ward was a principal figure in the formative years of the Corporation for Public Broadcasting and more recently was president and vice-chairman of the Washington, D.C. public broadcasting enterprise.

CHAMBERLIN: We have built up a terrific loyalty in this country. Maybe we're not where you and I hoped twenty years ago that we would be, but we're a significant part of life in this democracy, and a lot of people depend upon us.

It's an elitist thing to say, perhaps, but a lot of people who do important things in life rely upon public television—and that's not an insignificant achievement.

~

True. But let's not inadvertently add to the mistaken impression that only upper-middle class intellectuals watch PBS and its member stations. The accompanying graph validates its own caption: public television's audience does indeed reflect *all* demographic segments of our American population.

Public Television's Audience Mirrors the Population

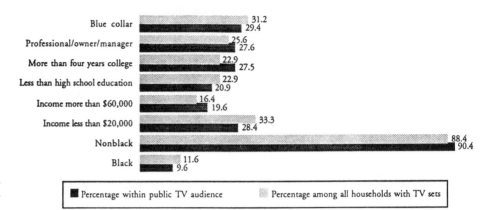

Blue collar — 31.2 / 29.4
Professional/owner/manager — 25.6 / 27.6
More than four years college — 22.9 / 27.5
Less than high school education — 22.9 / 20.9
Income more than $60,000 — 16.4 / 19.6
Income less than $20,000 — 33.3 / 28.4
Nonblack — 88.4 / 90.4
Black — 11.6 / 9.6

■ Percentage within public TV audience   ▓ Percentage among all households with TV sets

Graph courtesy of APTS, National Audience Handbook, January 1992.

While these facts and figures portray an impact on American life well beyond what the pioneers in public television may have imagined back in mid-century, there is a down side: public television audiences *did not grow* from 1985 to 1990.

Those were the years when the "new technologies" of cable and home VCRs gained wide popularity. In 1986 to 1987, instead of 54 percent of TV households watching public television weekly (the figure in 1990 to 1991), audience studies had reached a high of more than 56 percent. In the same year, the average number of minutes spent each day viewing public television stood at 198, or three hours and eighteen minutes. By 1990 to 1991 it had receded to 161 minutes per day, two hours and forty-one minutes, a drop of 18 percent!

During these years a similar drop in viewing of all types of television broadcasting created havoc among the commercial TV networks and advertising agencies. This trend also caused considerable concern in public broadcasting. Thanks in large part to the advent of "new technologies," viewers could now choose from a much greater range of options. Visionary leaders in public TV began to analyze the effect of these "new technologies" on the single-channel public TV enterprise.

During my interviews in Washington in 1991, I was especially impressed by the views of Michael E. Hobbs on this point. I had first known Mike in 1966 as a bright young attorney whom Hartford Gunn had appointed to represent Boston's WGBH. In the intervening years, he held many responsible positions before being awarded the first Hartford N.

Gunn Fellowship, a study grant allowing him time and leisure to think deeply about the status of public broadcasting. Just prior to that appointment in 1991, he was senior vice president for policy and planning at PBS. From this vantage point, after twenty-five years in the field, Mike described public TV as "a much more mature institution." He expanded his views as we talked, amid piles and piles of documents and research reports in his office at PBS in Alexandria, Virginia.

HOBBS: It's all due to the people in the field. The nature of the enterprise which the pioneers created has attracted those who want to perform a public service, as other TV has become principally an entertainment and advertising business.

~

Hobbs pointed out two major accomplishments: the first, that well over a million people have now earned college credit through courses offered on public television; the second, that the usual audience for public television now stands at "upwards of 100 million viewers per week. Those people," he remarked, "must certainly experience some effect on their lives."

His views about the future of the single-channel public television station reflected not only his own conclusion but that of other leaders as well.

HOBBS: To the extent public television thinks of itself only as broadcasting of the old style but better than other channels, I think it will not thrive (in this new environment). Also, to the extent public television thinks of itself merely as the manager of a cafeteria of technologies, more interested in its *array* of technologies than in the *content* of its public service, it will not thrive.

Public TV has established its hallmark in the realm of *superior quality*, the excellence of both the content and the purpose of what it does. If it loses that, it will disappear in the welter of available means of video delivery.

~

But Hobbs was optimistic about the outcome.

HOBBS: Public TV has nothing to fear from the multi-channel environment. Over time there's going to be an inexorable deterioration in the commercial channels as they reach for the lowest common denominator. And, as the plethora of choices overwhelms the viewer and stultifies excellence in the competing commercial media, I think the quality and purpose of public TV will become all the more distinctive and apparent. And if it is made accessible through *all* of the technologies that people use to access their video choices, I think it will prevail.

~

I hope Mike Hobbs is right that more and more of the public will begin to sense the differences between what the commercially-supported channels offer in order to bring profit to their owners, and what public television provides for the sole purpose of enriching our lives and helping us to understand ourselves and our world. But we must do more than hope.

We must try to comprehend the amazing educational and cultural possibilities in the uses of videocassettes, videodiscs, interactive computer learning systems, two-way satellite transmissions between business offices, factories, schools, and homes and more. We must not be satisfied merely with gradual improvement of the single-channel public broadcasting station, even though that must also be a continuing objective. People of all ages are already affected by these new ways of delivering television. The commercially-motivated entertainment world is making them available to shoppers in every supermarket as well as in video stores and elsewhere. If those of us who are aware of the needs of people beyond mere entertainment do not also employ these new technological tools for educational and cultural purposes, we shall all be overrun by those whose motivations are purely for profit.

Challenges to be Faced

Public television's greatest challenge, from day one, has been to find ways to raise the money to pay for it. Public television needs adequate funding so that it can provide this essentially free service to all.

William J. McCarter, a veteran of this struggle since his early days in public TV in Philadelphia and later at NET in New York, WETA in Washington, and for many years as president and general manager of Chicago's WTTW, stated the problem in colorful terms when we visited him in 1981. His remarks are cogent today.

McCARTER: We seem, from the very beginning up until today, to be plagued by a fatal flaw. Why is it that we built this [public television] without an admissions gate of any sort?

An admissions gate is enjoyed by every university, hospital, dance company, symphony orchestra, and theater in the country. Everyone else has a box office. We tried to do this without a box office, and that is our Achilles' heel.

I find the gate analogy surprises a lot of people, because we describe ourselves like these other non-profit institutions but everyone has a tuition gate except us.

We are a perfect example here [in Chicago]. We have two million homes watching; 150,000 subscribing. You have no way to enforce the payment. Your best means of support is in the home that makes a conscious decision to contribute on an annual basis. In many ways, it's pay television by the honor system.

We're right at the point where, although it has been a remarkable achievement, it could blossom into one of the most stunning accomplishments the nation has had. The irony is that the audiences want it, the private sector wants to get behind it on some sort of *quid pro quo* basis, and the artistic community desperately wants to participate in it. It's just a missing link. If we can only close that link, it'll just be absolutely remarkable.

~

McCarter would be the first to acknowledge that through the years, many have been striving to forge that missing link. Initially, stations came into being using funds provided by school systems or colleges and universities or through state appropriations, plus modest citizen support. Compared with the billions available for commercial television, public television's funds were infinitesimal.

Over a period of forty years—largely due to its own increasing quality and impact—public television has generated financial support from a dozen different sources, as shown in the accompanying table.

Public Television Income by Source

Fiscal Year 1990, in thousands of current dollars

Source of public TV Income	FY 1990 Amount	Percent of total
Corporation for Public Broadcasting	$ 168,602	13.5
Federal grants and contracts	33,767	2.7
Local governments	46,072	3.7
State governments	241,077	19.3
State colleges and universities	81,815	6.6
Other public colleges and universities	9,868	.8
Private colleges and universities	19,536	1.6
Foundations	57,692	4.6
Businesses (underwriting)	209,808	16.8
Subscribers (members)	273,297	21.9
Auctions	21,527	1.7
All others	84,967	6.8
TOTAL INCOME	$ 1,248,030	100.0
Total non-federal income	$ 1,045,661	83.8
Total federal income	202,369	16.2

Note: Totals are rounded off. Source: Corporation for Public Broadcasting, November 1991

The creation of the Corporation for Public Broadcasting in 1967 and subsequent federal appropriations funneled through that agency have helped, but cannot be depended upon. There always seem to be elements in the Congress urging the freezing of funds because of disagreements concerning the alleged lack of balance and objectivity in a few PBS public affairs programs. Perhaps this always will be an issue, for one person's view of balance and objectivity is not likely to be the same as the next man's. In fact, the *Oxford English Dictionary* gives thirty-nine uses of the word "balance," and twenty-six uses for the word "objective."

It was the hope of those who helped to create the Corporation for Public Broadcasting that it could function as a "heat shield" against political pressures, and it tries to do that. But the annual arguments always seem to leave future funding in jeopardy, even when criticisms are leveled at a very small proportion of program offerings, and despite the fact that nearly all viewers surveyed say they are unaware of any consistent bias. Without funding guarantees for a period of years, planning for improvements can be difficult at best.

Moreover, federal funding through CPB provides less than 15 percent of public television's revenues. As the table shows, state governments supply about 25 percent of total support through both legislatively-established state commissions and through the budgets of state-supported institutions of higher education.

Underwriters, benefitting in an institutional way through on-air credits, furnish more financial support than does Congress through CPB, but this is in the form of program production dollars for specific series of telecasts—important and useful, but not a dependable source of funds since each underwritten project must be negotiated independently.

Subscribers—those viewers who contribute to their local public television station—provide only a little more than 20 percent of public television's revenue nationally. Fortunately, their support steadily increased during the the 1980s. The number of such members rose from 2.6 million in 1980 to 5.2 million in 1990. Contributions from these members in 1980 amounted to $78 million; by 1990 the figure was $273 million. In the same period, the average contribution in-

This cartoon by San Francisco artist Tom Tomorrow, which appeared in the San Francisco Chronicle/Examiner, reflects the dissatisfaction of many viewers with the aggravating pleas for funds.

creased from $29.96 to $52.40. Obviously, there remains a great potential for growth from viewers.

The problem, as yet unresolved, is how to secure financial support from the four-out-of-five viewers who watch but who contribute nothing. The most effective method so far has been the one used periodically by your own local public television station—and in all probability, you deplore it.

Concentrated on-the-air pleas for contributions are probably the single most criticized aspect of every local public television station's programming.

Why do they do it? Because it works! But there surely is a need for a less painful and more effective way to persuade *all* those who enjoy public broadcasting to pay their fair share. As McCarter says, there is no admission gate. Viewers can watch public television, day after day, year after year, and never contribute a dime. This must be acknowledged as just one of the principal challenges faced by every public TV enterprise today.

The answer to the overall funding problem may well be in focusing on increasing *all* of the sources of income shown in the table. Surely an enterprise with many different sources of support is better off than dependence upon a single source.

The federal government was identified by the Carnegie Commission on Educational Television as the one which could and should provide basic financing, although not a majority of the funding. The Carnegie Commission's preliminary recommendation was an excise tax on all TV sets, the method used successfully to finance noncommercial broadcasting in Britain, Japan, and several other countries. There was such a tax in effect in the United States during the Korean War to assist in funding the war effort, and it was repealed shortly after the end of the war. During those years it caused no upheaval or taxpayer revolt. Those who recommended it be retained for public broadcasting argued that everyone benefits from education, particularly when it is available through radio and television, and that the collection of a very small amount on each sale would furnish a strong fiscal foundation completely free from political interference.

The record shows that some of the leaders in Congress felt they could not support such a dedicated tax, and certain advisors to the U.S. Treasury Department also objected to it.

So the Carnegie Commission's initial proposal was put aside as not politically expedient, and Congress substituted the system of periodic authorizations and annual appropriations which is in effect today.

That occurred in 1966, when public television was not nearly so pervasive a part of American life. Several thoughtful leaders among our TeleVisionaries still believe that a dedicated excise tax would be the best way to build a solid financial floor under public broadcasting. This method should be investigated again, for it could insulate public television programming from any political influence. But that may also be the reason why certain politicians fear it.

Another approach to more adequate funding—aside from a constant effort to increase the dollars flowing from already identified sources–may well exist in the new services which the so-called new technologies make possible. Financial support comes as the result of recognized services of true value. If public television stations embrace these new methods of distribution and provide specially-designed educational materials in many forms to a host of agencies and groups—albeit in the form of videocassettes, cable transmission, and satellite interconnections—users should be expected to pay for these services, just as school systems in early years had to pay for classroom television.

Single-channel broadcast television seems destined to be only a part of many new services which can be performed by utilizing the new technologies which already are changing both the commercial and noncommercial video field.

The new challenge, then, to every public TV station is to transform itself into a multi-media telecommunications institution, able to offer even greater and more diversified services to its community.

What do I mean by a multi-media telecommunications institution? Most of us think of public TV as the one channel on our television set that is an oasis in what Newton Minow called "a vast wasteland."

If you already own a videocassette recorder (VCR), you have one example of what is meant by emerging new technologies. You already have experienced the convenience of using that machine to capture a TV broadcast you otherwise would miss and playing it back when you are able to watch. In schools,

colleges and libraries, hundreds of television programs, many initially broadcast by PBS, are played back on VCRs at viewers' convenience.

Cable television also comes under the heading of new technologies, even though it has been around for quite a time. It provides subscribers with clear reception of an assortment of TV broadcasting stations, and offers a wider and wider choice of programs not broadcast over the air. Some systems use as many as 100 channels, many featuring a type of programming called narrowcasting, aimed at the needs of highly specialized audiences, such as live coverage of Congress, or continuous weather information, or twenty-four hour news. Several public television stations are completing arrangements to furnish programs for special audiences to cable channels as a supplement to their on-air broadcasts.

Soon, people with satellite dishes in their yards will also be receiving program materials designed for specialized audiences, just as businesses and educational institutions utilize dedicated satellite channels to receive specialized information from a central source or to arrange two-way satellite conferences. This technique was pioneered by public television twenty years ago, and is now growing in popularity and usefulness.

There will also be more use of videodiscs, the TV version of the audio compact disc which is in some ways superior to the VCR. Home shopping and banking by TV are coming into greater use. Computers are being connected to television transmissions to enable students of all ages to interact with instructors hundreds of miles away. All of these applications of television are already in operation in some areas and are expected to become commonplace.

David Brugger, once in charge of television activities for CPB and in recent years president of the Association of America's Public Television Stations (APTS), encapsulated this during our conversation in Washington in 1991.

BRUGGER: We are service providers. We are not merely one technology; we are not just broadcasters. Very gradually, stations are becoming multi-media centers but [they] are ten years late. Our boards still think of us as merely broadcasters. Wrong! We must learn to promote the image of a community institution using all media.

~

As stations undertake this broader and more varied service by utilizing videocassettes, videodiscs, cable, microwave, satellites, and whatever other new technologies come upon the scene, two of their present problems may become less severe.

The single-channel broadcaster always has faced the vexing problem of trying to cram into the hours of the day the many kinds of programs which meet the varied needs and interests of viewers. For example, there are undoubtedly individuals who would welcome excellently-produced prime-time courses for credit which feature top professors. But stations hesitate to broadcast college courses in prime hours because the number of viewers thus served is far less than those who wish to watch "The MacNeil/Lehrer News Hour," "Washington Week in Review" or "Evening at Pops." But credit courses are relegated to fringe time and therefore are not easily available to many who otherwise might welcome them.

These courses can be provided on videocassette or videodisc or on a cable channel or by satellite without interfering with programs serving larger audiences on the standard broadcast channel. Public television stations could use their professional staffs and production facilities to create courses and informational programs designed to serve educational needs more limited than those that would qualify for broadcast time, and thereby provide a whole additional range of educational services for the benefit of more people. One result should be additional means of financial support.

Customers could include businesses in need of in-service training, community agencies anxious to get their messages to the public, and governmental agencies. Because there seems endless need for effective communication, the local public television station can become the institution looked to by those in need to help them solve their educational communications problems.

There is yet another challenge as new technologies emerge: the challenge to protect future capabilities from over-commercialization. We must not make the mistakes of the past.

In 1924, before most people had bought their first radio, President Herbert Hoover called a conference to discuss radio. He said he considered it "inconceivable that we should allow so great a possibility for service to be drowned in advertising chatter." But as potential profits loomed, AM radio frequencies were gobbled up by enterprising commercial broadcasters. To prevent reoccurrence in FM two decades later, the FCC was persuaded to set aside a handful of FM frequencies for noncommercial educational use. This precedent proved helpful to those pioneers who petitioned the FCC in the 1950s to reserve a few TV channels for noncommercial television.

We owe a debt to those visionaries for their foresight and the fight goes on today. As new technologies develop, we simply must not allow them to be dealt with as irresponsibly as were radio and television frequencies at first.

Many leaders in public broadcasting are aware of this. In 1981, I interviewed Donald E. Ledwig, then president of the Corporation for Public Broadcasting, about his concerns. He called my attention to an observation made by futurist author, John Naisbitt: that while in the past major wars have been fought over *land*, in the future the big struggles for power will be over *control of information*. Aware of this possibility and past problems, public broadcasting proponents now urge that thirty percent of any communications capabilities (such as satellite channels) be reserved for noncommercial educational use.

If we truly believe in the importance of education and the dissemination of reliable information, surely 30 percent of the public airwaves (which belonged to all of us in the first place) is a nominal figure. But all of us must carry on the fight so that regulatory agencies do not succumb to pressure from far-sighted profiteers.

How Can Each of Us Help?

Public television often has been described as "the people's business." That's why it is known as *public* television. Each of us can play a role in putting this remarkable technology to greater use. This is what the TeleVisionaries tried to do. We need to consider how we can continue to expand public television's role as the force for good in society.

Here are my suggestions for some questions to ask yourself, depending on your relationship to public broadcasting.

If you don't watch public television at all, will you try it? More than 100 million fellow Americans have discovered it has something to offer.

If you watch but have never made a contribution, will you think about doing so? Maybe you haven't realized that your support is needed. Consider what it offers you and your family, and join with those who make contributions, however modest, to keep this kind of television available. Don't allow others to pay for what you are getting for nothing.

If you are a contributor, are you taking full advantage of the programming? Program guides provide detailed listings so you do not miss some features of personal interest. Maybe you'll discover a fresh idea, a new thought, or a different perspective.

If you are already a fan of public television, might you encourage your friends to watch? Might you write a letter to your congressmen and senators and to your state legislators to let them know how much you appreciate public television? The main reason that Congress finally approves appropriations for CPB is because constituents express support. Have you done so?

If you are working at a public television station, are you taking pride in everything you do, knowing that you carry on a great tradition and follow in the footsteps of the TeleVisionaries?

If you are a station manager, are you allowing yourself time to set aside day-to-day problems in order to think about goals and objectives — about what direction you are taking your station? Believe me, I know from personal experience how hard this is. You may ask how you can plan while you're trying to cope. There are no easy solutions, but I'm sure you are aware how important planning is to the future of public television, even on a local level.

If you serve on the board of directors of a public television station or a state agency responsible for a network of stations, how can you find more time to give this responsibility the attention it deserves? Your personal capabilities are needed on that board. Consider how many people are now benefitted and how many more might be aided as the enterprise for which you are responsible gains strength and capability, thanks to your leadership.

If you are a high school or college student, are you considering a career in educational communications? As many of us have learned, there probably will be more income available elsewhere, but we learned there are other rewards from a career in public television. My South Carolina friend, Henry J. Cauthen, began working in this field when he was very young. At this time he not only heads the extensive educational telecommunications complex in South Carolina but also is a member of the board of directors of the Corporation for Public Broadcasting. He told me this when we visited him in Columbia:

CAUTHEN: I think there are very few areas of work any more where, to use a really corny turn of phrase, you can make the world a little better place to live in. There are very few places where you can have any real impact on that any more in [our] complex society. But this is one where you can still do that.

~

If you need additional college credit instruction, have you investigated the courses already broadcast by your public TV station? Ask about their courses on videocassette. You could join the more than one million adults who have successfully earned college credit by television.

If you are in need of employment re-training or in-service education, have you conferred with your local public TV station or state telecommunications agency? Several states already are bringing course instruction by satellite or microwave to people in occupations where new information is mushrooming faster than most people can keep up with it. Perhaps, through television, you can secure the instruction you need without the necessity for long distance travel.

If you are a parent or a grandparent, are you sharing the fun of public television programming with your children or grandchildren — or are they sharing it with you? It's a great way of doing things together. Your local public TV station can acquaint you with their schedule of programs for various age groups. You just may get hooked on "Sesame Street" or "Mister Rogers" yourself.

Parents, are your local school officials aware of the resources which public television offers now at every level from pre-school day care to college credit courses? If not, how about urging them to ask local public television people about the new learning resources in which public television is playing a leading role?

If you do not fit any of these categories, you may at least sense the variety of services which public television is offering. And you may wish to join today's Televisionaries simply because it is everyone's responsibility to see that our airwaves are properly used, not to *manipulate* viewers but to *serve* them.

My purpose in sharing the personal testimonials and commentary in this book has been to suggest how vital noncommercial television has been, is now, and can become. We all seem so busy these days that we may not take time to consider what television is doing to us as individuals and to our way of life. Its promise will be fulfilled only if more people understand its tremendous potential for good in this beautiful but tragically shadowed world in which we find ourselves.

Looking back over my forty-five year involvement, I believe most of us have taken television for granted.

This thought was also expressed by my long-time friend, Jim Day, of KQED, then WNET, and more recently a member of the teaching faculty at New York University. Near the end of our cross-country trip, I spent part of an afternoon visiting with him in New York City. He was his usual cryptic self.

DAY: My argument is that Americans expect too little from their television set. That's why they get what they get.

~

Jim Day is right. The airwaves once belonged to all of us, but while we weren't looking they got turned into an incredibly effective marketing machine—except for the channels which a few TeleVisionaries managed to establish for noncommercial use.

Public television in the early 1990s is a significant part of American life, but its future is more fragile than most people realize. And public television is accomplishing only a small part of what it could accomplish if its financial base could be greatly increased and made more steady and reliable.

Sylvester L. "Pat" Weaver, a top advertising agency executive with unusual creative ability, is one who wants to see better commercial and noncommercial television. In the 1950s, Pat was president of NBC Television, where he originated such programs as "Today" and "Tonight." Long retired, he lives in California and continues to argue for television improvements. In 1989, after he had appeared on a PBS special and I had corresponded with him about this book, he wrote me a plaintive note:"I don't watch much, and even as an adman as well as a TV program creator, I still think lovingly of my seasons where I laid down the law: no laxatives, toilet paper, etc. And we made a fortune."

In 1977, Weaver wrote thoughts appropriate to today, even though his beginning reference is to commercial TV:"I believe we have cause for alarm in evaluating the home TV services and their use today in America. Television was built in its first ten years by a group of us who really believed we could bring about a mutation in the human condition. And we still can. But television has failed its promise, become over commercialized, without standards of taste that once applied in commercial and program acceptance, taste with lesser rather than greater enriching impact on its habit viewers...."

"Public television has brought many bright moments and hours, but the role of the service is diminished over what it should be. And the need for a stronger service grows as the commercial service withers."

Another of the early visionaries in commercial television was the superb reporter and commentator, Edward R. Murrow. He did his best to persuade CBS Television in its beginning years to use its capabilities for the public good, just as did Weaver at NBC. Murrow's convictions about the power of television were shared by all of us who had a role in creating public television.

Of television, Murrow said: "This instrument can teach; it can illuminate. Yes, and it can even inspire. But it can do so only to the extent that humans are determined to use it to those ends. Otherwise, it is merely lights and wires in a box."

Index

* Indicates individuals interviewed personally and quoted in the book.
To locate general subjects, also see the Table of Contents and its subheadings.